IRISH GENEALOGY
A RECORD FINDER

IRISH GENEALOGY
A RECORD FINDER

Edited by

Donal F. Begley

Heraldic Artists Ltd.
Genealogy Bookshop, Trinity Street, Dublin 2, Ireland.

I.S.B.N. 0 9502455 7 7

A Publication in The Heraldry and Genealogy Series by HERALDIC ARTISTS LTD., Trinity Street, Dublin 2.

Printed in Ireland by Mount Salus Press Ltd., Dublin 4.

Dedication

Gerard & Leo O'Beirne

ABBREVIATIONS

Add.Ms.	Additional Manuscript	M.	Munster
A.H.	*Analecta Hibernica*	Marr.Art.	Marriage Article
B.L.	British Library	Ms.	Manuscript
B.M.	British Museum	Mss.	Manuscripts
c.	about	Nat.Lib.	National Library (of Ireland)
C.	Connacht		
Co.	County	NLI	National Library of Ireland
Cos.	Counties		
d.	died, pence	No.	Number
DKPRI	Deputy Keeper of Public Records in Ireland	Nos.	Numbers
		P.	Positive (microfilm)
ed.	edited	p.	page
e.g.	for example	pp.	pages
esq.	esquire	Parl.	Parliamentary
G.O.	Genealogical Office	P.C.C.	Prerogative Court of Canterbury
G.P.O.	General Post Office		
GRO	General Register Office	PRO	Public Record Office (of Ireland)
H.M.	His (Her) Majesty	PRONI	Public Record Office of Northern Ireland
i.e.	that is		
IMC	Irish Manuscripts Commission	q.v.	which see
		RCB	Representative Church Body
Ir.	Irish		
Irl.	Ireland	RIA	Royal Irish Academy
JCHAS	Journal of the Cork Historical and Archaeological Society	s.	shilling
		SPO	State Paper Office
		St.	saint, street
		TCD	Trinity College Dublin
JCLAS	Journal of the County Louth Archaeological Society	U.	Ulster
		viz.	namely
L.	Leinster	Vol.	Volume
£.	Pound Sterling	Vols.	Volumes

CONTENTS

FOREWORD

This book may be regarded as a sequel to the *Handbook on Irish Genealogy* published by Heraldic Artists Ltd. in 1980 (5th edition). It differs from the Handbook, an elementary and general guidebook on Irish genealogy, in as much as it consists of contributions from a number of specialists on the subject, mainly in fact by individuals connected with the Genealogical Office, founded in 1552 as the Ulster Office of Arms, though its functions related to all Ireland and not specifically to the province of Ulster.

As to the contributors themselves: Donal F. Begley has been administrative assistant at the Genealogical Office for a number of years; Dr. William Nolan is lecturer in geography at Carysfort Training College; Rosemary ffolliott is editor of *The Irish Ancestor*; Eileen O'Byrne is research assistant at the Genealogical Office and Beryl Phair has edited a number of works for the Irish Manuscripts Commission.

I have nothing to add myself to this valuable work since what I would have to say already appears in the opening six chapters of the first volume of my "Irish Families" series. I might add that I get many letters regarding genealogical research and the present work will certainly help to answer such questions. *Go n-éirí an t-ádh leis an obair*: Good luck to the work.

Edward MacLysaght

November 1981

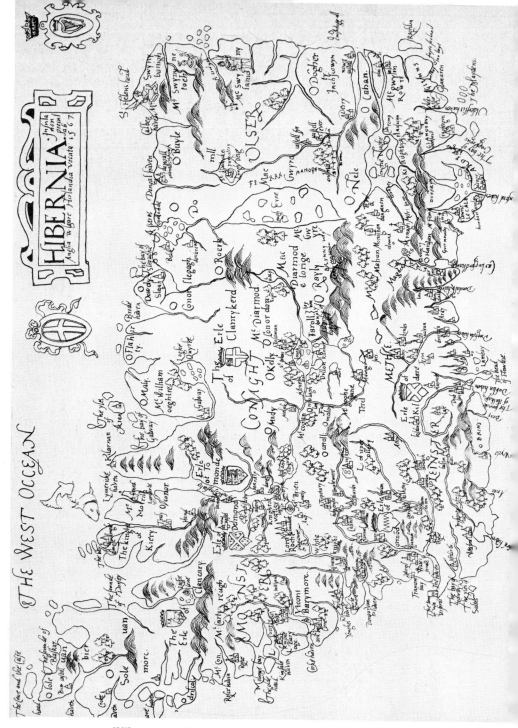

'Hibernia, an island close to England generally called Ireland'
—*by John Goghe, 1567.*

CHAPTER 1

The Peoples of Ireland

DONAL F. BEGLEY

All through the course of civilisation, the past has held a peculiar fascination for man. In particular he has shown a constant interest in the human lines of ancestry which, generation upon generation, determine, in large measure, who he is, what he is and where on the face of the earth he finds himself. It is perhaps the fact that he experiences within himself something of the past that impels him to explore it. All about him, historic landmarks on the landscape, fashioned by unseen hands, provide a physical stimulus to his curiosity. Few emerging into the sunlight from the "Cave in the field of the Great God" or *Uam Achaid Alldui* — as New Grange was known in the Gaelic tongue — have not quietly speculated to themselves about the identity of the builders of that great prehistoric mound.

Celts

Regarding the earliest arrivals in Ireland many thousands of years ago, next to nothing is known. The likelihood is that in origin they were Celtic, belonging to that comity of rural communities which, for well over twenty centuries before the birth of Christ, extended from the Black Sea to the Atlantic Ocean. These communities, enjoying a common culture and language, were known to Xenophon and Herodotus as *Keltoi,* a term which for the Greek authors was essentially linguistic in connotation. According to the findings of modern research four distinct settlements in Ireland by Celtic peoples can be traced to the centuries immediately prior to the coming of Christ. To these settlements can be attributed the Celtic element in the present day population of this island.

Cruithin

The first of the Celtic peoples to settle in Ireland to whom a name can be assigned were the Pretani, or *Cruithin,* as they were called by the Irish annalists. The Pretani appear to have made their way to Ireland directly from Britain, possibly by way of south-west Scotland — exactly when we cannot say — although we do know they were in occupation of the country by the time the second wave of Celtic settlers arrived here about 500 B.C. Those of the Pretani who inhabited the area north of the Caledonian Canal were designated *Picti* by the Roman writers on account, it is suggested, of the practice among their fighting men of tatooing their bodies. The Irish Pretani or *Cruithin* whose ancestral father-figure was Conall Cernach, were located mainly in east Ulster where their representatives in historical times were known as *Dál nAraide* and the *Uí Echach.* Elsewhere in Ireland the Loiges, a powerful branch of the *Cruithin,* established themselves in the midlands, eventually lending their name to the modern county of Leix. From the Loiges, of course, derive the important sept of O'More, whose heraldic crest and motto bear testimony to their Cruithnean origins.

Érainn (Iverni, Fir Bolg)

Regarding the second of the authenticated Celtic settlements in Ireland, we have considerable knowledge. Among themselves the new settlers were known as *Euerni,* a name which was represented in old Irish documents as *Érainn.* To their adopted homeland they gave the name *Eueriio,* rendered *Iepvn* by the fourth century Greek geographer Pytheas, and *Iovepvia* by Ptolemy. From the latter form was derived the Latin classical name for Ireland, *Ivernia,* which later, by popular etymology, became *Hibernia.* In due course *Eueriio* — the Celtic name for Ireland — dissolved into the old Irish *Eriu* and the modern Irish *Éire.*

On the evidence of the tribal names recorded by Ptolemy in his geography of Ireland — the oldest documentary account of the country we possess — the *Érainn* appear to have been widely spread throughout Ireland in districts as far apart as Antrim and Kerry. Among the branches of the Érainn prominent in early historical times in the north-east of the country were the *Dál Riada,* the *Dál Fiatach* and the *Uluti* or *Ulaid,* after whom the province of Ulster was named. In the south-east the *Uí Bairrche,* whose original home was in south Wexford — where they bequeathed their name to the Barony of Bargy — may be taken to be the historical representatives of Ptolemy's *Bpiyavtes.*

It is, however, with the south of Ireland that the *Érainn* are believed to have had particularly close connections. The association of the *Érainn* with the south of the country is reinforced by Ptolemy who located the *Iverni* — whom he treats as a single tribe — in the present county of Cork. The late Professor T. F. O'Rahilly has identified several Ernean tribes who inhabited the south and south-west of the country, among them the *Corcu Loígde, Corcu Duibne, Ciarraige, Múscraige, Fir Maige, Uí Liatháin* and *Déisi.* Considerations such as these incline one to the view that the strength of the *Érainn* lay in the south of the country where we may suppose they first established themselves, probably in the fifth century B.C., before extending their conquest to the rest of Ireland.

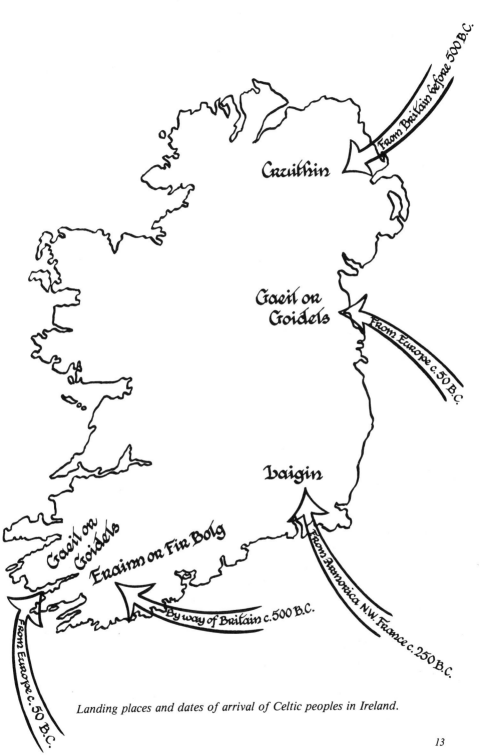

Cruithin

From Britain before 500 B.C.

Gaeil or Goidels

From Europe c. 50 B.C.

Laigin

Gaeil or Goidels

Eranin or Fir Bolg

By way of Britain c. 500 B.C.

From Aramorica N.W. France c. 250 B.C.

From Europe c. 50 B.C.

Landing places and dates of arrival of Celtic peoples in Ireland.

As to the identity of the *Érainn* or *Iverni,* available evidence tends to suggest that they were in fact *Belgae,* the name applied by the Roman writers to a large section of the Continental Celts. A study of early Irish genealogical tracts shows that the *Érainn* were distinguished by being made to descend from certain divine ancestors, notably *Daire, Eterscél (a quo* O'Driscoll) and *Bolg.* Of particular interest to us here is the name *Bolg,* which was one of the many appellations of the Celtic sun-god, giving rise to the forms *Bolgi* (Celtic), *Belgae* (Latin) and *Fir Bolg* or *Builg* (Irish). The conclusion, therefore, would appear to be that *Érainn, Euerni, Fir Bolg* and *Builg* were merely different names for the one people, who in origin were remotely an offshoot of the *Belgae,* and more immediately descendants of Belgic tribes that had settled in Britain.

Laigin

The migration of Gallic tribes from Armorica on the western edge of modern Normandy to the Celtic Sea areas of these islands resulted, it is believed, in a further substantial settlement of Celtic people on this island in the third century B.C. That the new arrivals were an Iron Age people is suggested by their name, viz. *Laigin* — so designated in early Irish manuscripts because of the *láigne* or spears with which they were armed when they first arrived in Ireland. A legend handed down amongst themselves recounted that their warrior-king, Labraid Loingsech (i.e. Labraid "the Seafarer") led a force of Gauls to Ireland about 300 B.C. The *Laigin,* who have left their name on the Province of Leinster, where we may suppose they first landed, gradually extended their conquest in a north-westerly direction as far as the Atlantic seaboard. In the process, the *Érainn* or *Fir Bolg* were forced into the remoter parts of the country, for example the Aran Islands, where tradition ascribes to them the building of the great stone forts still to be seen on Inishmore and Inishmaan.

Among the branches of the *Laigin,* consistently prominent all through the Irish Annals, were the *Osraige,* whence the modern toponym Ossory; the *Uí Drona,* after whom the Barony of Idrone in Co. Carlow is named, and the *Uí Ceinnselaigh,* who lent their name to the territory later known as Hy-Kinsella.

In the west of Ireland the Laiginian tribes were also well established. The *Gálioin,* for example, are represented by the Barony of Gallen in Co. Mayo, while the *Domnainn* are commemorated in the place-name *Irrus Domnann,* i.e. Erris, in the same county. Elsewhere, the *Conmaicne,* who settled around the upper reaches of the Shannon, are believed to be the remote ancestors of the historical septs of O'Farrell and MacRannall (Reynolds). Lastly, the *Uí Maine,* an important tribe whose territory in historical times comprehended the eastern half of Co. Galway and the southern portion of Co. Roscommon, may well have been of Laiginian descent.

Gaeil or **Goidels**

The last of the major Celtic settlements effected in Ireland followed upon Roman attempts to dominate Gaul, and the consequent uprooting and dispersal of many Gaulish tribes. The remnants of one such tribe (the Helvetic *Quariates* — in the opinion of T. F. O'Rahilly) are thought to have made their way directly from the Continent to Ireland about the year 50 B.C. Popular tradition points to the Kenmare River in south Kerry and the Boyne estuary as the landing places of this final wave of Celtic peoples to settle in Ireland.

The newly arrived Celts knew themselves as *Feni,* but the older inhabitants of the country, notably the *Érainn,* who vehemently resisted their intrusions, gave them the name *Gaodhail* (*Gaeil*), anglicized Goidels — from the language they spoke, i.e. *Gaedelg.*

An account of the several Celtic settlements in Ireland will be found in the ninth century Irish treatise known as *Lebor Gabála Érenn* — "The Book of the Conquest of Ireland." This compilation, which purports to give the history of Ireland from earliest times down to the coming of St. Patrick, is, in the opinion of modern Irish scholarship, largely mythological in character. Thus, for example, the Goidelic settlement is represented in terms of invasion of this island by one *Mil Espáine* (the Soldier from Spain, i.e. Milesius) and his sons, Eremon and Eber. The latter, it would appear, are merely inventions of the ninth and tenth century *literati.* They represent, in fact, the two traditional ancestors of the *Gaeil,* Conn and Eogan.

The southern *Gaeil* gave themselves the name *Eoganacht,* in honour of their ancestor-deity, Eogan. From the extreme south-west, where they landed, they gradually moved northwards into the fertile lands of east Limerick and the adjoining part of Tipperary, eventually establishing themselves at Cashel, probably in the early part of the fifth century. From the *Eoganacht,* of course, descend the powerful families of later historical times, such as O'Connell, O'Sullivan and McCarthy. Eogan, we should add, was also known as Mug Nuadat; hence, all through Irish literature, the southern half of Ireland is known as *Leth Moga Nuadat,* or shortly *Leth Moga* — whence *Muma* or Munster, the name of our southern province.

Similarly, the *Gaeil* of the midlands, out of respect for their ancestor Conn, styled themselves *Connachta* (i.e. Conn's people) — a term which was later applied in a more restricted sense as the Gaelic name for the province of Connacht. Gradually, and at the expense of the *Laighin* or Leinstermen, they carved out for themselves the midland kingdom of Meath, eventually establishing their royal residence at Tara. By the beginn-

Ireland: Provinces and Royal residences.

ing of the fifth century the king of Tara was styling himself "King of Ireland."

The first of the "Kings of Ireland" to emerge from the fabled past into the light of history was Niall, known as *Noigiallach,* i.e. Niall of the Nine Hostages. In the Book of Ballymote he is called *Niallus Magnus* or Niall the Great. The son of one Eochu Mugmedon and Caireann, a Britannic princess, Niall had the distinction of being the ancestor of all but two of the long line of Irish kings who ruled from the second quarter of the fifth century down to the battle of Clontarf. Two reputed brothers of his, namely Fiachra and Brian, established themselves in the present province of Connacht, giving rise to the designations *Uí Fiachra* and *Uí Briúin,* the principal septs of the latter being O'Reilly and O'Rourke.

It was Niall's son, Laoghaire, who received the newly-arrived Christian apostle, Patrick, at Tara, shortly after the year 432. A few years later three of his more adventurous sons, Eogan, Conall and Enda, described in Irish literature as the *Collas* (princes), undertook a campaign of aggressive warfare against the *Ulaid* who, at that time, were the dominant power in the north of Ireland. That warfare finally resulted in the destruction, about the year 450, of *Emain Macha,* principal stronghold of the *Ulaid,* who were thereafter confined to land east of the River Bann. In the north-west, two kingdoms established by Eogan and Conall afterwards rose to great prominence under the names Tír Eogain and Tír Conaill. According to the scribe of the Book of Leinster, Eogan took possession of Aileach and reigned there for forty years.

In the Irish annals the descendants of Eogan, Conall and Enda are referred to as the Northern *Uí Néill,* in contradistinction to the Southern *Uí Néill,* who were descended from the other sons of Niall, such as Laoghaire, who ruled the province of Meath. From the beginning of the seventh century onwards the kingship of Ireland was, by mutual agreement, shared alternately by the two branches of Niall's descendants. This arrangement ended in 1002 when Maelseachlainn stood down from the throne to allow Brian Boru lead the Irish to a decisive victory over the Norsemen at Clontarf in 1014.

Of the Celtic settlers who made their home on this island the influence of the *Gaeil* or Goidels eventually proved to be the most enduring. To them we probably owe the introduction of the linear script we call ogham — a characteristic feature of early Irish pillar and other demarcation stones. Their particular dialect of Celtic — linguistically known as Q-Celtic, and fore-runner of modern Irish, Manx and Scottish Gaelic — gradually replaced the Ivernic P-Celtic, the dialect which lies at the root of modern Welsh, Breton and Cornish. When patronymics began to be taken and given in the tenth century, this development was effected by prefixing the kinship particle *Ua,* meaning grandson or descendant, to the numerous Goidelic personal names, e.g. Cormac Ua Ceallacháin. Finally, their basic unit of political organization, the *Tuath,* or district subject to the rule of a petty king, in later days became the geographic basis for many of our baronies, e.g. Clankelly, Tirkennedy, Clanmahon and Iraghticonnor, to instance just a few.

The civilisation of this island remained uniformly Celtic until the ninth century when a fresh ethnic strain was injected into the population following the Viking settlements.

Vikings

Who exactly were the Vikings, those seafaring Scandinavians whose longships suddenly cut into the beach just below St. Columcille's monastery on Lambay Island in the year 795? Ethnically they were Teutons and their German language, known as the "Danish Tongue," was common to all Scandinavians up to the end of the Viking Age, that is about A.D. 1000. That era, which was profoundly disturbing for much of Western Europe, was ushered in when, in the eighth century, over-population and shortage of arable land forced many of the inhabitants of Scandinavia on to the open seas in search of a livelihood. Generally speaking, the Norwegian Vikings operated in the North Atlantic area, the Swedish Vikings in the Baltic Sea and Russian rivers, while the main thrust of the Danes was in a southeasterly direction towards the English and French coasts. First as plunderers, later as traders and finally as settlers, the Vikings reached almost every part of the known world in their time. It is easy to understand how Ireland could not, and did not, long escape their attentions. A marginal verse from the quill of a monastic scribe in an old Irish manuscript reflects the fear of the Vikings:

> Bitter is the wind tonight
> It ruffles the ocean's white hair
> Tonight I fear not the fierce Norwegians
> Coursing the Irish seas.

Norwegians

Our principal source of information on the Scandinavian settlements in Ireland is a twelfth century Irish manuscript entitled *Cogadh Gaedhil re Gallaibh* or "The War of the Gaeil with the Foreigners." The reputed author of this work, Mac Liag, a bard at the court of King Brian at Kincora, carefully distinguishes between two groups of Scandinavian incomers to Ireland. The first he terms *Lochlainn,* i.e. Norwegians, the second *Danair,*

Kings of the Ostmen of Dublin.

	Kings of Dublin	from.	death.	years.
1	Amlave, or Aulaffe	853	871	18
2	Ivar Mac-Aulaffe	871	872	1
3	Ostin Mac-Aulaffe	872	875	3
4	Godfred Mac-Ivar	875	888	13
5	Sitric Mac-Iver	888	896	8
6	Aulaffe Mac-Iver — for part of a year	896	896	"
7	Reginald Mac-Ivar	896	921	25
8	Godfred Mac-Reginald	921	934	13
9	Aulaffe Mac-Godfred	934	941	7
10	Blacar Mac-Godfred	941	948	7
11	Godfred Mac-Sitric	948	951	3
12	Aulaffe Mac-Sitric 1	951	981	30
13	Guniaran Mac-Aulaffe	981	989	8
14	Sitric Mac-Aulaffe, (Hyman an usurper for part of a year, while Sitric was in banishment)	989	1029	40
15	Aullaffe Mac-Sitric 2	1029	1035	6
16	Sitric Mac-Aulaffe 2	1035	1042	7
17	Aulaffe Mac-Sitric 3, deposed by Godfred Croven	1042	1066	24
18	Godfred Croven	1066	1076	10
19	Godfred Meranagh (Murtagh King of Ireland, governed the Ostmen of Dublin).	1076 / 1095	1095 / 1120	19 / 25
20	Torfin Mac-Torcall	1120	1125	5
21	Donald Mac-Gillehodmock	1125	1134	9
22	Reginald Mac-Torcall	1134	1147	13
23	Octer, or Oiter (by others Godfred Mac-Olave, King of Man)	1147	1149	2
24	Brodar Mac-Torcall	1149	1161	12
25	Asculph Mac-Torcall, in whose time Dublin became subject to the English, and he slain.	1161	1171	10

List of the Ostman (Danish) Kings of Dublin, 853-1171.

i.e. Danes. Elsewhere in the work, these two groups are distinguished as white or fair-haired foreigners (Ir. *Fionn-Gaill*) and black or dark-haired foreigners (Ir. *Dubh-Gaill*) — the Norwegians being the white race, the Danes the dark.

Initially, that is to say over the first fifty years of the ninth century, the Viking intrusions into this island were of a plundering nature and almost exclusively the work of the Norwegians or Norsemen. Time after time, the great ecclesiastical centres of Clonmacnois, Bangor, Lismore, Clonfert, Lorrha and Terryglass were pillaged, their sacred possessions carried off, their monks made prisoners and slain. Thorgils (Ir. Turgéis), King of the Norsemen in Ireland, established his headquarters at Armagh, after ousting the successor of St. Patrick. With a view to subjugating the entire country, he strategically posted fleets of Viking longships on Loughs Neagh and Ree but was arrested in the midst of his campaign and drowned in Lough Owel by Maelseachlainn, King of Meath. The year was 845.

Danes

Having chronicled the devastations of the Norwegians or Norsemen, Mac Liag goes on to record the arrival of the *Dubhgaill* or Danes. In 852 the Norwegians, he informs us, perceive the approach of a vast fleet. The newcomers prove to be Danes: a sea battle ensues in which the Danes are victorious and subsequently (853) take possession of the Norwegian military and trading post at Dublin. Their leader, Olaf (Amhlaoimh to the Irish annalists), heads a list of twenty-five kings of the Danish kingdom of Dublin, which endured for three hundred years down to the coming of the Anglo-Normans.

Elsewhere in Ireland the Danes occupied and developed the existing Norse *longphuirt* or harbour trading posts at Wexford, Waterford, Cork and Limerick, thereby laying the foundation stones, as it were, of our most important present-day urban centres. If the general pattern of Viking trading centres is mirrored in the Danish settlement at Dublin, then what remains of that settlement would imply the existence there, in the ninth and tenth centuries, of a shallow water-front full of characteristically Viking longships and behind it a jumble of buildings crowding in on narrow, dirty wood-paved lanes, all jammed with goods, animals and people, the whole encircled by a town wall punctuated with numerous wooden defensive gates.

In the eyes of the older inhabitants of Ireland the Danes were *danair* or barbarians. Their constant aggression on all sides gradually set in train a sequence of events, dramatically described by Mac Liag, that eventually led to a decisive confrontation between the Celtic and Viking civilisations of this island. By the evening of April 23, 1014 the massed might of the Norwegian and Danish forces had been pushed back to the sea at Clontarf by the confederate Gaelic army led by King Brian Boru. The Viking grip on Ireland was broken with many of the erstwhile adventurers opting for a settled life among the local population. Indeed, when the advance party of yet another group of invaders arrived in the south-east corner of Ireland in May 1169 the first blows in defence of the homeland were struck by — the Danes of Waterford!

Normans

Speak of the Normans and immediately armour, castles and heraldry should spring to mind. Ethnically, the Normans were an admixture of Viking and Celt, the descendants of mainly Danish adventurers who themselves had settled in north-western France in the ninth century and there intermarried with the local population. In the course of time these Viking Northmen — whence the term Norman — became Christians and played a leading role in the Crusades. By the time their ruler William — thereafter known as the Conqueror — made himself king of England, following the battle of Hastings in 1066, they were thoroughly French in outlook and language.

Following their king's example, the Norman noblemen lost little time in consolidating their grip on their latest acquisition. They pushed westward as far as South Wales where they took in marriage daughters of the Welsh princes. Visible in the distance across the sea from Pembrokeshire were the Wicklow mountains and it was merely a matter of time — and opportunity — until the Normans continued on their westward trail. That opportunity came in 1166 when Dermot MacMurrough, after being ousted from the kingship of Leinster, sought their assistance in his struggle to regain his lost domain.

The first Norman settlers to arrive in Ireland were led by Robert Fitzstephen, who in May 1169 put ashore at Baginbun, just south of the present village of Fethard in Co. Wexford. In the next two years there followed a succession of knightly adventurers bearing names like de Prendergast, Fitzgerald, Fitzmeiler and de Clare. In origin, a number of these early Norman leaders, such as Fitzgerald, Fitzstephen and Fitzmeiler, were half Norman, half Welsh, being descended from Nesta, daughter of Rhys, Prince of South Wales. Using the south Leinster area as a springboard for their attacks, the Normans were quick to establish themselves in other parts of Ireland, until by 1250 there were few areas of the country that had not felt the impact of their presence.

The Normans settled for the most part on the rich plains of Ireland and in

A Norman knight returns to his castle.

the process many of the Gaelic ruling families were driven from their native territories. The powerful *Eoganacht* families of O'Sullivan and McCarthy, whose ancestors had ruled at Cashel, were forced out of the plains of Tipperary and into the extreme south-west of the country. Likewise, the Kavanaghs, O'Tooles and O'Byrnes were gradually driven from the fertile plains of Leinster into the mountainous country of Co. Wicklow. Concomitantly, the thirteenth century witnessed the rise of the great Hiberno-Norman houses such as Fitzgerald of Desmond, Butler of Ormond, de Burgo of Connacht, de Lacy of Meath and de Courcy of Ulster — to name the more important.

It was the practice of the Normans, once they took possession of an area, to erect a strong fortification in order to control the surrounding countryside. They can rightly be regarded as the architects of the stone castle, a fortress equally effective for purposes of attack or defence. In town and country we can still admire the often extensive, and indeed imposing, remains of those Norman military fortifications. Foremost among them stands the castle of Trim in Co. Meath, enclosing over three acres within its walls, which have a perimeter of some fifteen hundred feet. This castle, which was constructed by Hugh de Lacy about the year 1200, must surely rank among the wonders of medieval Ireland.

Following the initial shock of the Norman advances, the Gaelic rulers, having organized themselves, began to exert pressure on the colonists. Employing weapons and tactics similar to those of their opponents, the Irish forces actually bested the Normans in a number of decisive encounters. What followed was a gradual integration of the Celtic and Norman stocks. By the close of the fourteenth century many of the Norman settlers had adopted Irish customs and dress, as well as the Irish language. In summary, captive Ireland had in turn taken captive her rude conqueror.

English

Englishmen, whose involvement in Irish affairs really began with the accession of the Tudor kings to the throne of England in the closing years of the fifteenth century, trace their origins to the Angles, Saxons and Jutes, three north German tribes who, under pressure from the Huns, settled in the Roman province of Britain in the middle of the fifth century A.D. Like Ireland, they too suffered invasion and settlement by the Danes and the Normans.

The Tudor kings, notably Henry VII and Henry VIII, established a centre of civil administration at Dublin for the purpose of furthering their policy of conquest in Ireland. The business of government required the settlement of large numbers of English in the city of Dublin and its immediate neighbourhood, thereby creating a centre of English influence around the Irish capital which became known as the Pale. A comprehensive statement on the English establishment in Ireland will be found in *Liber Munerum Publicorum Hiberniae* — "the Book of Public Offices of Ireland" — which includes a bewildering catalogue of local and central government offices as well as the names of the succession of office-holders.

A number of significant English settlements in Ireland were effected through a method of colonization known as plantation. In the 1550's Henry VIII's daughter, Queen Mary, succeeded in ousting the Gaelic ruling families of O'Connor, O'More and O'Dempsey from their ancestral holdings in the midlands. She encouraged settler families and their retainers from England to make their homes in the more fertile portions of the territory of the former rulers. Henceforward, these particular areas of the Irish midlands would be known as Queen's County and King's County, with their principal towns of Maryborough and Philipstown also named after the Tudor Queen and her Spanish consort, Philip.

A plantation of more sweeping proportions was attempted in Munster towards the end of the same century. Large tracts of land in Cork, Limerick, Tipperary, Waterford and Kerry were confiscated by the English government, following the unsuccessful rebellion of the old Norman family of Fitzgerald of Desmond. Estates, carved out of the confiscated land, were offered, at the nominal rent of a penny per acre, to would-be settlers, who undertook to bring with them from England their tenants, servants and farm stock. Among the numerous families that established themselves in Munster at that time were those of Spenser, Ralegh, Courtney, Clifton, Hatton, Hyde, St Leger, Boyle, Carew, Denny and Browne.

At the beginning of the seventeenth century, following the defeat of Hugh O'Neill and Hugh O'Donnell at Kinsale, there followed the plantation of Ulster, the consequences of which remain with us to this day. Farmers, merchants and craftsmen from England and Scotland began to settle in considerable numbers on the confiscated territory of the former Ulster chieftains. After the rebellion of 1641 a further two and a half million acres of Irish land was declared forfeited in order to satisfy Cromwell's debts to his financial sponsors, army officers and common soldiers. By the time the Williamite plantation — the last in Irish history — was completed towards the end of the seventeenth century, a mere fifteen per cent of Irish land remained in Irish hands.

Scots

Of the numerous organized groups of incomers to this island, the ingress of the Scots was perhaps the most natural, considering the narrow channel that separates the south-west of Scotland from the north-east of Ireland. The story of Scoto-Irish interaction goes back to the sixth century when Columcille founded Ireland's first missionary house on the island of Iona, at a time when the kingdom of Dal Riada on the Antrim plateau extended over the North Channel to embrace the Western Highlands and Isles of Scotland. By the time the first stream of Scottish immigrants began to reach Ireland in the middle of the thirteenth century, Western Scotland had, of course, absorbed the shock of the ravaging Norsemen, so that the incoming settlers were essentially an intermixture of Dalriadic Irish, Viking and Pict. To the medieval Irish annalists they were known as *galloglaigh.*

Gallowglass motif from 'Hibernia' by John Goghe, 1567.

As their name implies, the *galloglaigh,* anglicized Gallowglasses, were "foreign young fighting men" — in simple language, mercenaries. As professional soldiers, they found ready employers among the heads of the great Irish houses, notably O'Neill, O'Donnell and Maguire of Ulster, De Burgo and O'Conor of Connacht, and Fitzgerald of Munster. We are told they were men of great stature, that they were courageous and fierce in battle, that they were dressed in coats of mail to the knee and were armed with battle-axes. Among the principal gallowglass families to make their mark in the Irish annals were MacDonald, MacSweeney, MacSheehy, MacRory and MacCabe.

In 1603 when James, King of Scotland, succeeded to the throne of England, he was determined to undo the close association — of which the institution of the *galloglaigh* was a manifestation — that existed between the west of Scotland and Ulster, an association that had long been a source of worry to him as King of Scotland. Accordingly, he encouraged his subjects in that other Scotland — the anglicized south, centred on Edinburgh — to take up unlimited quantities of land in Ulster at six pence an acre. Thousands of farmers and labourers from the lowlands of Scotland, led by James Hamilton and Hugh Montgomery, were settled in Counties Antrim and Down on the forfeited lands of O'Neill of Clandeboy. The plantation of the northern counties accounts for the frequent appearance there of surnames such as Stewart, Ross, Patterson, Frazer, Morrison, Kerr, Graham, Sinclair and Gordon.

Welsh

The movement of Welsh people to Ireland, while admittedly lacking the intensity and significance of the English and Scottish settlements here, was nonetheless a recognized phenomenon from early historical times. The seventeenth-century Irish historian, Geoffrey Keating, in a passage in *Forus Feasa ar Éirinn,* maintained that "Ireland was a place of refuge for the Welsh whenever they suffered persecution from the Romans or Saxons." "Large numbers of them," he goes on to say, "with their families, followers and cattle used to repair for refuge to Ireland where the Irish nobles would give them land." In the ninth and tenth centuries the Viking harrassment of Wales was responsible for a considerable influx of Welshmen into Ireland: an entry in the Annals of the Four Masters for the year 874 even records that Roary Mac Murmine, king of the Welshmen, sought refuge in Ireland from the Black Danes.

It was, however, the Cambrian element in the Anglo-Norman invasion of Ireland that accounts, in the main, for the infusion of Welsh stock into the native population. It will be remembered that many of the leaders of that invasion, like Fitzgerald and Fitzstephen, were themselves partly Welsh. Giraldus Cambrensis, the chronicler of the invasion, tells us that Robert Fitzstephen, who landed in Ireland in 1169, was accompanied by three hundred archers on foot, representing, as he put it, "the flower of the south of Wales." Almost certainly many of these soldiers, who came from south Wales and especially Pembrokeshire, eventually settled as tenants on the feudal manors of their Norman masters.

Irish tradition points to a number of other settlements by the Welsh in

Ireland in the twelfth and subsequent centuries. The seventeenth century antiquary and genealogist, Duald MacFirbis, in a tract on the Welshmen of Tirawley, gives an account of a Welsh settlement in the thirteenth century in north-west Connacht. According to him, the Irish families of Walsh, Barrett, Joyce, MacHale, Wallace, Tomlin, Hosty and Lawless, so characteristic of the area, are descended from these Welsh settlers. In addition to this Connacht settlement, there is also a tradition of a Welsh colony in Co. Antrim. Conell MacGeoghagan, the seventeenth-century translator of the Annals of Clonmacnoise, notes that the families of Barrett, Cusack and McQuillin of the Route, in north Antrim, "are Welsh and came from Wales to this land."

Lastly, among the Cromwellian soldiery there can be identified a fair sprinkling of Welshmen. They were mainly "marcher Welsh," originating in those parts of Wales abutting on the English border. By temperament dissenters and free worshippers, their natural dislike of establishment religion had inclined them to support the puritanical Cromwell. A number opted to take up land in Ireland in lieu of payment for army service: the Evanses, Morgans and Morrises who settled in Munster fall into this category.

Flemings

Mention may be made here of the movement of a small but interesting group of people from South Wales to Ireland just before and also during the Norman invasion of Ireland. When in 1167 Dermot MacMurrough returned to Ireland from Wales, where he had gone to elicit Norman support for his campaign to re-establish himself as King of Leinster, he was accompanied by a knight from Pembrokeshire named Richard Fitzgodebert. Almost certainly the Fitzgodeberts or Godeberts belonged to the colony of Flemings planted in the province of Ros in Pembrokeshire by Henry I in the early twelfth century. Later generations of the family of Godebert "the Fleming," Orpen states, took the name of de la Roche, from the rock-castle near Haverford in Pembrokeshire.

A close reading of the sources suggests that the Flemings of South Wales played a considerable role in the invasion. In their record of the events of 1169 the Four Masters speak of *Loingeas na Fflemendach do thocht . . . . ,* that is to say "the coming of the Flemish fleet . . . ." Moreover, the little band of warriors who joined Maurice de Prendergast on his expedition to Ireland were, no doubt, largely composed of mercenaries drawn from the Flemish settlement in the neighbourhood of Haverford. Maurice's native place was Haverford, while Orpen notes that the name Prendergast survives as that of a suburb of Haverford.

In Ireland the Flemish element among the invasion settlers impressed itself most strongly on Co. Wexford, notably the baronies of Forth and Bargy. The peninsular position of these baronies — the sea on one side, the mountain of Forth on the other — ensured that the descendants of the original settlers preserved their way of life and language right up to the eighteenth century. While names cannot always be taken to be conclusive evidence of origin, nevertheless surnames like Codd, Colfer, Howe, Quiney, Rossiter, Sinnott, Stafford, Stephen and Whitty — all traditionally associated with the "Barnies" — would seem to constitute a link with the medieval settlement of Flemings in south Wexford.

The seventeenth century brought a selection of Flemish and Dutch merchants to Ireland. The religious troubles caused by first Spain's and then France's designs on the Reformed Low Countries adversely affected commerce and many local merchants departed to overseas trading centres like London or Dublin. At the end of the century others of their countrymen followed them in the shadow of William III's army. These entrepreneurs, who established themselves in the various Irish ports, are readily identifiable from contemporary testamentary documents, in which they frequently describe themselves as "merchant," and sign by such names as Van Cruyskercken, Vanwycke, Vereker, Vernezobre and Van Homrigh. Of the last named family was Esther Van Homrigh, immortalized as Vanessa in letters by Jonathan Swift, Dean of the Cathedral Church of St Patrick, Dublin.

Huguenot French

The religious and political upheavals in Europe during the sixteenth and seventeenth centuries lay at the root of small but selective settlements here, beginning in the late 1600's, of members of the Reformed Church in France — the Huguenots, as they were called. In the course of the Reformation, traditionalists and reformers engaged in a bloody struggle — particularly vicious in France — on the question of whether the institutional Church or the Bible was to be regarded as the canon of Christian truth. The Edict of Nantes, promulgated by Henry IV of France in 1598, allowed the Huguenots, after sixty years of persecution, liberty of conscience and freedom of worship. But the revocation of that Edict in 1685 resulted in a renewed persecution of the Huguenots, so much so that thousands upon thousands of French Protestant refugees sought asylum in Switzerland, Germany, Holland, England and Ireland.

The origin of the term *Huguenot,* first applied as a nickname to the French Protestants, is extremely obscure. Some authorities suppose it to be derived from *Huguon,* a word used in Touraine to signify persons who

The Huguenot Settlers in Ireland.

NAME.	COUNTY.	PARTICULARS.
Meinhardt Christain,	Longford	549 acres, reserved rent £6 17s 5d.
Nathaniel Philipot,	Longford and Dublin	6103 acres, reserved rent £76 5s 2d.
John Exham,	Cork	213 acres, reserved rent £1 19s 9d.
Daniel Hignette,	Cork	680 acres, reserved rent £2 2s 6d.
Richard Covert,	Cork	1633 acres, reserved rent £15 6s 3d.
John Mascal, clk,	Cork	Impropriate tithes of Cork beg.
Charles Nicholette,	Cork	398 acres, reserved rent £3 14s 8d.
Anne Wybrowe,	Limerick and Kerry	723 acres, reserved rent £6 15s 6d.
Ahasuerus Reigmort,	Limerick	148 acres, reserved rent £2 5s.
John Turin,	Limerick	745 acres, reserved rent £19 13s
Abel Guilliams,	Wexford	1591 acres, reserved rent £19. 17s 11d.
Christain Borr,	Wexford	304 acres, reserved rent £3 15s
Richard Izod,	Kilkenny	619 acres, reserved rent £7 14s 10d.
William De la Mere,	Galway	2472 acres, reserved rent £15 9s 0d.
Fredrick Trench.	Galway	670 acres, reserved rent £6 1s 3d.
John Gaick,	King's County	1055 acres, reserved rent £19 8s 0d.
John Holland,	King's County	1529 acres, reserved rent £19 2s 5d.
Philip Bigoe.	King's County & Clare	2569 acres, reserved rent £32 4s 3d.
Ferdinando Weeden,	Clare	70 acres, reserved rent £11 13s 2½.
Henry Ivers,	Clare	1050 acres, reserved rent £9 17s 0d.
Faustine Cubbaidge,	Cavan	1597 acres, reserved rent £12 11s 4d.
Thomas Guyllyms,	Cavan	3667 acres, reserved rent £80 11s 3d.
Andrew Ricard,	Waterford & Tipperary	3485 acres, reserved rent £32 4s 3d.
Robert Mercier,	Waterford and Kerry	240 acres, reserved rent £2 5s
John Paris,	Tipperary	995 acres, reserved rent £30 4s 10d.
Ambrose Aungier,	Longford	Was possessed of an estate in fee.
John Jerones,	Wexford	Had a burgage in the town of Wexford.

Table detailing settlement of Huguenot families in Ireland.

walked the streets at night — the early Protestants, like the early Christians, preferring the late evening for their religious assemblies. Others are of the opinion that the term derives from the word *Eignote* — the name given to a confederacy of Swiss cantons that entered into an alliance to resist attempts on their liberties by the Duke of Saxony. A third surmise is that the term was derived from one Hugues, the name of a Genevese Calvinist.

The main body of Huguenots, whose family names are best remembered today, came to Ireland between 1685 and 1700 from the countryside around the city of La Rochelle in the present day department of Poitou-Charentes. Some came directly, others via England, while a considerable number arrived here as officers and privates in the army of King William of Orange. Following the end of the Williamite war in Ireland, substantial Huguenot settlements were effected in Portarlington, Youghal, Waterford, Cork, Lisburn and Dublin. In the latter, the settlers established themselves, for the most part, in the "Liberties," where they began the manufacture of tabinet which later became well known as Irish poplin.

In the fields of commerce, manufacture and banking the Huguenots introduced an entirely new but welcome expertise to Ireland. In this connection names like Fontaine, La Touche and D'Olier immediately spring to mind. In other areas of human endeavour, such as the ministry and literature, descendants of Huguenots bearing names like Saurin, Chevenix, Trench, Le Fanu and Boucicault made notable contributions. When French names such as Boissere, Blanc, Bouhereau, Fleury, Goulin, Ligonier and Vignoles began to be anglicized in the early nineteenth century, it is easy to understand how, in the Irish situation, some curious misnomers resulted. To take just one example, the Huguenot name Couchancex was rendered "Coach-and-six!"

Early in this century church registers and historical documents relating to the Huguenots were deposited in the Public Record Office, Dublin. Fortunately,before catastrophe struck in 1922, many of these had been published by the Huguenot Society of London, viz., the registers of the French Conformist Church of St. Patrick and St. Mary, Dublin (ed. by J. J. Digges La Touche, 1893), the registers of the French Nonconformist Church of Lucy-Lane and Wood-street, Dublin (ed. by T. P. Le Fanu, 1901), and the registers of the French Church of Portarlington (ed. by T. P. Le Fanu, 1908). With the help of these sources and some published family histories, it is possible to construct a reasonably accurate picture of the Huguenot settlements in Ireland.

Palatine Germans

The movement of several hundred German-speaking families from the Palatinate of the Rhine to Ireland in 1709 is a subject that has attracted the attention of a number of scholars and researchers in recent years. The migrations of the Palatines were occasioned, in the first instance, by the destruction caused in their homeland by the wars between Louis XIV of France and a European confederacy that included England. In early May, 1709, thousands of farmers and vine-dressers from the countryside of Hesse and Baden, west of the city of Mannheim, made their way down the River Rhine to Rotterdam, whence they were transported in English ships to the port of London.

The English government of the day, its finances at a low ebb due to the cost of the campaign against Louis XIV, appears to have been ill-prepared to deal with the sudden influx of German Protestant refugees from the Rhineland. From Whitehall correspondence of 12 May 1709, we learn that "German Protestants lately come from the Palatinate are in a starving condition and several have died of want." The mayor of Canterbury, when requested to accommodate some of the poor Palatines, replied that he did not have enough to give his own poor. In June, Queen Anne gave orders that tents be pitched on Blackheath to accommodate the refugees. The Board of Ordnance wrote that tents would be required for 6,520.

The dispatch of over eight hundred Palatine families to Ireland in September 1709 was a direct response to the Council of Ireland's request of 7 July to Queen Anne that five hundred such families be sent to Ireland. In making such a request the English establishment in Ireland was motivated by two considerations, first the desire to strengthen the Protestant interest there, and secondly the prospect of introducing a measure of continental expertise in agriculture and industry into the home economy.

The Government-appointed "Commissioners for the settling of the poor Palatines in Ireland," in the course of correspondence with the Irish authorities, reported the numbers of Palatines arriving at Dublin as follows:—

	Number of Families	Number of Persons	Persons over 14 years	Persons under 14 years
4-7 Sept. 1709	794	2,971	1,836	1,135
14 Oct. 1709	25	100	62	38
24 Jan. 1710	2	2	—	2
Total	821	3,073	1,898	1,175

The Commissioners succeeded in placing a total of 538 Palatine families on the estates of forty-three sympathetic Irish landlords but, to the dismay of the Commissioners and the annoyance of the well-meaning landed gentlemen, 352 of these families deserted their new holdings, some by night, most without a fair reason. The Commissioners' reports indicate that between April and December 1710 a total of 232 Palatine families returned to England. In 1712 Sir Thomas Southwell, one of the forty-three proprietors who had already befriended ten Palatine households, succeeded in inducing a further one hundred and thirty families to settle on his estate at Rathkeale in Co. Limerick. Southwell's inducements were clearly decisive; they included fallow land at half rent, free materials to build houses as well as cash grants. In 1716 Sir Thomas, in a letter to the Lord Lieutenant of Ireland,was apparently able to report that all the families had settled in well and were fully engaged in the production of hemp, flax and cattle. Another sizeable settlement of Palatine families was made on the estate of Abel Ram near Gorey in Co. Wexford.

Aside from their looks, language and customs, the Palatines could, of course, be readily identified from their family names — and surnames like Bovenizer, Delmege, Fitzell, Reinhardt, Ruttle, Shire, Sparling, Teskey and Switzer found in the current edition of the Irish telephone directory represent descendants of the original settlers on Southwell's estate.

Jews

We have seen how, over the centuries, layer upon layer, the population of Ireland has been laid down. And still our island continues to attract newcomers. Within the past hundred years racial intolerance and war lie at the root of small settlements here of Jews, Italians, Hungarians and, most recently of all, Vietnamese. Of the four, Jewish immigration from eastern Europe in the closing decades of the last century was in terms of numbers the most significant.

In the aftermath of the promulgation of the Russian anti-semitic laws of 1881, thousands of Lithuanian, Polish and Russian Jews were compelled to seek asylum in these islands. The Irish census returns for 1881 and 1901 reveal that in that twenty-year period the number of Jews resident in Ireland rose from 472 to 3,769. Most were listed as resident in the larger cities like Dublin, Belfast, Cork, Limerick and Waterford. The census statistics of 1901 for Dublin show that there were 261 drapers, 223 pedlars and hawkers, 200 students, 88 commercial travellers, 72 tailors, 66 domestic servants and 64 dealers among the Jews of foreign birth.

In his *Special Report* for 1909 the Registrar-General tabulates the following examples of names of the Jewish settlers from the Marriage and Birth Indexes of his office:

Coplan	Maisell	Statsumsky	Wedeclefsky
Fridberg	Matufsky	Stuppel	Weiner
Greenberg	Rabinovitch	Wachman	Winstock
Hasselberg	Rossen		

The Irish People today.

A comprehensive account of the Jewish settlement in Ireland from earliest times to 1910 can be read in *The Jews in Ireland,* by Louis Hyman, published by Irish University Press, 1972.

Conclusion

History, as Bronowski reminds us in *The Ascent of Man,* is not, in the final analysis, about events but people. In turn, man is not merely the embodiment of his present and future but, in his day to day life, also acts out a little of the past. In a sense, some among us could be said to be people who have been living on this island for over two thousand years. New arrivals intermarrying with the descendants of earlier settlers in the fullness of time produced a common identity: the peoples of Ireland merged to become the Irish people.

Over the ages there is no telling how many individuals wind and wave have thrown up upon our shores, and one can only hope that those who made the shore could truly say of the land they found that it became for them, in Homer's words, "a rough country but a good nurse."

A Dé 7 a Muire is mor do na genelacaib sin nac bfuil fis agam ar bith cé h-iad: O God, many are the generations I have no knowledge whatsoever about.

Scribe's marginal entry in Manuscript VI,
Advocates Library, Edinburgh.

Bibliography

Almgren, B., *The Vikings,* Gothenburg, 1966.
Bronowski, J., *The Ascent of Man,* London, 1973.
Hyman, Louis, *The Jews in Ireland,* Irish University Press, 1972.
MacNiocaill, G., *Ireland before the Vikings,* Dublin, 1972.
O'Rahilly, C., *Ireland and Wales,* London, 1924.
O'Rahilly, T. F., *Early Irish History and Mythology,* Dublin, 1946.
O'Rahilly, T. F., *The Goidels and their Predecessors,* London, 1935.
Smiles, S., *The Huguenots,* London, 1881.
Todd, J. H. (ed.), *War of the Gaedhil with the Gaill,* Dublin, 1867.

CHAPTER 2

Historical and Administrative Divisions of Ireland

DR. WILLIAM NOLAN

Research in Irish source materials, whether these be literary, historical or genealogical in character, presupposes an acquaintance with Irish historical and administrative geography, especially with geographical and administrative divisions, maps and place-names. This requirement is most pressing for those contemplating work in the field of genealogical research because so many of our records were based on territorial denominations such as the townland, the parish and the barony. In this connection, if there is one work more than another that should be at the hand of every researcher, it is surely one of the editions of that monumental government publication entitled *General Alphabetical Index to the Townlands and Towns, Parishes and Baronies of Ireland.* Any good reference library will have a copy.

On the subject of maps, it is useful to know that the Irish Government's Ordnance Survey has published a set of five sectional maps covering the entire country, on a scale of one quarter inch to the mile, and a more detailed series of twenty-four maps covering the entire country on a scale of one half inch to the mile. These show not only the natural physical features — hills, lakes and rivers — but also a wide range of man-made features — roads, churches, antiquities and, of course, towns and villages.

This article is concerned with the evolution of some of the more important administrative divisions of Ireland. Its aim is to assist the research worker to acquire a deeper understanding and appreciation of the various types of record he or she must inevitably come to handle in the course of research. It is hoped that it will enable those engaged in genealogical research to narrow the field of their endeavours and to confidently identify the locality of their forebears. The treatment of divisions is selective, and only those units which are important for historical research are examined.

Provinces

The four provinces of modern Ireland — Ulster in the north, Leinster in the east, Munster in the south and Connacht in the west — form the largest units of geographical reference in Ireland. The origins of these provinces (of which there were five in existence prior to the coming of the Normans) can be traced to the overriding influence exerted in their respective territories by the great Irish dynastic families of O Neill (Ulster and Meath), O Brien (Munster), O Conor (Connacht) and MacMurrough-Kavanagh (Leinster). In the post-Norman period the historic provinces of Leinster and Meath gradually merged, mainly due to the impact of the Pale which straddled both, thereby forming our present-day province of Leinster. In the Irish Annals these five ancient political divisions were invariably referred to as *cúigí*, i.e. "fifth parts," such as the fifth of Munster, the fifth of Ulster and so on. The English administrators and record-makers, on the other hand, dubbed them "provinces," in imitation of the Roman imperial *provinciae*. Very occasionally the province was used as an entity for official surveys of land and estates: an obvious example is the Earl of Strafford's Survey into the titles to estates in Connacht, 1635-6.

Dioceses

During the fourth and fifth centuries the Christian Church in Europe organized itself within the framework of a territorial or geographical episcopate, in which the bishop became the principal administrator of a well-defined area known as a diocese. In Ireland, on the other hand, ecclesiastical discipline, jurisdiction and organization were essentially monastic in character, and remained so until the twelfth century. By that time the number of monasteries was excessively high in relation to the size of the Christian community, while at the same time in matters of church government the position of the abbots, whether bishops or not, was supreme. With a view to imposing the continental-type diocesan organization on the Irish church, three ecclesiastical synods were convened in Ireland in the first half of the twelfth century, and it is to these great reforming synods that we owe the present formal diocesan structure of the Irish church.

The first took place at Cashel in the year 1101 and was presided over by Muirchertach Ua Briain, great-grandson of Brian Boru. Gilbert, the papal legate, outlined a plan for a hierarchical structure to embrace all Ireland, based on the model of the Universal Church. He declared that the Irish Church, including the abbots and monasteries, should be ruled by bishops, and parishes should be administered by priests and not by monks.

The subsequent synods of Rathbreasail (near Templemore, Co. Tipperary) in 1111 and Kells in 1152 were the instruments whereby Gilbert's plan was put into effect. The hierarchical arrangement, as decreed at Kells, provided for four ecclesiastical provinces, Armagh, Cashel, Dublin and Tuam, each headed by an archbishop, and under these were to be twenty-two suffragan bishops in charge of as many dioceses. It is, perhaps, worthy of note that the diocesan boundaries set down at these two synods appear in several

IRELAND,

Showing the Ecclesiastical Division into
PROVINCES AND DIOCESES;
WITH THE EPISCOPAL SEES.

*From the Rev.ᵈ W. Beaufort's Map
published in 1792.*

Boundaries of the 4 Arch bishopricks
of Armagh Dublin Cashel & Tuam
Boundaries of the Bishopricks

Scale of English Miles
0   10   20   30   40   50   60

Longitude West ‡ from Greenwich

W. Hughes.

instances to be aligned with old Irish tribal territories. Thus, for example, the Diocese of Limerick is parallelled by the ancient territory of Uí Fidhgente, the Diocese of Lismore by the territory of the Deise and the Diocese of Cork by that of the Ui Eachach. Moreover, the Dioceses of Ossory and Ferns take their names from similar territorial entities. Apart from occasional minor modifications, the ecclesiastical geography of Ireland, as mapped at Kells, has remained constant to the present day and is in use by both Catholic and Anglican churches.

Counties

The gradual imposition of the English shire system on Ireland gave rise, in due course, to our modern administrative divisions. The development of the territorial framework of counties was interrelated to the process of political colonization which began with the shiring of Dublin in the late twelfth century. Professor Otway-Ruthven has suggested that in 1211-12 there were still only three shires, namely Dublin, Waterford with Cork, and Munster (which included Limerick, Tipperary and Thomond). Kerry appeared as a shire as early as 1232-3, while Oriel, or Louth, also became a shire about this time. The counties of Tipperary and Limerick date from 1254; Connacht, shired in 1247, was subdivided into the shires of Connacht and Roscommon in 1292. Representatives from these shires attended the Parliament of 1297, one of whose first enactments was the creation of two new shires, Kildare and Meath. Part of north-east Ulster was divided into the shires of Antrim and Down about 1300. In 1306 the Liberty of Carlow reverted to the Crown and was thereafter considered a shire.

The evolution of the shire system represents the encroachment by the central government on the great lordships originally formed at the beginning of the Anglo-Norman conquest. Shires were instruments of local government. They were administered by sheriffs who had a wide variety of functions, including the holding of shire-courts on a fixed day of the week, the collection of subsidies and other revenues due to the Crown, and the maintenance of bridges and highways. The delimitation of their territorial jurisdiction was an important process in fixing definitive boundaries.

The shiring process slowed down in the following two centuries, and the impetus to proceed was directly related to the vigorous policy of Plantation in the period from 1550 to 1600. The shire of Westmeath was created in 1543. In 1557 the historic "countries of Leix, Slievemarge, Irry, Glinmaliry and Offaly" were shired. Legislation contained in the Acts known as 3rd and 4th Philip and Mary tells us much about the government's perception of the value of the process:

"and to the end the said countries may be from henceforth the better conserved, and kept in civil government, be it enacted . . . that the new fort in Leix be from henceforth forever called and named Maryborough, and that the said countries of Leix, Slewmarge, Irry, and such portion of Glinmaliry as standeth and is situate on that side of the river Barrow, whereupon the said Maryborough standeth and is situated . . . be from the first day of this Parliament, one shire or county, named, known, and called the Queen's County, and shall from the said day be taken, reputed and used as a county or shire, to all purposes for ever, and that there shall be appointed, ordained, and made within the said shire or county, for the rule thereof, and execution of things there, sheriff, coroners, escheator, clerk of the market, and other officers and ministers of Justice yearly, as in other shires or counties in this Realm of Ireland be or should be.''

Successive governments reiterated the necessity of bringing this uniform administrative system to the whole country as a means of extending common law and of reducing the autonomous power of both Gaelic and Anglo-Norman families. The O'Farrells of Annaly were subjugated by 1565 and their "country" became henceforth the county of Longford. Between 1568 and 1578 the Lord Deputy, Sir Henry Sydney, subdivided the existing shire of Connacht into the counties of Clare, Galway, Mayo and Sligo. Clare, which geographically belongs more to Connacht than to Munster, was carved out of the medieval territory of the O'Briens which was known as Thomond. It was returned to Munster in 1639.

The shiring of Ulster, under Sir John Perrott, was the last major addition to the county system. The Lordships of the Gaelic families of O'Cahan, O'Neill, Maguire, O'Reilly, MacMahon, O'Hanlon and O'Donnell were submerged into the counties of Coleraine, Tyrone, Fermanagh, Cavan, Monaghan, Armagh and Donegal respectively. The creation of Wicklow by statute in 1606 completed the county framework as we know it today. The tenacity of the O'Tooles and O'Byrnes in maintaining their grip on the great glens and remote mountain fastnesses adjoining the anglicized Pale is a reminder not to regard the colonization as a simple east to west progression.

It is evident that the counties were invariably formed as convenient administrative units out of a group of Anglo-Norman Lordships and Gaelic "countries" or "nations." The longevity of the county as an administrative division, and its role today as an important concept, is due to a number of factors. During the seventeenth century the county was taken as a leading unit of area when framing the great plantation schemes. The Strafford Inquisition of Connacht c. 1635, the Down Survey, Civil Survey and Books of Survey and Distribution were all major enquiries concerning land, its location, quality and ownership. The county became a standardized term of reference in the location, distribution and sale of land and this, more than anything else, led to its permanence. Sir William Petty's atlas, *Hibernia Delineatio,* served as the standard Irish atlas until the publication, in 1776, of Bernard Scalé's *Hibernian Atlas*. Moreover, the Grand Jury system, which developed in the eighteenth century, served to reinforce the concept of the county as an administrative region since, however undemocratic, Grand Juries were an embryonic form of local administration. Their members, drawn mainly from the landed gentry, met in the county towns where they administered hospitals and gaols, besides being responsible for the development and maintenance of the local road-system. The use of the county towns as meeting places augmented their existing importance and ensured their survival and that of the county unit which they served.

The present status of the county as an administrative division is the result of a vast body of legislation ranging from the Poor Relief (Ireland) Act of 1838, through the County Management Act of 1940 and the more recent Local Government Planning and Development Act of 1963. The recurrent crises of the nineteenth century led to the more direct involvement of central government in the administration of national valuation and taxation schemes, and in the relief of distress. The mapping of the country on the basis of six inches to the statute mile was completed in 1846, and this official cartographic recognition of county boundaries fossilized them as units of convenience. The Valuation (Ireland) Act of 1852 provided for one uniform valuation of lands and tenements throughout Ireland. This was completed in 1865 and, together with the Ordnance Survey maps, provided a vast compendium of information on counties and their contents. The administrative counties were formed in 1898 by the Local Government (Ireland) Act. County Councils, of which there are twenty-seven in the Republic, consist of elected representatives and a number of administrators, overseen by county managers. They have a wide, but declining, range of responsibilities and their existence has given the county unit a function and a personality.

The Gaelic Athletic Association, through its provincial and national competitions in Gaelic football and hurling, has been one of the most important generators of county consciousness. Other elements too have cemented loyalties and affection between people and place. Dialect, local tradition, shared history and even physical appearance differentiate people on a county basis. Some counties have their own anthems, redolent of the spirit of the place. For many the song "Boolavogue" sums up the character and aspirations of the people of Wexford, while "Slievenamon" captures the flavour of Tipperary. The vitality of county associations overseas is irrefutable evidence of the durability of the county unit as a distinctive region.

A reprint of the thirty-two maps, one for each county, which were drawn for Lewis's *Topographical Dictionary of Ireland* in 1837, is included in *Handbook on Irish Genealogy*.

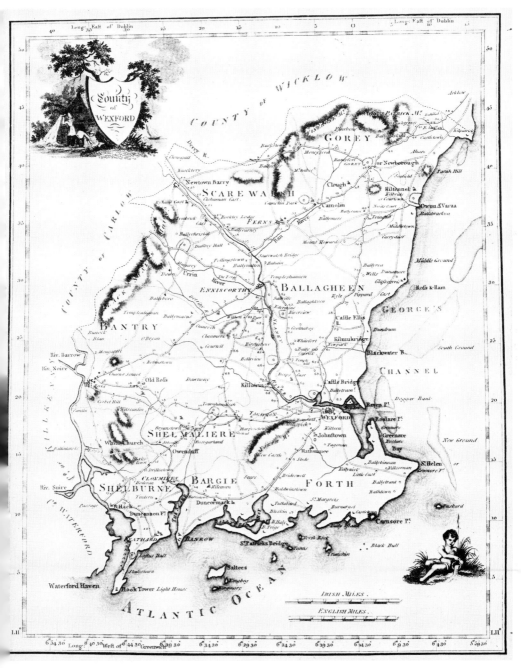

Wexford County and Barony Divisions.

Small Baronies not shown on map

St. Mullin's Upper (Co. Carlow), Courceys (Co. Cork), Dublin (Co. Dublin), Callan & Kilculliheen (Co. Kilkenny), North Liberties & Kilmallock (Co. Limerick), N.W. Liberties of Londonderry & N.E. Liberties of Coleraine (Co. Londonderry), Drogheda (Co. Louth).

Ireland: Counties and Baronies.

Baronies

Celtic Ireland's basic territorial division was the *tuath* (tribe or people). In their book, *The Celtic Realms,* Dillon and Chadwick noted the resemblance between barony names and *tuath* names. They found, however, that in the eleventh century the Book of Rights lists only ninety-seven *tuaths,* although to-day Ireland has a total of two hundred and seventy-three baronies. The modern barony is a superimposed division which can represent single or multiple units, either Gaelic or Anglo-Norman. From the sixteenth century onwards the barony was widely employed as an administrative, tax and regional entity within the county. The steady use of baronies during the seventeenth century, both as cadastral bases and convenient subdivisions of the county, standardized their shape and function. The baronial geography of seventeenth century Ireland is to be found set out in the three great series, the *Civil Survey,* the *Down Survey* and the *Books of Survey and Distribution.* In the numerous transactions concerning land in that century, the townland, barony and county were all employed as references to locate and identify property, and this legal recognition ensured their survival.

During the eighteenth century, county rates, as levied by the Grand Juries, were paid on a barony basis. The Grand Jury Act of 1836 authorized the holding of presentment sessions in each barony and each barony was represented in the county-at-large presentment sessions. The barony was used as a unit in the printed census summaries until 1901, and the general Valuation of rateable property in the mid-nineteenth century was largely organized and published by barony. The reorganization of local government at the end of the century heralded the demise of the barony as a meaningful territorial division.

Though the barony never had the local significance of either county or parish, nonetheless in cases where it coincides with a district of distinctive physical character, the barony name can still proclaim both a heritage and an identity. The baronies of East and West Inishowen (Donegal), Erris (Mayo), Moycullen (Galway), Burren (Clare), Iveragh (Kerry), Carbery (Cork), Bargy and Forth (Wexford), Mourne (Down) and Dunluce (Antrim) are all situated in coastal areas and have retained meaning as spatial entities. Other barony names such as, for example, Clanmorris (Macmorris), Costello (MacCostello), both in Mayo, Eliogarty (O'Fogarty) in Tipperary, the Oneillands in Armagh and Upper and Lower Talbotstown in Wicklow commemorate family surnames.

Parishes

In origin, the parish is an ecclesiastical administrative division of great

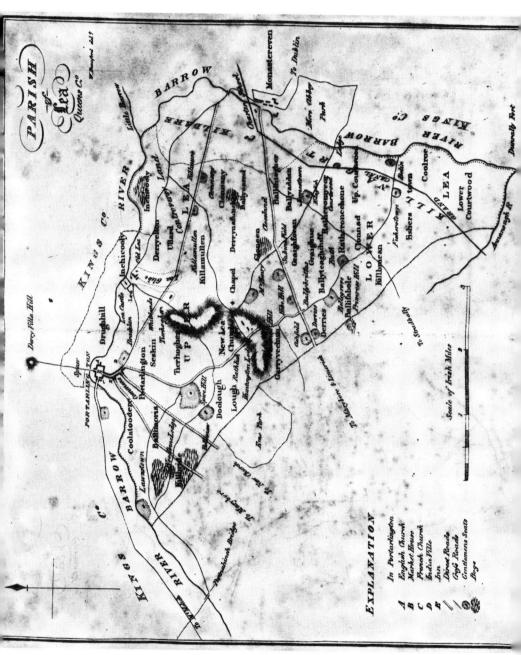

Civil parish of Lea, Queen's County (Leix).
Parochial Survey of Ireland, William Shaw Mason, 1814.

antiquity, and indicates the area over which a clergyman exercised spiritual jurisdiction. The early Christian churches, often found in association with a burial ground and holy well, were rarely destroyed. The density of early Christian parish centres is surprisingly high in what must have been sparsely populated countryside. However, they may not have functioned in the same way as modern parochial centres. Some churches may have been administered by specific families; others may have served primarily as safe housing for the shrine of a local saint and thus become places of pilgrimage. It would seem that by the thirteenth century a network of parishes existed across the island. The Anglo-Normans did little to alter the existing framework, apart from rededicating churches to universally acknowledged saints. The break in continuity from the early Christian period to modern Ireland occurred in the sixteenth century, with the extension of the Reformation to Ireland and the dissolution of the monastic orders. The armed conflicts of the seventeenth century and the suppression of the Catholic clergy further eroded the status of the medieval parish, allowing the old structures to be adapted by the new religious administration and also to be used as civil territorial divisions in the land surveys. The sparsity of the Protestant community in some parts of the country meant that many ancient parish centres were neglected and failed to attract settlement. There are numerous examples to-day of these isolated, ruined churches.

From the Reformation onwards, the two major religious communities had separate parochial structures. In general, the medieval parish became the civil parish and the parish of the Established Church: sometimes two or more small civil parishes would be combined to make one church parish. The Catholic Church, deprived of its great resources of buildings and land by the Reformation, had to adapt itself to a new parochial system. The poverty of the population and the restrictions on priests ensured that the new units were large and unwieldy. Old focal points were abandoned and the new Catholic parishes were focused on the rapidly developing network of towns and villages, often taking the village name instead of the old parochial one. The evolution of the contemporary Catholic Church owes little to the medieval world, though it retains the ancient ecclesiastical lay-out from the Synod of Kells, and has to be seen in terms of population changes and especially with the re-emergence of the Catholic Church in the early nineteenth century.

The relative ages of the parish systems become apparent when they are mapped. The civil parishes frequently break both the barony and county boundaries, indicating that they were drawn up with scant reference to either. On the other hand, Catholic parishes, though constructed on a diocesan basis, faithfully observe the county boundaries.

The creation of Catholic parishes still continues, particularly in the rapidly developing suburban areas of the cities. Between 1975 and 1980 no fewer than twenty-six new parishes were created in the Archdiocese of Dublin. Because of the religious homogeneity of the population, the Catholic parish has always been a unit of great significance and the parish church and its ancillary buildings, such as the parish hall, are focal points in Irish life. In rural areas the Catholic parish is also used as the spatial base for sporting organizations such as the Gaelic Athletic Association.

It may be relevant here to indicate the major sources available that list civil and Catholic parishes. Because of its utilization as a cadastral and organizational unit in the various surveys of the seventeenth and nineteenth centuries, the civil parish is particularly well documented, as the following list shows:

Civil Parishes

1600-1700. The Civil Survey, 1654-6.
"Census" of Ireland, c. 1659.
The Down Survey, 1655-7.
The Books of Survey and Distribution, 1664-8.
Hearth Money Rolls, 1664-7.
1800-1901. Tithe Applotment Books, 1824-1838.
A Topographical Dictionary of Ireland, by Samuel Lewis, 1837 (arranged alphabetically by civil parish).
Summaries of Census of Population, 1821, 1841, 1851, 1861, 1871, 1881, 1891, 1901.
The Primary Valuation of Tenements, by Sir Richard Griffith, 1848-1864.
Townlands Index, 1841, 1851, 1871, 1901.
Parochial Survey of Ireland, 1814-19, by William Shaw Mason.

Catholic Parishes

1836 *et seq.* Catholic Directory, Almanack and Registry (issued annually since 1836, and arranged by Diocese).
A Topographical Dictionary of Ireland, by Samuel Lewis, 1837 (name(s) of corresponding Catholic parish(es) shown under each civil parish).

Townlands

The townland is the smallest administrative division in the country and all other territorial divisions are collections of townlands. The contemporary townland is representative of a great variety of units of measurement which were used locally to identify lands. O'Donovan assumed that the "denominations of land in modern times called townlands are generally quarters of the ancient Irish bally betaghs." They may also relate to land divisions such as ploughlands, quarters, cartrons, gneeves, trines and tates. The townland became standardized as a basic division in the seventeenth century through repeated usage in surveys and land transactions. From then onwards townlands were named in leases and great estates were listed and mapped by townlands. The tithe applotment books took the townland as their smallest division, as did the subsequent Valuation, and it was also used as an enumeration unit in the censuses. A most important record of townland names, shapes and sizes exists in the townland maps of the Ordnance Survey to the scale of six inches to the mile. The Ordnance Survey created a number of new townlands, and we can identify some of these by the use of such suffixes as Upper, Lower, North, South, East and West. These detailed maps, completed before the Famine, are an invaluable record of the lay-out of townlands at that heavily populated stage in our history.

There are approximately 64,000 townlands in Ireland. Great variations occur in townland sizes which range from three roods and one perch in Mill Bank, Co. Dublin, to 7,012 acres in Sheskin, barony of Erris, Co. Mayo. Townland quantity may be regarded as a rough guide to land quality, the bigger townlands being usually found in the poorer areas. Townland boundaries may coincide with either physical or man-made features: hill-tops and running water were widely used, as were roads, ancient hedges, estate walls and large ditches. In less mobile times, people identified closely with their townland or village, but even now townlands, because of their intimacy and association with home, are our most meaningful micro-regions.

Townland Names

The majority of townlands were named at an early period and denoted a place where people lived and the lands they owned. The standardization of territorial divisions in the seventeenth century greatly reduced the number of townlands and many place-names were lost in the process. Furthermore, these names were written down by people who had little knowledge of the Irish language and in many cases the place-names which have survived bear little similarity in meaning or construction to the original name. Because the primary purpose of place-names is to distinguish between places, they usually refer to permanent, visible and easily identifiable features of the landscape. These features may be divided into two groups. The first group consists of toponyms referring to physical or natural features, usually of a topographical or botanical nature. The second group refers to features which are man-made. The following are the major name elements in each group:

Topographical Features

Druim, ridge; *cnoc,* hill; *cúil, corner, angle; tulach,* mound; *gleann,* glen; *carraig,* rock, rocky place; *árd,* height; *mullach,* summit, height; *mor,* big; *beg, small.*

Botanical Features

Cluain, field cleared in a bog or forest, meadow; *doire,* oak-wood; *currach, corrach,* marsh, moor; *moin,* bog; *eanach,* marsh; *garran,* shrubbery; *muine,* shrubbery.

Land Units

Baile, place, land, farm, town; *gort,* field; *ceathramha,* quarter; *achadh,* field; *pairc,* field, demesne; *ceapach,* tillage, plot; *garrdha,* garden, cultivated plot.

Places of Settlement

Cill, church; *lios,* enclosure, fort; *rath,* fort; *dún,* fort; *cathair,* stone fort.

Place-names may be further classified according to age, an analysis which may reveal interesting regional patterns. In Ireland, place-names can be divided into Irish, Old-English and New-English names. Old-English names are those bestowed during the medieval period and include such elements as castle, court, farm, field, hill, park, town and wood. The New-English place-names may be defined as those given during the sixteenth and seventeenth century confiscations. They include brook, dale, lodge, mount and ville. Christian names and patronymics are sometimes commemorated in place-names and may give clues to the history of a district or the identity of the former owners. The following examples will serve to illustrate the different classes of place-names:

Examples of Place-names

Irish: Tullowglass, Donaghmore.
Old-English (1200-1600): Clinstown, Moatpark.
New-English (1600 onwards): Webbsborough, Swiftsheath.
Irish and Old-English: Castlecomer, Ballyraggett.
Irish and New-English: Firoda Upper, Dunmore West.
Old-English and New-English: Castlemarket East, Damerstown West.

In the rather complex subject of Irish place-names, the reader could do worse than to dip into P. W. Joyce's *Irish Local Names Explained,* Dublin 1884 (reprinted 1979), for guidance on the derivations and meanings of the commoner Irish toponyms. A more intimate treatment of local place-names will be found in the "Name Books" for each of the counties which were compiled from the letters and notes of John O'Donovan, collected in the course of the Ordnance Survey in the 1830's.

Maps

The six inch to the mile maps of Ireland, made c. 1833-1846, are very detailed maps of townlands, and also show parish and barony boundaries. These maps have, of course, been revised and updated. Due to their large scale they are difficult to handle for general purposes.

Half and quarter inch to the mile contoured maps give a good working impression of the physical aspects of the country. They show county boundaries but not those of parish or barony.

Bibliography

Andrews, J. H., *A Paper Landscape,* Oxford, 1975.
Curtis, E., *History of Medieval Ireland from 1086 to 1513,* 2nd ed., London, 1938.
Dillon, M. and Chadwick, N. K., *The Celtic Realms,* London, 1967.
Evans, E. E., *Irish Heritage,* Dundalk, 1942.
Green, A. S., *The Making of Ireland and its Undoing, 1200-1600,* London, 1908.
O'Donovan, John, *Genealogies, Tribes and Customs of Hy-Fiachrach,* Dublin, 1844.
Orpen, G. H., *Ireland under the Normans, 1169-1333,* 4 vols., Oxford, 1911-20 (reprinted 1968).
Orme, A. R., *Ireland,* London, 1969.
Otway-Ruthven, A. J., *A History of Medieval Ireland,* Dublin, 1968.

CHAPTER 3

Irish Census Returns and Census Substitutes

ROSEMARY FFOLLIOTT

Irish census returns are a peculiarly fragmented and widely dispersed body of records. For this reason they tend to be avoided or overlooked as a source of genealogical information. The country-wide returns made over the centuries for the central government which were once comprehensive now only survive for certain areas. Other returns made at the behest of private individuals such as bishops and landlords were necessarily local in character and related only to specific places. As might be expected, local returns vary widely in scope and content. Consequently there now exists an intricate hotch-potch of pieces of census in addition to what may be termed census substitutes. This article is an attempt to set down the main items available on a county basis. Almost certainly some items have been overlooked, and equally so, new items will come to light in the future.

In the first section of this article the various censuses, beginning with the oldest, are set down chronologically under date heading and discussed separately. The second section consists of detailed references to surviving returns for each of the counties. The amount of census material now available for individual counties varies considerably as will be seen from the lists below. It is instructive to compare, say, Londonderry, which has a great deal to offer, with Mayo, which has very little. The earliest census now surviving for the whole island is that of 1901.

Precise references to specific documents in individual libraries and offices are given as follows: PRO (1A 46 49), G.O.539, British Library Add. Ms. 4770.

Irish Census Returns 1630-1981

c. 1630

The Add. Ms. 4770 in the British Library contains a Muster Roll for

Ulster. It is undated, but there is general agreement that it stems from about 1630-1631. Arranged by county and by area within each county, it lists the undertakers (large landlords) and the names of men each could produce in time of need, plus a list of the available arms. No ages are shown, but by its nature the Roll must represent able-bodied males between about 16 and 50. The lists for three counties — Cavan, Donegal and Fermanagh — have been printed: details are given in the census lists arranged by county.

1652

In 1652 a list of the inhabitants of a large part of south Co. Dublin was compiled. Arranged by area, not parish, it extends roughly from Tallaght to Dalkey. Precise address within each area is not stated. Details provided include age, occupation, personal description and relationships, as for example, this family at "Tyrrenure: John Strong, labr, 24, a little low man, Kath his wife 23, med brown; Elizabeth Roiers his dau, 12, small brown woman". A copy of the list is at the Public Record Office (1A 41 100).

1654-6

Sir William Petty's *Civil Survey of Ireland* lists the then landlords of each townland as well as their predecessors in 1641, prior to the Cromwellian alterations. Arranged by county, barony, parish and townland, it supplies most interesting topographical details and the great tragedy is that so little of it survives. Providentially it includes Co. Tyrone which is missing from the 1659 "Census". It must be stressed, however, that for both 1641 and 1657 it refers only to substantial landlords, those of 1641 being, if anything, the more substantial. All the extant sections have been printed by the Irish Manuscripts Commission: exact details are given under each county.

1659

The *Census of Ireland circa 1659,* also compiled by Sir William Petty, was edited by Séamus Pender and published by the Dublin Stationery Office in 1939. It is not a true census, giving only the names of the tituladoes (those with title to land) and the total number of persons (English and Irish) resident on each townland. Its arrangement is similar to that of the Civil Survey, but no descriptions of property are supplied. The counties of Cavan, Galway, Mayo, Tyrone and Wicklow are wholly omitted, and only three baronies are given from Co. Meath. It is only useful for sizeable landlords, though it does descend a little lower in the economic scale than the Civil Survey. It also lists the "Principall Irish Names and their Number" in each barony, e.g. for Raphoe, Co. Donegal: "Browne 09, 0

Boyle 07, McCormick 07, Cunyngham 27, McCallin 07, McClintock 08, McCarter 07, McConnell 11'', and so on.

1664, 1665, 1666

Some of the Hearth Money Rolls from these years survive. Arranged by county and parish, they list only the name of the householder and the number of hearths on which he was taxed. Most houses had only one, but a substantial house might rise to six, a mansion to perhaps eleven, while the Duke of Ormonde's manor house and castle at Carrick-on-Suir admitted to thirty. It appears to have been a fairly comprehensive list, dealing with all economic levels, and the sad thing is that it has not survived for the entire island. Much of the extant portions are in print, and full details are given under the relevant counties.

1702

There are some partial lists of male householders in Kilkenny city for 1702. They are divided into five sections and obviously some portions are missing. The first gives the "Papists in St. Mary's Hightown Ward", numbering 1-194. The second gives the Protestants in St. Canice's In Gate, numbering 204-267. The third gives the Protestants in St. Canice's Outgate, numbering 268-287. The fourth gives the "Papist Inhabitants in St. Canice's Ingate", numbering 476-580. The fifth gives the "Papist Inhabitants in St. Canice's Outgate", numbering 581-709. Details supplied differ: the first, second and third of these lists provide only the householder's name, and no other particulars or detailed address. The fourth gives the householder's occupation, e.g. Michaell Burns, weaver; Luke Murphy, tanner. The fifth gives address (Butts, Fenners Town, etc.) but no occupation. PRO (1A 55 82).

1708

In 1708 James Maguire made a survey of the town of Downpatrick, Co. Down, which is printed in *The City of Downe* by R. E. Parkinson. Arranged by quarter, it describes each premises by name, giving its size (rear, front and depth), its principal tenant, the tenant in possession, the half yearly rent due, and adds in many cases a brief description of the building.

1715

There is a list of the male Protestant inhabitants of the parish of St. John

Parish of	Place of Abode	Names and Religion	Profession	Children under 14 Prot.	Pap.	Children above 14 Prot.	Pap.	Men Serv. Prot.	Pap.	Women Serv. Prot.	Pap.
Taunagh	Carneha	Manus Brady pa	Labr								
		Felim Brennan pa:	labr		2						
		Danie Lowny pa	labr				1				
		Peter Gilner pa	maltster		1						
		Bryan mcDonogh pa	cottier				1				
	Carrowkeel	Hugh Cone pa:	herd		3				1		1
		Js Gibbon prot:	labr	5		1				1	
		Edm Rowlatt prot:	aleseller	4		2					
		Ec Rowlatt wd prot:	farmr			1		2			
	Behy	Ja Dorcan pap:	shoemr		3			1		1	
		Cha Duke prot:	farmer					2		l	
		Patt Long pa:	labr		1	2					
		Pat Gilmer pa	labr		4						
		Wm Boyce prot:	herd	3							
		Laur Bolton pa:	labr								
	Oaghan	Alex Middleton pa:	labr		4	2					
		Miles Coyle pa	farmr		2						
		Wm Connel wid pa	farmr			2					
		Edm Lavin pa:	labr		1	1					
		Js Davey pa;	farmr			1					
		Farrel Guinan pa	labr		1						
		Patt Feeny wd pa	brogesh		1						
		Bry Guinane pa	labr		2						
		Ja Gilmr pa	labr								
		Laur Gilmer pa	labr		1						
		Ja Dyer pa:	labr			3					
		Margt Hara pa	cottier		2						
		Laur mcDonogh pa	farmr			1					1
		Matt Lavin pa			1						
		Ows Feeny pa:	labr		2						
		Jo Fawny pa:	labr		4						
	Whitehill	Morgan White pro	Gent			2			2	1	l
		Hugh Banaghan pa	plowmr		3	2					1

Elphin Diocesan Census 1749: Returns for townlands in the parish of Taunagh, Co. Sligo.

Courtesy Deputy-Keeper, Public Record Office of Ireland.

Within Gates, Kilkenny city, from the ages of 16 to 60 years. 46 individuals are given with their occupations, but no detailed addresses. PRO (1A 55 82).

1740

1740 saw the compilation of a list of Protestant householders in parts of Cos. Antrim, Armagh, Donegal, Londonderry and Tyrone. It is arranged by county, barony and parish, but is not usually sub-divided into townlands, which is a pity. It covers an area of rather dense population and is therefore valuable. It has not been printed. The portion at the Genealogical Office (G.O. 539) is typed and indexed: that at the Representative Church Body Library is unindexed. No details of any sort are given, just the bare names of the householders, and these are limited to persons of the Protestant faith.

1749

In 1749, at the behest of Edward Synge, Church of Ireland Bishop of Elphin, a census of his diocese was taken. This covered most of Co. Roscommon, part of Co. Sligo and nine parishes in Co. Galway. Arranged by parish and townland, it lists the heads of households, with their occupation, religion, the number and religion of their children, plus the number, sex and religion of their servants. Some parishes supply the Christian name of the householder's wife, others merely phrase the entry as "Patt Plunkett and wife". All religions and all economic classes are covered, and the census appears very complete. It is still only in manuscript and unindexed, and is held at the Public Record Office. (1A 36 13).

1750

In 1750 the High Constable of the Half Barony of Ikerrin, Co. Tipperary, listed the "Popish Inhabitants" of his district in order to facilitate the levying of a tax to offset Whiteboy depredations on local property. Sub-divided into nine parishes, it shows the names of householders and the acreage held by each, though not their townland addresses. Taken from Ms. 8913 in the National Library of Ireland, it was printed in *The Irish Genealogist,* 1975.

1753

The Church of Ireland registers of the small parish of St. Nicholas in Cork city include a Valuation in the form of a list of householders, dated 6th March 1753. Arranged by street, it consists of about 500 names, the bulk of them obviously belonging to Catholics. The form is: "On West side of ye Main Street from South Bridge: A house in the possession of John Power £12: Ditto Andrew Donohoo £8: Ditto Robert Egar £6: Ditto John Skeys £8."

The same source also contains parish valuations dated 5th July 1770, 14th May 1782 and 5th May 1791. All these are extremely small, and at best include only the Protestant householders and at worst only some of the more prosperous Protestant householders.

1757

In 1757 the matter of raising local militia regiments was active and male Protestants were required to present themselves before the Commissioners of Array and "take the usual Oaths". Lists of these worthies from seven parishes in north Cork survived in the Mallow Castle estate records and were printed as Appendix IV in *An Anglo-Irish Miscellany* by Maurice D. Jephson, 1964. They appear to contain all the able-bodied Protestant men in the parishes concerned, but give neither age nor townland address.

1766

In 1766 the Government instructed the Church of Ireland rectors to draw up a return of householders in their respective parishes, showing their religion (whether Protestant, Dissenter or Papist), with details of such Catholic clergy or friars as might be active in the area. Some rectors fobbed off the authorities with numerical totals (so many Protestants, so many Papists, one priest and no friars), with no mention of proper names or townlands. The most diligent rectors listed every townland and every householder on it. Between these two extremes there were various permutations. The work seems to have been mostly carried out during March/April. Sadly, the whole of this original treasure trove was destroyed in the Four Courts in 1922. Transcripts survive for certain areas, notably Tipperary, north Cork, Limerick, Louth, Londonderry and Wicklow. A few of the transcripts give only the Protestant householders, and I have tried to note these: most of the transcripts give all religions. I have not listed parishes for which only numerical totals survive. The transcripts are scattered, some at the P.R.O., some in the Genealogical Office, some in the R.C.B. Library and a few have been printed. Details are given under the counties.

1782

A list of persons in the parish of Culdaff, Co. Donegal, drawn up on 8th

March 1782, is printed on pp. 159-60 of *Three Hundred Years in Inishowen,* by Amy Isabel Young, 1929. Arranged by townland, the details vary from "Jo. Elliott & Family" to "Robt Dickey, his wife and several children, his wife's mother the widow Chittock". No ages are stated.

1791

A list of landholders in the parish of Dromiskin, Co. Louth in 1791 is printed in the *History of Kilsaran Union of Parishes,* by Rev. J. B. Leslie. No details beyond the names are given.

1799

A detailed census of the town and suburbs of Carrick-on-Suir, Co. Tipperary, was made in 1799. It is arranged by street and gives the name, age, religion and occupation of the 10,907 inhabitants, together with their relationship to the head of each household. The manuscript of the census is now in the British Library (Add. Ms. 11,722) and there is a microfilm copy at the National Library of Ireland (P. 28). It is the earliest true census now extant for any part of Ireland.

1801

The tithe applotment book for the parishes of Stabannon and Roodstown, Co. Louth, lists the landholders and their acreages, and is printed in the *History of Kilsaran Union of Parishes,* by Rev. J. B. Leslie.

1802-3

With the energy of a new broom, Thomas O'Beirne, Church of Ireland Bishop of Meath, swept round his disordered diocese. The questionnaires he sent out to his clergy included requests for a census of Protestant parishioners. His clergy responded variously. Many ignored all demands; others, such as the rector of Kells, painstakingly listed their flock street by street, townland by townland; others supplied their parishioners' ages, and the rector of Navan even proffered comments. In all, 27 parishes from Counties Meath, Westmeath and Offaly and one from Co. Cavan produced useful returns. Only members of the Church of Ireland are shown (Dissenters seem to have been definitely omitted) but all economic levels are involved. The original manuscript is in the Meath Diocesan Office at Trim, and all 28 parishes were printed in *The Irish Ancestor,* 1973.

A list of Protestant parishioners on 14 of the 33 townlands in the parish of Culdaff, Co. Donegal, in 1802 or 1803, was printed on pp. 186-7 of

Three Hundred Years in Inishowen by Amy Isabel Young. Ages of children are shown, but not those of adults.

1814

The Church of Ireland parish register for the united parishes of Drung and Larah, Co. Cavan, includes a list of "the young and unmarried" Protestant parishioners. It shows townland address and the name of the children's father, but no ages. It was printed in *The Irish Ancestor,* 1978.

1821

On 28th May 1821 Government-appointed enumerators set forth to take a census of the population. Their returns were assembled by county, barony, parish and townland. For each household they were told to list the names, ages, occupations and relationship to the householder of all the occupants, plus the acreage held by the householder, and how many storeys high the dwelling-house was. No information as to religious persuasion was noted. A goldmine of information, it was perhaps the single most disastrous loss in the 1922 burning of the Four Courts. A few volumes survived the holocaust (parts of Cavan, Galway, Offaly, Meath and Fermanagh) and these are in the Public Record Office. There also exist some transcripts and extracts relating to Cos. Waterford and Kilkenny. These items seem complete and accurate except with regard to the ages of adults. The ages of children are apparently pretty correct, but the number of adults whose age is entered in round figures (40, 50, 60, 70) is manifestly absurd. These persons must therefore be assumed to be in their 40s, 50s and so on.

1824

The Catholic parish registers of Lusmagh, in Offaly, include a list of Catholic parishioners, taken 1st November 1824. Arranged by townland, it gives the heads of households but no other information.

1827

The Church of Ireland registers of Aughrim, Co. Galway, include a census of parishioners in 1827. It lists the names of parents and the names and ages of their children, but it does not give townland address. There is a copy at the Public Record Office (M.5359).

1831

Another government census was taken this year, following the same general system as that of 1821, omitting the number of storeys in the houses, but including the religion of the occupants. It too, was lost in the Public Record Office in 1922. Returns for many parishes in Co. Londonderry survive and are in the Public Record Office.

The 1831 census for St. Bride's parish, Dublin city (of which there is a microfilm at the National Library, P. 1994) may be based on the official census, but gives much less information. Arranged by street, it includes only the name of the householder and his religion, with the number and religion of the children and adults in each household.

1834-35

These years saw the compilation of a number of small, locally produced censuses, the precise purpose of which is obscure. Information given also varies widely, and details are therefore supplied below for each parish under the various counties.

The tithe applotment books, now held in the Public Record Offices of Dublin and Belfast (Belfast having the books for the counties of Northern Ireland), range in date from about 1824 to 1838. Arranged by parish and then by townland under each parish they list the occupiers of titheable land, but are *not* a list of householders. Tithe books exist for almost all parishes, the date of the book varying per parish. The surnames shown have been indexed in the Index to Surnames compiled by the National Library. It is instructive to compare a tithe book of the 1820s with the 1821 Census for the same parish, for it then becomes clear what a small section of the population was caught in the tithe net, the labourers, weavers and cottiers being all omitted, in addition to all purely urban dwellers.

1841

The government census was taken on 6th June and though it followed the same general lines as that of 1831, the returns were compiled by the householders themselves. Additional information requested included date of marriage, ability (or otherwise) to read and write. Also included were sections requesting details as to absent members of each household and of those who had died since 1831, their ages and relationships to the householder, and the cause and year of their decease. The only original return to survive the 1922 fire is that for the parish of Killeshandra, Co. Cavan, now in the Public Record Office. A transcript of the return for most of the parish of Aglish, Co. Kilkenny, was printed in *The Irish Ancestor,* 1977. The transcripts of parts of four Co. Cork parishes are an edited copy, arranged by townland, showing ages and relationships, but giving no details concerning the actual building and wholly omitting the sections relating to absent and dead members. It contains some additional notes regarding marriages and deaths of individuals in 1851-3. The version at the Public Record Office is a photostat copy (1A 30 76).

Dr. Stephen Royle has prepared a detailed list of the surviving individual copies of returns extracted from the 1841 and 1851 censuses, mostly for purposes of obtaining old age pensions. His list shows the parish, townland and surnames involved. The bulk relate to Ulster. He also lists the many Walsh Kelly fragments from the 1821, 1831, 1841 and 1851 censuses for Cos. Kilkenny, Waterford and Wexford, which are so disjointed and fragmentary as to be of little value save for the actual surnames Mr. Kelly concentrated on. Dr. Royle's unpublished list is held in Queen's University, Belfast.

1851

Taken on 30th March, this government census followed the formula of 1841 but added a column for religious affiliation, while retaining the sections for absent and dead members of the household. A good number of original returns survive for parishes in Co. Antrim and are in the Public Record Office in Dublin. Transcripts for the parishes of Aglish and Portnescully, Co. Kilkenny, were printed in *The Irish Ancestor,* 1977.

1848-1864

These years cover the publication of Sir Richard Griffith's *Primary Valuation of Ireland,* the date of publication varying for individual counties. Arranged by county, barony, poor law union, civil parish and townland, it lists every householder and every occupier of land. It gives no personal particulars at all other than name, townland address, acreage held and the estimated value of the holding, and from whom the land was leased. If the 1851 census had survived, the valuation would be of little genealogical importance, but in the absence of the census it is an invaluable guide to where people lived and what property they held. The surnames in each parish have been indexed in the Index to Surnames compiled by the National Library.

1861

This census was destroyed by government order. The Catholic parish registers of Enniscorthy, Co. Wexford, include a census of the inhabitants of the parish, dated 17 April 1861, which seems to be based on the official census. It is arranged by street and townland. It notes the numbers of Protestants in Protestant households, but gives no details. For Catholics it gives name and religion, indicates relationships, but gives no indication of age other than the occasional "infant". An example of an entry is:

"Vinegar Hill Lane — John Dillon, Mary his wife, Anne, John, all Catholics".

1871

Taken on 2nd April, this census also was officially destroyed. What is apparently a full transcript for two parishes in Co. Meath (Drumcondra and Loughbraclen) is contained in the Catholic parish registers. The entries relating to Protestant families are given in full, notwithstanding its source. Dated 2nd April and arranged by townland, it gives name, age, relationship, occupation, religion and absent members of the family.

1901

On 31st March 1901 a census was again taken of the whole island, and this is now the earliest extant return for the entire country. It is held by the Public Record Office, including the returns for Northern Ireland. Arranged by county, district electoral division and townland, it gives the usual data — name, age, religion, occupation, ability (or otherwise) to read and write, marital status, relationship to householder, county of birth (country if born outside Ireland) and ability (or otherwise) to speak English and/or Irish. Absentees are not listed. Ages of adults are suspect: most adults were actually older than they admitted, as can readily be seen by checking against the 1911 return. (I found one woman who actually gained no less than twenty years during the decade, i.e. she was thirty years older in 1911 than in 1901!). Details concerning the houses are also given: number of rooms occupied by each family, type of roof, and total number of windows in front. If one is familiar with the local type of house one can deduce a pretty fair picture of the dwelling concerned. Never underestimate the 1901 Census. It is a mine of useful information, and lists a lot of hardy 80-90 year-olds who were born during the reign of George III.

1911

Taken on 1st April, this followed the lines laid down in 1901 with one important addition. Married women were required to state the duration of their present marriage, the number of children born and how many of these were still alive. As a quick guide to a marriage date this is marvellous. Moreover, numerous widows also dutifully supplied these particulars: the authorities deleted the numerals entered but it is usually quite possible to read the deletions. The return is also a most useful check on the ages of adults as alleged in 1901: remarkably few of them tally. 1911 is the latest census available for public consultation, though a census has been taken in each of the following years since: 1926, 1936, 1946, 1951, 1956, 1961, 1966, 1971, 1981.

19   *Gortboy.*

Name	Age	Occupation
Mary Keane	40	Housekeeper
Jane Keane	7	daughter. School Girl
Ellie Keane	5½	,, ,,
Patrick Bergin	35	Farmer
Mrs Bergin	70	Mother, Housekeeper
John Shanahan	65	Mason
Mrs Shanahan	50	Wife, Housekeeper
John Shanahan	22	Son, Mason
Dan Shanahan	19	Son, ,,
Ellie Shanahan	16	daughter. dress maker
Patrick Shanahan	14	Son. apprentice to Drapery
Annie Shanahan	13	daughter. School Girl
Denis Shanahan	12	Son.
James Shanahan	7	Son. School boy
Delia Shanahan	6	daughter. ,, Girl
Cissie Shanahan	4½	,,
Wm. Shanahan	3	Son
Dan Shanahan	60	Mason.

Local Census: Parish of Kilmallock, townland of Gortboy, c. 1902 NLI Ms. 7997.

Surviving Census Records arranged by County

It will be evident from the foregoing that Irish census source materials are diverse and widely scattered. In order to facilitate consultation of these materials, references to surviving census records as well as to census substitutes have been assembled for each of the thirty-two counties of Ireland. The reference lists, which now follow, are in chronological order beginning with the oldest known source for each county.

Co. Antrim

1659.   "Census" of Ireland.
1669.   Hearth Money Roll. PRONI, and Nat. Lib. Ms. 9584.
1740.   Parishes of Aghoghil, Armoy, Ballintoy, Ballymena, Ballymoney, Bellewillen, Billy, Clogh, Drumaul, Dunean, Dunkegan, Dunluce, Finvoy, Kilraghts, Loghall, Manybrooks, Rasharkan, Rathlin, Remoan. (G.O. 559).
1766.   Parish of Aghoghill. RCB Library.
        Parish of Ballintoy. G.O. 536.
1851.   Parishes of Aghagallon, (townlands Montiaghs to Tiscallen only), Aghalee, Aghohill (townland of Craigs only), Ballinderry, Ballymoney (townland of Garryduff only), Carncastle, Dunaghy, Grange of Killyglen, Killead (townlands of Ardmore to Carnagliss only), Kilwaughter, Larne, Rasharkin (townlands of Killydonelly to Tehorny only), Tickmacrevan.
1861-2. Griffith's Valuation.
1901.   Census.
1911.   Census.

Co. Armagh

1659.   "Census" of Ireland.
1664.   Hearth Money Roll. G.O. 538, Nat. Lib. Ms. 9586, and PRONI. Also printed in *Archivium Hibernicum*, Vol. 8, 1936.
1740.   Parishes of Derrynoose, Lurgan, Shankill, Tynan. PRO (1A 46 100).
1766.   Parish of Creggan. G.O. 537.
1821.   Parish of Kilmore (townlands of Balleney, Corcreevy, Crewcat, Derryhale, Drumnahushin, Listeyborough and Maynooth) PRONI. T.450.
1864.   Griffith's Valuation.
1901.   Census.
1911.   Census.

Co. Carlow

1659.   "Census" of Ireland.
1852-3. Griffith's Valuation.

1901.   Census.
1911.   Census.

Co. Cavan

1630.   Muster Roll, c. 1630. Printed in *Breifne,* Vol. V, No. 18.
1664.   Hearth Money Roll for parishes of Killeshandra, Kildallan, Killenagh, Templeport, Tomregan. PRONI.
1766.   Protestants in parishes of Kinawley, Lavey, Lurgan, Munterconnaught. RCB Library.
1802.   Protestants in Enniskeen parish.
1814.   Youthful Protestants in parishes of Drung and Larah.
1821.   Parishes of Annageliffe, Ballymacue, Castlerahan, Castleterra, Crosserlough, Denn, Drumlumman, Drung, Kilbride, Kilmore, Kinawley, Larah, Lavey, Lurgan, Mullagh, Munterconnaught.
1841.   Killeshandra parish, *except* townlands of Corranea Glebe and Drumberry.
1856-7. Griffith's Valuation.
1901.   Census.
1911.   Census.

Co. Clare

1659.   "Census" of Ireland.
1855.   Griffith's Valuation.
1901.   Census.
1911.   Census.

Co. Cork

1654.   Parishes of Aghabullog, Aghina, Aglish, Ballinaboy, Ballyvorney, Carnaway, Carrigrohanbeg, Clondrohid, Currykippane, Desertmore, Donoughmore, Drishane, Garrycloyne, Granagh, Inchigeelagh, Inniscarra, Kilbonane, Kilcolman, Kilcorny, Kilmihil, Kilmurry, Kilnamartyr, Knockavilly, Macloneigh, Macroom, Matehy, Moviddy, Templemichael, Whitechurch. *Civil Survey,* Vol. VI.
Cork city, with north and south suburbs and liberties. *Civil Survey,* Vol. VI.
1659.   "Census" of Ireland.
1753.   List of householders in St. Nicholas parish, Cork city.
1757.   Male, able-bodied Protestants in parishes of Brigown, Castletown Roche, Clonmeen, Farrihy, Glanworth, Kilshannig, Marshallstown, Roskeen.
1766.   Parishes of Aghabullog, Aghada, Ardagh and Clonpriest (names wife and children of householder), Ballyhea, Ballyhooly and Killathy, Brigown, Britway, Carrigdownane, Castlelyons, Castlemartyr, Castletown Roche, Churchtown, Clenor, Clonfert, Clondrohid, Clondullane, Clonmeen, Ruskeen and Kilcummy, Clonmult and Kilmahon, Cloyne and Ballintemple, Coole, Farrihy, Templemologga, Kildorrery, Nathlash and

Carrigdownane, Garrycloyne, Whitechurch and Grenagh, Glanworth, Ightermurragh, Imphrick, Inniscarra and Matehy, Killogrohanbeg, Kilnamartyr, Kilshannig, Kilworth and Macrony, Knockmourne and Ballynoe, Lisgoold and Ballykeary, Litter, Macroom, Magourney and Killcolman, Mallow, Marshalstown, Midleton, Mourne Abbey, Shandrum, Youghal. PRO (1A 41 67).

Parishes of Rathbarry, Ringrone. PRO (1A 46 49).

Parish of Dunbulloge. Printed in *Journal of the Cork Historical and Archaeological Society,* Vol. 51.

Parish of Kilmichael. Printed in *Journal of the Cork Historical and Archaeological Society,* Vol. 26.

1834. List of Protestant parishioners in the Ballymodan part of the town of Bandon, arranged by street, and listing the children of each householder. National Library Ms. 675.

1851. Parish of Kilcrumper, *except* the townlands of Glenwood, Lisnasallagh and Loughnakilly.

Parish of Kilworth.

Parish of Leitrim, *except* the townlands of Ballymamudthogh, Cronahil and Propogue.

The townlands of Castle Cooke, Kilclogh, Macrony and Shanaclure in the parish of Macrony.

1851-3. Griffith's Valuation.

1901. Census.

1911. Census.

Co. Donegal

1630. Muster Roll. Printed in *The Donegal Annual,* Vol. X, No. 2.

1654. Civil Survey, Vol. III.

1659. "Census" of Ireland.

1665. Hearth Money Roll. G.O. 538 and Nat. Lib. Ms. 9584 and PRONI.

1740. Parishes of Cloncaha, Clonmeny, Culdaff, Desertegney, Donagh, Fawne, Movill, Templemore. G.O. 539.

1766. **Parish of Donoghmore. PRO M.207-8.**

Protestants in parish of Leck. PRO (1A 41 100).

1782. Persons in Culdaff parish.

1802-3. Protestants in part of Culdaff parish.

1857. Griffith's Valuation.

1901. Census.

1911. Census.

Co. Down

1659. "Census" of Ireland.

1708. Householders in the town of Downpatrick.

1766.   Parish of Kilbroney and Seapatrick. RCB Library.
         Parish of Shankill. PRO (1A 46 100).
1863-4. Griffith's Valuation.
1901.   Census.
1911.   Census.

Co. Dublin

1621.   List of householders in St. John's parish who were rated for parish cess. Printed as Appendix II in the *Registers of St. John's 1619-1699,* Vol. I. of the Parish Register Society, 1906. Arranged by street, it lists the householders with their occupations and the tax due.
1646.   A similar list for St. John's parish, included in the same source, which also has a list of 1687 for the same parish.
1652.   Inhabitants of the Baronies of Newcastle and Uppercross, districts of Ballyfermot, Balliowen, Ballidowde, Belgard, Bellemount, Blundestown, Butterfield, Carranstown, Crumlin, Dalkey, Deane Rath, Esker, Feddenstown, Finstown, Gallanstown, Great Katherins, Irishtown, Killnemanagh, Killiney, Kilmainham, Kilmatalway, Kilshock, Loughstown, Lucan, Milltown, Nanger, Nealstown, Newcastle, Newgrange, Newland, Oldbawn, Palmerstown, Rathgar, Rathfarnham, Rowlagh (Ranelagh), Rockstown, Shankill, Symon, Tallaght, Templeogue, Terenure.
1654-6. *Civil Survey,* Vol. VII.
1659.   "Census" of Ireland.
1663.   Hearth Money Roll. Printed in the *Journal of the Kildare Archaeological Society,* Vol. X.
1766.   Parishes of Crumlin and Donnybrook. RCB Library.
1831.   Householders in St. Bride's parish.
1848-51. Griffith's Valuation. (The parishes in Dublin city are not included in the Index to Surnames, which covers the county only.)
1901.   Census.
1911.   Census.

Co. Fermanagh

1631.   Muster Roll. Printed in *History of Enniskillen* by W. C. Trimble.
1659.   "Census" of Ireland.
1665.   Hearth Money Roll. National Library Ms. 9583.
1766.   Parish of Boho and Derryvullen. RCB Library.
         Parishes of Devenish, Kinawley and Rossory. G.O. 536.
1821.   Parish of Aghalurcher (townlands of Altamartin, Altamullaboy, Altdwark, Attaclenobrien, Aughavory, Augheetor, Carahoney, Cavanalack, Cleen, Colebrooke, Comnohy, Corlacky, Corrafat, Cran, Corckadreen, Currylongford, Derrintony, Derrychrum, Dordrany, Drumrock, Dunavoghy, Esnasillong, Esthomas, Feavanny, Foglish,

Grogy, Killarbin, Killybawn, Lamphill, Legtiladay, Lisavinick, Moughly, Mount Gibbon, Owenskerry, Ranult, Stripe, Tatenahoglish, Tattyreagh, Tereaghan, Tullaharney, Tullichanie, Tulnavarin).
Parish of Derryvullen.

1851.	Townland of Clonee, parish of Drumkeeran.
1862.	Griffith's Valuation.
1901.	Census.
1911.	Census.

Co. Galway

1749.	Parishes of Ahascragh, Athleague, Ballynakill, Drimatemple, Dunamon, Kilbegnet, Kilcroan, Killian, Killosolan.
1806-1.	Catholic householders in Killallaghten parish, arranged by townland. A few marked "dead" or "gone" but no other details. In the Catholic parish registers of Killallaghten.
1827.	Protestants in Aughrim parish.
1855.	Griffith's Valuation.
1901.	Census.
1911.	Census.

Co. Kerry

1657.	Parishes of Dysart, Killurry, Rathroe. *Civil Survey,* Vol. IV.
1659.	"Census" of Ireland.
1821.	Parish of Kilcummin. Royal Irish Academy: McSwiney Papers (Parcel F, No. 3).
1834-5.	Householders in parishes of Dunquin, Dunurlin, Killemlagh, Kilmalkedar, Kilquane, Marhin, Prior. Arranged by townland, it lists the householders with numerical totals for the males and females in each establishment. Printed in the *Journal of the Kerry Archaeological and Historical Society,* 1974-5.
1852.	Griffith's Valuation.
1901.	Census.
1911.	Census.

Co. Kildare

1654-5.	*Civil Survey,* Vol. VIII.
1659.	"Census" of Ireland.
1840.	Census of Castledermot parish. Arranged by townland or street, it gives names and relationships, but not age, e.g. "Main Street: Charles M'Donald, sons John, Thomas, wife Bridget". National Library P.3511.
1851.	Griffith's Valuation.
1901.	Census.
1911.	Census.

Co. Kilkenny

1654-6. Kilkenny City. *Civil Survey,* Vol. VI.

1659. "Census" of Ireland.

1664. Hearth Money Roll for parishes of Agherney, Aghavillar, Bellaghtobin, Belline, Burnchurch, Callan, Castleinch, Clone, Coolaghmore, Coolcashin, Danganmore, Derrinahench, Dunkitt, Earlstown, Eyvk, Fartagh, Inishnagg and Stonecarthy, Jerpoint, Kells, Kilbecon and Killahy, Kilcolm, Kilferagh, Kilkredy, Killamery, Killaloe, Killree, Kilmoganny, Kiltackaholme, Knocktopher and Kilkerchill, Mucklee and Lismatigue, Outrath, Ratbach, Rathpatrick, Tullaghanbrogue, Tullaghmaine, Tullahaght, Urlingford. Transcript in the Carrigan Mss., Kilkenny. Printed in *The Irish Genealogist,* 1974-5 (Vol. 5, Nos. 1 and 2).

1702. List of Catholics in St. Mary's Hightown Ward, and of inhabitants of St. Canice's Ingate and Outgate, city of Kilkenny.

1715. List of Protestant males between ages of 16 and 60 in the parish of St. John, City of Kilkenny.

1797. The chief Catholic inhabitants of the parishes of Graigenemanagh and Knocktopher. Printed in *The Irish Ancestor,* 1978.

1821. Parishes of Aglish and Portnascully. Printed in *The Irish Ancestor,* 1976. Extracts from the parish of Pollrone. Printed in *The Irish Genealogist,* 1977 (Vol. 5, No. 4).

1841. Townlands of Aglish and Portnahully, parish of Aglish. Printed in *The Irish Ancestor,* 1977.

1849-50. Griffith's Valuation.

1851. Parish of Aglish. Printed in *The Irish Ancestor,* 1977.

1901. Census.

1911. Census.

King's Co. (Offaly)

1659. "Census" of Ireland.

1766. Parish of Ballycommon. Printed in the *Journal of the Kildare Archaeological Society,* Vol. VII, pp. 274-6. Also G.O. Ms. 537.

1802. Protestants in parishes of Ballyboggan, Ballyboy, Castlejordan, Clonmacnoise, Drumcullin, Eglish, Gallen, Killoughey, Lynally, Rynagh, Tullamore.

1821. Parishes of Aghacon, Birr, Ettagh, Kilcolman, Kinnitty, Letterluna, Roscomroe, Roscrea, Seirkieran.

1824. List of Catholic householders in Lusmagh parish on November 1st. Arranged by townland, it gives no other information. Included in the Catholic registers of Lusmagh.

1830. List of contributors to the new Catholic Church at Lusmagh: a sizeable list with townland address and sum subscribed, but no other details. Included in the Catholic registers of Lusmagh.

1835. Census of Tubber parish. Arranged by townland, it gives ages, occupation and religion of each person, but no relationships. National Library P. 1994.

1840.   Parishes of Eglish and Drumcullin. Taken in August and arranged by townland, it shows heads of households, their occupation, the number of males and of females in each household, the number over 15 years and the number under 15 years, the number of male servants, the number of female servants. Included in the Catholic parish register of Eglish.

1854.   Griffith's Valuation.

1901.   Census.

1911.   Census.

Co. Leitrim

1659.   "Census" of Ireland.

1821.   Parish of Carrigallen (it is called 1831, but this is incorrect, even though religion is stated for the individuals, which was not done in 1821: the religion has apparently been added in the transcript). National Library P. 4646.

1856.   Griffith's Valuation.

1901.   Census.

1911.   Census.

Co. Limerick

1570.   List of the Freeholders and Gentlemen in Co. Limerick. Printed in the *Journal of the North Munster Archaeological and Historical Society,* 1964.

1654-6.   *Civil Survey,* Vol. IV.

1659.   "Census" of Ireland.

1766.   Parishes of Abington, Cahircomey, Cahirelly, Carrigparson, Clonkeen, Kilkellane, Tuogh. PRO (1A 46 49).
Protestants in the parishes of Croagh, Kilscannel, Nantinan and Rathkeale. Printed in *The Irish Ancestor,* 1977.

1834.   Parish of Templebredin. Arranged by townland, it lists the heads of households with numbers of males and females in each establishment. Printed in the *Journal of the North Munster Archaeological and Historical Society,* 1975.

1851-2.   Griffith's Valuation.

1901.   Census.

1911.   Census.

Co. Londonderry

1628.   *Houses and Families in Londonderry, 15 May, 1628,* edited by Rev. R.G.S. King, 1936.

1654-6.   *Civil Survey,* Vol. III.

1659.   "Census" of Ireland.

1663.   Hearth Money Roll. National Library Ms. 9584.

1740.   Protestant householders in the parishes of Aghadowy, Anlow, Artrea, Arigall, Ballinderry, Ballynascreen, Ballyscullion, Balten, Banagher, Beleaghron, Belerashane, Belewillin, Boveva, Coleraine, Comber, Desart, Desartlin, Desartmartin, Drummacose, Dunboe, Dungiven, Faughanvale, Glendermot, Killcranoghen, Killowen, Killylagh, Kilrea, Lissan, Macosquin, Maghera, Magherafelt, Tamlaghtfinlaggan, Tamlagh o Creely, Tamlatard, Tamloght, Templemore, Termoneny. G.O. 539.

1766.   Parishes of Artrea, Desertlin and Magherafelt. PRO (1A 46 49).

        Parishes of Bovah, Comber, Drumacoose and Inch. PRO (1A 41 100).

        Parish of Desertmartin. RCB Library.

        Protestants in parishes of Ballymascreen, Banagher, Dungiven and Leck. RCB Library.

1831.   Parishes of Aghadowey, Aghanloo, Agivey, Arboe, Artrea, Ballinderry, Balteagh, Banagher, Ballyaughran, Ballymoney, Ballynascreen, Ballyrashane, Ballyscullion, Ballywillin, Boveagh, Clondermot, Coleraine, Cumber, Desertlyn, Derryloran, Desertmartin, Desertoghill, Drumachose, Dunboe, Dungiven, Errigal, Faughavale, Kilcrea, Kilcunaghan, Killeagh, Killowen, Lissane, Maghera, Magherafelt, Macosquin, Tamlagh, Tamlagh Finlagan, Tamlaght O'Crilly, Tamlaghtard, Templemore, Termoneeny.

1858-9.   Griffith's Valuation.

1901.   Census.

1911.   Census.

Co. Longford

1659.   "Census" of Ireland.

1731.   Protestants in the parish of Shrule. RCB Library.

1766.   Protestants in the parishes of Abbeylara and Russough. RCB Library.

1834.   List of heads of households in the parish of Granard, showing numbers of males and of females in each household with their religion (i.e. Catholic, Protestant, Presbyterian). Included in the Catholic parish registers of Granard.

1854.   Griffith's Valuation.

1901.   Census.

1911.   Census.

Co. Louth

1659.   "Census" of Ireland.

1663-4.   Hearth Money Roll. Printed in the *Journal of the Co. Louth Archaeological Society,* Vol. 6,Nos. 2 and 4.

1666-7.   Hearth Money Roll of Dunleer parish. Printed in *The Irish Genealogist,* 1969.

1760.   Census of Ardee parish. Printed in *The Irish Genealogist,* 1961.

1766.   Parishes of Ardee, Ballymakenny, Beaulieu, Carlingford, Charlestown, Clonkeehan, Darver, Drumiskan, Kildermock, Killeshiel, Louth,

Mapestown, Phillipstown, Shanliss, Smarmore, Stickallen, Tallonstown and Termonfecken. PRO (1A 41 100).

Parish of Creggan. PRO (1A 46 49), and also printed in the *History of the Parish of Creggan,* by Rev. L. P. Murray, Dundalk, 1940.

1782-92. Cess payers in the parishes of Cappagh, Drumcar, Dysart, Moylary and Monasterboice. Printed in *Journal of the Co. Louth Archaeological Society,* Vol. 9, No. 1.

1791. List of landholders in the parish of Dromisken.

1801. Tithe applotment of the parishes of Stabannon and Roodstown.

1834. Census of the parish of Tallanstown. Printed in the *Journal of the Co. Louth Archaeological Society,* Vol. 14.

1852. Census of the townland of Mosstown, parish of Mosstown, and of the townland of Phillipstown, parish of Phillipstown. Printed in the *Journal of the Co. Louth Archaeological Society,* 1975.

1854. Griffith's Valuation.

1901. Census.

1911. Census.

Co. Mayo

1856-7. Griffith's Valuation.

1901. Census.

1911. Census.

Co. Meath

1654-6. *Civil Survey,* Vol. V.

1659. "Census" of parishes of Abbey, Athlumney, Ardcath, Ardmulchan, Ballygart, Ballymagarvey, Ballymaglassan, Brownstown, Clonalvy, Colpe, Cruckstown, Donoghmore, Dowestown, Duleek, Dunshaughlin, Dunowre, Dunsany, Fennor, Grenock, Julianstown, Kentstown, Kilbrew, Kilcarne, Kilkervan, Killeen, Killegan, Kilmoon, Knockamon, Macestown, Moorchurch, Monkstown, Paynstown, Rathbeggan, Rathfeagh, Rathregan, Ratoath, Skryne, Staffordstown, Stamullen, Tara, Trevett, Templekeran.

1766. Protestants in parish of Ardbraccan. RCB Library.

1802-6. Protestants in parishes of Agher, Ardagh, Clonard, Clongill, Drumconrath, Duleek, Emlagh, Julianstown, Kells, Kentstown, Kilbeg, Kilmainhamwood, Kilskyre, Laracor, Moynalty, Navan, Robertstown, Raddenstown, Rathcore, Rathkenny, Rathmoylon, Ratoath, Skryne, Slane, Syddan, Tara, Trim. Printed in *The Irish Ancestor,* 1973.

1813. Protestant children at Ardbraccan School. Printed in *The Irish Ancestor,* 1973.

1821. Parishes of Ardbraccan, Ardsallagh, Balrathboyne, Bective, Churchtown, Clonmacduff, Donaghmore, Donaghpatrick, Kilcooly, Liscartan, Martry, Moymet, Navan, Newtownclonbun, Rathkenny, Rataine, Trim, Trimblestown, Tullaghanoge.

1871. Census of parishes of Drumcondra and Loughbraclen. Transcript included in the Catholic parish registers.
1901. Census.
1911. Census.

Co. Monaghan

1659. "Census" of Ireland.
1666. Hearth Money Roll, printed in *A History of Monaghan,* by D. C. Rushe.
1858-60. Griffith's Valuation.
1901. Census.
1911. Census.

Queen's Co. (Leix)

1659. "Census" of Ireland.
1850-1. Griffith's Valuation.
1901. Census.
1911. Census.

Co. Roscommon

1659. "Census" of Ireland.
1749. Parishes of Aughrim, Ardcarn, Athleague, Ballintober, Ballynakill, Baslick, Boyle, Bumlin, Cam, Clontuskert, Clooncraff, Cloonfinlough, Cloonygormican, Creive, Drimatemple, Dunamon, Dysart, Estersnow, Elphin, Fuerty, Kilbride, Kilbryan, Kilcolagh, Kilcooley, Kilcorkey, Kilgefin, Kilglass, Kilkeevin, Killinvoy, Killuken, Killumnod, Kilmacallan, Kilmacumsy, Kilmore, Kilnamagh, Kilronan, Kiltoom, Kiltrustan, Lissonuffy, Ogulla, Oran, Rahara, Roscommon, St. John's Athlone, St. Peter's Athlone, Shankill, Taghboy, Termonbarry, Tibohine, Tisrara, Tumna.
1857-8. Griffith's Valuation.
1901. Census.
1911. Census.

Co. Sligo

1659. "Census" of Ireland.
1664. Hearth Money Roll. Printed by the Irish Manuscripts Commission, 1967.
1749. Parishes of Aghanagh, Ahamlish, Ballynakill, Ballysumaghan, Drumcliff, Drumcolumb, Killadoon, Kilmacallan, Kilmactranny, Kilross, Shancough, Sligo, Tawnagh.
1858. Griffith's Valuation.
1901. Census.
1911. Census.

Co. Tipperary

1654-6. East and South, *Civil Survey,* Vol. I. West and North, *Civil Survey,* Vol. II.
1659. "Census" of Ireland.

1666.
1667. } Three Hearth Money Rolls. Printed as *Tipperary's Families,*
1668. edited by Thomas Laffan,Dublin, 1911.

1750. Catholics in parishes of Barnane, Bourney, Corbally, Killavanough, Killea, Rathnaveoge, Roscrea, Templeree, Templetouhy. Printed in *The Irish Genealogist,* 1973.

1766. Parishes of Athassel, Ballintemple, Ballycahill, Ballygriffin, Boytonrath, Brickendown, Bruis, Clerihan, Clonbeg, Cloneen, Clonoulty, Cloonbolloge, Clonpet, Colman, Cordangan, Corrogue, Cullen, Dangandargan, Drum, Dustrileague, Erry, Feathard, Gaile, Grean, Horeabbey, Killardry, Killbrugh, Killea, Kilconnell, Kilfeacle, Killevinogue, Knockgrafton, Killnerath, Kiltynan, Lattin, Magorban, Mealiffe, New Chapel (gives numbers of children per household), Pepperstown, Railstown, Rathcoole, Relickmurry, Redcity, Shronell, St. John's Cashel, St. Patrick's Rock, Solloghodmore, Templebeg, Templemore, Templeneiry, Templenoe, Tipperary, Toom. PRO (1A 46 49).
Parishes of Ballingarry and Uskeane. G.O. 536.

1799. Census of Carrick-on-Suir.

1834. Parish of Templebredin. Arranged by townland, it lists the heads of households with numbers of males and females in each establishment. Printed in the *Journal of the North Munster Archaeological and Historical Society,* 1975.

1835. Census of parishes of Birdhill and Newport. Arranged by townland or street, it gives the name of the householder with numbers of males and of females in each household, but no ages. National Library P. 1561.

1851. Griffith's Valuation.
1901. Census.
1911. Census.

Co. Tyrone

1654-6. *Civil Survey,* Vol. III.
1664. Hearth Money Roll. National Library Mss. 9583-4. (The portion covering Clogher Diocese was printed in *The Clogher Record,* 1965.)
1740. Protestants in the parishes of Derryloran and Kildress. RCB Library.
1766. Parishes of Aghalow, Artrea, Carnteel, Clonfeacle, Derryloran, Donaghendry, Errigalkerrouge, Kildress. PRO (1A 46 49).
Parishes of Drumglass, Dungannon, Tullynishan. PRO (1A 41 100).
1860. Griffith's Valuation.
1901. Census.
1911. Census.

Co. Waterford

1664-6. *Civil Survey,* Vol. VI.

1659.   "Census" of Ireland.

1663.   Inhabitants of Waterford city, showing trade or profession. Printed in the *Journal of the Cork Historical and Archaeological Society,* Vol. 51.

1766.   Parish of Killoteran. PRO (1A 46 49).

1821.   Extracts from the census of the city of Waterford. Printed in *The Irish Genealogist,* 1968-9.

1848-51. Griffith's Valuation.

1901.   Census.

1911.   Census.

Co. Westmeath

1659.   "Census" of Ireland.

1666.   Hearth Money Roll of Mullingar. Printed in the *Franciscan College Journal,* 1950.

1802-3. Protestants in the parishes of Ballyloughloe, Castletown Delvin, Clonarney, Drumraney, Enniscoffey, Kilbridepass, Killallon, Kilcleagh, Killough, Killua, Killucan, Leney, Moyliscar, Rathconnell. Printed in *The Irish Ancestor,* 1973.

1835.   Census of the parish of Tubber. Arranged by townland, giving the age, occupation and religion of each person, but no relationships. National Library P. 1994.

1854.   Griffith's Valuation.

1901.   Census.

1911.   Census.

Co. Wexford

1654-6. *Civil Survey,* Vol. IX.

1659.   "Census" of Ireland.

1766.   Parish of Ballynaslaney. PRO (1A 41 100).
          Protestants in parish of Edermine. G.O. 537.

1853.   Griffith's Valuation.

1861.   Census of Catholics in parish of Enniscorthy. Included in the Catholic parish registers.

1901.   Census.

1911.   Census.

Co. Wicklow

1669.   Hearth Money Roll. G.O. 667.

1766.   Protestants in parishes of Ballymaslaney, Dunganstown (with the surnames of Catholics), Rathdrum (with surnames of Catholics) and Wicklow. G.O. 537.

1852-3. Griffith's Valuation.

1901.   Census.

1911.   Census.

CHAPTER 4

Guide to Irish Directories

ROSEMARY FFOLLIOTT

DONAL F. BEGLEY

Whatever may be said about other Irish genealogical sources, it is undeniable that Irish directories are excellent. Actual copies are, of course, in short supply. Most can now be obtained only in the larger reference libraries. Some of the earliest have been reprinted in various periodicals while the very rare can be extremely hard to locate. Under these circumstances, it becomes difficult to trace the many small, locally-printed directories that were issued in the nineteenth century, and undoubtedly some of these have been omitted from the lists given here.

One of the most comprehensive collections of directories is that in the National Library of Ireland. The search-room at the Public Record Office has a complete run of the annual Dublin directories, as well as Pigot's provincial directories of 1820 and 1824 and Slater's provincial directories of 1846 and 1894.

For convenience, directories will be dealt with under the following headings:

1. Dublin Directories — issued annually.

2. Directories of Provincial Towns — issued occasionally.

3. Country-wide Directories — listing the names of occupants of substantial houses and gentlemen's seats.

4. Professional Directories — devoted to a single category of persons such as medical practitioners or the clergy of a particular denomination.

1. Dublin Directories

The first trade directory for Dublin was the pamphlet issued in 1751 by Peter Wilson of Dame Street, entitled "An Alphabetical List of Names and Places of Abode of the Merchants and Traders of the City of Dublin," priced at 3d. A similar list appeared the following year, being described as a "Proper Supplement to the Gentleman's and Citizen's Almanack and suitable to be bound with it." This Almanack had been produced by John Watson every year since 1729.

HAL   *Merchants and Traders.*

Grehan (Thady) Brewer, 55, *James's-street.*
Greir (James) Joiner, *Joseph's-lane.*
Greffon (William) Merchant, 135, *King-street, oxm.*
Grierfon (William) Tobacconift, 40, *Meath-street.*
Griffin (James) Tanner, 33, *James's-street.*
Griffith (Humphrey) Grocer, 99, *Capel-street.*
Grilley (John) Shoe-maker, *City-bafin.*
Gripen (Hartwick) Grocer, 5, *George's-street, George's-quay.*
Grogan (Edward) Mercer, 7, *Dame-street.*
Grubb (Widow and William) Tobacconifts, 146, *Capel-street.*
Grumley (Michael) Taylor, *Wood-quay.*
Grumley (Nicholas) Currier, 36, *Nicholas-street.*
Grumley (Peter) Tallow-chandler, 93, *James's-street.*
Grundy (Samuel) Dyer and Manufacturer, *Pimlico.*
Gueft (Frederick) Hatter, 92, *Dame-street.*
Guile (Thomas) Mafter of the *Charlotte,* Chefter Trader, *George's-quay.*
Guinnefs (Arthur) Brewer, 1, *James's-gate.*
Guinnefs (Benjamin) Merchant, 22, *Werburgh-street.*
Guinnefs (Samuel) Gold-beater, 4, *Crow-street.*
Gunne (Benjamin) Book-feller, 3, *Lurgan-street.*
Gunfton (John) Upholder, 107, *Capel-street.*
Gunfton (Joshua) Joiner, 14, *Arran-quay.*
Gunfton (Thomas) Coach-maker, 114, *King-street, oxm.*

H.

Hacket (Thomas) Breeches-maker, 153, *Capel-street.*
Hadfor (George) Lace-feller, 30, *Caftle-street.*
Hagan (Henry) Apothecary, 17, *great Longford-street.*
Hagarthy (Matthew) Linen-draper, 26, *Suffolk-street.*
Hagarthy (Thomas) Lapidary, *Cole-alley, Caftle-street.*
Haighton (John) Merchant, 13, *Jervis-street.*
Hale (Alice) Silk-dyer, 68, *Meath-street.*
Hale (John) Coach-maker, 30, *S. great George's-street.*
Hale (Richard) Ironmonger, 41, *Meath-street.*
Halfpen (John) Herald-painter, 161, *Britain-street.*
Hall (Daniel) Carpenter, 17, *Henry-street.*
Hall (Daniel)Shoe-maker, 22, *Caftle-street.*
Hallam (Robert) Houfe-painter, 57, *Capel-street.*
Halligan (William) Merchant, *Ballybough-bridge.*
Hallwood (Lancelot) Linen-draper, 8, *Bride-street.*

List of Merchants and Traders
The Gentleman's and Citizen's Almanack, Samuel Watson, 1775.

Wilson published a third edition in 1753 and none in 1754. In 1755 he embarked on an annual publication that was to continue until 1837. It was regularly bound in with Watson's *Almanack* and in 1787 the entire production was re-titled *The Treble Almanack*: it then contained Watson's Irish Almanack, Exshaw's English Court Registry and Wilson's Dublin Directory, with "a new correct plan of the city."

Though the 1752 list of merchants and traders had contained only about 840 entries, by 1760 this had risen to an alphabetical list of 1,800 names, addresses and occupations, exclusive of separate lists for lawyers and medical practitioners. The merchants list continued to grow and in 1783 amounted to over 2,800 items. By 1799 the list was in excess of 4,300. The entries were in the following form:

O'Brien (Thomas) Undertaker and Auctioneer, 159 gt-Britain-st
O'Brien (Valentine) Apothecary, 51, Moore-st
O'Callaghan (Thomas) Merchant, 26, Fleet-street
O'Connor (Andrew) Timber-merchant, 5 Bonham-st
O'Connor (Christopher) Printseller, 15, Aston's Quay

In addition to the Merchants and Traders, the late eighteenth-century editions contained separate lists of Judges and Barristers, Attornies, Public Notaries, members of the Royal College of Physicians and the Royal College of Surgeons, lists of the Church of Ireland clergy and churchwardens of the Dublin city parishes, and the Masters, Wardens and Clerks of the City Guilds.

A listing in these directories indicates a fair degree of prosperity: disappearance suggests the death of a trader but in rare instances can mean either his retirement from business or removal elsewhere. Directories are often the only source that state a man's exact occupation: a will or a registered deed may describe him simply as "merchant," whereas the directory will identify him as an iron-monger or grocer or wine-merchant or whatever.

In 1815, when the list of merchants and traders was verging on 5,000 entries, a new section was added, entitled "Nobility and Gentry," which that year gave the full street address of some 1,500 persons. It was enlarged in subsequent editions, reaching about 2,400 in 1827.

Other small lists were also included in early nineteenth-century editions — linen-hall factors, pawnbrokers, hotel-keepers and the masters of regular packets and trading ships plying between Ireland and England. In the 1820s there were also some useful lists of the Revenue officials stationed throughout Ireland. Some of the lists occur irregularly, being given in some years and omitted or contracted in others. This is particularly true of the lists of Irish militia officers. By the early nineteenth century most editions carried an alphabetical list of Dublin streets and alleys, although not indicating the parishes in which they were situated.

Although the *Treble Almanack* lasted until 1837, in 1834 Messrs. Pettigrew and Oulton issued a new *Dublin Almanac and General Register of Ireland.* This, for the first time, included a house-to-house listing of the main streets, showing the civil parish for each. The 1835 and subsequent editions carried both an alphabetical list of individuals and a house-to-house list arranged by street. The scope of the latter widened yearly until it encompassed not only the entire city but also the big suburban area around it. Unfortunately a large proportion of the smaller householders who were listed in the street directory were omitted from the alphabetical list. Consequently it can be very hard to trace persons who moved house at frequent intervals. This was at that time a fairly common practice, since houses could easily be rented for a year or two.

Another of Pettigrew and Oulton's innovations in 1834 was the printing of lists entitled "Official Authorities of Counties," which included the names and addresses of the magistrates for each county as well as various other local dignitaries.

Pettigrew and Oulton survived until 1849 but in 1844 there appeared the first edition of Alexander Thom's *Irish Almanac and Official Directory,* price 10s. 6d. This preserved all the main features of its rival, as well as much miscellaneous information. It continued in annual publication, growing in size as the city grew, and extending its scope ever further into the fast-spreading suburbs.

In addition to its own annual directories, Dublin city was also included in the composite directories issued during the nineteenth century by Pigot and Slater. These publications provide useful lists of persons arranged under their various trades, an arrangement that was never used by the annual Dublin directories. Details of these directories are given in the following section.

2. Directories of Provincial Towns

The first provincial city to issue a directory was Limerick, where John Ferrar produced a splendid directory in 1769. This was followed in 1787 by Richard Lucas's directory of Cork city and of six towns in the south of that county, and in 1788, by his directory of a sizeable selection of towns in Munster and Leinster. In 1797, John Nixon produced a good trade directory of Cork city. With the coming of the nineteenth century, directories proliferated.

In 1820 J. Pigot & Co. issued *The Commercial Directory of Ireland,* the first of a series of composite directories covering the main towns, and arranged under trades rather than alphabetically by surname. From such directories one can readily ascertain what architects, auctioneers, bakers, bankers, bellows makers etc. there were in each town. Further editions appeared in 1824 and (under the name Slater's *Directory*) in 1846, 1856, 1870, 1881 and 1894 — each edition embracing more towns than its predecessor.

The format and contents of the provincial directories are discussed hereunder in chronological order, followed by a list of directories for towns and cities arranged by county.

List of Trade Directories covering more than one Town

1787. Richard Lucas's *Cork Directory*. This has an alphabetical list of Cork merchants, with separate lists of the city officers and aldermen, bankers, barristers, physicians and surgeons, and revenue collectors. It was reprinted in the *Journal of the Cork Historical and Archaeological Society, 1967*. The section covering six towns in the south of the county gives only lists of merchants: these were reprinted in *The Irish Genealogist, 1968*.

1788. Richard Lucas's *General Directory of the Kingdom of Ireland*. This, despite its title, does not extend beyond Munster and Leinster. It consists of short alphabetical lists of traders, but the cities of Limerick, Waterford and Kilkenny have additional professional lists similar to those for Cork in 1787. All were reprinted in *The Irish Genealogist*: the seven towns from Co. Tipperary in 1966, Limerick city in 1967, Ennis, Co. Clare in 1968, and the others in 1965.

1809. Holden's *Triennial Directory* covered the cities of Cork, Limerick and Waterford, again with alphabetical lists of traders.

1819. Thomas Bradshaw's *General Directory of Newry, Armagh, Dungannon, Portadown, Tandragee, Lurgan, Waringstown, Banbridge, Warrenpoint, Rosstrevor, Kilkeel and Rathfryland*. This gives alphabetical lists of traders but does not include local gentry.

1820. J. Pigot's *Commercial Directory of Ireland*. Laid out alphabetically by towns, the traders are arranged, also alphabetically, under their various trades. The names of nobility and gentry resident in or near each town are also given. Dublin alone has an alphabetical list of nobility and gentry. Though the lists in 1820 are small compared with those given in 1824, nonetheless this directory can be useful, particularly in locating persons who had left a district by 1824. For example, the 1820 directory of Newry shows one "William Tosh, Sugar-island" among the "Grocers, Spirit Dealers, etc.," whereas no Tosh at all appears in the 1824 lists for Newry.

1824. Pigot and Co's *City of Dublin and Hibernian Provincial Directory*. Arranged by province, it includes over 220 urban centres. Its lay-out is similar to that of 1820 but it has the important addition of a composite

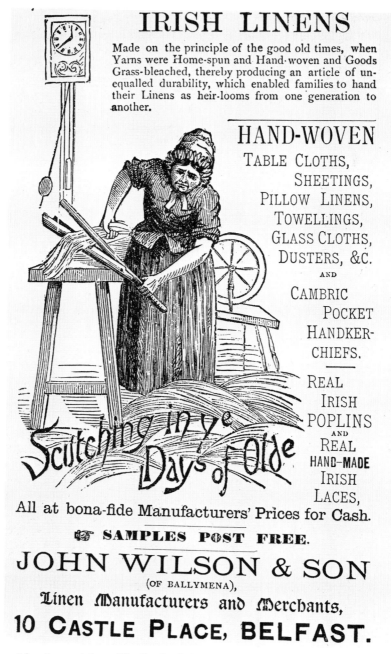

IRISH LINENS

Made on the principle of the good old times, when Yarns were Home-spun and Hand-woven and Goods Grass-bleached, thereby producing an article of unequalled durability, which enabled families to hand their Linens as heir-looms from one generation to another.

HAND-WOVEN

TABLE CLOTHS,
SHEETINGS,
PILLOW LINENS,
TOWELLINGS,
GLASS CLOTHS,
DUSTERS, &C.

AND

CAMBRIC
POCKET
HANDKER-
CHIEFS.

REAL
IRISH
POPLINS
AND
REAL
HAND-MADE
IRISH
LACES,

All at bona-fide Manufacturers' Prices for Cash.

☞ **SAMPLES POST FREE.**

JOHN WILSON & SON
(OF BALLYMENA),

Linen Manufacturers and Merchants,

10 CASTLE PLACE, BELFAST.

Advertisement from The Book of Antrim by George Henry Bassett, 1888.

alphabetical index to all the nobility, clergy and gentry listed under each town. There are also separate alphabetical indexes to the merchants and tradesmen in the cities of Belfast, Cork, Dublin and Limerick.

1839. *Directory of the Towns of Sligo, Enniskillen, Ballyshannon, Donegal,* etc. This excellent little directory gives for each town an alphabetical list of traders and a further list of traders arranged under their own individual trades.

1839. T. Shearman's *New Commercial Directory for the Cities of Waterford and Kilkenny, Towns of Clonmel, Carrick-on-Suir, New Ross and Carlow.* Each town in this directory has an alphabetical list of nobility, gentry and clergy, an alphabetical list of traders and a list arranged by trades.

1841. Matthew Martin's *Belfast Directory.* For Belfast there is a house-to-house list of the principal streets; a list classified by professions and trades; an alphabetical list of gentry, merchants and traders; and a list of noblemen, magistrates etc. resident in Cos. Antrim and Down. The provincial towns in the province of Ulster have alphabetical lists only.

1842. Matthew Martin's *Belfast Directory.* This has the same arrangement as the 1841 edition.

1846. Slater's *National Commercial Directory of Ireland.* This follows the lay-out of Pigot in 1824, but is very much larger; regrettably it omits the composite index to the country gentry. For Dublin there are alphabetical lists of nobility, clergy and gentry, of attornies and of physicians, surgeons and dentists.

1852. James Alexander Henderson's *Belfast and Province of Ulster Directory.* There are three lists for the city of Belfast: a good house-to-house street list, an alphabetical list of the ''principal inhabitants,'' and a list arranged under trades and professions only, together with a list of country residents in the vicinity of each town. Further editions appeared in 1854, 1856, 1858, 1861, 1863, 1865, 1868, 1870, 1877, 1880, 1884, 1887, 1890, 1894 and 1900, with only a few minor additions to the list of towns and no other alterations in lay-out.

1856. Slater's, late Pigot & Co's, *Royal National Commercial Directory of Ireland.* Arranged by province in the manner of the 1846 edition, each town starts with a list of nobility, clergy and gentry and shows the business people under their trades. The names of the National, Parochial and Free schoolmasters for each town are also given. This edition has an alphabetical index to the towns and villages not specifically mentioned in the alphabetical headings. For instance, the index shows that the village of Graigue is included under the town of Carlow, and the village of Banteer under the town of Kanturk — though it may be noted that not a single trader in Banteer is actually mentioned by name. In general, the information given for these very minor villages is not of much genealogical significance.

1865. R. Wynne's *Business Directory of Belfast.* For Belfast there is an alphabetical list of merchants, manufacturers and traders, and a further list arranged under professions and trades. These lists also cover the suburbs of Ardoyne, Ballysillan, Dundonald, Dunmurry, Greencastle, Hannastown, Ligoniel, Newtownbreda, Sydenham, the Knock, Whiteabbey and Whitehouse. Other towns are listed by trades only.

1866. *Directory of the City and County of Limerick and of the principal Towns in the Cos. of Tipperary and Clare,* by George H. Bassett. This has a house-to-house street directory for Limerick city, while the lists for other towns are shown under trades. There are alphabetical lists of the gentry in each of the three counties.

1870. Slater's *Directory of Ireland.* This follows the customary lay-out, arranged by province with trade lists for each town. There are also lists of nobility, gentry and clergy, though there is no composite alphabetical index to these. The principal farmers are not listed. Local magistrates, however, are shown under each county town. The main cities — Belfast, Cork, Dublin and Limerick — are each supplied with alphabetical indexes to both their traders and nobility, gentry and clergy.

1872. George Griffith's *County Wexford Almanac.* Enniscorthy is listed by trades, whereas Ferns has an alphabetical list of traders. There is also an alphabetical list of medical practitioners in the county.

1875. Francis Guy's *Directory of the County and City of Cork.* This superb production is arranged alphabetically by postal district. Each district has an alphabetical list of residents, traders and landholders, i.e. the sizeable farmers. For Cork city there is both a house-to-house street directory and an alphabetical list of persons.

1879. *Limerick Directory,* by George Henry Bassett. For Limerick city there is an alphabetical list of persons and a list arranged by professions and trades. Included also are directories for all the towns and villages in the county, these being arranged under trades. Also included is a list of gentlemen in the county.

1881. Slater's *Royal National Commercial Directory of Ireland.* The format is as usual, arranged by province, with the business community of each town classified by trade. This edition, however, also carries lists of farmers arranged by parish adjoining their nearest town, albeit lacking the farmers' individual townland addresses.

1882. *Omagh Almanac.* This carries four alphabetical lists: a list of National Schools in the Omagh district together with the names of managers and teachers; lists of local clergy — Anglican, Catholic and Presbyterian; a list of medical and surgical practitioners, and a list of country gentry. For the town of Omagh there is both a street directory and an alphabetical list. The directories of Cookstown and Strabane are arranged under trades while Fintona has an alphabetical list of traders and Dungannon has a street directory. Similar *Omagh Almanacs* were issued in 1885 and 1888.

1883. S. Farrell's *County Armagh Directory and Almanac.* There are street directories for Armagh and Newry but the other towns have alphabetical lists only. There is also a list of judicial rents in Co. Armagh for 1882, showing tenant and landlord, but *not* address.

1884. *Kilkenny City and County Guide and Directory,* by George Henry Bassett. There is an alphabetical list of gentlemen in the county, and an alphabetical list of persons in Kilkenny city. Every town and village is listed, showing not only the traders but also the farmers and landowners within each postal district. The book contains a mass of local information.

1885. *Wexford County Guide and Directory,* by George Henry Bassett. For Wexford Borough there is both an alphabetical list of persons and a list arranged by trades. There are directories of all the postal districts in the county, showing traders, farmers and landowners. The volume also contains much history and general local information.

1886. Francis *Guy's Postal Directory of Munster.* This covers the six counties of Munster. Arranged under counties and then by postal district, it gives lists of gentry, clergy, traders, principal farmers, heads of national schools and police sergeants. For each county there are separate lists of magistrates, clergy, solicitors, physicians and surgeons.

1886. *Louth County Guide and Directory,* by George Henry Bassett. There are alphabetical lists of persons for the towns of Ardee, Drogheda and Dundalk; the other villages have lists arranged under trades, with lists of farmers and landlords. There is also county history and local information.

1887. *Derry Almanac and Directory.* For Londonderry there are both street lists and lists arranged under trades. The other towns are listed under trades only. This *Almanac* was produced annually from 1891.

1888. *The Book of Antrim,* by George Henry Bassett. This is arranged by postal district, but omits the city of Belfast. It contains history and local information.

1889. Guy's *City and County Cork Almanac and Directory.* This follows the same lay-out as Guy's Munster Directory in 1886, being arranged by postal district. As from 1889 it was issued annually.

1889. *Sligo Independent County Directory.* For the town of Sligo there is a street directory, a list arranged under trades and an alphabetical list of gentry and clergy. The other towns are arranged under trades only. There is also a list of police sergeants at Ballymote, Colloony, Easkey, Sligo and Tobercurry, and a list of petty session clerks and another of schoolmasters.

1889. *The Book of County Tipperary,* by George Henry Bassett. This is a directory of the whole county, giving places as small as New Inn (population 133 in 1881), and listing the traders, farmers and residents. Also includes history and much local information.

1891. *Derry Almanac and Directory.* For Londonderry there is both a street list

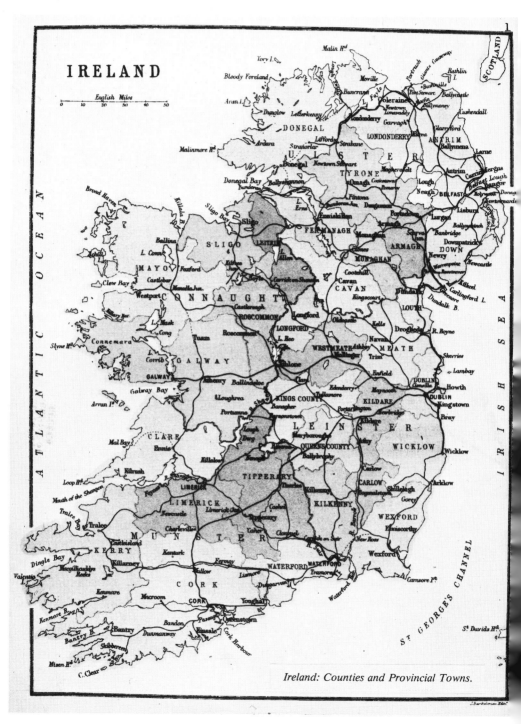

Ireland: Counties and Provincial Towns.

and a list arranged by trades. Two other towns have lists by trades only. This *Almanac* was issued annually as from 1891.

1891. *Omagh Almanac.* For Omagh, there is both a street list and an alphabetical list of persons. Aughnacloy and Drumquin have alphabetical lists only, Augher has a street list only, while the other towns have lists arranged under trades only.

1893. Francis *Guy's Directory of Munster.* Arranged under each of the six counties, and then divided by postal district containing lists of traders and farmers. There is also an alphabetical list of persons for each of the counties at large.

1894. Slater's *Royal National Directory of Ireland.* This has a new lay-out for Slater, being arranged by province as usual, but then alphabetically by parish, town or village. It lists the names of National schoolmasters, police head-constables and sergeants, private residents, commercial persons and farmers. It appears to include every parish in Ireland. There is also a list of magistrates for each county, as well as an alphabetical list of the "principal seats" throughout Ireland (though only those of considerable importance are included).

Directories for Towns and Cities, listed by County

Co. Antrim

1819. Bradshaw's *Directory* of Belfast, Lisburn.

1820. Pigot's Directory of Antrim, Belfast, Lisburn.

1820. Joseph Smyth's *Directory of Belfast and its Vicinity.*

1820. *Belfast Almanack* (contains alphabetical list of traders with their addresses, and also an alphabetical list of streets, etc.).

1824. Pigot's *Directory* of Antrim, Ballycastle, Ballymena, Ballymoney, Belfast, Carrickfergus, Larne, Lisburn, Portglenone, Randalstown.

1835. William T. Matier's *Belfast Directory* (contains alphabetical list of gentry, merchants and traders residing in Belfast, and an alphabetical list of noblemen and gentlemen residing in the neighbourhood of Belfast, and also a list classified by trades and professions).

1839. Matthew Martin's *Belfast Directory* (contains alphabetical list of gentry, merchants, traders etc; a list of persons classified by professions and trades, and a house-to-house list of the principal streets; also a list of noblemen and gentry residing in Cos. Antrim and Down).

1841. Martin's *Belfast Directory* of Antrim, Ballymena, Belfast, Carrickfergus, Crumlin, Lisburn.

1842. Martin's *Belfast Directory* of Antrim, Ballymena, Belfast, Carrickfergus, Crumlin, Larne, Lisburn.

1850. James Alexander Henderson's *Belfast Directory* (contains an alphabetical list of nobility and gentry in and about Belfast; a street list of the principal houses in the principal streets; an alphabetical list of gentry, merchants and traders; a list of persons classified by trades; the suburbs of Ballymacarrett, Holywood, Whiteabbey and Whitehouse).

1852. *Belfast & Province of Ulster Directory* of Antrim, Ballycastle, Ballymoney, Carrickfergus, Larne, Lisburn, Randalstown.

1854. *Belfast & Province of Ulster Directory* of Antrim, Ballyclare, Ballycastle, Ballymena, Ballymoney, Bushmills, Carrickfergus, Crumlin, Dromara, Glenarm, Larne, Lisburn, Randalstown. Further editions issued in 1856, 1858, 1861, 1863, 1865, 1868, 1870 without alteration to its scope.

1856. Slater's *Directory* of Antrim, Ballycastle, Ballyclare, Ballymena, Ballymoney, Belfast, Carrickfergus, Crumlin and Glenavy, Cushendall, Glenarm, Larne, Lisburn, Portglenone, Randalstown.

1860. Hugh Adair's *Belfast Directory* (contains a good house-to-house street list; also covers the suburbs of Ardoyne, Ligoniel, Ballynafeigh, Ballymacarrett, Dundonald, the Knock, Newtownbreda, Sydenham, Whiteabbey, Whitehouse).

1865. Wynne's *Directory* of Antrim, Ballymena, Ballymoney, Carrickfergus, Larne, Lisburn, Portrush.

1870. Slater's *Directory* of Antrim, Ballycastle, Ballyclare, Ballymena, Ballymoney, Belfast, Carrickfergus, Crumlin and Glenavy, Cushendall, Glenarm, Larne, Lisburn, Portglenone, Portrush, Randalstown, Whiteabbey.

1877. *Belfast & Province of Ulster Directory* of Antrim, Ballyclare, Ballycastle, Ballymena, Ballymoney, Bushmills, Carnlough, Carrickfergus, Crumlin, Dromara, Glenarm, Larne, Lisburn, Randalstown. Further editions in 1880, 1884, 1887, 1890, 1894, 1900.

1881. Slater's *Directory* of Antrim, Ballycastle, Ballyclare, Ballymena, Ballymoney, Belfast, Carrickfergus, Glenarm, Larne, Lisburn, Portrush, Randalstown, Whiteabbey.

1887. *Derry Almanac* of Portrush.

1888. Bassett's *Book of Antrim* (omitting Belfast).

1894. Slater's *Directory*.

Co. Armagh

1819. Bradshaw's *General Directory* of Armagh, Lurgan, Markethill, Portadown, Tandragee.

1820. Pigot's *Directory* of Armagh.

1824. Pigot's *Directory* of Armagh, Blackwatertown, Lurgan, Portadown, Tandragee.

1841. Martin's *Belfast Directory* of Armagh, Lurgan, Portadown, Waringstown.

1842. Martin's *Belfast Directory* of Armagh, Lurgan, Markethill, Portadown, Waringstown.

1846. Slater's *Directory* of Armagh, Blackwatertown, Loughgall, Lurgan and Moira, Portadown, Tanderagee.

1852. *Belfast & Province of Ulster Directory* of Armagh, Blackwatertown, Lurgan, Portadown.

1854. *Belfast & Province of Ulster Directory* of Armagh, Blackwatertown, Keady, Lurgan, Moira, Portadown, Richhill, Tandragee. Further editions issued in 1856, 1858, 1861, 1863, 1865, 1868, 1870 without alteration to its scope.

1856. Slater's *Directory* of Armagh, Keady, Middletown, Richhill, Tynan and Markethill, Blackwatertown and Loughgall, Lurgan, Moira and Waringstown, Portadown, Tanderagee.

1865. Wynne's *Directory* of Armagh, Lurgan, Portadown.

1870. Slater's *Directory* of Armagh, Crossmaglen, Lurgan, Moy, Newtown Hamilton, Portadown, Tanderagee.

1877. *Belfast & Province of Ulster Directory* of Armagh, Blackwatertown, Keady, Lurgan, Moira, Portadown, Richhill, Tandragee, Waringstown and Donaghcloney. Further editions in 1880, 1884, 1890, 1894, 1900.

1881. Slater's *Directory* of Armagh, Crossmaglen, Lurgan, Moy, Newtown Hamilton, Portadown, Tanderagee.

1883. Farrell's *Directory* of Armagh, Lurgan, Portadown, Richhill, Tandragee.

1888. Bassett's *Book of Armagh,* with directory of Armagh town and all postal districts in the county.

1894. Slater's *Directory.*

Co. Carlow

1788. Lucas's *Directory* of Carlow, Old Leighlin, Leighlinbridge.

1820. Pigot's *Directory* of Carlow.

1824. Pigot's *Directory* of Carlow, Hacketstown, Leighlinbridge, Tullow.

1839. *New Commercial Directory* of Carlow.

1846. Slater's *Directory* of Carlow, Hacketstown, Leighlinbridge, Bagnalstown and Royal Oak, Tullow.

1856. Slater's *Directory* of Carlow, Hacketstown, Leighlin Bridge, Bagnalstown, Borris and Royal Oak, Tullow.

1870. Slater's *Directory* of Bagnalstown and Leighlinbridge, Carlow, Hacketstown, Tullow.

1881. Slater's *Directory* of Bagnalstown and Leighlinbridge, Borris and Old Leighlin, Carlow and Graigue, Hacketstown, Tullow.

1894 Slater's *Directory.*

Co. Cavan

1824. Pigot's *Directory* of Bailieborough, Ballyconnel, Belturbet, Cavan, Cootehill, Killeshandra, Kingscourt.

1846. Slater's *Directory* of Bailieborough, Belturbet, Cavan, Cootehill, Killeshandra, Kingscourt.

1852. *Belfast & Province of Ulster Directory* of Cavan.

1854. *Belfast & Province of Ulster Directory* of Bailieborough, Belturbet, Cavan, Cootehill. Further editions issued in 1856, 1858, 1861, 1863, 1865, 1868, 1870, 1877, 1880, 1884, 1890, 1894, 1900.

1856. Slater's *Directory* of Bailieborough, Ballyconnell, Belturbet, Cavan, Cootehill, Killashandra, King's Court.

1870. Slater's *Directory* of Bailieborough, Ballyconnel, Bawnboy and Swanlinbar, Ballyjamesduff, Belturbet, Cavan, Cootehill, Killeshandra, Kingscourt.

1881. Slater's *Directory* of Bailieborough and Kingscourt, Ballyconnell, Bawnboy and Swanlinbar, Ballyjamesduff, Belturbet, Cavan, Cootehill, Killeshandra.

1894. Slater's *Directory*.

Co. Clare

1788. Lucas's *Directory* of Ennis.

1824. Pigot's *Directory* of Ennis, Killaloe, Kilrush.

1846. Slater's *Directory* of Ennis, Kilkee, Killaloe, Kilrush, Tulla.

1856. Slater's *Directory* of Ennis, Ennistymon, Kilkee, Killaloe, Kilrush, Milltown Malbay, Tulla.

1866. Bassett's *Directory* of Ennis, Killaloe, Kilrush.

1870. Slater's *Directory* of Ennis, Ennistymon, Kilkee, Killaloe, Kilrush, Miltown Malbay, Newmarket-on-Fergus, Sixmilebridge and Cratlow, Tulla.

1881. Slater's *Directory* of Ennis, Ennistymon, Kilkee, Killaloe, Kilrush, Milltown Malbay, Newmarket-on-Fergus, Tulla.

1886. Guy's *Postal Directory of Munster*.

1893. Guy's *Postal Directory of Munster*.

1894. Slater's *Directory*.

Co. Cork

1787. Lucas's *Directory* of Bandon, Cork, Cove, Innishannon, Kinsale, Passage, Youghal.

1797. John Nixon's *Cork Almanack* (alphabetical list of merchants and traders in Cork city).

1809. Holden's *Triennial Directory* of Cork.

1810. William West's *Directory of Cork* (contains alphabetical lists of gentry, merchants and traders, attornies, physicians and surgeons, etc.).

1812. John Connor's *Cork Directory* (alphabetical list of merchants and traders).

1817. John Connor's *Cork Directory* (alphabetical list of merchants and traders, and a list of streets, lanes etc. divided by parish).

1820. Pigot's *Directory* of Bandon, Cork, Kinsale, Youghal.

1824. Pigot's *Directory* of Bandon, Bantry, Castle-lyons, Castlemartyr, Charleville, Clonakilty, Cloyne, Cork, Cove, Doneraile, Fermoy, Kanturk, Kilworth, Kinsale, Macroom, Mallow, Midleton, Millstreet, Mitchelstown, Newmarket, Rathcormac, Skibbereen, Youghal.

1826. John Connor's *Cork Directory* (alphabetical list of merchants and traders).

1828. John Connor's *Directory of Cork* (ditto).

1846. Slater's *Directory* of Ballincollig, Bandon and Innishannon, Bantry, Charleville, Clonakilty, Cloyne and Castlemartyr, Cork, Cove, Doneraile, Fermoy, Kanturk, Kilworth, Kinsale, Macroom, Mallow, Midleton, Millstreet, Mitchelstown, Newmarket, Rathcormac, Skibbereen and Castletownsend, Youghal.

1856. Slater's *Directory* of Ballincollig, Bandon and Innishannon, Bantry and Glengariff, Charleville, Clonakilty, Cloyne and Castlemartyr, Cork, Doneraile, Dunmanway, Fermoy, Kanturk, Kilworth, Kinsale, Macroom, Mallow, Midleton, Millstreet, Mitchelstown, Newmarket, Passage and Monkstown, Queenstown (Cove), Rathcormac and Castlelyons, Ross, Skibbereen, Castle-Townsend and Baltimore, Skull and Ballydehob, Youghal.

1870. Slater's *Directory* of Ballincollig, Bandon, Bantry, Charleville, Clonakilty, Cloyne and Castlemartyr, Cork, Doneraile, Dunmanway, Fermoy, Kanturk, Kilworth, Kinsale, Macroom, Mallow, Midleton, Millstreet, Mitchelstown, Newmarket, Passage, Queenstown (Cove), Rathcormac and Castlelyons, Rosscarbery, Skibbereen and Ballydehob, Youghal.

1875. Guy's *Directory of the County and City of Cork.*

1881. *Slater's Directory* of Bandon, Bantry and Glengariff, Charleville, Clonakilty, Cloyne and Castlemartyr, Cork, Dunmanway, Fermoy, Kanturk, Kinsale, Macroom, Mallow, Midleton, Millstreet, Mitchelstown, Newmarket, Passage and Monkstown, Queenstown (Cove), Rathcormac and Castlelyons, Rosscarbery, Skibbereen, Castletownsend and Leap, Skull and Ballydehob.

1886. Guy's *Postal Directory of Munster.*

1889. Guy's *City and County Cork Almanac,* issued annually thereafter.

1894. Slater's *Directory.*

Co. Donegal

1824. Pigot's *Directory* of Ballybofey, Ballyshannon, Donegal, Letterkenny, Lifford, Pettigo, Raphoe, Stranorlar.

1839. *Directory* of Ballyshannon, Donegal, Stranorlar and Ballibofey.

1846. Slater's *Directory* of Ballyshannon and Bundoran, Buncrana, Donegal, Killybegs and Dunkineely, Letterkenny, Lifford and Castlefinn (see under Strabane, Co. Tyrone), Moville, Raphoe, Rathmelton, Stranorlar and Ballybofey.

1854. *Belfast & Province of Ulster Directory* of Ballyshannon, Lifford. Further editions issued in 1856, 1858, 1861, 1863, 1865, 1868, 1870, 1877, 1880, 1884, 1890, 1894, 1900.

1856. Slater's *Directory* of Ballyshannon and Bundoran, Buncrana, Donegal, Killybegs and Dunkineely, Letterkenny, Lifford and Castlefinn, Moville, Pettigoe, Raphoe, Rathmelton, Stranorlar and Ballybofey.

1870. Slater's *Directory* of Ballyshannon, Buncrana, Donegal, Dunfanaghy, Glenties and Ardara, Killybegs, Letterkenny and Manorcunningham, Lifford, Moville, Pettigoe, Raphoe and Convoy, Ramelton, Stranorlar.

1881. Slater's *Directory* of Ballyshannon, Buncrana and Clonmany, Donegal, Dunfanaghy, Glenties and Ardara, Killybegs, Letterkenny and Manorcunningham, Lifford, Moville, Pettigoe, Raphoe, Rathmelton, Stranorlar and Ballybofey.

1887. *Derry Almanac* of Ardara, Ballintra, Ballybofey, Ballyshannon, Buncrana, Carndonagh, Carrigans, Castlefin, Donegal, Donemana, Dunfanaghy, Glenties, Killygordon, Letterkenny, Lifford, Manorcunningham, Milford, Mountcharles, Moville, Ramelton, Raphoe, Rathmullen, Stranorlar, St. Johnstown (issued annually thereafter).

1894. Slater's *Directory*.

Co. Down

1819. Bradshaw's *General Directory* of Banbridge, Newry, Rathfriland, Rosstrevor, Kilkeel, Warrenpoint.

1820. Pigot's *Directory* of Newry.

1824. Pigot's *Directory* of Ballynahinch, Banbridge, Bangor, Castlewellan, Comber, Donaghadee, Downpatrick, Dromore, Gilford, Hillsborough, Killileigh, Loughbrickland, Newry, Newtownards, Portaferry, Rathfryland, Rosstrevor, Saintfield, Strangford, Warrenpoint.

1841. Martin's *Belfast Directory* of Banbridge, Bangor, Comber, Downpatrick, Dromore, Hillsborough, Holywood, Killileagh.

1842. Martin's *Belfast Directory* of Banbridge, Bangor, Castlewellan, Comber, Crawfordsburn, Donaghadee, Downpatrick, Dromore, Hillsborough, Holywood, Killileagh, Kircubbin, Newtownards, Portaferry, Rathfriland, Saintfield, Strangford.

1846. Slater's *Directory* of Ballynahinch, Banbridge, Bangor, Castlewellan, Clough and Newcastle, Comber, Donaghadee, Downpatrick, Dromore, Gilford and Loughbrickland, Hillsborough, Killyleagh, Newry, Newtownards, Portaferry, Strangford and Kircubbin, Rathfryland, Saintfield, Warrenpoint and Rosstrevor.

1852. *Belfast & Province of Ulster Directory* of Ardglass, Ballynahinch, Banbridge, Bangor, Donaghadee, Downpatrick, Dromore, Hillsborough, Newry, Newtownards, Saintfield.

1854. *Belfast & Province of Ulster Directory* of Ardglass, Ballynahinch, Banbridge, Bangor, Castlewellan, Comber, Donaghadee, Downpatrick, Dromore, Gilford, Hillsborough, Holywood, Killyleagh, Loughbrickland, Newcastle, Newry, Newtownards, Rathfriland, Rosstrevor, Saintfield, Strangford. Further editions in 1856, 1858, 1861 (with Kilkeel added), 1863, 1865, 1868 (with Laurencetown added), 1870, 1877, 1880, 1884, 1890, 1894, 1900.

1856. Slater's *Directory* of Ballynahinch, Banbridge, Bangor, Castlewellan, Comber, Donaghadee, Downpatrick, Dromore, Gilford, Loughbrickland and Laurencetown, Hillsborough, Kilkeel, Killyleagh, Newry, Newtownards and Grey Abbey, Portaferry, Strangford and Kircubbin, Rathfryland, Saintfield, Warrenpoint and Rosstrevor.

1865. Wynne's *Directory* of Ballynahinch, Banbridge, Bangor, Comber, Downpatrick, Donaghadee, Dromore, Hillsborough, Holywood, Newry, Newtownards, Rathfriland, Warrenpoint.

1870. Slater's *Directory* of Ballynahinch, Banbridge, Bangor, Castlewellan, Comber, Donaghadee, Downpatrick, Dromore, Gilford, Hillsborough, Hollywood, Kilkeel, Killyleagh, Newry, Newtownards, Portaferry, Rathfryland, Saintfield, Warrenpoint and Rosstrevor.

1881. Slater's *Directory* of Ballynahinch and Saintfield, Banbridge, Bangor, Castlewellan, Donaghadee, Downpatrick, Dromore, Holywood, Kilkeel, Newry, Newtownards, Portaferry, Rathfryland, Warrenpoint and Rosstrevor.

1883. Farrell's *Directory* of Newry.

1894. Slater's *Directory*.

Co. Dublin
(see also Dublin Directories)

1820. Pigot's *Directory* of Dublin.

1824. Pigot's *Directory* of Dublin, Howth, Lucan, Swords.

1846. Slater's *Directory* of Balbriggan and Skerries, Blackrock, Booterstown, Dalkey, Dublin, Howth, Kingstown (Dun Laoire), Monkstown, Swords and Malahide, Williamstown.

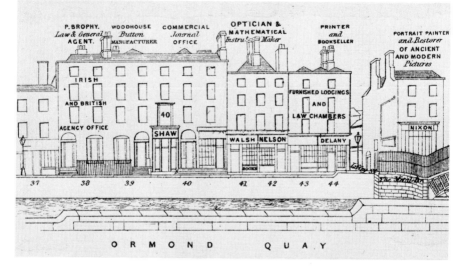

New City Pictorial Directory of Dublin city, Henry Shaw, 1850.

1850.   Henry Shaw's *New City Pictorial Directory of Dublin city* (contains a house-to-house street list, an alphabetical list of persons, alphabetical lists of attornies and barristers and many line drawings showing street frontages, etc.).

1856.   Slater's *Directory* of Balbriggan and Skerries, Dublin and Kingstown (Dun Laoire), Howth, Swords and Malahide.

1870.   Slater's *Directory* of Balbriggan and Skerries, Dalkey, Dublin, Dundrum, Howth, Rathfarnham, Swords and Malahide.

1881.   Slater's *Directory* of Balbriggan and Skerries, Donabate and Malahide, Dublin, Howth and Baldoyle, Rathfarnham, Swords.

1894.   Slater's *Directory*.

Co. Fermanagh

1824.   Pigot's *Directory* of Churchhill, Enniskillen, Irvinestown, Maguiresbridge.

1839.   *Directory* of Enniskillen.

1846.   Slater's *Directory* of Enniskillen, Lisnaskea, Maguire's Bridge and Brookeborough, Lowtherstown.

1852.   *Belfast & Province of Ulster Directory* of Enniskillen. Further editions in 1854, 1856, 1858, 1861, 1863, 1865, 1868, 1870, 1877, 1880, 1884, 1890, 1894, 1900.

1856. Slater's *Directory* of Enniskillen, Lisnaskea, Lowtherstown.

1870. Slater's *Directory* of Enniskillen, Lisnaskea, Maguiresbridge and Brookeborough, Lowtherstown.

1881. Slater's *Directory* of Enniskillen, Lisnaskea, Lowtherstown.

1891. *Derry Almanac* of Enniskillen.

1894. Slater's *Directory*.

Co. Galway

1820. Pigot's *Directory* of Galway.

1824. Pigot's *Directory* of Ballinasloe, Eyrecourt, Galway, Gort, Loughrea, Tuam.

1846. Slater's *Directory* of Athenry, Ballinasloe, Castleblakeney, Clifden, Dunmore, Eyrecourt, Galway, Gort, Headford, Loughrea, Portumna, Tuam.

1856. Slater's *Directory* of Athenry, Ballinasloe, Clifden, Dunmore, Eyrecourt, Galway, Gort, Headford, Loughrea, Portumna, Tuam.

1870. Slater's *Directory* of Athenry, Ballinasloe, Clifden, Dunmore, Eyrecourt, Galway, Gort, Headford, Loughrea, Portumna, Tuam.

1881. Slater's *Directory* of Athenry, Ballinasloe, Clifden, Eyrecourt, Galway, Gort, Loughrea, Portumna, Tuam.

1894. Slater's *Directory*.

Co. Kerry

1824. Pigot's *Directory* of Dingle, Kenmare, Killarney, Listowel, Tarbert, Tralee.

1846. Slater's *Directory* of Castleisland, Dingle, Kenmare, Killarney, Listowel, Miltown, Tarbert, Tralee.

1856. Slater's *Directory* of Cahirciveen and Valentia, Castleisland, Dingle, Kenmare, Killarney, Listowel, Milltown, Tarbert, Tralee and Blennerville.

1870. Slater's *Directory* of Cahirciveen and Valentia, Castleisland, Dingle, Kenmare, Killarney, Listowel, Milltown and Castlemaine, Tarbert and Ballylongford, Tralee.

1881. Slater's *Directory* of Cahirciveen and Valentia, Castleisland, Dingle, Kenmare, Killarney, Listowel, Milltown and Castlemaine, Tarbert and Ballylongford, Tralee.

1886. Guy's *Postal Directory of Munster*.

1893. Guy's *Postal Directory of Munster*.

1894. Slater's *Directory*.

Co. Kildare

1788. Lucas's *Directory* of Athy.

1824. Pigot's *Directory* of Athy, Celbridge, Kilcock, Kilcullen, Kildare, Leixlip, Maynooth, Monastereven, Naas, Rathangan.

1846. Slater's *Directory* of Athy, Celbridge, Leixlip and Lucan, Kilcullen, Kildare, Maynooth and Kilcock, Monasterevan, Naas, Rathangan.

1856. Slater's *Directory* of Athy, Celbridge, Leixlip and Lucan, Kilcullen, Kildare, Maynooth and Kilcock, Monastereven, Naas and Newbridge, Rathangan.

1870. Slater's *Directory* of Athy, Kilcullen, Kildare, Maynooth and Kilcock, Monastereven, Naas, Newbridge, Rathangan.

1881. Slater's *Directory* of Athy, Celbridge, Kildare, Maynooth and Kilcock, Naas.

1894. Slater's *Directory*.

Co. Kilkenny

1788. Lucas's *Directory* of Kilkenny, Thomastown.

1820. Pigot's *Directory* of Kilkenny.

1824. Pigot's *Directory* of Ballyragget, Callan, Castlecomer, Kilkenny, Thomastown.

1839. Shearman's *Directory* of Kilkenny.

1846. Slater's *Directory* of Ballyragget, Callan, Castlecomer, Durrow, Kilkenny, Thomastown.

1856. Slater's *Directory* of Ballyragget, Callan, Castlecomer, Durrow, Kilkenny, Thomastown.

1870. Slater's *Directory* of Ballyragget, Callan, Castlecomer, Durrow, Kilkenny, Thomastown.

1881. Slater's *Directory* of Callan, Castlecomer, Durrow, Kilkenny, Thomastown.

1884. Bassett's *Directory* of Ballyhale, Ballyragget, Bennett's Bridge, Callan, Castlecomer, Clonmantagh, Cuff's Grange, Dungarvan, Ferrybank, Freshford, Glenmore, Goresbridge, Gowran, Graigue, Inistioge, Jenkinstown, Johnstown, Johnswell, Kells, Kilfane, Kilkenny, Kilmacow, Kilmanagh, Kilmoganny, Knocktopher, Luke's Well, Mooncoin, Mullinavat, Piltown and Fiddown, Rosbercon, Slieverue, Stonyford, The Rower, Thomastown, Three Castles, Tullaroan, Tullogher, Urlingford, Whitehall, Windgap.

1894. Slater's *Directory*.

King's County (Offaly)

1824. Pigot's *Directory* of Banagher, Birr, Cloghan, Edenderry, Frankford, Philipstown, Tullamore.

1846. Slater's *Directory* of Banagher, Birr, Clara, Cloghan, Edenderry, Frankford and Ballyboy, Philipstown, Tullamore.

1856. Slater's *Directory* of Banagher, Birr, Clara, Cloghan and Ferbane, Edenderry, Frankford and Ballyboy, Philipstown, Tullamore.

1870. Slater's *Directory* of Banagher, Birr, Cloghan and Ferbane, Clara, Edenderry, Frankford, Philipstown, Tullamore.

1881. Slater's *Directory* of Banagher, Cloghan and Ferbane, Birr, Edenderry, Frankford, Tullamore.

1894. Slater's *Directory*.

Co. Leitrim

1824. Pigot's *Directory* of Ballinamore, Carrick-on-Shannon, Drumsna, Jamestown, Manor-Hamilton.

1846. Slater's *Directory* of Carrick-on-Shannon, Dromahaire, Drumsna and Jamestown, Manorhamilton, Mohill.

1856. Slater's *Directory* of Ballinamore, Carrick-on-Shannon, Dromahaire, Drumsna and Jamestown, Manor-Hamilton, Mohill.

1870. Slater's *Directory* of Ballinamore, Carrick-on-Shannon and Leitrim, Dromahaire, Drumsna, Manorhamilton, Mohill.

1881. Slater's *Directory* of Ballinamore, Carrick-on-Shannon, Manorhamilton and Dromahaire, Mohill.

1894. Slater's *Directory*.

Co. Limerick

1769. John Ferrar's *Directory of Limerick* (alphabetical list of merchants and traders, list of aldermen and burgesses, list of military establishment of the city, 5th, 27th and 47th Regts., list of Anglican clergy and church-wardens; list of revenue officers at Limerick, Scattery, Kilrush and Tarbert; lists of barristers, attornies and public notaries; list of masters and wardens of the guilds; lists of physicians, surgeons and apothecaries; list of masters and wardens of the Lodges of Freemasons).

1788. Lucas's *Directory* of Limerick.

1809. Holden's *Triennial Directory* of Limerick.

1820. Pigot's *Directory* of Limerick.

1824. Pigot's *Directory* of Castleconnell, Kilmallock, Limerick, Newcastle, Rathkeale.

1846. Slater's *Directory* of Adare, Bruff, Castleconnell and O'Brien's Bridge, Croom, Kilmallock, Limerick, Newcastle, Rathkeale.

1856. Slater's *Directory* of Adare, Bruff, Castleconnell and O'Brien's Bridge, Croom, Kilmallock, Limerick, Newcastle, Rathkeale.

1866. Bassett's *Directory* of Adare, Castleconnell, Kilmallock, Limerick, Newcastle, Rathkeale.

1870. Slater's *Directory* of Adare, Askeaton, Bruff, Castleconnell, Croom, Kilmallock, Limerick, Newcastle, Rathkeale.

1879. Bassett's *Directory* of Abbeyfeale, Adare, Ardagh, Ashford, Askeaton, Athea, Broadford, Bruff, Caherconlish, Castleconnell, Croom, Drumcollogher, Foynes, Glin, Hospital, Kilmallock, Limerick, Murroe, Newcastle West, Oola, Pallaskenry, Rathkeale, Shanagolden, Tounafulla.

1881. Slater's *Directory* of Adare and Croom, Askeaton, Castle-connell and O'Brien's Bridge, Foynes (see Tarbert, Co. Kerry), Kilmallock, Limerick, Newcastle West, Rathkeale.

1886. Guy's *Postal Directory of Munster.*

1893. Guy's *Postal Directory of Munster.*

1894. Slater's *Directory.*

Co. Londonderry

1820. Pigot's *Directory* of Coleraine, Londonderry.

1824. Pigot's *Directory* of Castledawson, Coleraine, Dungiven, Kilrea, Londonderry, Maghera, Magherafelt, Moneymore, Newtown-limavady.

1842. Martin's *Belfast Directory* of Castledawson, Coleraine, Magherafelt, Moneymore.

1846. Slater's *Directory* of Castledawson and Bellaghy, Coleraine, Portstewart, Bushmills and Port Balintrae, Dungiven, Garvagh and Ballinameen, Kilrea, Londonderry, Maghera, Magherafelt, Moneymore and Coagh, Newtown-Limavady.

1852. *Belfast & Province of Ulster Directory* of Castledawson, Coleraine, Londonderry, Maghera.

1854. *Belfast & Province of Ulster Directory* of Castledawson, Coleraine, Londonderry, Maghera, Magherafelt, Moneymore. Further editions issued in 1856, 1858, 1861 (with Newtownlimavady added), 1865, 1868, 1870, 1877, 1880, 1884, 1894, 1900.

1856. Slater's *Directory* of Castle-Dawson and Bellaghy, Coleraine, Portstewart, Bushmills and Port Balintrae, Dungiven, Garvagh and Ballinameen, Kilrea, Londonderry, Maghera, Magherafelt, Moneymore and Coagh, Newtown-Limavady.

1865. Wynne's *Directory* of Coleraine, Londonderry, Newtown-Limavady, Maghera, Moneymore.

1870. Slater's *Directory* of Castledawson, Coleraine, Dungiven, Garvagh, Kilrea, Londonderry, Maghera, Magherafelt, Moneymore, Newtownlimavady.

1881. Slater's *Directory* of Coleraine, Dungiven, Kilrea, Limavady, Londonderry, Maghera, Magherafelt, Moneymore and Coagh.

1887. *Derry Almanac* of Coleraine, Dungiven, Kilrea, Londonderry, Limavady, Portstewart.

1894. Slater's *Directory*.

Co. Longford

1824. Pigot's *Directory* of Granard, Lanesborough, Longford.

1846. Slater's *Directory* of Ballymahon, Granard, Longford, Mostrim or Edgeworthstown.

1856. Slater's *Directory* of Ballymahon, Granard, Longford and Newtown-Forbes, Mostrim or Edgeworthstown.

1870. Slater's *Directory* of Ballymahon, Edgeworthstown, Granard, Longford.

1881. Slater's *Directory* of Ballymahon, Edgeworthstown, Granard, Longford.

1894. Slater's *Directory*.

Co. Louth

1820. Pigot's *Directory* of Drogheda, Dundalk.

1824. Pigot's *Directory* of Ardee, Carlingford, Castlebellingham, Drogheda, Dundalk.

1830. McCabe's *Directory* of Drogheda.

1846. Slater's *Directory* of Ardee and Louth, Carlingford, Castlebellingham and Dunleer, Drogheda, Dundalk.

1856. Slater's *Directory* of Ardee and Louth, Carlingford, Castlebellingham and Dunleer, Drogheda, Dundalk.

1870. Slater's *Directory* of Ardee, Carlingford, Castlebellingham, Drogheda, Dundalk.

1881. Slater's *Directory* of Ardee and Louth, Carlingford, Castlebellingham and Dunleer, Drogheda, Dundalk.

1886. Bassett's *Louth County Guide and Directory*.

1894. Slater's *Directory*.

1896. Tempest's *Almanac and Directory of Dundalk* (thereafter issued annually: note that the 1890-95 editions have no lists of traders).

Co. Mayo

1824. Pigot's *Directory* of Ballina, Ballinrobe, Castlebar, Killala, Swineford, Westport.

1846. Slater's *Directory* of Ballina, Ballinrobe, Castlebar, Claremorris, Killala, Newport, Swineford, Westport.

1856. Slater's *Directory* of Ballina, Ballinrobe, Castlebar, Claremorris, Killala, Newport, Swineford, Westport.

1870. Slater's *Directory* of Ballina, Ballinrobe and Hollymount, Castlebar, Claremorris and Ballyhaunis, Killala, Newport, Swineford, Westport.

1881. Slater's *Directory* of Ballina and Killala, Ballinrobe and Hollymount, Castlebar, Claremorris, Ballyhaunis and Knock, Swineford and Bellaghy, Westport and Newport.

1894. Slater's *Directory*.

Co. Meath

1824. Pigot's *Directory* of Athboy, Duleek, Kells, Navan, Ratoath, Summerhill, Trim.

1846. Slater's *Directory* of Athboy, Duleek, Kells, Navan, Ratoath, Ashbourne and Dunshaughlin, Trim and Summerhill.

1856. Slater's *Directory* of Athboy, Duleek, Kells, Navan, Oldcastle, Ratoath, Ashbourne and Dunshaughlin, Slane, Trim and Summerhill.

1870. Slater's *Directory* of Athboy, Duleek, Kells, Navan, Oldcastle, Ratoath, Slane, Trim.

1881. Slater's *Directory* of Duleek, Kells, Navan, Oldcastle, Ratoath, Ashbourne and Dunshaughlin, Trim and Athboy.

1894. Slater's *Directory*.

Co. Monaghan

1824. Pigot's *Directory* of Ballybay, Carrickmacross, Castleblayney, Clones, Monaghan.

1846. Slater's *Directory* of Ballybay, Carrickmacross, Castleblayney, Clones and Newtown-Butler, Monaghan.

1852. *Belfast & Province of Ulster Directory* of Ballibay, Clones, Monaghan.

1854. *Belfast & Province of Ulster Directory* of Ballibay, Carrickmacross, Castleblayney, Clones, Monaghan. Further editions issued in 1856, 1858, 1861, 1863, 1865, 1868, 1870, 1877, 1880, 1884, 1890, 1894, 1900.

1856. Slater's *Directory* of Ballybay, Carrickmacross, Castle-Blayney, Clones and Newtown-Butler, Monaghan.

1865. Wynne's *Directory* of Clones, Monaghan.

1870. Slater's *Directory* of Ballybay, Carrickmacross and Shercock, Castleblayney, Clones, Monaghan.

1881. Slater's *Directory* of Ballybay, Carrickmacross and Shercock, Castleblayney, Clones, Monaghan.

1894. Slater's *Directory*.

Queen's County (Leix)

1788. Lucas's *Directory* of Mountmellick, Portarlington.

1824. Pigot's *Directory* of Ballinakill, Durrow, Maryborough, Montrath, Mountmellick, Portarlington, Stradbally.

1846. Slater's *Directory* of Ballinakill, Maryborough, Mountmellick, Mountrath, Portarlington, Stradbally.

1856. Slater's *Directory* of Ballinakill, Maryborough, Mountmellick, Mountrath, Portarlington, Rathdowney and Donaghmore, Stradbally.

1870. Slater's *Directory* of Abbeyleix, Maryborough, Mountmellick, Mountrath, Portarlington, Rathdowney, Stradbally.

1881. Slater's *Directory* of Abbeyleix, Ballinakill and Ballyroan, Maryborough and Stradbally, Mountmellick, Mountrath, Portarlington, Rathdowney.

1894. Slater's *Directory*.

Co. Roscommon

1824. Pigot's *Directory* of Boyle, Castlerea, Elphin, Roscommon, Strokestown.

1846. Slater's *Directory* of Boyle, Castlerea, Elphin, Roscommon, Strokestown.

1856. Slater's *Directory* of Boyle, Castlerea, Elphin, Roscommon, Strokestown.

1870. Slater's *Directory* of Boyle, Castlerea, Elphin, Roscommon, Strokestown.

1881. Slater's *Directory* of Boyle, Castlerea, Elphin, Roscommon, Strokestown.

1894. Slater's *Directory*.

Co. Sligo

1820. Pigot's *Directory* of Sligo.

1824. Pigot's *Directory* of Ballisodare, Ballymote, Collooney, Sligo.

1839. *Directory* of Sligo.

1846. Slater's *Directory* of Ballymote, Coloney and Ballysadare, Sligo.

1856. Slater's *Directory* of Ballymote, Collooney and Ballysadare, Sligo.

1870. Slater's *Directory* of Ballymote, Collooney and Ballisodare, Sligo.

1881. Slater's *Directory* of Ballymote, Collooney and Ballysodare, Enniscrone and Easkey (see Ballina, Co. Mayo), Sligo.

1889. *Sligo Independent Directory* of Ballymote, Cliffoney, Easkey, Coolaney, Drumcliff, Collooney, Carney, Dromore West, Riverstown and Bunnemadden, Rosses Point and Enniscrone, Sligo, Tubbercurry.

1894. Slater's *Directory*.

Co. Tipperary

1788. Lucas's *Directory* of Borrisoleigh, Carrick-on-Suir, Cashel, Clonmel, Nenagh, Thurles, Tipperary.

1820. Pigot's *Directory* of Clonmel.

1824. Pigot's *Directory* of Caher, Carrick-on-Suir, Cashel, Clogheen, Clonmel, Fethard, Killenaule, Nenagh, Roscrea, Templemore, Thurles, Tipperary.

1839. Shearman's *Directory* of Carrick-on-Suir, Clonmel.

1846. Slater's *Directory* of Borrisoleigh, Caher, Carrick-on-Suir, Cashel, Clogheen, Clonmel, Fethard, Killenaule, Nenagh, Newport, Roscrea, Templemore, Thurles, Tipperary.

1856. Slater's *Directory* of Borrisoleigh, Caher, Carrick-on-Suir, Cashel and Golden, Clogheen, Clonmel, Fethard, Killenaule, Nenagh, Newport, Roscrea, Templemore, Thurles, Tipperary.

1866. Bassett's *Directory* of Clonmel, Cashel, Nenagh, Newport, Thurles, Tipperary.

1870. Slater's *Directory* of Borrisoleigh, Caher, Carrick-on-Suir, Cashel, Clogheen, Clonmel, Fethard, Killenaule, Nenagh, Newport, Roscrea, Templemore, Thurles, Tipperary.

1881. Slater's *Directory* of Caher and Ballylooby, Carrick-on-Suir, Cashel, Clogheen, Clonmel, Fethard, Killenaule, Nenagh, Newport, Roscrea, Templemore, Thurles, Tipperary.

1886. Guy's *Postal Directory of Munster*.

1889. Bassett's *Book of Co. Tipperary*.

1893. Guy's *Postal Directory of Munster*.

1894. Slater's *Directory*.

Co. Tyrone

1819. Bradshaw's *Directory* of Dungannon.

1820. Pigot's *Directory* of Strabane.

1824. Pigot's *Directory* of Aughnacloy, Cookstown, Dungannon, Moy and Charlemont, Newtown-stewart, Omagh, Stewartstown, Strabane.

1842. Martin's *Belfast Directory* of Cookstown, Dungannon, Stewartstown.

1846. Slater's *Directory* of Aughnacloy, Cookstown and Desertcreat, Dungannon, Coal Island and Donaghmore, Moy and Charlemont, Newtownstewart, Omagh, Stewartstown, Strabane.

1852. *Belfast & Province of Ulster Directory* of Aughnacloy, Cookstown, Dungannon, Moy and Charlemont.

1854. *Belfast & Province of Ulster Directory* of Aughnacloy, Bellaghy, Clogher, Cookstown, Dungannon, Moy and Charlemont, Omagh, Stewartstown, Strabane. Further editions issued in 1856, 1858, 1861, 1863, 1865, 1868, 1870, 1877, 1880, 1884, 1890, 1894, 1900.

1856. Slater's *Directory* of Aughnacloy and Ballygawley, Clogher and Five-mile-town, Cookstown, Dungannon, Coal Island and Donaghmore, Moy and Charlemont, Newtown-stewart, Omagh, Stewartstown, Strabane.

1865. Wynne's *Directory* of Cookstown, Dungannon, Omagh, Strabane.

1870. Slater's *Directory* of Aughnacloy, Caledon, Castlederg, Clogher and

Fivemiletown, Cookstown, Moy, Newtownstewart and Gortin, Omagh, Stewartstown, Strabane.

1881.   Slater's *Directory* of Aughnacloy, Castlederg, Clogher and Five-mile-town, Cookstown and Stewartstown, Dungannon, Newtownstewart and Gortin, Omagh, Strabane.

1882.   *Omagh Almanac* of Cookstown, Dungannon, Fintona, Omagh, Strabane.

1885.   *Omagh Almanac* of Cookstown, Dungannon, Fintona, Omagh, Strabane.

1887.   *Derry Almanac* of Castlederg, Fintona, Gortin, Newtown-Stewart, Omagh, Strabane (issued annually from 1891).

1888.   *Omagh Almanac* of Cookstown, Dungannon, Fintona, Omagh, Strabane.

1891.   *Omagh Almanac* of Aughnacloy, Augher, Ballygawley, Beragh, Clogher, Cookstown, Dromore, Drumquin, Dungannon, Fintona, Gortin, Newtownstewart, Omagh, Sixmilecross, Strabane, Trillick.

1894.   Slater's *Directory*.

Co. Waterford

1788.   Lucas's *Directory* of Dungarvan, Passage, Waterford.

1809.   Holden's *Triennial Directory* of Waterford.

1820.   Pigot's *Directory* of Dungarvan, Waterford.

1824.   Pigot's *Directory* of Cappoquin, Dungarvan, Kilmacthomas, Lismore, Tallow, Tramore, Waterford.

1839.   Shearman's *Directory* of Waterford.

1839.   T. S. Harvey's *Directory* of Waterford (alphabetical lists of gentry and merchants and traders; house-to-house street directory).

1846.   Slater's *Directory* of Dungarvan, Dunmore, Kilmacthomas, Lismore, Portlaw, Tallow, Tramore, Waterford.

1856.   Slater's *Directory* of Bonmahon, Dungarvan, Dunmore, Kilmacthomas, Lismore and Cappoquin, Portlaw, Tallow, Tramore, Waterford.

1866.   T. S. Harvey's *Waterford Almanac and Directory* (alphabetical list, and list arranged by trades, also map of the city).

1869.   Newenham Harvey's *Waterford Almanac and Directory* (house-to-house directory, alphabetical list of persons, and list arranged by trades).

1870.   Slater's *Directory* of Bonmahon, Dungarvan, Dunmore, Kilmacthomas, Lismore and Cappoquin, Portlaw, Tallow, Tramore, Waterford.

1881.   Slater's *Directory* of Dungarvan, Dunmore, Kilmacthomas, Lismore, Cappoquin and Tallow, Portlaw and Fiddown, Tramore, Waterford.

1886.   Guy's *Postal Directory of Munster*.

1893.   Guy's *Postal Directory of Munster*.

1894.   Slater's *Directory*.

Co. Westmeath

1820. Pigot's *Directory* of Athlone.

1824. Pigot's *Directory* of Athlone, Ballymore, Castletown Delvin, Kilbeggan, Kinnegad, Mullingar.

1846. Slater's *Directory* of Athlone, Castlepollard, Kilbeggan and Ballinagore, Kinnegad, Mullingar.

1856. Slater's *Directory* of Athlone, Castlepollard, Castletowndelvin, Kilbeggan and Ballinagore, Kinnegad, Moate, Mullingar, Tyrrell's Pass.

1870. Slater's *Directory* of Athlone, Castlepollard, Castletowndelvin, Kilbeggan, Kinnegad, Moate, Mullingar.

1881. Slater's *Directory* of Athlone, Castle-Pollard, Castletowndelvin, Kilbeggan and Tyrrell's Pass, Moate, Mullingar.

1894. Slater's *Directory*.

Co. Wexford

1788. Lucas's *Directory* of Enniscorthy, Gorey, New Ross, Taghmon, Wexford.

1820. Pigot's *Directory* of New Ross, Wexford.

1824. Pigot's *Directory* of Enniscorthy, Gorey, New Ross, Taghmon, Wexford.

1839. Shearman's *Directory* of New Ross.

1846. Slater's *Directory* of Enniscorthy and Ferns, Gorey, New Ross and Rosbercon, Taghmon, Wexford.

1856. Slater's *Directory* of Enniscorthy and Ferns, Fethard, Gorey, New Ross and Rossbercon, Newtownbarry, Taghmon, Wexford.

1870. Slater's *Directory* of Enniscorthy, Fethard, Gorey, New Ross, Newtownbarry, Taghmon, Wexford.

1872. Griffith's *Directory* of Enniscorthy, Ferns.

1881. Slater's *Directory* of Enniscorthy and Ferns, Fethard, Gorey, New Ross, Newtownbarry, Wexford.

1885. Bassett's *Wexford County Guide and Directory*.

1894. Slater's *Directory*.

Co. Wicklow

1788. Lucas's *Directory* of Arklow, Bray, Wicklow.

1824. Pigot's *Directory* of Arklow, Baltinglass, Blessington, Bray, Newtown Mount Kennedy, Rathdrum, Wicklow.

1846. Slater's *Directory* of Arklow, Baltinglass, Blessington, Bray, Newtownmountkennedy and Delgany, Rathdrum, Wicklow.

1856. Slater's *Directory* of Arklow, Baltinglass, Blessington, Bray and Enniskerry, Newtown-Mount-Kennedy, Delgany and Kilcoole, Rathdrum, Wicklow and Ashford.

& from DUBLIN to CARRICK on Suire.

From Kilkenny to Carrick on Suire 19.2 M F

CALLEN
West Court
Galway Esq.r
Ballytoban
Baker Esq.
Dungarmore
Chapel Izod
Izod Esq.
Wray Esq.
Cas Eve
Newtown
Welsh Esq.
Desart
L.d Desart
Killnea Ch.
Kells
Ballymack
Hood Esq.
Turnpike
Waterford P.K.
Thomastown R.d
Ennisnag Ru.r
Farm
R.t Hon.H. Hood
Mount Juliet
Pk of Carrick
Grange
Purcel Esq.
Ballydur Cas.
Grange Esq.
Shearman Esq.
Danes Fort Ch.
Newland
Cas. Inch
Tina Park
Wemyss Esq.
Lanamult Cas.
Birchfield
R.d M.r Mulder
Gostinstown
Kennls
Cas.Bhoden
Maidenhall
Hood Esq.
2 Bartonl.s
Blunden Bar.t
Kilcreen
Thomastown R.d P.133
Bennets Br.
R.t M.r Broderick
Morres Bar.t
Scheestown
Ishee Es.
KILKENNY
Archers Grove
IRISH-TOWN
Killfaara Ryan Esq.r
Blunt Esq.
Cooke Esq.r
Hunt Esq.
Sion
Turnpike
R.t M.r Chandler
Ballinabola
Ragarran
Knaresborough Esq.r
Temple-martin
Wheeler Cuffe Esq.r
Clashwilliam
Blunt Esq.
Blanfieldstown
Mathew Esq.r
Clara Cas.
GOWRAN
Bayly Esq.

Maps of the Roads of Ireland, Surveyed 1777
George Taylor and Andrew Skinner, Dublin, 1778.

1870. Slater's *Directory* of Arklow, Baltinglass, Blessington, Bray, Newtown Mount Kennedy, Rathdrum, Wicklow.

1881. Slater's *Directory* of Arklow, Baltinglass, Donard and Dunlavin, Blessington, Bray and Enniskerry, Newtown-Mount-Kennedy, Greystones and Delgany, Rathdrum, Wicklow.

1894. Slater's *Directory*.

3. Country-wide Directories

Directories of country gentlemen are far less numerous than the trade directories of towns and cities. For the eighteenth century there are two publications that can be used as substitutes for directories, namely,

1778. George Taylor and Andrew Skinner's *Road Maps of Ireland* (reprinted by Irish University Press, 1969). This marks the names of the gentlemen's seats along the principal highways, adding the surname (but not the Christian name) of their owners. There is an alphabetical index to these surnames at the end of the book.

1783. *The Post Chaise Companion through Ireland* was first issued in this year but went into several subsequent editions, virtually unamended. It describes the countryside as it might be observed while travelling along the main coaching roads and includes the names of the country seats with their owners' surnames.

The nineteenth century brought the first real attempt to produce a country directory with the publication of Ambrose Leet's Directory in 1814, entitled,

1814. *A Directory to the Market Towns, Villages, Gentlemen's Seats and other Noted Places in Ireland.* Alphabetically arranged, it contains a miscellaneous but useful mixture, listing such seats, villages and townlands as occurred to the compiler — the selection seems quite arbitrary — and showing the county and the nearest post-town of each. In the case of the gentlemen's residences, the names of the owners are given, and the owners themselves are indexed alphabetically at the end of the book. The volume has two specific uses: (1) to locate a substantial house where its name was not the same as that of the townland on which it stood and which therefore cannot be found in a Townlands Index, and (2) to determine the name of the resident on a particular property.

Leet's entries take the following form:

Knocknacarron, Co. Clare, post town Kilrush, Signal Station
Knocknacarry, Co. Antrim, post town Newtown-Glens, Town-land
Knocknacullagh, Co. Cork, post town Youghal, Richard Seymour esq
Knocknacollagh, Co. Mayo, post town Ballinrobe, Village

1824. As already mentioned, Pigot's *Directory* of 1824 has an alphabetical index to nearly 7,000 nobility, clegy and gentry scattered through its pages.

1837. The list of subscribers printed in the first edition of Samuel Lewis's *Topograhical Dictionary of Ireland* gives over 9,000 alphabetically-arranged names and addresses, covering most of the prosperous gentry.

1834. In 1834, Pettigrew and Oulton's annual *Dublin Directory* began listing the "Official Authorities of Counties," which included a list of magistrates for each county. These sizeable lists give the addresses of the principal gentlemen and appeared every year from 1834.

Many of the trade directories issued during the nineteenth century include lists of country gentry, and these have been noted in the previous section.

4. Professional Directories

Professional directories concentrating on a specific category of persons arose out of the need to make generally available detailed and accurate information on clergymen, doctors, apothecaries and such like. By the middle of the last century the three main Christian churches in Ireland — Church of Ireland, Catholic Church and Presbyterian Church — had their own ecclesiastical directories.

Church of Ireland Directories

Ecclesiastical Registry, by Samuel Percy Lea, 1814. Arranged by diocese, it lists the parishes and incumbents only, omitting the curates. It is indexed.

Irish Ecclesiastical Register, 1817. Also arranged by diocese, it lists both the incumbents and the curates, and is indexed. Further editions, following the same lay-out, appeared in 1818, 1824 and 1827.

Ecclesiastical Register, by John C. Erck, 1830. Arranged by diocese and indexed, it shows each incumbent's year of induction, and names the curates.

The Churchman's Almanack and Irish Ecclesiastical Directory, by John Medlicott Bourns, 1841. This is arranged by diocese, shows incumbents and curates and is indexed.

Irish Ecclesiastical Directory, 1842. Arranged by diocese, showing incumbents and curates, but is not indexed.

The Irish Clergy List, 1843, by John Medlicott Bourns. Arranged by diocese, showing incumbents and curates, and is indexed.

Clerical Directory of Ireland, 1858, by Samuel B. Oldham. Arranged by diocese, it shows incumbents and curates and is indexed.

James Charles's Irish Church Directory, 1862. Arranged by diocese, showing patron, incumbent and curate, and indexed. Since 1862 an *Irish Church*

Directory has been issued annually. A section at the end of each volume shows the succession of bishops in each diocese, with dates of their episcopate, from the earliest known times.

Catholic Church Directories

The Catholic Directory, Almanack and Registry was first issued in 1836. It lists the clergy by diocese, giving an alphabetical list of parish priests (accompanied by their curates), the names of their parishes and the location of the various chapels with their post towns.

The *Directory* has been issued annually every year since.

The 1838 edition contains a list of "Popish Priests registered in Ireland in July 1704," which is arranged by county, giving alphabetical lists of the parish priests and showing their abode, parish, year of ordination and by whom they were ordained, as well as in some instances the 1704 sureties for their good behaviour.

Presbyterian Church Directories

Little success has been achieved in tracing Presbyterian church directories. Simm's and M'Intyre's *Belfast Almanack* of 1837 gives a list of the members of the Presbyterian Synod of Ulster, showing the congregational address of the members.

In 1857, William M'Comb issued a *Presbyterian Almanack* which gives an alphabetical list of the General Assembly of the Presbyterian Church, showing the Presbytery, Congregation and post town of each of the members.

Medical Directories

Almost all the trade directories of towns and cities list medical practitioners, either in the general list or else as separate lists. Specific medical directories seem to have begun only in the middle of the nineteenth century.

The Irish Medical Directory for 1846, by H. Croly, gives alphabetical lists of bachelors of medicine, of the Royal College of Surgeons, of Licentiate Apothecaries of Ireland (some without addresses) and of certified practitioners of the Lying-in Hospital. There is also a list of dispensaries and their medical officers, arranged by county, and a general register of Medical Practitioners in Ireland, which is arranged by towns under each county.

The Medical Directory for Ireland, 1852, gives an alphabetical list of doctors, showing address, qualifications and where these were obtained, position currently held and professional works published. There is also an obituary list of those who died the previous year, giving address and date of death. Appended is a list of coroners arranged by county.

The Medical Directory for Ireland, 1853, is similar, but omits the coroners list, and the Irish obituary gives fewer dates of death. Further similar editions were issued in 1854, 1856, 1857, 1858, 1859 and 1860.

In 1872 the *Irish Medical Directory* was issued for the first time. It gives an alphabetical list of doctors, showing their addresses and qualifications. This directory thereafter appeared annually.

CHAPTER 5

Genealogical Matter in the Publications of the Irish Manuscripts Commission

DONAL F. BEGLEY

People who desire to deepen their knowledge of the life and times of their forefathers might, to their advantage, thumb through some of the many publications of the Irish Manuscripts Commission. It must be stressed at once, however, that the great bulk of the Commission's works are for the advanced research student and not for the uninitiated. Nevertheless, the discerning amateur will gain much useful information on the origin and background of important record collections, for example, the Tithe Applotment Books and the Hearth Money Rolls — which should lead to a fuller and more intelligent use of such records.

The Irish Manuscripts Commission was established under a government warrant in October 1928. Its function was (and is) to survey and report on collections of manuscripts and papers of literary, historical and genealogical interest relating to Ireland, and to arrange and supervise a programme of publication. In addition, the Commission issues a periodical entitled *Analecta Hibernica* in which are published from time to time various documents unsuitable for publication as separate volumes. To date, twenty-eight issues of this periodical have appeared.

Thanks to the efforts of the Commission some of the more remarkable of the old Irish manuscripts are now more generally available, having been reproduced by a reflex facsimile process. Among those that have been so duplicated are the Great Book of Lecan, one of the Royal Irish Academy's most treasured manuscripts, and probably the earliest and most authoritative compilation of Irish genealogical material extant; the Book of Uí Máine, otherwise known as the Book of the O'Kellys, compiled towards the end of the fourteenth century and containing a considerable corpus of information on the history of Connacht families; and the Book of Armagh (Patrician Documents only) written by Ferdomhnach in the year 807 and containing our oldest and most important collections of documents relating to St. Patrick.

The loss of historical manuscript material which may be regarded as normal from generation to generation has, over the past number of years, accelerated to an alarming degree. Many country houses which were the repositories of manuscript collections have been destroyed, old estates have been broken up and family papers dispersed beyond recall. The Commission was quick to foresee the possible loss of valuable papers and had surveys carried out of such collections of manuscripts as still survived in private keeping. Three series of reports on papers and manuscripts in private hands will be found in *Analecta Hibernica,* Nos. 15, 20 and 25.

Since the destruction of the Public Record Office, Dublin in 1922, by far the largest single collection of records now extant in Ireland are the papers of the Butler family of Ormond. While these papers in the main relate to the affairs of the Ormonds, they contain, in addition, large numbers of deeds relating to other Anglo-Irish families in Tipperary, Kilkenny, Carlow, Waterford and elsewhere. The collection also includes charters of Irish towns, pedigrees of important families side by side in Latin, French, Irish and English and — incredibly — the original foundation charter of Holycross Abbey given in the year 1187 by Donal Mor O'Brien, King of Thomond. The Butler papers long preserved by the family in Kilkenny Castle are now deposited in the National Library of Ireland. A summary of the contents of this outstanding collection will be found in the Commission's publication entitled *Calendar of Ormond Deeds* in six volumes running to over 2,500 pages.

How much were our ancestors paid for their day's work? What did they take for the common cold? The answers to these and a hundred similar questions will be found in a remarkable volume, published by the Commission in 1942, entitled *The Kenmare Manuscripts*:

> 9 May, 1722
> An average of about 25 labourers, besides a large number supplied by Mr. Brown were employed, the rate of pay being 4d. per day in winter and 5d. in summer.
>
> circ. 1770
> Receipt for a cold.
> L'Oximel. Take a naggin of white vinegar, a naggin of honey, one ounce of sugar candy and a half pint of spring water: boil them together in a tin saucepan on a slow fire and then take off the scum. Take a teaspoonful every hour.

The Kenmare Manuscripts, the subject of which is the private collection of papers of the Browne family, Earls of Kenmare, directs our attention to some interesting features of that collection. The collection, for example, contains a remarkable series of rental books through which certain families still living in Co. Kerry can be traced back to the seventeenth century. The estate accounts and agents' reports throw considerable light on the state of agriculture in Ireland in the eighteenth century. The age-old struggle between landlord and tenant can be sensed in the private notebook of Thomas, 4th Viscount Kenmare, containing his remarks on some of the tenants on his estates in Cork, Limerick and Kerry:

> He is a skilful farmer and as well capable of making rent as any man in his country but spoilt by keeping company with rakish gentry, horse racing, etc., which has deprived him of most of his leases and rendered him a most unpunctual wrangling tenant.

> I took a fancy to this fellow upon the notion of his being a very industrious cottier under one of my tenants and though I knew him to be very poor set him this interest which was worth him £30 per annum profit rent. Instead of making his fortune by it he instantly took to drunkenness and roguery and was less than three years obliged to sell it. . . .

One further item included in *The Kenmare Manuscripts* is a collection of over one hundred letters written by one of the most interesting of the Brownes, namely Katherine, daughter of Valentine Browne, 1st Viscount Kenmare, and wife of Don Lois da Cunha, Portuguese ambassador in London. The letters, as well as being of great historical value, are often somewhat amusing:

> 1 Dec. 1724
> I'm astonished to hear Lord Kerry was at church, for neither he nor his lady troubled it much here, [London] and pray tell him I'm very glad the County Kerry air has inspired him with so much piety; but I fear it was either some young lass he wanted to ogle, or he has nothing else to do, was the cause of his devotion.

The seventeenth century in Ireland might well be regarded as the century of surveys. Three spring to mind readily, namely, the Civil Survey, the Books of Survey and Distribution and the Down Survey, the latter carried out by Sir William Petty being the mapped expression of the first two. All three surveys originated in the requirement of the English government for a nationwide stocktaking of land preparatory to the distribution of about two and a half million acres forfeited after the Rebellion of 1641.

In addition to mapping the confiscated lands, i.e. the Down Survey, Petty mapped virtually the entire country with the exception of three counties in Connacht for which maps had already been drawn in the course of the Strafford Survey. From the official parish and townland maps — alas now all destroyed — Petty constructed a set of barony, county and provincial maps with a view to producing a comprehensive geography of Ireland. This manuscript set of maps, known as Hibernia Regnum, is in the Bibliotheque Nationale, Paris. According to its table of contents the set ought to contain

Sir William Petty, 1623-1687.

Petty

Arms: Ermine on a bend azure a magnetic needle proper
pointing at the pole star or.
Crest: A beehive and bees proper.
Motto: Ut Apes Geometriam (To measure as the bees).

Recorded in Genealogical Office Ms. 97.

216 barony maps, 32 county maps and 4 province maps. The county and province maps were, however, retained by Petty for use in the preparation of his Atlas of Ireland known as *Hiberniae Delineatio* published in 1685. Taken in conjunction, Hibernia Regnum and *Hiberniae Delineatio* are an important repertory of Irish place-names in the seventeenth century at a time when these were undergoing thorough anglicisation. A topographical index comprising some 2,000 parish, and over 25,000 townland, names abstracted from these two sources was published by the I.M.C. in 1932.

Based on the knowledge and evidence of "the most able and ancient inhabitants of the country," the Civil Survey was a descriptive record of the land and its owners in 1640. Written down in the course of the years 1655-57 from the testimony of juries representative of Gael and Norman, the Civil Survey set forth the estates of landed proprietors in almost every county in Ireland. Herein Gaelic and Norman ancestral tenures were recorded as well as titles by patent from the Crown. For barony, parish and townland the 'meares and bounds' were described. Many names of places that had long gone out of use are set down in this detailed description which took account of streams, rivers and woodland areas. The valuable local particulars given for each townland included the name of the owner, a description of the larger houses, valuations, areas in tillage and pasture, mills, antiquities and so forth. Independent dealings in land were likewise written down, particulars of deeds and wills being frequently specified. Extraordinarily rich in place-names and in information regarding Irish families, the Civil Survey was further distinguished by separate returns of Church lands, Crown lands and tithes, the entire compilation representing a record of a most precious kind.

What has survived of the Civil Survey has been published in ten volumes, a task which took more than thirty years to complete and is undoubtedly one of the I.M.C.'s more formidable achievements. These volumes cover the following counties: Cork, Derry, Donegal, Dublin, Kildare, Kilkenny, Limerick, Meath, Tipperary, Tyrone, Waterford and Wexford.

The Books of Survey and Distribution readily disclose the position in relation to the ownership of land in each barony and parish prior to, and subsequent to, the forfeitures under Cromwell and William III. The names of the old proprietors, the lands forfeited, the extent profitable and unprofitable, and the areas distributed to the specified new owners are exhibited, column by column, in wide folios. To date, the Books for Roscommon, Mayo, Galway and Clare have been published by the Commission. The Books for the remaining counties not yet in print can be consulted on microfilm in the National Library of Ireland.

The seventeenth century also saw the first attempt at census making in

Ireland when about the year 1659 returns of the inhabitants were compiled under the direction of William Petty. Petty's returns were arranged by county, barony, parish and townland. In addition to mere numbers, the returns supply the names of prominent occupiers of townlands under the title of 'Tituladoes' or large property holders. An edited version of the census was published by the I.M.C. in 1939 in a volume running to over a thousand pages.

The Elphin Diocesan census of 1749, which the Commission hopes to publish, is a valuable source of reference for people attempting to trace ancestors over a wide area of the province of Connacht. The manuscript of the census is now in the Public Record Office and was compiled by Edward Synge, bishop of Elphin between 1740 and 1762. In its four hundred and fifty pages details of householders and families living in the diocese of Elphin are given for fifty-two parishes in Co. Roscommon, thirteen parishes in Co. Sligo and nine parishes in Co. Galway. The manuscript gives the names of heads of households, their professions, e.g. broguemaker, pumpmaker, weaver, etc., and the number of children and servants in each household. In all there are approximately seventeen thousand five hundred entries.

Of particular interest to those whose forebears were in the Quaker tradition is *Guide to Irish Quaker Records,* 1654-1860, I.M.C., 1967. This book is essentially a guide to the manuscript collections at present housed at the Society of Friends' premises at 6, Eustace St., Dublin. The archive, which consists of an accumulation of materials from 1670, includes original registers of births, marriages and deaths, lineage books, certificates of removal and school roll-books. Appended to the book is a list of 2,500 names found in Irish Quaker registers.

It is manifestly impossible within the compass of a short article to do justice to the work the Irish Manuscripts Commission has done over the past sixty years and continues to do. Thanks to the devoted scholarship of its members, many rare and valuable records hitherto inaccessible to historian and genealogist alike are now readily available in print. Unfortunately, some of the Commission's early publications, available some thirty years ago for the proverbial song, are now collectors' items. Incredible as it may seem, the Book of Armagh (Patrician Documents) was published in 1937 for fifteen shillings: a copy recently changed hands in Dublin for £115. People interested in the work of the Commission should first procure a copy of the *Catalogue of Publications,* issued and in preparation, 1928-1966. The fly sheet of the catalogue states that the publications of the Commission can be obtained from the Government Publications Sales Office, G.P.O. Arcade, Dublin 1.

Lastly, scattered throughout the various issues of the Commission's periodical, *Analecta Hibernica,* are numerous items of obvious genealogical value. Because of the high standard of index making which characterises the Commission's publications, it should be a relatively simple task to locate specific items across the entire range of its published work. Appended below is a table of references to genealogical matter scattered throughout all the numbers, issued to date, of *Analecta Hibernica.* The purpose of the table is twofold: first, to convey a general impression of the scope of the work of the Irish Manuscripts Commission, and secondly, to identify and isolate certain items which are apt to be of assistance to researchers in the field of genealogical research.

References to Genealogical Matter in *Analecta Hibernica,* Nos. 1-28

1200-1599. Survey of the Memoranda Rolls of the Irish Exchequer, 1294-1509.

A.H. 23, pp. 51-134

1400-1899. Survey of documents relating to the Wardenship of Galway, including much information on Co. Galway families, e.g. register of householders in the parish of Ballinrobe, 1783; list of inhabitants of the parish of Moycullen, 1793.

A.H. 14

Surveys of manuscript collections in private keeping, including papers of the following families: Colclough 1538-1818; Dillon 1589-1820; Mansfield 1565-1848; Nugent 1488-1865; Power O'Shee 1499-1763; St. Leger 1589-1910; Shirley 1573-1706; Smyth 1639-1827; Vigors 1727-1828.

A.H. 20, pp. 3-310

1500-1899. Surveys of manuscript collections in private keeping, including the collections of the following families: Bowen 1640-1840; O'Grady 1564-1815; Ussher 1562-1844; Brown 1667-1765; Herbert 1640-1792; Pakenham 1689-1845; Harold-Barry 1700-1898; Longfield 1628-1864; Roche 1556-1870; Conner 1659-1843; St. Leger 1611-1774; O'Brien 1558-1770; O'Gorman 1618-1790; Vere Hunt 1761-1816; Daly 1665-1724.

A.H. 15

Index of Will Abstracts in the Genealogical Office, Dublin Castle.

A.H. 17, pp. 151-348

Surveys of manuscript collections in private keeping, including the collections of the following families: Acton 1643-1850; Kavanagh 1572-1768; Loftus 1639-1832; Power 1629-1681; Mahon 1663-1838; Bayly 1657-1827; Dunne 1617-1886; Gormanston 1626-1802; O'Malley 1576-1842; Plunkett 1538-1850.

A.H. 25, pp. 3-214

1500-1799. Papers of the old Corporation of Kinsale, including rent-roll dated 29 Sept. 1731.

A.H. 15, pp. 163-225

1500-1699. Corporation Book of the Irishtown of Kilkenny, with mention of very many old Kilkenny and South Leinster family names, 1537-1628.
A.H. 28, pp. 3-78

1500-1599. Survey of O'Kane Papers, including lists of parish clergy, Diocese of Derry, 1569-1603. *A.H. 12,* pp. 69-127

Visitations of the Dioceses of Clonfert, Tuam and Kilmacduagh, 16th century. *A.H. 26,* pp. 144-157

1600-1899. King's Hospital (Bluecoat School) manuscripts, including the names of masters of the guilds of the city of Dublin, 1673.
A.H. 15, pp. 325-331

1600-1799. Documents relating to the Irish in the West Indies, with extensive accounts of Irish settlements in those parts, 1612-1752.
A.H. 4, pp. 140-286

1600-1699. *Cin Lae O Meallain:* Account of the Rebellion of 1641, 1641-1647.
A.H. 3, pp. 1-49

Ulster Plantation Papers, from T.C.D. Library Ms. N.2.2., with the names of servitors and native families, 1608-1612.
A.H. 8, pp. 181-297

Two articles relating to copies of the maps of Sir William Petty's Survey of Lands forfeited under the English Commonwealth, generally known as the Down Survey, 1654-1656. *A.H. 8,* pp. 419-430

The Adams Rental: a seventeenth century record, with maps, of a large Co. Westmeath estate, 1697. *A.H. 10,* pp. 253-286

The term "titulado" in a "Census" of Ireland, c. 1659.
A.H. 12, pp. 177-178

Documents relating to the Jacobite War in Ireland, with indexes, 1689-1691. *A.H. 21,* pp. 1-240

List of outlawed Irish Jacobites, with indexes of persons and places, 1689-1699. *A.H. 22,* pp. 11-230

Lists of outlaws, 1641-1647, from the Oireachtas Library, Leinster House, Dublin.
A.H. 23, pp. 319-367

Seventeenth century hearth money rolls, with full transcript relating to Co. Sligo, 1665. *A.H. 24,* pp. 1-89

Fragments of the Civil Survey of Counties Kerry, Longford and Armagh, 1654-1656. *A.H. 24,* pp. 227-231

List of Irish Ecclesiastical Visitations, seventeenth century.
A.H. 28, pp. 81-102

Account of Books of Survey and Distribution for Co. Westmeath, 1661-1700. *A.H. 28,* pp. 105-115

1700-1899. Account of the Applotment Books of St Michan's Parish, Dublin City, 50 vols., 1711-1843. *A.H. 10*, pp. 241-243

1700-1799. Calendar of the Dunalley Papers, including the names of the commissioners of the peace, Co. Tipperary, 1715; roll call of Col. Sadleir's Cromwellian Company, 1649; returns of voters for Counties Tipperary, Kilkenny and Waterford, 1775; list of tenants of the Earl of Charleville, Tullamore, 1763. *A.H. 12*, pp. 131-154

List of the names of the United Irishmen, 1791-1794. *A.H. 17*, pp. 7-143

The Duke of Devonshire's Irish Estates, 1794-1797. *A.H. 22*, pp. 271-327

Irish appeals to the Lords in the eighteenth century. *A.H. 22*, pp. 245-255

1800-1899. Background to the compilation of the Tithe Composition Applotment Books, c. 1825. *A.H. 10*, pp. 295-298

State-aided Emigration Schemes from Crown Estates in Ireland, c. 1850. *A.H. 22*, pp. 331-394

Report on Ordnance Survey manuscripts of the nineteenth century. *A.H. 23*, pp. 279-296

Reports of Fenian Trials in the Library of the Oireachtas, Leinster House, Dublin, 1865-1866. *A.H. 23*, pp. 279-301

Sources Referenced in *A.H.*, Nos. 1-28, for the Genealogy of Gaelic Families

Fermanagh Genealogies, including pedigrees of the Maguires and allied families, 1303-1626. *A.H. 3*, pp. 62-150

A Guide to Irish Genealogical Collections, 700-c.1850. *A.H. 7*, pp. 1-167

Treatise on the O'Donnells of Tirconnell, being R.I.A. 23 D 17, including genealogical tables, 1207-1834. *A.H. 8*, pp. 375-418

Description and composition of Roger O'Ferrall's *Linea Antiqua*, 1709. *A.H. 10*, pp. 289-299

The O'Clery Book of Genealogies, being R.I.A. Ms. 23 D 17. *A.H. 18*, pp. 1-194

References to Libraries in *Analecta Hibernica*, Nos. 1-28

Manuscripts in the Representative Church Body Library. *A.H. 23*, pp. 307-309

List of Reports in the National Library of Ireland on manuscript collections in private keeping. *A.H. 20*, pp. 311-318 and *A.H. 23*, pp. 371-387

Guide to the Records of the Genealogical Office, Dublin Castle. *A.H. 26*, pp. 3-43

Description of the library and manuscripts of Sir William Betham, Ulster King of Arms. *A.H. 27*, pp. 3-99

CHAPTER 6

Newspapers as a Genealogical Source

ROSEMARY FFOLLIOTT

Though newspapers were published in Ireland from the late 17th century they do not assume genealogical importance until the 1750s. For genealogical purposes "early" newspapers may be regarded as those published between about 1750 and 1830, and "later" newspapers as those published post-1830. There is a marked difference between the two periods, the earlier being in many ways more difficult to handle while the later is marked by a bewildering proliferation of publications.

Newspapers 1750-1830

Early newspapers contain two main sources of genealogical information. The first, and most important, is the obvious one: the announcements of marriages and deaths which occur with increasing frequency from about 1750. These are almost wholly absent, save for a few references to the nobility, before that date. The second source, much less obvious but not necessarily less useful, is the information to be gleaned from the advertisements. Actual mention of persons in news items is minimal: the occasional brutal murder or a spectacular law suit might rate a few lines, but such events would usually be more easily traced in other sources, e.g. the Law Reports.

Dublin, as might be expected, was the first Irish city to publish newspapers. By the 1760s bi-weekly publications were appearing in such places as Belfast, Cork, Limerick and Kilkenny, to be followed in the 1780s by Tralee, Ennis, Waterford, Clonmel and Newry. Dublin maintained a regular minimum of four tri-weekly papers. Provincial centres were not necessarily limited to one paper each: Cork always maintained at least two, Ennis always had two and Limerick sometimes two or more. By the 1780s Belfast also had two.

Dublin Newspapers

For genealogical purposes the best 18th century Dublin papers are *Faulkner's Dublin Journal* (1725), the *Freeman's Journal* (1763), the

The Dublin Evening Post.

SATURDAY, APRIL 12, 1834.

PRICES OF IRISH STOCKS.

	Monday.	Tuesday	Wednes.	Thrsday	Friday.	Saturdy
Bank Stock........	217	217½	217½	217½	217½	—
Irish 3 p.Ct. Consols	90	90⅛	90	90⅛	90⅛	—
Gov. Deb. 3½ p.Ct...	89¾	89¾	89⅞	89¾	89¾	—
Do. Stock, 3½ p.Ct...	97½	97½	97⅝	97½	90½	—
Do. New, 3½ p.Ct.	97⅝	97½	97⅝	97⅝	97⅛	—
G. Canal L. 4 p.Ct...	—	—	—	—	60½	—
Do. do. 6 p.Ct...	90	89¾	89⅞	89⅞	90	—
Royal Canal Stock..	—	—	41¾	41¾	42	—
Grand Canal Stock	—	24½	—	24½	—	—
Mining Co. Ireland	—	—	—	—	—	—
Dublin Steam Com.	—	—	—	—	—	—

TO OUR SUBSCRIBERS.

In consequence of the alteration in the Post Office, the Clerks of the Roads have handed to us a list of those Gentlemen who had hitherto subscribed for this Journal through their Agency. It is, therefore, necessary to apprise such Subscribers, that three days before their subscriptions expire, they will receive THE DUBLIN EVENING POST *wrapped in a blue cover: when they are requested to renew their subscriptions, by transmitting the money to our Office in Trinity-street, or giving direction to some friend in town to have it renewed.*

☞ Sir George Cockburn's Letter on Tuesday.

THE LATE RIOTS IN BRUSSELS,

We are again indebted to the activity of our London Correspondent for communicating, *exclusively*, to the readers of The Dublin Evening Post the following very interesting letter from Brussels. The absurdity of the Orangemen *every where* is quite curious and characteristic. But we have not room to run the parallel between the Continental and the insular tribes of this common genus :—

London, Thursday Evening, half-past Seven, April 10.

The following letter is from our private correspondent at Brussels, dated Tuesday evening, April 8 :—

" Everything is now as quiet, and apparently as secure as it was before the events which two days back excited such alarm in the few, and such indignation in the many. No new attempt at disorder of any kind has taken place. The streets have resumed their wonted air, with the exception of some small bodies of foot soldiers still standing to their arms in the principal quarters. The artillery and cavalry have been withdrawn from their yesterday's position. The whole of the military force in the city amounts to 7,000 infantry, 1,000 cavalry, and several pieces of cannon. Every account from the large towns are favourable. No imitations of the scenes acted here have taken place. The people seem to have been satisfied with having struck the blow at the head-quarters of Orangeism. About 100 prisoners were secured by the troops on Sunday evening. With the exception of a few seized in attempts to steal some article of property, they were arrested in a state of drunkenness, and in order that they might be kept out of the way of doing harm. It would be

DANIEL'S LETTER.

Thanks, a thousand thanks—O'Connell—for your mo valuable—*to us*, most valuable letter—inasmuch as it ju tifies the course we have taken, and demonstrates the tru of every position we have ever laid down, in regard to yo and your agitation. The letter is printed in full. We wis we could give it in characters that all Ireland migh read, and *understand*. But, indeed, it is sufficient intelligible. Jack, Jem and Jerry will understand it. You public men with political lives, who have been lecturing yo will comprehend its drift but too well. At present, how ever, we can do little more than to reiterate our thanks f this timely publication. Still we think it rather too lon Would not the following passages, extracted from the spi of your epistle, be sufficient ?

HEADS OF A LETTER TO THE PEOPLE OF IRELAND.

Men of Ireland,

In disappointment, but not in despair, I announce to yo that after all my bragging about a million of signatures, t coercive system, (*my* coercive system of denouncing eve man who dares to contradict me), has only produced, forger and all, 80,000!! Now, this is your fault. You thoug when you had filled my Begging-Box you had done the jo To be sure I told you so; but then why did you belie me?—

> Hereditary Bondsmen know you not
> Who trusts to others surely goes to pot—
> The begging box, alas! was but a go,
> Who would be free *themselves* must strike the blow.

Well, there is no use in mincing the matter—the Rep hoax is over for this year; and I—I by telling you so befo hand, insure its not having a single chance in the House not that this ass's kick at the dead lion was necessary. Bu no matter, do you get your purses ready for October, and my hopes will be fulfilled.

There were many causes for your (excusable) apathy.

First—The Cholera. Oh! by the Jagers, I know th myself. Didn't I run away from London when the Chole arrived in Wapping—and back to London when it arrived Dublin ?

Secondly—You were so very unanimous, that you ea left the business to your neighbour. Very like a whale!

Thirdly—You were all so satisfied in being protected person and property by the Coercion Bill that you had room in your hearts for Repeal.

Fourthly—In the districts proclaimed (how many we there ?) no assemblies could be had, and this fully expla why the signatures were so few from *the rest of the island*.

Fifthly—The Coercion Bill prevented me from getting so cleverly my factitious agitation, and goading and driving t people into discontent and turbulence, which shows that, wh left to themselves, the said people of Ireland are very deep desirous of carrying the Repeal.

I say nothing about any disinclination in any of the s millions nine hundred and twenty thousand non-subscriber It would not have been thus, if I had been in Ireland; b when the cat's away the mice will play: I am the alpha a the omega of Repeal; and if I were bought (*absit omen*

Dublin Hibernian Journal (1771) and the *Dublin Evening Post* (1719). In the mid-1750s these papers began to carry regular and fairly numerous batches of marriage and obituary notices relating not only to the Dublin population but to persons all over the country. Many of these items were culled from provincial papers. The provincial announcements in the Dublin press appear to be slightly abridged from their original form. Consequently, if the local paper still happens to exist, it is better to seek the notice there. However, if it does not, the Dublin paper may provide an invaluable substitute. Normally the notice appeared in Dublin papers between five and ten days after its appearance in the provincial press. The result is, of course, that the substance of a great many notices from the country papers survives in the Dublin re-print even though no copy of the provincial paper now exists. Of the four papers just mentioned, the *Dublin Hibernian Journal* carried the largest number of notices from 1771 to about 1787. Before that date, *Faulkner's Dublin Journal* is probably the best, although it disimproves markedly in the 1780s, when the *Freeman's Journal* picks up. Notices tail off sadly in the Dublin papers of the early 19th century, and become especially meagre for items actually relating to Dublin itself. This situation does not really improve again until the 1820s. It presents a serious genealogical gap for Dubliners but happily the same situation did not apply in the provinces, where announcements were universally on the increase. The only index to early Dublin newspapers is a card-index to the *Freeman's Journal* for 1763-1771 made by the National Library.

In the early 19th century Dublin papers multiplied. The more notable newcomers were the *Dublin Morning Post,* the *Dublin Evening Herald* and the *Dublin Evening Mail.* Some of the papers, too, began to be published daily rather than tri-weekly. Dublin papers are more plentiful than provincial papers, and both the National Library of Ireland and the British Library have fine collections.

Advertisements in the Dublin press were almost entirely confined to the businesses in or near the capital: provincial advertisements appeared only in provincial papers. In the 18th century the Dublin advertisements were numerous and extremely interesting: there is much genealogy to be gleaned from them as well as social history. Unfortunately, when the biographical notices tail off in the early 19th century the advertisements became less informative, as businesses became less personal.

Provincial Towns that issued Newspapers before 1830

There is difficulty in ascertaining details of early provincial papers and some of those mentioned here may well be older than stated. In contrast to the Dublin tendency towards tri-weekly publication, most of the provincial papers appeared bi-weekly.

BALLINA. The *Ballina Impartial* or *Tyrawley Advertiser* began in 1823 but was discontinued in 1835, to be succeeded in 1840 by the *Ballina Advertiser*. Good runs of both these papers are now in the British Library.

BALLINASLOE. In 1828 a paper was issued called the *Western Argus and Ballinasloe Independent,* which in 1830 was re-titled the *Western Argus and Galway Commercial Chronicle*. In 1845 this was joined by the *Western Star and Ballinasloe Advertiser.*

BELFAST. Belfast produced the earliest and one of the best provincial papers in Ireland, the *Belfast Newsletter,* beginning in 1737. It covered a wide geographical area, extending as far south as Carlingford in Co. Louth. It is full of information and during the second half of the 18th century carried particularly interesting advertisements and "occasional items". An excellent run is held at the Linenhall Library, where there is also an index, though most unfortunately this is not arranged alphabetically. In 1783 the *Belfast Mercury* appeared and in 1786 this became the *Belfast Evening Post.* Then followed the *Northern Star* in 1792, the *Belfast Commercial Chronicle* in 1805, the *Belfast Mercantile Register* in 1822, the *Northern Whig* in 1824, the *Guardian* in 1827 and the *Banner of Ulster* in 1842.

BOYLE. In 1822 the *Roscommon and Leitrim Gazette* was produced in Boyle. The British Library has an almost complete set until its close in 1882.

CARLOW. Considering its circumstances, Carlow came late into the newspaper business, starting with the *Carlow Morning Post* in 1817, copies of which are now exceedingly scarce. Apart from some fragments, the British Library only has the issues for 1834. However, the *Carlow Sentinel* began in 1832 and there is a complete run at the British Library.

CASTLEBAR. Castlebar produced the *Mayo Constitution* in the 1790s but the British Library set only begins in 1828. The *Telegraph or Connaught Ranger* followed in 1830 and the British Library has an almost complete run of this.

CLONMEL. Clonmel supported a number of papers, beginning with the *Clonmel Gazette* (1788) and the *Clonmel Herald* (1802), followed by the *Clonmel Advertiser* (1813) and the *Tipperary Free Press* (1826). The papers carried a lot of interesting material but unfortunately the earliest issues have had a low survival rate. The British Library holds both the *Clonmel Herald* and the *Clonmel Advertiser* from 1828 to their demise in 1841 and 1838 respectively, and also the *Tipperary Free Press* from its beginning in 1826, as well as the *Tipperary Constitution* from 1835 to 1848. All the Clonmel papers deal with the south Tipperary/Waterford area.

CORK. Cork issued more newspapers than anywhere else outside Dublin, starting with the excellent *Corke Journal* (1753), the *Corke Evening Post* (1757), the *Corke Chronicle* (1765), the *Hibernian Chronicle* (1769), the *Cork Gazette* (1793), the *Cork Advertiser* (1800), the *Cork Mercantile Chronicle* (1802), the *Southern Reporter* (1807), the *Cork Morning Intelligence* (1815) and the *Constitution* (1822) as well as the short-lived late 18th century *Volunteer Journal*. Of these, where they exist, the *Corke Journal,* the *Cork Evening Post,* the *Hibernian Chronicle,* the *Cork Mercantile Chronicle,* the *Southern Reporter* and the *Constitution* are probably the best. The *Southern Reporter* lived up to its name by carrying large numbers of notices relating to every county in Munster, and is very good for Limerick and Tipperary.

An alphabetical card-index has been compiled by the writer to all the Cork and Kerry biographical notices (plus the most useful advertisements) that appeared in the Cork papers up to 1827, and a copy of this is held both in the National Library and in Cork. The Irish Genealogical Research Society has an Index to the *Hibernian Chronicle* only.

Holdings of the Cork papers are widely scattered. The National Library has good runs of the *Hibernian Chronicle* and the *Cork Mercantile Chronicle.* Trinity College, Dublin, has an excellent run of the *Cork Evening Post,* while the best run of the *Constitution* is in the British Library. Others are in the National Library and in Cork. By and large, Cork papers have survived well and are reasonably accessible.

DROGHEDA. There was a *Drogheda Journal* in 1788 and a *Drogheda Newsletter* in 1801, but early issues are in short supply, which is a tragedy as they were good papers with particularly interesting advertisements. The British Library has a complete run of the *Drogheda Journal* from 1823 to 1843 and also the *Drogheda Argus* from its beginning in 1835.

ENNIS. For a small town, Ennis was quite remarkable in constantly maintaining two papers in the late 18th century, the *Clare Journal* (1787) and the *Ennis Chronicle* (1788), both of which have a high survival rate. The geographical scope of these publications was wide, taking in not only Limerick and Galway but extending north-east into Mayo, Longford and Leitrim. The 18th century *Ennis Chronicle* is short on biographical notices but rich in informative advertisements: by the first years of the 19th century both it and the *Clare Journal* contained copious biographical items. The best run of the *Clare Journal* is held in the office of the *Clare Champion* in

FASHIONABLE INTELLIGENCE.

The Marquis of Sligo, the Marquis of Clanricarde, the Earl of Howth, the Earl of Pembroke, and Lord St. Lawrence, are among the latest arrivals at the Baths of Homburg.

Robert French, Esq., Miss Blake, and suite, have left Salt town for Kilmore Palace, county Cavan.

The Earl of Lucan is expected at Castlebar House, on or before the 15th instant.

The Lord Chief Justice has left Old Connaught for Carriglass.

BIRTHS.

At Ballincurrig, Douglas, county Cork, the wife of Lawrence O'Callaghan, Esq., of a daughter.

At Bray, the wife of Edward S. Corry, Esq., Sub-Inspector of Constabulary, of a son.

MARRIAGES.

At Moylough, by the Rev. William Digby, Rector of Clongish, county of Longford, assisted by the Rev. Charles H. Seymour, Provost of Tuam, W. J. Digby, Esq., of Moate Lodge, to Sarah Rebecca, only child of the Rev. W. LePoer Trench, D.D., Rector of Moylough.

In the Metropolitan Church, Marlborough-street, Dublin, by the Rev. Canon Pope, Major Talbot, of Castle Talbot, county Wexford, brother of the late Countess of Shrewsbury, to Charlotte, youngest daughter of the late Macarius John Kennedy, Esq., of Gloncester-terrace, Dublin.

In Ennis, Michael Moloney, Esq., Solicitor, to Lucie, the amiable and accomplished daughter of Marsus Talbot, Esq., Chairman Ennis Town Commissioners.

DEATHS.

Sept. 9, at Loughrea, after a short illness, which she bore with exemplary patience and resignation, Catherine, the dearly-beloved wife of John Fahy, Esq., merchant, and general stockmaster. Her unostentatious charities—her mild and unassuming manners, and lady like deportment—endeared her to all her acquaintances—to whom her demise, in the prime of life, will be long a source of sorrow and regret.—May her soul rest in peace.

On the 25th ultimo, on board s. s. Circassian, on her homeward voyage from New York to Galway, Mr. John Moore Thistle, of Newark. New Jersey, eldest surviving son of the late Mr. James Thistle, of Londonderry, Ireland.

At New York, on Saturday, August 13th Margaret, wife of Mathew Kehoe, Esq., and daughter of the late Mr. Wm. Kane, of Ballybane, aged 30 years.

The Galway Vindicator, 10 Sept. 1859.

Ennis while the National Library has a long run of the *Ennis Chronicle*. Excluding the issues that are only available in Ennis, the extant copies of both papers have been included in my index to biographical notices in Limerick and Ennis newspapers up to 1820. As might be expected, it is virtually impossible to separate the coverage of Ennis and Limerick papers as the overlap is quite considerable.

ENNISKILLEN. The *Enniskillen Chronicle* began in 1808 and the best early holding is that at St. Macartan's College in Monaghan. The British Library has a complete run from 1824 and the Linenhall Library some issues from 1817. The *Impartial Reporter* appeared in 1825, of which the British Library has a full run, and the *Enniskillener* followed in 1830.

GALWAY. Galway papers are now rare commodities. They began in 1813 with the *Connaught Journal* of which the British Library has a fair run from 1823. It was followed in 1818 by the *Galway Weekly Advertiser* and the British Library has a complete run from 1823 to 1843. 1825 saw the publication of the *Galway Independent Paper,* which was discontinued in 1832. In the same year the *Galway Free Press* commenced publication and was joined in 1835 by the *Galway Patriot*. The *Galway Vindicator* dates from 1841.

KILKENNY. From the 1760s Kilkenny was served by *Finn's Leinster Journal*. Though the advertisements are marvellous, the 18th century marriages and deaths are disappointing, being both few in number and sparse in information. Indeed, they look as if they had been shamelessly cribbed from the Dublin press, a reversal of the usual procedure. The area covered is primarily Kilkenny/Carlow with forays into Wexford and Waterford. In 1814 *Finn's Leinster Journal* was joined by the *Kilkenny Moderator*. The best run of *Finn's Leinster Journal* is held in Kilkenny while the British Library has a complete run of the *Kilkenny Moderator* from 1828.

LIMERICK. The first Limerick publication was the *Munster Journal* in 1749 but the real landmark was the advent of the *Limerick Chronicle* in 1768, a paper which lasted for two centuries. The best surviving run is that owned by the *Limerick Leader* but the National Library also has a number of early issues. In 1804 there appeared the *General Advertiser* or *Limerick Gazette,* of which there is a good run in the British Library. In 1811 came the valuable but short-lived *Limerick Evening Post*, which in the 1830s became the *Limerick Star*. The *Limerick Herald* dates from 1831, the

Limerick Standard from 1837 and the *Limerick Reporter* from 1839. The survival rate of these papers is generally good.

Early Limerick papers covered a wide area outside the home county, extending not only into Tipperary and Clare but also into Kerry, Galway and King's County. They are a mine of information, both in biographical notices and in advertisements, and are particularly important because other sources for the area tend to be lacking. As already mentioned, the overlap with the Ennis papers is great and the two cannot be separated. Many of the Limerick publications up to 1820 are included in my card-index to biographical notices in Limerick and Ennis papers. This card-index currently runs to about 35,000 items.

LONDONDERRY. The excellent *Londonderry Journal* began in 1772 and there is a good run of this paper at the National Library. Its circulation extended into Donegal and Tyrone so it is a valuable source for north-west Ulster. The *Londonderry Sentinel* dates from 1829 and there is a good run of this at the British Library.

NEWRY. Almost nothing now exists of the *Newry Journal* published in the 1770s and 1780s, and though the *Newry Commercial Telegraph* began in 1812, little survives of it before the start of the set owned by the Public Record Office of Northern Ireland which begins in 1823. The *Newry Examiner* came into being in 1830 but in 1844 became the *Dundalk Examiner,* published in that town.

ROSCOMMON. The *Roscommon Journal* began in 1828 and the British Library possess a complete run. In 1848 it was joined by the *Roscommon Weekly Messenger.*

SLIGO. The *Sligo Journal* was in existence in 1810, though the British Library set only begins in 1828. The *Sligo Observer* dates from 1828 and the *Champion or Sligo News* from 1836: the former seems to have died in 1831, but the latter prospered indefinitely and the British Library has a complete run.

STRABANE. Virtually nothing survives of the *Strabane Journal* (1771) but the Linenhall Library has some issues of the *Strabane Morning Post* (1812). The British Library has a full run of the latter from 1823 to 1837.

TRALEE. The *Kerry Evening Post* began in 1771 but nothing is known to have survived before the start of the British Library set in 1828. It seems, however, that both the Cork and Limerick papers culled liberally from their

Kerry neighbour, thus preserving some of its biographical notices though not, of course, its advertisements. The *Western Herald* was in existence in 1811 but again the British Library run dates only from 1828. The *Kerry Examiner* began in 1840 and the *Tralee Chronicle* in 1843, both of which have excellent runs at the British Library.

The biographical notices in the *Kerry Evening Post* from 1828 to 1864 were published in Vol. 6 of Dr. Albert Casey's *O'Keif, Coshe Mang, etc.,* and their use is discussed in the post-1830 section of this article.

WATERFORD. Though Waterford published several early newspapers, their survival rate is very poor. The earliest was the *Waterford Chronicle* (1770), then the *Waterford Herald* (1791), the *Waterford Mirror* (1804) and finally the *Waterford Mail* (1823), of which there is a complete run at the British Library. The notices from the surviving 18th century issues have been re-printed in the *Irish Genealogist* 1974, 1976, 1977, 1978, 1979 and 1980. I have included any available Waterford papers in my Limerick/Ennis card-index. The British Library has certain years of the *Waterford Chronicle* after 1811. The Waterford press was not strong on early biographical notices, but those that are given are informative. The area covered extends into both south Tipperary and Wexford.

WEXFORD. The earliest paper, the *Wexford Herald* (1788) has survived badly. The British Library has the *Wexford Evening Post* from its beginning in 1826 to 1830, the *Wexford Independent* from its beginning in 1830 and the *Wexford Conservative* from its beginning in 1832.

Birth Notices in Newspapers

Of the three types of biographical notices, births are by far the least important. Infants were born and died in such numbers that to have listed their names would have filled the entire paper. The late 18th century Dublin papers carried few notices of births: these referred mainly to wealthy families. This practice was discontinued in the first years of the 19th century but resumed again in ever increasing volume in the late 1820s. By contrast Cork papers reported relatively few births until the 1820s although Limerick and Ennis papers printed a fair number after about 1805. Kilkenny newspapers carried few notices of birth. Even where birth announcements occur they are of little genealogical value since the details given are generally pathetically meagre, as for example, the *Dublin Hibernian Journal* of 8th July 1787: "the lady of Arthur Ormsby Esq of a son". This, it will be observed, gives neither date nor address: in actual fact, Mr. Ormsby was living in Limerick.

A birth notice never provides the Christian name of either mother or child. The usual formula was on the lines of this item from the *Clonmel Herald* of 1st May 1816: "At Wilton in this county, the lady of William Poe junior Esq of a son". Occasionally one may be lucky enough to glean some other useful snippet, perhaps in respect of the infant's maternal grandfather, as in an item from the *Limerick Chronicle* of 8th July 1815: "yesterday at her father's (John Gabbet Esq.) Corbally, the lady of Francis H. Bindon Esq of a son".

In general birth announcements are of limited use — though an amazing number of people believe otherwise — since there is always the problem of identifying the child in question, — a next to impossible task unless there is a baptismal register available. There is also the depressing fact that birth notices tended to be restricted to the more wealthy families, who were in any event easier to trace. In short, if a birth notice turns up, it may just be useful: it is certainly not worth expending hours of work seeking it.

Marriage Announcements in Newspapers

Marriage announcements, in contrast to announcements of births, are well worth seeking. They are an extremely valuable source of information, being more numerous, more informative and less economically select. The details proffered vary widely from a bald statement such as the following in the *Drogheda Journal* of 21 November 1795: "married John Ferguson of Carrickmacross to Miss Pace of Balbriggan", to an elaborate announcement such as this from the *Ennis Chronicle* of Wednesday, 25 September 1816: "married on Saturday by special licence at Newgrove, the seat of Thomas Browne Esq, by the Rev. Mr Whitty, Cornelius O'Callaghan of Ballynahinch Esq to Frances, second daughter of the late Henry Brady of Raheens Esq". The more usual type of announcement is midway between these two extremes, somewhat on the lines of the following from the *Cork Advertiser* of Thursday, 23 July 1801: "on Saturday last, Mr David Hare of Barrack Street, woollen draper, to Miss Ward of White Street". It can happen that even more information than in the O'Callaghan/Brady item is elicited, as in this item in the *Hibernian Chronicle* of 3 August 1772: "married Thomas Horan Esq of Newcastle, Co. Limerick, to Miss Meredith, daughter of the late Richard Meredith Esq and niece to Counsellor Robert Fitzgerald, member for Dingle". This provides excellent clues as to the identity of the bride's mother.

The majority of marriage announcements will give the name of the bride's father and his address, but even in the early 19th century only an exceptional item will provide the name of the bridegroom's father, and this generally only for a person of considerable means, say, the *Ennis Chronicle* of 28 December 1816: "married by the Rev. Ralph Stoney, A.M., a few days ago, Robert Johnston Stoney, only son of Major Stoney of Grayford, Co. Tipperary, to Frances Margaret, youngest daughter of Thomas Stoney of Arran Hill in said county Esq".

Happily, little religious discrimination existed and the papers contain an abundance of Catholic marriages belonging to the merchant and gentry classes. Consequently, the papers are one of the very best ways of tracing the Catholic professional and middle classes as they emerge from the obscurity of the Penal Laws in the 1770s and 1780s. Not that the parties' religion is necessarily specified, indeed, it is usually left obscure after the manner of this announcement from the *Limerick Evening Post* of 3 March 1813: "married on Wilson's Quay in this city, Mr James O'Dea of Ennis, linen and woollen draper to Miss Bridget O'Dwyer, daughter of the late Thomas O'Dwyer Esq of this city". On other occasions the religion is delicately indicated by the style and identity of the officiating cleric as in this item from the *Constitution* of Friday, 18 April 1823: "married on Tuesday morning by the Right Rev. Dr Murphy, William Lalor Esq of Johnstown, Co. Kilkenny, to Catherine, eldest daughter of the late Timothy Murphy Esq of this city". It is rare for a Catholic marriage notice to specify the actual *place* of wedding (usually a private house), whereas it is commonplace for a Protestant notice to do so.

Weddings that took place outside Ireland were sometimes reported, with of course a greater time-lag between the event and the announcement than would otherwise occur. The *Wexford Herald* of 4 September 1788 reported "married in Scotland, John Snow Esq of Waterford to Miss Eliza Wyse, second daughter of John Wyse of Newton Esq". The registers of Portpatrick show that this wedding took place there on 8th August. During the 18th century a marriage in Ireland would be reported in the local paper within a week or ten days — and occasionally, the next day. An additional week to ten days would elapse before it was repeated in the Dublin papers.

Lastly it must be pointed out that for many marriages, particularly those contracted in the 18th century, a newspaper notice may well be the only surviving record. This would be true where the appropriate church register was non-existent, no marriage settlement registered and no marriage licence bond available. The value of marriage notices in newspapers is very high.

Obituaries in Newspapers

Understandably, this is by far the largest of the three types of announcement and also the one that covers the widest range of social classes. As with marriages, the information given varies greatly. As examples of the briefest form of announcement, one may take *Finn's*

Leinster Journal of 20 February 1771: "died at Feathard, Mr Pierce Mountain", or the *Freeman's Journal* of 10 October 1789: "died at Waterford the widow Smithwick", — which leaves the poor lady nameless and almost unidentifiable. The happily, in this particular case the local paper has survived and the *Waterford Chronicle* of Tuesday 6 October 1789 adds the date and place: "on Sunday night died in George's Street widow Smithwick". The address may provide the clue to the identity of the lady.

Occasionally there is a surfeit of information, as for instance in the *Cork Advertiser* of Thursday 4 June 1812: "died on Tuesday in Marlborough Street at 6 o'clock in the afternoon. John Callanan Esq M.D. . . . in the 64th year of his age . . . was twice married to Misses Coppinger and O'Kelly, and by the former had four sons, professional men, now advanced in manhood, and by the latter a daughter . . . ". Sometimes an additional bonus linking two families may be obtained from an obituary, as the following cases show: *Limerick Chronicle*, 22 March 1815: "died at her brother's, Nicholas Clarke Esq, Doonass, Mrs Walplate relict of the late John Walplate." *Limerick Chronicle*, Wednesday 1 November 1815: "died at the house of his father-in-law, George Davis Esq, at O'Brien's Bridge on Monday, Luke Gardiner Tomkins Esq, formerly Major in the Royal Irish Artillery, and late of H.M. 27th Regiment." *Limerick Evening Post*, Saturday 9 April 1814: "died last Saturday at her brother-in-law's, John Keating of Clonngunna, Mrs Mary Finney, wife of Lieutenant Hamilton Finney of the 11th Royal Veteran Battalion."

Newspapers may carry obituaries of Irish persons who died outside the country, not only of officers serving in the army or navy but also of those who had gone abroad to England or Europe on business or for medical reasons. Occasionally one may find a notice of the death of a notable trans-Atlantic emigrant. Notices of such events would naturally appear somewhat later than in the case of local deaths. Some examples of this type of notice now follow. *Drogheda Newsletter*, 16 June 1802: "died at Bath of a decline, Miss Davis, daughter of James Davis of this town Esq." *Belfast Newsletter*, 1 June 1804: "died on the 1st ult. in the 23rd year of his age, on his passage from Gibraltar to Lisbon, where he had gone for the recovery of this health, Ross Balfour of Carlingford in the Co. of Louth Esq." *Waterford Herald*, 1 November 1791: "died at Malaga, Captain Lurgan of the 'Unity' belonging to this port." *Ennis Chronicle*; 27 January 1816: "died on the 2nd of November at New York (in the States of America) at the advanced age of 87, Mrs Elizabeth Maunsell, relict of the late Lieutenant General Maunsell and sister-in-law of the Rev. Dr William Maunsell formerly of Limerick deceased." *Cork Evening Post*, 26 July 1804: died on the 18th April last in Honduras in the prime of life, John O'Connor Esq of Midleton in this county after three days illness; his widow and only child about five years survived the Father but a few days.''

Exact age tended to be stated only if the deceased was very old or tragically young, as in the entries above for Mrs Maunsell and Mr Balfour. 18th century papers had a tedious habit of dismissing all the elderly as having ''died at an advanced age,'' a convenient phrase which seems to have covered anything between sixty and ninety! Until the second half of the 19th century the burial place of the deceased was hardly ever mentioned, the object of the obituary being to notify the public of the death not, as became the fashion later, to summon them to the funeral.

For the majority of the middle classes, a newspaper obituary is the only existing record of death at this period. The alternative sources such as wills, burial registers and gravestones may or may not exist whereas the newspapers provide obituaries for a whole section of merchants and traders whose deaths are not recorded elsewhere. This is particularly true of women, who left fewer wills and are less frequently mentioned on tombstones, whereas the papers carry numerous obituaries of females.

Advertisements in Newspapers

Apart from biographical notices, the early newspapers are crammed with treasures in the shape of advertisements. Their variety is almost infinite. At a time when businesses were privately owned by the individuals who ran them, the advertisements concerning those businesses produce a lot of information about the owners. Sometimes one can find a young man starting up in business or an old man retiring from business. Frequently one finds a business being moved from one place to another, and sometimes even the succession of a business from father to son or uncle to nephew. Disputes concerning ownership of property also found their way into the press via advertisements setting out the claims of one or other of the contestants, or even of both of them. Husbands might insert an advertisement disclaiming any debts that might be contracted by a wife who had absconded, and such an item frequently provides the woman's maiden surname as well as the husband's address.

Deaths, for which no actual obituary can be found, may be deduced from an advertisement. Such notices may take the form of a widow or son announcing that they will continue the deceased's business, or a notice to his creditors to present their claims, or an advertisement offering the deceased's house or effects for sale or to let.

Bankruptcies — of which there were many — can also be traced in the papers by way of an advertisement requesting an assembly of creditors, or by the bankrupt himself announcing his surrender on a certain date.

[WEDNESDAYS AND SATURDAYS.]

ESTABLISHED A. D. 1795.

O'SHAUGHNESSY,

WATCH AND CLOCK-MAKER, SILVERSMITH,

AND

JEWELLER,

HAS the honor of assuring his numerous patrons that for many years past there has not been so large a carefully assorted a Stock presented to their inspection in this city, as he will be found supplied with present, consisting of Gold and Silver, Horizontal, Duplex, Lever, Geneva, and Vertical WATCHES, of prices ; Gold and Silver Guard Chains, Gold Demi Guards, and Drop Chains, Seals and Keys, &c.

Jewellery.

O'S. having made considerable addition to his Jewellery Stock, will now be found supplied with some of t newest and most fashionable articles from the London Markets, viz.—Magnificent Stone and Cameo Brooch Lockets, Fancy and Set Rings, Ear-Rings, Bracelets, Pins and Shirt Studs, &c.

SILVER PLATE.

9000 Ounces best sterling Silver Plate, amongst which will be found Table, Desert, and Tea Spoons, Ta and Desert Forks, Soup Ladles, Gravey Spoons, Egg, Salt, and Mustard Spoons, Marrow Spoons, &c., all the newest patterns, and best possible manufactures.

EIGHT-DAY CLOCKS, IN MAHOGANY CASES,

Warranted—Only £4 10s.

WATCH AND CLOCK REPAIRS.

The greatest attention paid to to the repairs and time-keeping of all Watches and Clocks done in this Esta lishment, and from the moderation of the charges, the Proprietor hopes for a continuation of the patrona which the public have so long and kindly extended to him.

FISHING TACKLE.

☞ *Facts are Stubborn Things.*

O'SHAUGHNESSY has the honor of informing the Piscatorial world that he is now the ONLY Person in existen manufacturing the *real* O'Shaughnessy's Hooks and Flies ; and any other Person professing to sell Hooks Flies as O'Shaughnessy's, is imposing on the Public. There is but ONE Establishment for getting the r genuine article in, which has attained so much celebrity, and that is solely at O'SHAUGHNESSY's.

O'S. has at present an unrivalled assortment of Flies suited for the various Lakes and Rivers of the th Kingdoms ; also, the celebrated Archimedian Minnow, the artificial Par (or Graveling), the *Loach* or *Coll* Hibernice Callagh Rue. These unique baits have met the approval of the most scientific as well as the b practical Anglers, and are the only effective ones as yet discovered for

SALMON, TROUT, PIKE,

And other Fishing. They present the exact appearance of the natural bait ; are about the same weight, all co posed of one durable material, and the outside appearance can be easily renewed when discoloured fom use. Rods, Wheels, Lines, &c. of every description, and all engaged.

OBSERVE!

No connection with any other House in the Trade.

ROBERT O'SHAUGHNESSY,

18, George's-street,

PROPRIETOR.

Limerick, March 8

Limerick Chronicle, 8 March 1848.

Changes of ownership of inns were regularly notified by advertisement. Small schoolmasters advertised for pupils and the medical profession advertised endlessly for new apprentices. The scope and interest of these items is best shown by actual examples.

DROGHEDA NEWSLETTER, 30 October 1802: Michael Flanigan, horse-shoer and farmer, is removed from Loughcrew to Listoke within one mile of Drogheda . . .

FINN'S LEINSTER JOURNAL, 5 May, 1770: The noted Inn at Urlingford known by the Sign of the Munster Arms, lately kept by Mr Thomas Faye, is now opened by Mr Justin Fox . . .

ENNIS CHRONICLE, 9 April, 1790: John Judd has taken out licence as an auctioneer in Ennis and will keep an auction room next door to Mr Finucane's . . .

BELFAST NEWSLETTER, 3 December, 1779: John Gelston, clock and watch maker, who served his apprenticeship to Mr Wilson, Belfast, and since followed Business for himself in Dublin and Newry these 22 years past, has commenced Trade in Church Lane, Belfast . . .

DROGHEDA JOURNAL, 20 November, 1813: Michael O'Ferrall successor to his father, Francis O'Ferrall, and original proprietor of the Drogheda Foundry, is to obtain possession of his house in Shop Street and intends carrying on the hardware and ironmongery business, and as his brother John removes to West Street with the present stock in trade, there will be an entire supply of new and fashionable goods . . .

BELFAST NEWSLETTER, 8 March, 1782: John Ball of Newry in the Co. of Down gent was this day sworn and admitted an Attorney of His Majesty's Court of Exchequer . . . 23 February.

FINN'S LEINSTER JOURNAL, 16 February, 1771: John Fennessy, son of Richard Fennessy of Ballynatting, nurseryman, has lately opened a seed shop in the city of Cashel . . .

CORKE JOURNAL, 23 November, 1761: Whereas Joanna Maria Fitzgerald, wife of Richard Fitzgerald of Castle Ishin in the co. of Corke Esq, having thought proper to live separate for some time past from her husband, on the 7th August last forceably conveyed away from the Boarding School of Mrs Leo in Charleville the said Richard Fitzgerald's son and daughter . . .

LIMERICK CHRONICLE, 29 March, 1773: Whereas it was reported lately that Dominick Burke, younger brother to Redmond Burke of Moyglass, co.

Galway gent, pretended he was entitled to the lands of Moyglass by power of attorney from the said Redmond . . . such attorney was done about February 1772 when I, the said Redmond, was suffering a disorder of the mind . . . I have now perfectly recovered my health and manage my own affairs . . .

LIMERICK CHRONICLE, 6 July, 1772: I caution the public from crediting my wife Catherine Connor as she has turned out contrary to my expectations. Michael Connor, Glinn.

ENNIS CHRONICLE, 15 November, 1802: I caution the public not to credit my wife Margaret Geren otherwise Cunningham as she is turned out a Learner of Arts, that is false histories feigned lunacies pretended madness and the Art of Scolding, an Ideler, a lyard and in general worse than a _____ (*sic*). Daniel Geren, Gurtlummer, parish of Tulla.

(Mr. Geran's indignation evidently got the better of his spelling! The accusation is presumably one of witchcraft, a very rare event.)

WEXFORD HERALD, 14 May, 1789: Mary Hobbs, widow and executrix of Michael Hobbs late of the town of Wexford merchant deceased, intends carrying on the business . . .

CLONMEL GAZETTE, 4 December 1790: William Taylor, apothecary, has removed to the house where his father (the late W. Taylor) lived near the West Gate, Clonmel . . .

BELFAST NEWSLETTER, 21 October, 1777: Arthur Dowdall, Surgeon Apothecary and Man Midwife, Rathfriland, now wants an apprentice . . .

LIMERICK CHRONICLE, 8 February, 1773: whereas on 26 December last the house of Maurice Connell of Fanningstown, Co. Limerick, was broke open by Charles Connor of Kilderry in said co. (son of Jerry Connor who acts as deputy and assistant to the sub sheriff) aided by John Savage, Michael Quane, Timothy Connors, Michael Murphy and James Connor brother to the said Charles, all of Kilderry, and John Hayes of the city of Limerick . . . and took away his daughter against her will . . . (reward of £5 offered for conviction of any of the participants).

DROGHEDA NEWSLETTER, 31 October, 1801: To be sold by auction on Monday, 9th November, all the Household Furniture which is new, neat and fashionable, of the late Mr Richard Marron, at his house in Fair Street, Drogheda.

LIMERICK CHRONICLE, 27 January, 1772: D. Sullivan mathematician and son-in-law to the late Mr Dorgan, continues the school kept by the said Mr Dorgan in company with Mr Flannedy, also son-in-law to Mr Dorgan . . .

DROGHEDA NEWSLETTER, 12 June, 1802: Bankrupt — John Page of Dundalk, Co. Louth, grocer, to surrender 19 and 21 inst and 20 July.

Occasional Items in Newspapers

Apart from what may be regarded as normal advertisements, newspapers also featured what may be termed "occasional items". These consist mainly of lists of names, sometimes with a precise address for each, at other times merely indicating that the persons listed were resident in a particular locality. Generally they take the form of an advertisement, the lists representing the signatories to a protest or a congratulation or some other such announcement. Such items occur more frequently in the provincial newspapers, comparatively few appearing in the Dublin Press. They vary greatly in type and, because they are so difficult to locate, a number of them have recently been reprinted. Among the items reprinted are the following:

The *Corke Journal* of 12 April, 1762 has a list of the chief Catholic merchants in Cork city (reprinted in *The Irish Ancestor,* 1971); the *Dublin Evening Post* of 11 September 1784 has a list of the Grand Jury of King's County (The *Kildare Archaeological Journal,* Vol. XIII, 1935-45); *Finn's Leinster Journal* of 25 November, 1797 and 6 December, 1797 has lists of the chief Catholic inhabitants of Graige and Knocktopher, Co. Kilkenny (*The Irish Ancestor,* 1978), and the same paper of 18 November, 1767 has a list of many Freeholders in Co. Carlow (*The Irish Ancestor,* 1980); the *Belfast Newsletter* of 5 April, 1754, 10 January, 1755, 2 October, 1761 and 24 July, 1764 all carried lists of linen-drapers operating in south-east Ulster (*The Irish Ancestor,* 1979) and on 26 October, 1765 the same paper carried a list of over forty passengers who sailed on the "Buchannon" from Newry to New York the previous August (*The Irish Ancestor,* 1980). Between 25 May and 6 July, 1807 the *Waterford Mirror* named those who voted in a parliamentary election for the city of Waterford (*The Irish Ancestor,* 1976). During August 1802 many provincial papers carried lists of such local persons as had taken out Game Licences and these (unlike all the lists previously mentioned) supply exact address: they were reprinted in *The Irish Ancestor,* 1976-7. Similar Game Licence lists occur in papers in later years: one for Co. Louth in 1813 was printed in *The Irish Ancestor,* 1980, and one for Co. Waterford in 1827 was printed in *The Irish Genealogist,* 1973.

Many more of these "occasional items" exist, awaiting discovery and reprinting. They are well worth reprinting simply because by their very nature they are so impossible to find when required.

People who appear in Newspapers

The general run of the early papers deal in biographical notices concerning the nobility and country gentry, the professional, merchant and trading classes in the towns, clergy of all denominations, army and navy

Names of Divisions.	Names of Persons proposed as Guardians.	Number of Votes given to each Candidate set opposite to his name.	Names of the Guardians elected for the Division mentioned in the first Column opposite hereto.	Residence and Post Town.
No.				
1. PARSONSTOWN	William Justin O'Driscoll ...	611	William Justin O'Driscoll ...	Rose Villa, Parsonstown
	Thomas Hackett	497	Thomas Hackett ...	Parsonstown
	Patrick Slattery ...	322	Patrick Slattery ...	Derrinduff, Parsonstown
	Michael Horan ...	153		
	Edward Harte ...	132		
	Michael Madden ...	2		
	John Smith ...	Resigned		
2. KILCOLEMAN...	John Davis ..	179	John Davis ...	Dromoyle, Parsonstewn
	William Costello	96		
3. SEIRKYRANS. ...	Denis Mooney ...	179	Denis Mooney ...	Oakley, Kinnity
	Sandford Palmer	54		
	John Ryall ...	Resigned		
	Michael Keating	6		Cadamstown House, Kinnity
4. KINNITY..........	Daniel Manifold ...	No Contest	Daniel Manifold ...	
5. LITTER............	John Head Drought ...	No Contest	John Head Drought ...	Lettybrook, Kinnity
	Michael M'Redmond ...	Resigned		
6. DRUMCULLEN..	Patrick Corcoran ...	326	Patrick Corcoran ...	Pass, Kinnity
	Thomas Manifold ...	Resigned		
	Richard Davis ...	63		
7. EGLISH.........	George Heenan ...	304	George Heenan ...	Parsonstown
	Charles Fury ...	260		
	John Guinan ...	Resigned		Broughhall Castle, Frankford
8. FRANKFORD. ...	Nicholas Fitzsimon ...	No Contest	Nicholas Fitzsimons ...	
	Andrew Stoney ...	No Contest	Andrew Stoney ...	Frankford
	William Whitfield ...	Resigned		
	Charles Burriss ...	Resigned		
9. FERBANE.........	William Petty ...	184	William Petty ...	Ferbane
	Abraham Bagnell ...	159		
10. LEMANAGHAN	Michael Kennedy ...	396	Michael Kennedy ...	Tombea, Ferbane
	Patrick Cantwell ...	289	Patrick Cantwell ...	Labeg, Ballycumber, Clara
	John Warneford Armstrong	71		
	Thomas Robinson ...	Resigned		
11. SHANNON-BRIDGE	Robert Dalton ...	234	Robert Dalton ...	Clongowney, Ferbane
	James Colclough ...	218	James Colclough ...	Cloniver, Cloghan
	John Drought Lawdor ...	54		
	William James Stanley ...	13		
12. TISSARIN.........	William L'Estrange ...	152	William L'Estrange ...	Kilcummin, Cloghan
	James Devery, jun. ...	139		
13. SHANNON-HARBOUR	Bernard Callaghan ...	No Contest	Bernard Callaghan ...	Millbrook, Cloghan
	James Devery ...	—	James Devery ...	Cloghan
14. BANAGHER.....	John Sherlock ...	206	John Sherlock ...	Miltown, Banagher
	Kiran Molloy ...	189	Kiran Molloy ...	Banagher
	John Doorley ...	99		
15. LUSMAGH.......	Patrick Larkin ...	No Contest	Patrick Larkin ...	Lr. Newtown, Banagher
16. DORHA............	Michael Meara ...	No Contest	Michael Meara ...	Annagh, Parsonstown
	John Lawlor ...	Resigned		
17. LORHA	Thomas Hemsworth ...	288	Thomas Hemsworth ...	Abbeyville, Borrisokane
	Patrick Hough ...	38	Patrick Hough ..	Ballincur, Lorha
	Daniel Meara ...	31		
18. LOCKEEN.....,...	Simpson Hackett ...	81	Simpson Hackett ...	Riverstown, Parsonstown
	Christopher Dignan ...	78		
	Michael Burke ...	26		
19. AGLISH-CLOGHANE	James Meara ...	No Contest	James Meara ..	Ballymassey, Borrisokane
	Benjamin Armitage ...	Resigned		
20. USKEANE........	John Cleary ...	75	John Cleary ...	Driminihane, Borrisokane
	William Stewart Trench ...	68		
	Samuel Barry, jun. ...	38		
21. BALLINGARRY	James Sheppard ...	218	James Sheppard .,	Clifton, Shinrone
	Michael Hoctor ...	30		

Election of Guardians for the Poor Law Unions, King's County (Offaly).
Dublin Evening Post, 18 June 1839.

officers, lawyers, doctors and the masters of schools. They are particularly useful for locating the Catholic middle classes as they come into evidence after the relaxation of the Penal Laws in the 1770s, and are one of the very best sources extant for tracing the many craftsmen — silversmiths, clock-makers, cabinetmakers and the like — who may be sought both in the advertisements and amongst the marriages and deaths. Papers are also one of the very few sources that give any information about those maddeningly mobile innkeepers. They do *not*, however, concern themselves at all with medium to small farmers or cottiers.

Except in the case of the few indexed papers, there is a great problem locating relevant items, since one hardly ever knows the exact date of the event sought. To examine a complete year of any one paper takes about two hours (three on microfilm), so that a long search — say, one covering twenty years — might last for a week and might well produce nothing. The extant papers are also scattered and hard to obtain. Many of them are now only available on microfilm and some of those on microfilm are next to impossible to read due to the thin paper of the original and the print from one side showing through to the next. To add to the hazards, the early papers did not print their biographical notices in one regular spot, but inserted them wherever convenient, so that every page may have to be searched in turn, which naturally delays progress, especially on microfilm.

Newspapers Post 1830

After 1830 newspapers proliferated. Not only were new papers produced in towns that already had papers but towns that had hitherto been paperless, so to speak, began to publish newspapers, as exemplified by the following list:

The Leinster Express (1831), published in Maryborough; *Ballyshannon Herald* (1832); *Athlone Independent* (1833); *Athlone Sentinel* (1834); *The Westmeath Guardian* (1835), published in Mullingar; *Downpatrick Recorder* (1836); *Tuam Herald* (1837); *Nenagh Guardian* (1838); *Longford Journal* (1839); *Northern Standard* (1839), published in Monaghan; *Armagh Guardian* (1844); *Coleraine Chronicle* (1844); *Tyrone Constitution* (1844), published in Omagh; *Meath Herald* (1845), published in Kells; *King's Co. Chronicle* (1845), published in Birr; the *Anglo Celt* (1846), published in Cavan; *Dundalk Patriot* (1847); *Lurgan Chronicle* (1850); *Leitrim Journal and Carrick on Shannon Advertiser* (1850); *Lisburn, Hills-borough and Dromore Gazette* (1851); the *Midlands County Advertiser* (1854), published in Roscrea; *Tipperary Leader* (1855), published in

Thurles; *Wicklow Newsletter* (1857); *Leinster Reporter* (1859), published in Tullamore; *Skibbereen Eagle* (1861); *Larne Weekly Reporter* (1865).

In the 1880s and 1890s still smaller towns began publications, so that by the turn of the century Ireland gives the impression of being beset with newspapers, since nearly every little town had one and the bigger towns two or three.

The best general Dublin paper from the 1830s on was the *Freeman's Journal*, and it remained unrivalled until the advent of the *Irish Times* in 1859. In the remaining years of the century the *Freeman's Journal* bore a somewhat more Protestant and Unionist flavour than the more Catholic and Nationalistic *Irish Times*. Both papers, however, carried substantial numbers of marriage and death notices.

In many ways the post-1830 papers differ from their predecessors and are considerably more straightforward to handle. The biographical notices become steadily more numerous and more detailed, as well as being regularly placed in one spot in the paper, often the front page. The number of birth announcements rises sharply, though they still give neither the name of infant or mother, the formula being on the lines of this from the *Irish Times*: "October 23, 1904, at 7 Carlisle avenue, Donnybrook, the wife of Thomas A. O'Brien, of a son."

From the 1860s onwards an obituary in Dublin newspapers will mention the time and place of the forthcoming funeral, which is a convenient guide when seeking either cemetery records or a tombstone. Such information was not always given in the country, being considered unnecessary, as the place of interment might be presumed to be the local churchyard. In the last quarter of the century discursive obituaries began to be awarded to men prominent in their own fields, usually supplying interesting details of their careers: these often appeared on the day of the funeral, a day or two after the actual announcement of death. While death notices in the Dublin papers usually give a reasonable amount of information, those in the provinces could still be depressingly brief, as this item from the 1886 *Meath Herald*: "Died 12th September, Samuel M. Kellett, Headfort Place, Kells. Aged 57 years."

Marriage notices tended more and more to supply the bridegroom's parentage as well as that of the bride, and continued to indicate the place of wedding, besides being careful to add the exact date. Their value, of course, diminishes with the coming of civil registration in 1864, as it is much easier to trace a marriage in the civil records than in the newspapers.

As family establishments began to decline, businesses became more impersonal and advertisements more severely commercial in nature. Consequently after about 1830 the value of advertisements as purveyors of genealogical information decreased sharply.

Which Newspapers to Consult

After 1830 newspapers are so abundant that the choice is bewilderingly wide. As already mentioned, by the 1880s almost every small town had a paper, many had several, and there were a great number in Dublin. Unfortunately only one paper has been indexed: Vol. 6 of Dr. Albert Casey's *O'Keif, Coshe Mang, etc.* contains the biographical notices from the *Kerry Evening Post* of 1828-1864. These consist mainly of items cribbed from Cork and Limerick papers, almost always in abridged form. Precise dates are omitted and there is a shortage of exact addresses, plus a lack of the precise place of marriage, even though the original announcement in the Cork or Limerick paper may well have supplied such particulars. A couple of comparisons will make the point. Where the *Kerry Evening Post* of 26 May 1852 gives simply "died at Limerick, George B. Dartnell", the *Limerick Chronicle* of 22 May 1852 gives "died on the 19th inst. at his father's residence, Mr George B. Dartnell aged 22 years, youngest son of Mr John Dartnell, Cappoquin". Where the *Kerry Evening Post* of 6 September 1856 gives "married at Cork, James Denehy of George's Street to Lizzie daughter of the late Richard Fenny", the *Constitution* of 4 September 1856 has "on the 2nd inst. at the South Chapel by the Rev. Dominick Murphy, P.P. and V.G., Mr James Denehy of Great George's Street to Lizzie daughter of the late Mr Richard Fenny of this city". What makes the rather truncated *Kerry Evening Post* notices important is that they are indexed, and can therefore be used as a quick guide to the approximate date before seeking the more informative announcement in a Cork or Limerick paper.

In general, the local paper still remains the best place to look, in preference to the more general Dublin papers, especially if there is any prospect of finding a discursive obituary. The discursive obituaries in the Dublin press were pretty well confined to Dubliners, although the Dublin press carried a wide selection of death notices from all over the country.

Recent years have seen a sharp decline in provincial papers, and nowadays only Belfast and Cork have a daily publication, the other survivors being weekly productions. Most counties, however, have at least one, though they are not necessarily required local reading.

Where to Find Newspapers

For Northern Ireland the Public Record Office of Northern Ireland and the Library Association have jointly produced an excellent booklet, *Northern Ireland Newspapers: Checklist with Locations*, which covers papers from 1737 to the present day. All the known papers, past and present, are listed alphabetically, with a clear guide as to where the various issues are now held.

In the Republic of Ireland the situation is very different, for there is no comprehensive guide at all, and newspapers are so widely scattered that no one person knows what exists where. Individual libraries, of course, have lists of their own holdings (and sometimes of the holdings of other large libraries), but there is no composite guide to the lot. In Dublin the National Library has by far the best over all collection, but there are some valuable items in the Library of Trinity College (notably very good 18th century runs of *Faulkner's Dublin Journal* and of the *Cork Evening Post*). Pearse Street Library has a fine collection of modern newspapers.

Libraries in provincial towns often have volumes of old local papers — this is certainly true of Cork, Waterford and Athlone. Existing newspapers may have inherited the old files of previously published newspapers, as has happened in Kilkenny, Ennis and Limerick, as well as in Dungannon and Londonderry.

The British Library has an impressive accumulation of Irish newspaper material at Colindale, and the National Library possesses a copy of their catalogue to this material. Before 1826 the papers are somewhat fragmentary but from then on the British Library was required to hold all the Irish papers, so moderately complete runs may be expected as from that date.

Finally it must be said that old newspapers — particularly those before 1830 — are one of the most absorbing sources a genealogist can study. One never knows what gem is around the corner and the social history that may be gleaned on the way has a fascination all its own. But to enjoy the quest as it should be enjoyed an abundance of patience is essential, for nothing can be found in a hurry, and truly this is a case where to travel hopefully is at least as good as to arrive.

CHAPTER 7

The Registry of Deeds for Genealogical Purposes

ROSEMARY FFOLLIOTT

The Registry of Deeds, unlike the Public Record Office, is fully intact. Of the various Irish record repositories it is perhaps the most difficult for the amateur to handle. In the first instance there is the actual physical problem posed by the large, heavy leather-bound volumes written in diverse hands. Some of these are a joy to read, particularly in the early 18th century, while others are extremely hard to decipher — an especially obscure hand having been at work in the 1790s. Additionally, the indexing systems are confusing, words are frequently written in an abbreviated form and a novice frequently finds the legal phraseology obscure. I have known all too many people, having turned up quite a straight-forward deed, try to read and understand it and — utterly defeated — end by asking me blankly, "What does it mean? What was he doing?" Because of all these hazards, the Registry is a place where it is advisable to employ an experienced researcher, for the amateur will certainly overlook almost as much as he finds. Work there is always slow and there may be little reward for a couple of hours snatched out of a brief visit to Dublin.

Deeds vary widely in their usefulness. Many, particularly straight leases, provide little genealogical information while others may supply particulars of up to three generations of a family. Some families were partial to registered deeds: others, for no very obvious reason, were not. The volume of registered transactions varied from county to county. Dublin, Cork, Tyrone, Tipperary and Offaly are especially rich in registered items while Mayo, Kerry and Armagh have appreciably fewer. Kilkenny and Limerick have a smaller number of registrations than one might expect, while the small farmers who abounded in Wexford and Down eschewed registration, which makes the deeds from these areas fewer than would otherwise be the case. Certain groups of people tended to avoid registered deeds: the Quaker community had few and there are no 18th century deeds relating to the many Palatine families who settled in Cos. Limerick and Wexford. Moreover, the number of deeds registered by Presbyterians from Ulster was small.

There was a strong economic element involved in the registration of deeds. Registered items are mainly those made between economic equals, or near equals, who might sue each other in the courts. A lease from a wealthy landlord to a small tenant hardly ever reached the Registry, though a lease from a medium-sized landlord to a not-so-small tenant easily might. It is therefore advisable to determine the economic standing of the family being researched by checking the size of the family holding in Griffith's Valuation or the Tithe Books before spending hours searching for deeds. If either source should show, say, a five-acre farm held from Lord Clanwilliam, the possibility of a registered deed can be dismissed forthwith. On the other hand, deeds contain a mass of information concerning merchants, traders, professional men, farming gentry and substantial farmers. Small farmers and cottiers rarely, if ever, figure in registered deeds.

How a Deed was Registered

The Registry was established in 1708 as part of the legislation designed to prevent land passing into Catholic hands. Only a few deeds recite back to transactions in the 1690s: I have never seen a recitation extend earlier than that. Up to 1730 relatively few deeds were registered, and all of them belonged to the richer section of the community. From about 1745 the number registered began to increase markedly and their economic level began to fall. Both these circumstances continued to prevail into the early 19th century. Until the Penal Laws were relaxed in 1778 few deeds relating to admitted Catholics were registered, but after this date there was a general move by Catholic landholders to register their rightful property. For genealogical purposes the prime period of the deeds runs from about 1750 to 1840, after which date their value steadily declines when better, sources become available.

The registration system worked as follows. A deed was executed between the contracting parties, duly signed and witnessed. Then one of the parties (usually the grantee) had a copy or "memorial" made, which he signed, and which was witnessed by two persons, at least one of whom had previously witnessed the deed itself. This witness, who had testified to both deed and memorial, then took the memorial before a Justice of the Peace and swore that it was a true copy of the original. The sworn memorial was promptly dispatched to the Registry, and entered there within a couple of days. The Registry retained the actual memorial, transcribed it into one of the great parchment volumes and indexed it. The original memorials are stored in files in the vaults, and the enquirer works on the transcript in the volume. It will thus be seen that the only original signatures preserved are those on the memorial, that of the person who registered the deed and the two memorial witnesses. A deed could be sworn and registered within two days of being made, but normally it was done within a couple of years. There are, however, innumerable cases of deeds being registered after a lapse of many years. Indeed, I have seen up to forty years elapse before registration. The sudden urge to register was usually caused by death, and the registration date of deeds registered more than six or seven years after their execution should be noted, as it can hold useful significance. The whole matter is of some importance, since the deeds are indexed under their date of registration, not under the date on which they were made.

As already mentioned, the great mass of registered deeds were those made between economic equals who were liable to sue each other in the courts. The Irish appear to have been fond of litigation and waged endless law suits both within and outside of the family, irrespective of whether or not they could afford them. Since a lease from a wealthy landlord to a small tenant held no prospect of a law suit, it was left unregistered — registration cost money, gave trouble and in a case such as this was of no advantage. I once checked the 18th century leases of the Jephson estate in Mallow, — mainly to the local shopkeepers and townsfolk — and of three hundred transactions preserved in the Estate Office, only six reached the Registry of Deeds. The low ratio of registrations to transactions in this instance will probably be found to be uniform for the country at large.

The Indexing System

The first problem that confronts a person trying to operate the Registry is to get to know the indexes, which are quite complicated. The deeds are indexed in two ways. There is an alphabetical Index to Grantors, and a county Index to Lands. *There is no alphabetical index to grantees.*

Up to 1833 the Index to Grantors offers no clue to the address or property involved. It merely shows the surname and Christian name of the grantor, followed by the surname of the first grantee and the three reference numbers (volume, page and deed number) needed to find the item. Thus, with no guidance as to address, seeking a name such as John Johnston one might be faced with several hundred references, all of which would have to be checked in order to extract those relating to, say, Co. Leitrim. In the case of a rare surname, or even a common surname and a rare Christian name (e.g. Gamaliel Fitzgerald or Aquilla Smith), the Index to Grantors works splendidly, but in the case of poor John Johnston it presents a daunting task. After 1833 the situation improves dramatically, when the Index shows the county in which the lands concerned were situated, though this is not necessarily the same as the county in which the parties resided.

The Index to Lands is divided into counties, and the townland references are assembled together under their initial letter, but are not arranged in any further alphabetical order. The length of a search, therefore, depends on

Darley	John	Crawford	303	87	203197
	Do. Van.	Vesey	305	507	203290
	Do. Van.	Reilly	316	145	210394
	Martha Van.	Darley Van.	271	26	173196
Darling	Robert	Gould	279	325	182991
	Do.	Naylor	279	326	182992
	Do.	Darling	282	589	186902
Darlington	Francis	Darlington	307	130	203390
	Grace	Do.	271	202	175665
	Joanna	Do.	308	60	203650
Darnley	Earl Vors	Hopkins	259	318	171772
	Do.	Lewis Van.	275	526	178927
	Do.	Hopkins	275	528	178928
	Do. Vors	Tighe	263	268	144109
	Do.	Blighe Vors	287	271	187129
	Do. Countess	Do. Van.	287	273	187130
	Earl	Bourne	292	592	192396
Darquier	William Vas	Roche	265	184	174597
	Do. Van.	Do.	261	621	175742
	Do. Van.	Morgan	276	91	176686

Index to Grantors, Vol. D 22, 1768-1776.

Courtesy of the Registrar of Deeds.

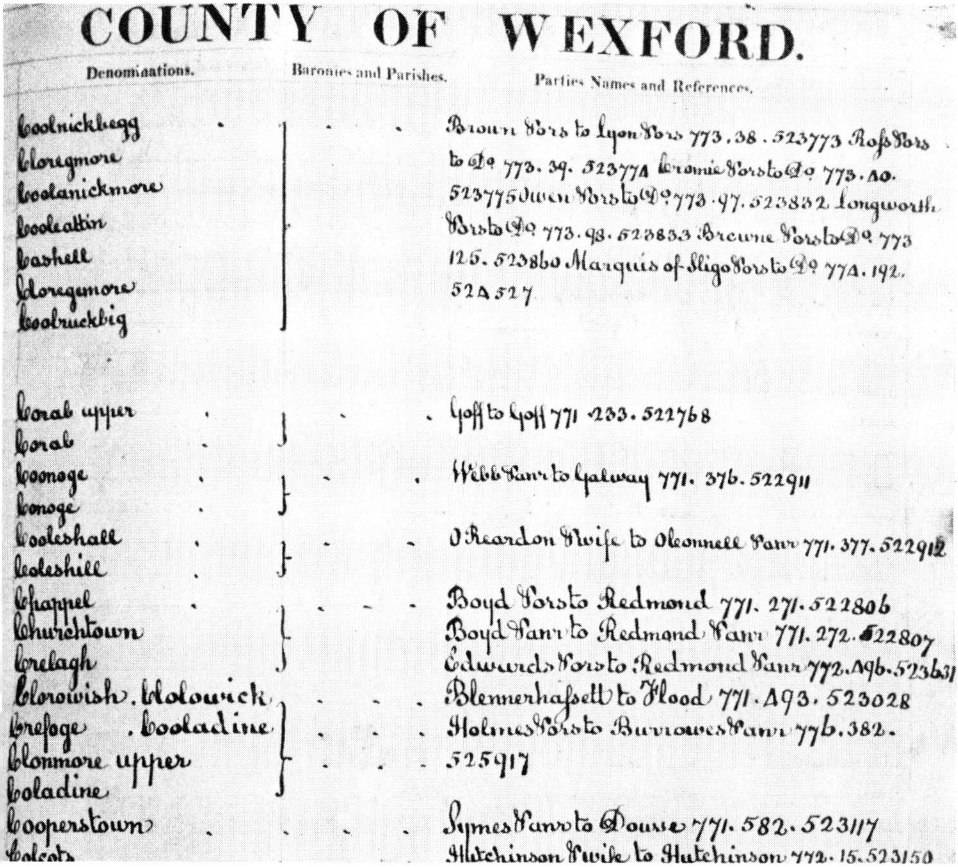

COUNTY OF WEXFORD.

Denominations.	Baronies and Parishes.	Parties Names and References.

The handwritten index entries:

Coolnickbegg
Cloregmore
Coolanickmore
Coolcattin
Bashell
Cloregmore
Coolruckbig

Brown &rs to Lyon &rs 773.38.523773 Ross &rs to do 773.39. 523774 Cromie &rs to do 773.40. 523775 Owen &rs to do 773.97. 523852 Longworth &rs to do 773.93. 523853 Browne &rs to do 773 125. 523860 Marquis of Sligo &rs to do 774.192. 524527

Coral upper
Coral
Coonoge
Conoge
Cooleshall
Coleshill

Coff to Coff 771 233. 522768

Webb &anr to Galway 771. 376. 522911

O'Reardon & wife to O'Connell &anr 771. 377. 522912

Chappel
Churchtown
Crelagh
Clonowish. Clolowick.
Crefoge   Cooladine
Clonmore upper
Cooladine
Cooperstown
Colcots

Boyd &rs to Redmond 771. 271. 522806
Boyd &anr to Redmond &anr 771. 272. 522807
Edwards &rs to Redmond &anr 772.196.523631
Blennerhassett to Flood 771.193. 523028
Holmes &rs to Burrowes &anr 771.382. 525917

Symes &anr to Douse 771. 582. 523117
Hutchinson & wife to Hutchinson 772. 15.523150

Index to Lands, 1821-1825.

the initial letter of the townland — B, C, D and K cover many pages, while A, N and O cover very few. The townland names are in the first column and are followed by a column intended to show the barony in which the various townlands lie. However, in many instances the barony is omitted, and the novice should sternly resist the temptation to skim down the barony column instead of reading the townland names. After 1828 the county indexes are further sub-divided into baronies, and from this date it is imperative to know in which barony the townland sought lay. Before 1828 this is of no great importance. After 1828 there is a further confusion in that there is an additional column for each county — "Where No Barony is Mentioned".

The actual references shown in the Indexes to Lands are brief, being

143

limited to surnames only, e.g. "Jones and ors (others) to Murphy and an (another)". Jones's grantor-partners will be indexed under their own names in the Index to Grantors, but Murphy's companion will not be indexed, and the only way to discover his name is to inspect the deed.

Cities and Corporation Towns have separate indexes. These are arranged by street or vicinity, but the arrangement can be so unusual that it is safer to read the entire Index for that particular town. The Index to Dublin City is notorious for its many omissions and curious lay-out. Indeed, it contains so many hazards that one tries hard to avoid using it. On the other hand, the big indexes for Cork and Limerick appear to work quite well.

Many of the Indexes to Lands are badly worn from constant usage and are difficult or impossible to read with the entire bottom lines of some pages rubbed away. Certain portions are missing, as for example the entire section A to C for Co. Cork from 1740 to 1780.

Sometimes, particularly when dealing with a rare surname, when the Index to Grantors has been exhausted, it will be worthwhile reading the entire Index to Lands for the relevant county over a given period. However, so long as the Index to Grantors can be managed, it is preferable to the Index to Lands, in that it covers all the stray pieces of property a man may have been dealing in (sometimes in an adjoining county), as distinct from the known townland where he habitually resided. The Index to Lands is, however, useful in the case of a medium-sized farmer who may — with luck — have held his farm by registered lease, but did not have the resources for dealing in stray pieces of land. The Index to Lands will establish whether or not he held a specific farm by registered lease. If, however, the name of the landlord can be found, say in Griffith's Valuation, then it is probably quicker to seek the lease under the landlord's name in the Index to Grantors.

There are six main types of transaction recorded at the Registry, and each is now dealt with in turn.

Deeds: Sales, Assignments or Conveyances

In the 18th century these were often disguised as a "Lease and Release" and they are best recognised by the proviso that the grantee is to hold the property "for ever". They are not over numerous. In general, the Irish were reluctant to actually part with freehold property! They preferred to have the hope of getting it back eventually. Sales of leases and conveyances of mortgages were, however, quite common, and will be dealt with later. The following is an example of a simple, direct sale. Like all the examples here quoted, it has been shorn of its legal verbiage, and appears deceptively plain. The actual memorials registered are not so simple, being wordy and repetitive.

Deed Reference: 94 164 65775

Sale dated 13 April 1738 whereby Francis Knox and Henry Darcus Esqs, Sheriffs of the City and Co. of Londonderry, by virtue of their Office, granted to Henry Dickson of Londonderry merchant a double messuage lately in the possession of Frederick Coningham Alderman deceased, situated in the liberties of Londonderry, to hold for ever.

Witnesses: Andrew Mackilwane senior and Andrew Mackilwane junior both of Londonderry gents.

Memorial witnesses: the said Andrew Mackilwane junior and Hamilton Benson of Londonderry gent.

Andrew Mackilwane junior swore 2 March 1738-9.

Sometimes the actual money paid — the consideration — is stated; more often, as in the above instance, it is not. Note that this particular deed provides extremely little genealogy, a not uncommon occurrence.

Property which had been the source of legal proceedings in the Courts of Chancery or Equity Exchequer, and which had been ordered to be sold by Decree of either Court was apt to be the subject of a registered Assignment. Such deeds are instantly recognizable since the first party is always the Master of the Court of Chancery in Ireland or the Chief Remembrancer of the Court of Exchequer in Ireland. They are frequently long and complicated, involving numerous parties with varying interests in the disputed lands. Sometimes they can be helpful in providing the names of a line of daughters and their husbands, if they were then married. Here is an example of a relatively simple, but very useful, Exchequer deed:

Deed Reference: 444 218 288182

Lease and Release dated 13 December 1791 made between (1) the Chief Remembrancer of H.M. Court of Exchequer in Ireland and (2) John Farrell of Sligo town Esq and (3) Robert Hillas eldest son and heir of Robert Hillas late of Doonecoy, Co. Sligo deceased, and Thomas Hillas, Richard Hillas gent, Jane Hillas, Mary Hillas and Helen Hillas spinsters and Catherine Cunningham otherwise Hillas widow, they being the younger children of the said late Robert Hillas, and (4) Robert Hillas of Seaview, Co. Sligo Esq.

Whereby in pursuance of a Decree in the Court of Exchequer (1), (2) and (3) granted the lands of Doonecoy to (4).

Witnesses: George Hillas of Dublin gent and Robert Faussett of Arkhill, Co. Sligo gent.

George Hillas swore 1 February 1792.

Sales of lands by persons on the point of emigration are — perhaps surprisingly — extremely rare. Either they had little to sell, or simply passed over their assets informally to a relative thereby enabling them to return to the homeland if they so desired. Sometimes, after a lapse of years, emigrants can be found disposing of their Irish property, having apparently decided to remain in their adopted country. Occasionally they will be found to have acquired an Irish property, possibly intending to return to Ireland at a future date. Such deeds are particularly interesting because they link the emigrant, with his new address, to a place — and even a family — in Ireland. An interesting early example of such a deed follows:

Deed Reference: 202 385 134389
   Indenture dated 6 October 1759 whereby Daniel Chambers of Rockhill, Co. Donegal, Esq, in consideration of £25 15s. sold to Redmond Coningham of the city of Philadelphia in America merchant two acres in the Quarters of Letterkenny, Co. Donegal, adjoining the Ballyboe and now in the possession of Catherine Coningham of Letterkenny widow.
   Witnesses: James Stevenson and Patrick Coningham both of Letterkenny. Patrick Coningham swore 1 November 1759.

The implication of the witnesses here is that Redmond Coningham must have been in Letterkenny at the time the deed was made, presumably on a visit from Philadelphia. Other deeds carry both Irish and trans-Atlantic witnesses, showing that the ocean sometimes divided the contracting parties.

Deeds: Rent Charges

Sometimes disguised as "Deed Polls" or "Leases and Releases", these were an arrangement whereby one party granted to another an annual payment of a specified sum charged on specified lands. Occasionally trustees were appointed to oversee proceedings. Rent charges could be a form of family settlement (to provide for a widowed mother or sister), to defray a mortgage by instalments or to satisfy an importunate creditor by agreeing to pay a certain sum at regular intervals.

A Rent Charge, once made, was a transferable asset, and was regularly assigned to a third party or fourth party, the object being either to make a little profit each time or else to raise some ready money, for example:

Deed Reference: 294 29 193631
   Assignment dated 4 November 1772 made between (1) William Gurly of the town of Wexford shopkeeper and (2) Rostocke Radford Jacob of the same town merchant.
   Reciting that by Deed dated 13 September 1772 Sir Vesey Colclough of Tintern Abbey, Co. Wexford, had granted to (1) an annuity of £9 2s. payable out of the tithes of the parish of St. Michael Muckrath in the Barony of Forth Co. Wexford, for the lives of the said (1) and of Mary Gurly his wife and of Mathew Gurly his brother.

Whereby (1) granted to (2) his interest in said Deed.

Witnesses: Michael Vicary and Thomas Jones both of the town of Wexford gents.

This is quite a useful specimen, providing the names of both William Gurly's wife and his brother. The two witnesses were in the legal profession and not relatives.

Deeds: Leases

Most Irish land was held by lease. Even the lesser gentry, who might reside on a freehold property, regularly took leases of outside lands with the result that leases are far the most numerous type of transaction on record at the Registry.

A lease might be for any term, one year, 999 years, or for a specified term such as 31 years or three lives, whichever was the longer. A lease for three lives renewable forever amounted to a lease in perpetuity. The only difference between it and an outright sale was that the rent remained due and on death, each of the three named lives had to be renewed, on payment of a heriot. The choice of lives could rest with either the lessor or lessee, but more usually with the latter.

A great deal of useful genealogy can be gleaned from leases especially from the lives mentioned in them. Fortunately, the custom of using the lives of royal personages was not widely followed. A lease may or may not recite the grantor's title to land or specify the annual rent due. An example of a straightforward lease now follows:

Deed Reference: 179 441 121746

Lease dated 27 June 1752 whereby John Moony and Edward Moony both of Doon, King's County, gents, set to Lewis Youell of Clonshanna, said county, farmer, part of the lands of Aghaten now in the occupation of William Youell, to hold for the lives of the said Lewis Youell and of Hugh Youell fourth son to William Youell of Aghatan and of Hugh Thomas eldest son of William Thomas of Cranasallagh weaver, or for 31 years.

Witnesses: Marlborough Sterling and Edward Colpoys both of the city of Dublin gents.

Registered by Lewis Youell and sworn by Marlborough Sterling 26th July 1756.

Occasionally, a lease will specify the ages of the three lives as in the following instance:

Deed Reference: 664 297 452916

Lease dated 5 September 1813 whereby John Strogen of the town of Galway Esq and Mary Strogen otherwise Mathews his wife and Osborne Strogen their eldest son and heir, set to Hyacinth Burke of Killemun, Co. Galway Esq, the lands at Curraghroe in the Half Barony of Loughrea, Co. Galway, to hold for the lives of Dominick Burke eldest son and heir of the said Hyacinth then aged about nine years and of Margaret Burke daughter of the said Hyacinth and then aged about four years and of Maria Burke daughter of the said Hyacinth and aged about three years, or for a term of 31 years.

Witnesses: Catherine Strogen of Galway spinster and Peter Ward of Dublin attorney.

Lands held by lease were regularly sub-let to other tenants, often only a few days intervening between the two transactions, the object being to make money. Deals of this kind were normal between economic equals.

Deeds: Mortgages

Mortgages were of immense importance in Ireland up to at least 1840. During a time when there was no stock market, a rather risky banking system, and an ever present acute shortage of hard cash, mortgages filled a dire need. If a man wanted ready money — perhaps for a daughter's dowry or to pay the builder of his new house — the only way he could get it was by raising a mortgage. Conversely, should a man happen to have funds in hand — say as the result of a successful bout of trading — the best temporary use he could make of it was to lend it on a sound mortgage. Mortgages were payable at "legal interest" and might be short term — a year or less — or for an almost indefinite period. If not redeemed, the mortgagee could finally foreclose — and often did, thereby making a substantial profit.

Like leases, mortgages were transferred from one party to another in a kind of stock market operation, each mortgagee aiming to make a profit. The original mortgage was more usually made between relatives or connections by marriage, the idea apparently being that such family links provided some additional security. This was a complete fallacy. Mortgages provided grounds not only for some of the most prolonged family law suits but also for some of the most bitter family quarrels. Once made, the mortgage often passed right out of the family through the transfer of interest to outsiders.

A mortgage, which is often disguised as a "Lease and Release" or an "Agreement", can be identified by the statement that the property has been conveyed "with a clause of redemption". Sometimes the money involved is specified, sometimes not. If it is, the size of the amount is of interest since it reflects not only the value of the mortgaged premises but the immediate financial needs of the owner. Mortgages were raised on both freehold and leasehold property. An example of a straightforward mortgage follows:

Deed Reference: 187 252 124810

Lease and Release dated 6 and 7 June 1757 whereby Robert Hamilton of Ballydoran, Co. Down gent in consideration of £260 granted to Isabella Reid of Ballowe, Co. Down widow, the lands of Ballydoran in the Barony of Duffran, Co. Down, to hold with a clause of redemption by 1st May next.

Witnesses: John Moore of Ballybregagh, Co. Dublin gent and William Gillespies of Cherryvalley, Co. Down, gent.

This particular mortgage was made on Ballydoran which was Mr. Hamilton's own residence, and would certainly have been speedily redeemed, since the demesne lands or "head lands" were only parted with in the most dire circumstances. They were therefore regarded as excellent security for a mortgage or a marriage settlement. A mortgage raised on some outlying farm might not be redeemed nearly so quickly. Sometimes the deed surrendering the mortgage is registered, the amount due having been repaid in full, but the number of surrenders registered is small compared to the number of mortgages — once the transaction was completed registration was not considered worth while.

Once a mortgage is transferred to a third party the deeds become more complicated, as for example in this case where the process was that Fowle leased the lands to Barter, Barter mortgaged them to Hayes and Hayes transferred them to Moore, viz.,

Deed Reference: 87 157 61059

Assignment dated 14 February 1736 made between (1) Thomas Hayes of Knockagore, Co. Cork gent and (2) John Moore of Inishonane, said county clerk and (3) John Barter of Cooldaniel, said county, gent.

Reciting that John Fowle of the city of Dublin by Lease dated 1 October 1714 set to (3) the lands of Killeene and Ballyhander in the Barony of Kinalea, Co. Cork (being 367 acres) to hold for 99 years, and Reciting that the said (3) by mortgage dated 14 February 1729 mortgaged same to (1) for £400.

Whereby (1) in consideration of £400 and at the discretion of (3), conveyed said mortgage to (2).

Witnesses: Thomas Barter of Annaghmore, Co. Cork and Robert Wallis of the city of Cork, public notary.

Thomas Barter swore 14 February 1736.

Marriage Settlements

From the genealogist's point of view these are usually the choicest items of all. They can be disguised as a "Lease and Release", or as an "Agreement" or a "Deed". Basically, they were designed as an insurance against improvidence, bankruptcy or other human vagary. From the trading classes upwards, it was customary for a father to bestow a dowry upon his daughter at her marriage. Once married, she could not hold property in her own right, and a prudent father did not wish to see the girl's fortune dispersed by a spendthrift husband. The granting of the dowry to trustees covered both difficulties, with the added advantage that should the husband become bankrupt the trust funds were immune from his creditors, and therefore provided some future security for the entire family. If the bride's father was dead, either her eldest brother or her mother might make the settlement on her. She might, of course, inherit a legacy under her father's will, which she herself, prior to marriage, could transfer to trustees. On the bridegroom's part, it was usual for him to make a grant to trustees of an annuity charged on his demesne lands, which was to be paid to his wife and her children, if she should survive him. The conditions of payment were varied and complicated, and are of little genealogical importance. It is, however, noteworthy that the heyday of registered marriage settlements (c.1790-c.1820) corresponds to the heyday of bankruptcies!

There are two main types of settlement. The more frequent was that made just before the wedding, generally a day or two beforehand. The less frequent was that made a year or two after the marriage — a post-marriage settlement. From the wording it is always quite clear which type one is dealing with. The pre-marriage settlement gives far more information, and may be confidently accepted as proof of the marriage since, had the ceremony not taken place for any unforeseen reason, nobody would have bothered to register the deed.

The pre-marriage settlement generally provides the name, address and occupation of the bride's father, as well as the name, address and occupation of the bridegroom. Sometimes the bridegroom's father joined with him in making available a settlement on the bride, but in many instances his name does not appear. The bride's dowry might be in the form of cash — £200 to £500 was the usual figure — or an annuity charged on her father's property. The amount of annuity may or may not be specified. The bridegroom's settlement on the bride was invariably charged on the demesne lands — outlying farms were not considered good security — and this is a valuable means of ascertaining the extent of the family's chief possessions. The two (or occasionally four) trustees were always relations by blood or marriage, a member often from each family. The bride's father rarely acted as a trustee but her brother often did. The trustees were almost always men. When, in later years, the bridegroom wished to lease or mortgage the lands on which his marriage settlement had been charged, the trustees of the settlement had to be parties to the new deed, and it was usual to take the precaution of making the wife a party to it also. The following is an example of a normal marriage settlement:

Deed Reference: 209 80 137626

Deed dated 19 January 1759 made between (1) Duke Barwick of Ballymahon, Co. Longford gent and (2) Samuel Potts of Tinemuck, King's County gent and Andrew McClaughry of Creagh, Co. Longford gent and (3) Catherine Potts spinster, daughter of the said Samuel Potts.

Reciting a marriage intended between (1) and (3).

Whereby (1) in consideration of £500 being the portion of (3), conveyed to (2) the lands of Ballynemanagh and Lisnecreevey, Co. Longford, to hold in Trust.

Witnesses: Thomas Laverock of Ballboughlin, Thomas Peacock and William Peacock both of Tinemuck and all in the King's County, gents.

Thomas Laverock swore 12 December 1760.

An equally informative type of marriage settlement is contained in the following example:

Deed Reference: 206 168 135550

Marriage Settlement dated 20 April 1751 made between (1) Francis Sargent of the city of Limerick Burgess and Francis Meares Esq Town Major of the same city as trustee for Jane Minchin of the same city spinster and (2) Jonathan Monsell of Donogroge, Co. Clare gent.

Reciting a marriage intended between (2) and Jane Minchin.

Whereby (2) agreed with (1) that (2) should by deed or will secure one third of his property unto the said Jane Minchin if she should survive him, and Reciting that (2) is entitled to the lands of Clonola under the will of his father William Monsell and as held for the lives of Richard Monsell and Angell Monsell and of the said (2) by Lease from John Westrop of Lismeehan, Co. Clare Esq.

Witnesses: William Gubbins of the city of Limerick burgess and Walter Cuff of the same city Esq.

The post-marriage settlement, which is less useful, may be worded along the following lines:

Deed Reference: 343 449 237434

Settlement dated 21 July 1780 made between (1) James Colhoun of Cross, Co. Tyrone Esq and (2) Catherine Colhoun otherwise Coghlan his wife and (3) Mathew Lyster of Newpark, Co. Roscommon Esq and James Lyster of Lysterfield, Co. Roscommon Esq.

Whereby (1) in persuance of a settlement made before his marriage with (2) granted to (3) the lands of Upper and Lower Laught, Upper and Lower Garvachallin, Tullymuck, Seraghey, Ballinree and his interests in Duntague and the one eighth part of Glassmullagh and Lismacreagh Mill, to hold in Trust.

Witnesses: William Burke of the city of Dublin gent and Thomas Pasley of the same city public notary.

Thomas Pasley swore 22 July 1783.

The pre-marriage settlement alluded to above was never registered. It should be stressed that — as with every other type of transaction — only a tiny proportion of the marriage settlements executed actually reached the Registry.

Finding these settlements in the Indexes presents special problems. Many, but by no means all, are indexed under the bride's name and they can be found readily enough. Virtually all are indexed under the bridegroom's name, but if he had a common name this may involve looking up perhaps fifty deeds over quite a short period in order to establish the existence of a settlement. Up to about 1810 the Index to Grantors simply contains the name of the first trustee in place of that of the grantee. If his name was the same as the bride's, then the deed is recognizable, but if not, there is no swift way of pinpointing the item. From about 1810 to about 1820 the Index to Grantors sometimes shows such a deed as ''Marr. Art.'', occasionally indicating the first trustee's name in the old manner. From about 1820 the Index is fairly consistent in marking these deeds as ''Marr. Art.'' Very few marriage settlements were registered after the 1840s.

Not all marriages were successful, and while divorce was difficult and expensive to obtain some unions reached such a pitch of disagreement that a separation was agreed upon. In such cases a deed was often executed appointing trustees to oversee maintenance payments to the wife. Rather like a marriage settlement, a deed of separation can be very instructive, as the following example bears out:

Deed Reference: 784 555 530890

Assignment dated 24 September 1823 made between (1) George Hillas of the city of Dublin Esq, youngest brother of Thomas Hillas of Seaview, Co. Sligo Esq and (2) Rebecca Hillas otherwise Mowbray of Dublin wife of the said Thomas Hillas and (3) James Hillas, John Cooke Rogers and Benjamin Swift, all of the city of Dublin, Esqs.

Reciting the settlement dated 19 October 1790 made prior to the marriage of the said Thomas Hillas with (2) the daughter of John Mowbray, the said Thomas Hillas being the eldest son of Robert Hillas late of Seaview, Co. Sligo.

Reciting that due to ''unhappy differences'' the said Thomas and Rebecca had agreed to live separate and apart, and that (1) had agreed to discharge all sums due to (2).

Where (1), on behalf of the said Thomas, granted to (2) an annuity of £130 payable out of the lands of Dunecloy, Co. Sligo, whereof (3) are to be the trustees.

Witnesses: John Barrett of the city of Dublin attorney and Thomas Tully of the same Esq.

Registration of Wills

During the 18th century a number of wills were registered, as if they had been deeds. Abstracts of these from 1708 to 1785 have been printed — *Abstracts of Wills at the Registry of Deeds,* edited by P. B. Eustace, 2 vols., Dublin, 1954, 1956. It should be noted that the abstracts do not contain the provisions of the wills although these are shown in the original memorials. The printed versions are therefore of strictly limited use.

Because of the tragic loss of wills in the Four Courts in 1922, this collection is, of course, of great value. It must, however, be constantly remembered that a will was only registered because it contained the makings of a good law suit. Registration of a will frequently carries with it the suspicion of disinheritance. The usual way of doing that was to omit all mention of the disinherited party. As a result registered wills should be viewed with caution. In particular, they should not be accepted as providing a full list of man's offspring since he is probably disinheriting (and not mentioning) a son or daughter with whom he has quarrelled. I recall one instance of an old lady who briskly — and silently — disinherited her eldest orphan grandson, a respectable linen draper with a socially acceptable wife and no visible crimes. But Granny didn't like him and he lost the estate, which — unfortunately for him — was hers in her own right to dispose of.

Wills are immediately identifiable in the Indexes, the words "His Will" or "Her Will" appearing in place of the name of a grantee. Very few wills were registered after 1785 and none after about 1810. The memorial of a will is generally written in the third person whereas the will itself would of course have been written in the first person:

Deed Reference: 565 243 377635
The last will and testament of Robert Pratt late of Killamullawn, Queen's County gent dated 13 April 1798 bequeathed to his sons Sergent, Robert and John Pratt the lands of Killamullawn and half of Eglish equally between them and if any of them die without issue then the other two to have his part in equal shares.
Witnesses: John Rudd and William Rudd both of Gragwalla and James Pratt of Killamullane.
Memorial witnesses: the said William Rudd and Henry Perry of Rathdowney, Queen's County, merchant.
William Rudd swore 14 July 1804.

Normally a will was not sworn and registered until after the death of the testator, and for this reason the date of swearing is important. I have, however, seen one strange case where a testator registered his will fourteen years before his eventual death! The usual practice was for the will to be registered shortly after the testator's death by the chief beneficiary — who had the most to lose if the will was contested.

Witnesses to Deeds
All registered deeds had to be witnessed by at least one person, usually by two and occasionally by more than two. As already mentioned, deeds

tended to be made "in the family" and witnesses too were apt to be relations, the chief exceptions being the use of the acting solicitor and/or his clerk, and the occasional use of servants. Even the solicitor could be a relation, for the Irish tended to give their abundant legal work to their relatives. Servants were apparently used when no more suitable candidate was to hand. Names, addresses and occupations of witnesses should therefore always be carefully noted, as their significance may suddenly emerge much later in the proceedings. Of course their significance may be instantly obvious, as in the following case:

> Deed Reference: 24 541 14658
> Lease dated 17 April 1713 whereby Hans Widman of Stroakestown, Co. Westmeath gent let to Thomas Batchelor of Stroakestown, carpenter, the Mill of Stroakestown and the lands adjoining, to Hold for the lives of the said Thomas Batchelor and of John Batchelor and of Ann Batchelor, son and daughter of the said Thomas Batchelor.
> Witnesses: Mary Widman mother of the said Hans Widman, and Jane Batchelor daughter of the said Thomas Batchelor.

It may be added that the use of *two* female witnesses is rare. Oddly, witnesses were not necessarily over the age of twenty one, but they were normally over sixteen, which was the usual age for a solicitor's clerk to begin his apprenticeship.

The term "gent" so widely used in the deeds covered a multitude of occupations, from farmer to merchant. An individual, particularly a witness to deeds, who resided in a town and persistently appears as "gent" may be suspected of being an attorney. By law, all Irish attornies were entitled to be termed gentlemen, and they made good use of this privilege. A few obligingly entered themselves as "gent attorney", clearly indicating their status. A "public notary" was a slightly superior brand of attorney, and was frequently used as a witness.

Women mentioned in Registered Deeds

Married women did not hold property and any assets that might be theirs by right of inheritance were automatically vested in their husbands. However, as a precaution, husbands were inclined to make their wives parties to any deeds that concerned either the wife's hereditary property or the lands on which her marriage settlement was charged. Such deeds often state the wife's maiden name. Any deed in which a wife appears falls into one or other of these categories.

Spinsters and widows, of course, regularly made deeds on their own account, many being made in conjunction with their brothers or sisters, sons or daughters, and therefore very helpful genealogically. By and large deeds to which females were party contain more family details than others. This is because they were so often involved in family settlements which can yield so much useful data. The point is well demonstrated by the following Hatton deed (which is indexed under the three Hatton women as well as under William Clifford and John Johnston).

Deed Reference: 330 662 220570

Release dated 5 June 1779 made between (1) William Clifford the elder of Castle Annesley Esq, acting executor of the will of the Rev. Robert Hatton late of Gorey, Co. Wexford deceased and (2) Margaret Hatton of Wexford spinster, William Clifford the younger of Wexford gent and Mary Clifford otherwise Hatton his wife and John Johnston of Wexford Doctor of Physick and Elizabeth Johnston otherwise Hatton his wife (which said Margaret, Mary and Elizabeth are the only children and co-heiresses of the said Rev. Robert Hatton) and (3) Anne Jackson of the city of Dublin, widow.

Whereby (1) and (2) in consideration of £400 sold to (3) the lands of Ballywoodick, Cloonevan and Baltivonny, Co. Wexford.

Witnesses: Arthur Meadows of Wexford Esq and Michael Vicary of same town gent.

Seals and Signatures on Deeds

As already explained, the only original signatures in the records of the Registry are those of the person who registered the memorial and his two memorial witnesses. The only original seal is that affixed by the individual who registered the memorial. Admittedly, these include a few fine armorial seals, but they belong mainly to the early years of the 18th century and thus to the top income bracket, whose arms are well known from other sources. The bulk of the seals used were fancy ones — a bird, a negroid head, a classical figure — with the occasional blank seal. In the late 18th century the blank seals became more and more favoured and by the 19th century were in universal use. In short, there is very little to be gained by a study of seals and signatures at the Registry of Deeds, although a surprising number of people delude themselves by imagining otherwise.

Deeds Providing for Illegitimate Children

In certain instances where a man, though married, had no legitimate offspring, he made his illegitimate children his heirs. This could be effected by will or by deed. Occasionally a wonderful deed will be found listing a string of children (probably by this stage young adults) and naming them as "my sons and daughters by Mary Molony my housekeeper". The purpose of such a deed was to settle property upon them. Deeds can also be found providing for the woman, sometimes so discreetly worded as to leave a doubt as to the actual relationship. Recognised illegitimate children took their father's surname as a matter of course: their mother retained her maiden surname.

Miscellaneous Points to be Noted

All parties to a deed had to be at least twenty-one years of age. A minor could only execute a deed through his guardian, and deeds will be found citing a minor acting by his guardian. This generally indicates that the minor is verging on his majority, as nobody would have bothered to involve a mere schoolboy, in which circumstances the guardian himself would no doubt have acted without involving his charge.

It is not generally feasible to trace the precise history of a specific plot or farm as it passed from hand to hand by lease, mortgage, sale, etc., because some of the relevant deeds are bound not to have been registered. The devolution of town property is particularly difficult to trace in this manner.

The spelling of place-names referred to in deeds is quite erratic, giving rise to some extraordinary transformations. The spelling of personal names is more reliable after allowance is made for some variations in surnames.

A number of deeds are wrongly indexed in that the volume or page number given in the Index Volumes is incorrect. This problem is particularly acute from about 1790 to 1810. The deed numbers, which are consecutive within each volume, tend to be accurate, so if the page number is wrong the required deed can be located by reference to its deed number within a given volume. If, however, the volume number is wrong then there is little one can do except perhaps try the volumes on either side of the alleged one. A mistake in the numbers given in the Index to Grantors is usually repeated in the Index to Lands. However, where the names but not the numbers can be read in the Index to Lands the required reference can be traced by recourse to the Index to Grantors. For example, the entry "Phillips to Snow" (number illegible) will suffice to make the deed identifiable in the Index to Grantors.

One final word of caution. Deeds as a source of genealogical information are unpredictable. They can provide a mine of information, and for no manifest reason they can provide very little. Families can make a host of deeds with no useful genealogical matter in them. Families may eschew deeds, even though their economic standing suggests they should have made use of them. In short, research at the Registry of Deeds should be undertaken in a spirit of speculation with the researcher equally prepared to savour the joy of discovery or taste disappointment of non-discovery.

CHAPTER 8

Wills and Administrations
A Prime Source for
Family Research

ROSEMARY FFOLLIOTT

EILEEN O'BYRNE

Wills, by their very nature, embodying as they do man's final instructions to his chosen ones, have always been among the most useful and reliable sources of genealogical information. In addition to the names of the testator, executor(s) and witnesses, wills normally give the names of spouse and children, and may also include those of parents, cousins and other relatives, either as beneficiaries or executors. Of further interest is the fact that until the early nineteenth century, witnesses to wills in Ireland were usually relations of the testator.

Perhaps unexpectedly, the wills richest in genealogy were often those made by women. Since they could not own property, married women did not make wills, but the will of a spinster or childless widow may mention numerous nephews, nieces and kinsfolk, thereby providing the basis for a substantial family tree. Wills also supply the address and occupation of the testator, give a good indication of economic status, and may well make useful mention of specific properties.

The date of a will and the date of probate combine to produce, in the first instance, a date when the testator was still alive, and secondly, a date by which he was most certainly dead. Up to the early nineteenth century the majority of wills were made shortly before the testator's death — generally within a year of decease. Many were proved within twelve months of the decease, although strange and unaccounted-for lapses of time could, and did, occur between death and probate, particularly where probate was in the Prerogative Court.

The provisions of a will can offer considerable insight into intimate family relationships. Exasperated parents have long attempted to impose sanctions on their offspring from beyond the grave. In his will dated 30th January 1476, Peter Higley of Dublin, "sound in mind though weak in body," left all his Dublin properties to his son Thomas Higley, "so long as my son Patrick Higley be not of good conduct and governance [but] if he be

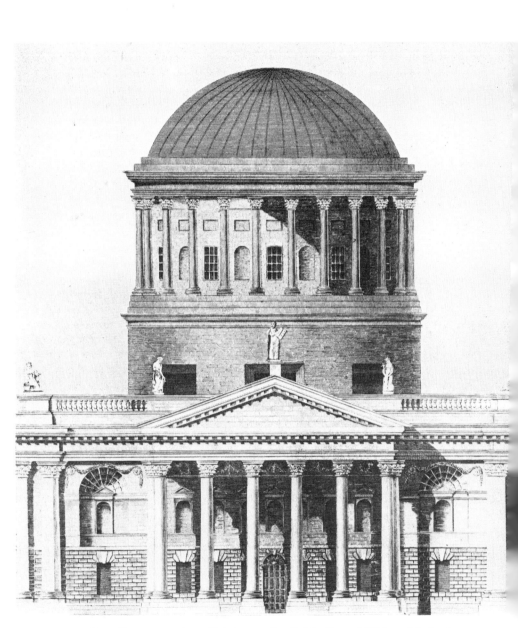

Four Courts complex which houses the Public Record Office of Ireland.

of good conduct then I will that the aforesaid lands etc. be distributed in equal division between them." Three centuries later, Walter Atkin of Ballinleaden alias Leadington, Co. Cork, in his will, dated 21st October 1741, cut off his "son Coningsby Atkin from all benefit under my will unless within one month after application he turn away, discharge and abandon a certain woman called Dorcas Roche otherwise Clarke."

In sharp contrast, one may find a will expressing great affection and tenderness, such as that of Emma Fleury who, in 1873, having disposed of all her personal treasures, wrote "And I now finish this my last will and testament by giving my earnest blessing to my darling and most beloved children telling them that they have indeed proved the greatest comfort and happiness of my troubled life and humbly praying a good and gracious God to bless, preserve and keep them as the apple of His Eye. I . . . also make it my most solemn and earnest entreaty that they dwell together in love, and that those who are comfortably off be ever ready to help their poorer brothers and sisters, and that with no niggardly hand."

Besides straightforward genealogy, there is a great deal of social history contained in wills; evidence of how people lived, how they managed their property, what objects they prized and on what sort of terms they stood with their family. Wills are thus of great value and importance from several points of view.

Testamentary Jurisdiction

From the time of the Norman invasion (1169) until the passing of the 1857 Probate Act (20 and 21 Vict. c. 79), testamentary jurisdiction in Ireland lay with the Church. As from the Reformation, this meant the Established Church of Ireland.

Each diocese had a Consistorial Court under the charge of the bishop, who might appoint a surrogate. It was this court that granted probate of the wills of the residents of the diocese as well as letters of administration on the estates of those who had died intestate. If, however, the deceased's property had a value of more than £5 in a second diocese, then his will had to be proved, or the administration granted, in the Prerogative Court. This was under the jurisdiction of the Archbishop of Armagh.

In 1858, the Probate Act mentioned above transferred testamentary jurisdiction to a new Court of Probate. A Principal Registry was set up in Dublin with eleven District Registries covering the remainder of the country. The wills previously filed by the Consistorial Courts were gradually deposited in the Public Record Office in accordance with the provisions of the Public Records (Ireland) Act, 1867, which required all documents of a public nature of twenty years of age and upwards to be transferred to a central location for safe keeping. There they were transcribed into Will Books and alphabetical indexes to testators were compiled.

Most tragically, this enormous collection of Irish wills — some dating from 1536 — was destroyed in the burning of the Four Courts in 1922. Since then, unremitting work has succeeded in collecting copies, abstracts and other substitutes to fill part of the enormous gap left by this irreparable loss.

It will be convenient to deal with the subject of Irish wills and administrations under the following principal headings:

1. **Testamentary Records before 1600**

2. **Prerogative Court Wills and Administrations**

3. **Consistorial Court Wills and Administrations**

4. **Testamentary Records after 1857**

5. **Will Abstracts and Copies of Wills**

1. Testamentary Records before 1600

Copies of only a few medieval or Tudor wills have survived, and these are mainly in the Library of Trinity College, Dublin, and in the Royal Irish Academy. One series from the former, edited by H. F. Berry, was published in 1898 as *Register of Wills and Inventories of the Diocese of Dublin, 1457-1483*. The documents are given in the original Latin, accompanied by an English translation, and provide revealing insight into the lives of those fifteenth-century gentry, merchants and farmers, who made ample provision for their funeral expenses and for the clergy, as well as for their next of kin. John Chever of Dublin even left £16 13s. 4d. "for a thousand Masses to be celebrated for my soul."

Unpublished early wills at T.C.D. include those of Robert de Moenes (1326), Gilian de Meonis (1348), Richard Stanyhurst (1501) and Alderman Robert Goldynge (1562), all in Ms. 1207.

The Royal Irish Academy has transcripts of the wills of three early citizens of Limerick — Richard Bultingford (1405), Geffry Galwey (1445) and John Stretch (1590), included in T. Westropp's manuscript volume "Notes on Clare" (ref. 3A 40, pp. 36-72).

The 55th *Report of the Deputy Keeper of the Public Records in Ireland* lists several other sources of early wills, such as the *Calendar of Christ Church Deeds* (printed in the 20th, 23rd and 24th *Reports of the Deputy Keeper*), John Gilbert's *Chartularies of St Mary's Abbey, Dublin* (1884), and his nineteen-volume *Calendar of Ancient Records of Dublin* (1889-1944). The *Reports of the Record Commissioners* (1810-1827) include abstracts of wills recited in Inquisitions post Mortem from the time of Henry VIII to that of Charles II. The Public Record Office also has an index to deeds and wills in Inquisitions.

An Index to about 550 Cloyne Wills from 1547 to 1628 was printed in the *Journal of the Cork Historical and Archaeological Society* in 1895 and reprinted in Albert Casey's *O'Keif, Coshe Mang etc.*, Vol. 8, 1965. Extracts from 21 of these wills were printed in the *Gentleman's Magazine* in 1861. In 1944 the same Journal printed the 1583 will of Garrett FitzRedmond Rochford. The 1580 will of Nicholas Ley was printed in the *Journal of the Waterford and South-East of Ireland Archaeological Society* in 1906.

Other printed sources for early wills include the six-volume *Calendar of Ormond Deeds, 1172-1603*, edited by Edmund Curtis, James Hardiman's edition of Roderick O'Flaherty's *Chorographical Description of West or H-iar Connaught* (1846), and John Begley's *History of the Diocese of Limerick* (1938). Richard Caulfield's *Council Book of the Corporation of Cork* (1876) includes a small collection of Tudor inventories of some of the city merchants.

There are a few fifteenth-century Irish wills in the Prerogative Court of Canterbury, and it has been estimated that this source has at least 40 wills prior to 1600 which show links with Ireland.

2. Prerogative Court Wills and Administrations

The Prerogative Court of the Archbishop of Armagh was the supreme court in all matters ecclesiastical in Ireland, though subordinate to the Prerogative Court of Canterbury. Originally the right of appointing its Judge or Commissary was vested in the Crown but in 1622 the Archbishop and his episcopal successors were appointed Judges and in 1644 they were empowered to appoint a Commissary instead of being obliged, as previously, to act in person.

Until 1816 the Court was held in the private residence of the judge, or sometimes in the Chapter Room of St Patrick's Cathedral in Dublin. The result of this mobility was that the records were not lodged in any one secure place, no permanent building being provided — and doubtless a good number of documents were mislaid over the years. In 1816 the Court was firmly established in Henrietta Street in Dublin, and the wills and other papers were then stored there until their final transfer to the Public Record Office in the second half of the nineteenth century.

Sir William Betham, 1779-1853.

Prerogative Wills

As already mentioned, a will qualified for the Prerogative Court if the testator left property worth over £5 in a second diocese. Prerogative wills, therefore, largely belong to (a) the wealthiest section of the population, (b) the merchant classes, whose unsold stock-in-trade was apt to extend beyond their own diocese, and (c) those persons who happened to live close to a diocesan border. This last nicety is often not clearly understood, but it accounts for the appearance in the records of the Prerogative Court of many persons whose means would not seem to warrant it. For example, while a highly prosperous landed gentleman, resident in the centre of Cork diocese — say, near Bandon or Kinsale — might very easily have no call for a Prerogative will, a relatively small farmer living near Youghal (on the border between the dioceses of Cloyne and Waterford) could very easily require one.

Until 1810 there was no guiding index to the Prerogative wills. In that year Sir William Betham, Ulster King of Arms, on behalf of the Record Commissioners, superintended the construction of an alphabetical index to testators. He also wrote out, in his own fine hand, brief genealogical abstracts of almost all those wills that pre-dated 1800, and later constructed sketch pedigrees from his notes.

The Prerogative Court was abolished by the Probate Act of 1857. The wills and other papers were moved to the Public Record Office, where the Prerogative wills were transcribed into Will Books. The Books were indexed in two series, the first ending at 1810 and the second covering the remainder of the period, 1811-1857. In 1897, Sir Arthur Vicars, Ulster King of Arms, edited a printed version of the first Index, 1536-1810. Arranged alphabetically, by surname and christian name, it shows the testator's address and occupation with the year of probate.

The destruction of the Public Rcord Office in 1922 resulted in the loss of all the original Prerogative wills and most of the Will Books into which they had been transcribed. The surviving volumes are the Will Books for 1664-84, 1706-8 (A-W), 1726-8 (A-W), 1728-9 (A-W), 1777 (A-L), 1813 (K-Z) and 1834 (A-E). The wills contained in these volumes are included in the P.R.O. Card Index to Testamentary Records. The manuscript index volumes also survived.

The loss of the Prerogative wills emphasised the importance of Betham's labours, and his original notebooks, containing the abstracts, were purchased by the Public Record Office. His volumes of Sketch Pedigrees constructed from these abstracts — with a few excusable misinterpretations — are in the Genealogical Office. There is another, but later, copy of the latter in the Public Record Office of Northern Ireland which, however, lacks the notes and marginal additions of the Genealogical Office set.

Betham's Prerogative will abstracts, although numerous (they amount to about 37,500) are brief. Most of them give the dates of will and of probate as well as the relations mentioned in the original will. The executors are only specified as such if they are relations, otherwise they are not mentioned. References to "friends" are habitually ignored. There is virtually no mention at all of property. The address of the testator is given but not the addresses of relatives or witnesses. The following is a typical Betham abstract:

> "William Walker of the city of Dublin, tanner, dat. 3 April 1740, pd 11 Nov. 1740 — wife Isabella — daus Anne and Allice — dau-in-law Mary Walker widow of son Thomas deceased — sons George and William."

It will, therefore, be apparent that while the Betham Collection is invaluable, nonetheless if another abstract of the required will can be traced elsewhere, it is likely to produce a lot more details. Fortunately, many of the various accumulations of will abstracts include numerous items from the Prerogative Court, giving copious information. In this connection, too, it is well to recall that in cases where the testator had property in England as well as in Ireland, the will itself was proved in the Prerogative Court of Canterbury and a *copy* only proved in Ireland.

The records of the Prerogative Court of Canterbury are now in the Public Record Office, Chancery Lane, London W.C.2. They include many wills with Irish connections, particularly during the seventeenth century when there were close trading links between the two countries. Moreover, many persons who had lately settled in Ireland still retained possessions in England. It is sometimes possible to discover from the Index entry in Ireland that a particular will was also proved in Canterbury. For example, in the entry "James Higgens, Ballykelly, Co. Londonderry, gent, 1635 (Copy)," the word "Copy" shows that the original was proved in England and only the copy in the Prerogative Court of Armagh: in the P.C.C. Index, Mr Higgens's will appears as 48 Sadler. Sometimes a double address in the Irish Index will provide the clue, as here: "Roger Dalton, sometime Kyrkbynnsperton, Yorkshire, now of Knockmoon, Co. Waterford, esq, 1603." His will was proved in the P.C.C. in 1597 and appears with the reference 25 Cobham. In other instances, however, the Irish Index gives no guidance at all, as in this case: "Sir Thomas Armstrong, knt., Dublin, 1662." Nevertheless, that will is to be found in the P.C.C. as 28 Bence. The fact is that the P.C.C. has a lot of Irish wills and, additionally, many more showing a connection with Ireland. Many of these are not recorded in any Irish Index to Wills, Prerogative or Consistorial — presumably having been mislaid before the general calling in of testamentary records under the Public Records (Ireland) Act of 1867.

Prerogative Administrations

On the death of an intestate person, the same conditions applied to the granting of Letters of Administration as to the proving of a will in respect of the jurisdiction of the Prerogative Court. Administration was normally granted to the widow or next of kin or to the principal creditor, and the grant often mentioned the names of the minor offspring of the deceased.

The original grants were all lost in 1922 as well as most of the Grant Books into which they had been transcribed. The Grant Books for 1684-88, 1748-51 and 1839 survived, as well as the Prerogative Day Books of 1784-88.

The ever-industrious Betham had, however, made abstracts of the approximately 5,000 grants before 1802. The notebooks into which he wrote his abstracts in an inconvenient arrangement that grouped the entries chronologically under each initial letter every few years are at the P.R.O. The Genealogical Office has a copy much more conveniently arranged in alphabetical order of surnames. The abstracts give the name, address and occupation of the deceased, the date of grant and to whom the grant was made. If the original administrator did not complete winding up the estate in his own lifetime, a second, and even a third, grant to another administrator might be required, and there are many confusing instances of this.

A Betham abstract of a Prerogative Grant of Administration will take somewhat the following form:

"Humphry Worthington, Dublin, timber merchant — 23 April 1790 — Joseph, Mary and Jane (minors) the children, Mary the widow."

The same regulations applied to Grants of Administration in the P.C.C. as to the probate of wills, and a considerable number of Irish Administrations can be traced in this source. These apart, there are very few abstracts of Prerogative Grants extant, other than Betham's pre-1802 collection, and the Irish Administration Registers of 1828-39 which include the entries from the Prerogative Court.

3. Consistorial Court Wills and Administrations

The testamentary affairs of persons who died leaving property in only one diocese were dealt with by the Consistorial Court of that diocese. In cases where two dioceses were united under a single bishop (e.g. Limerick and Ardfert or Leighlin and Ferns), property in both would not qualify the estate for the Prerogative Court. The matter would be dealt with by whichever diocese the deceased had lived in, even though the testamentary records of the two dioceses were administered separately.

After the abolition of the testamentary jurisdiction of the Consistorial Courts in 1857, the records held by these Courts were gradually deposited in the Public Record Office, transcribed into Will and Grant Books, and indexed. What the P.R.O. was able to collect depended to a marked degree on the care exercised over the centuries by the individual Consistorial Courts. None produced all the wills and administrations that had passed through their hands. Few produced much from the seventeenth century (Dublin, Cork, Cloyne, Cashel, Ossory and Limerick being among the best). Many produced a quantity so meagre as to be almost unbelievable (Glendalough, Ardfert, Killala, Leighlin and Meath being particularly sparse) while the general run of dioceses showed a notable scarcity of items that pre-dated 1780. It must, therefore, be constantly borne in mind that, despite the coverage dates shown on the volumes, the Indexes to Wills and to Administrations represent simply the documents delivered up to the P.R.O. authorities in the second half of the nineteenth century, and cannot be regarded as a complete list of the estates dealt with by the various Consistorial Courts.

The scale of the loss can be gauged in various ways, apart from such Indexes which are so small as to be nugatory. One is the substantial number of Irish wills in the P.C.C. for which no probate is recorded in Ireland. It is quite evident that these were by no means exclusively Prerogative wills. For instance, the P.C.C. probate of Christopher Alderman of Waterford, clothier, in 1666, mentions that the will was "first proved in Munster Court in 1654," whereas it is not given in the Indexes to either the Waterford or Prerogative Courts. More evidence of the loss of testamentary records appears at the Registry of Deeds, where a deed may mention an eighteenth-century will or administration as proof of title to property, even citing the precise year of probate or grant — and yet that item may not be in any Irish Will or Administration Index. Cork provides even more disturbing evidence. In 1895-6 the *Journal of the Cork Historical and Archaeological Society* printed a list of the original wills formerly in the Cork Registry. These are arranged chronologically under each initial letter and a random check suggests that perhaps as many as one-tenth of the entries are not in the P.R.O. Index to Cork and Ross Wills.

Consistorial Wills

With a single exception, all the original wills from the Consistorial Courts (like those of the Prerogative Court) were burned in 1922. Most of the Will

Books into which the wills had been transcribed were also lost. The surviving volumes are Connor (1818-20 and 1853-58) and Down (1850-58).

The series of Indexes to the Consistorial Wills likewise escaped destruction, though several volumes were severely damaged. Fortunately, some had already been printed. In 1895 and 1899 the Consistorial records of the united Dioceses of Dublin and Glendalough were printed in the appendices to the 26th and 30th *Reports of the Deputy Keeper of the Public Records in Ireland*. In 1905 the *Journal of the Kildare Archaeological Society* printed the Index to Kildare Wills. Between 1909 and 1920 Messrs. Phillimore of London printed five slim volumes of Consistorial Will Indexes, covering thirteen dioceses but regrettably repeating Kildare to 1800. Nine of their indexes stopped at 1800 instead of continuing to 1857. In two cases (Killaloe and Leighlin) the original Ms. Index was so badly mutilated in 1922 that the unprinted fifty-seven years were virtually lost. Since 1922 the Indexes to Wills from three further Dioceses (Ardagh, Clonfert and Kilmore) have been printed, and those from Cork, Cloyne and Ardfert have been reprinted complete to 1857. The remainder exist only in manuscript form in the search-room at the P.R.O. in Dublin with a few Betham copies in the Public Record Office of Northern Ireland.

The Indexes are arranged alphabetically by surname and christian name and give the testator's address (sometimes parish instead of townland), maybe occupation, and the year in which probate was granted.

List of Indexes to Consistorial Wills

Ardagh 1695-1858 (printed by *The Irish Ancestor,* 1971).

Ardfert and Aghadoe 1690-1858 (printed to 1800 by Phillimore and to 1858 by Albert Casey in *O'Keif, Coshe Mang, etc.,* Vol. 5, 1962).

Armagh 1666-1837 (A-L) and 1677-1858 (M-Y), together with the District of Drogheda 1691-1846.

Cashel and Emly 1618-1858 (printed to 1800 by Phillimore).

Clogher 1661-1858.

Clonfert 1663-1857 (printed in *The Irish Ancestor,* 1970, and from the Betham version in the PRONI as "Clonfert and Kilmacduagh" by P. Smythe-Wood, 1977).

Cloyne 1621-1858 (printed to 1800 by Phillimore, and reprinted to 1858 by Albert Casey in *O'Keif, Coshe Mang etc.,* Vol. 8, 1965. Cloyne Wills 1547-1628 were printed in the JCHAS 1895, and reprinted in *O'Keif,* Vol. 8).

Connor 1680-1856 (A-L) and 1636-1857 (M-Y). The PRO also has a second volume of combined wills and administrations 1810-58, which shows full date of probate and to whom it was granted).

Cork and Ross 1548-1858 (printed to 1800 by Phillimore and reprinted by Albert Casey in *O'Keif, Coshe Mang, etc.,* Vol. 8, 1965. A list of wills 1548-1833 formerly in the Cork Registry was printed in JCHAS 1895-8: arranged chronologically under each initial letter, it frequently gives occupation which can be omitted from the PRO version and sometimes gives a more detailed address (e.g. a street in Cork city), besides having about one-tenth more entries than the PRO version).

Derry 1612-1858 (printed to 1858 by Phillimore).

Down 1646-1858.

Dromore 1678-1858 with the Peculiar of Newry and Mourne 1727-1858 (both printed to 1858 by Phillimore).

Dublin and Glendalough 1536-1858 (printed in the appendices to 26th and 30th **Reports DKPRI, 1895 and 1899).**

Elphin 1650-1858 (badly mutilated).

Ferns 1601-1858 (badly mutilated). (Printed to 1800 by Phillimore. The PRO has a copy 1603-1838 for F-V, with unproved wills 1616-1842 for W only, ref. 1A 4 16).

Kildare 1661-1858 (printed to 1858 in the *Journal of the Kildare Archaeological Society,* 1905, and reprinted to 1800 by Phillimore).

Killala and Achonry 1756-1831.

Killaloe and Kilfenora 1653-1858 (fragments only surviving). (Printed to 1800 by Phillimore).

Kilmore 1682-1858 (mutilated). (Printed to 1858 by P. Smythe-Wood, 1975 from Betham transcript in PRONI).

Leighlin 1642-1858 (fragments). (Printed to 1800 by Phillimore).

Limerick 1615-1858 (printed to 1800 by Phillimore).

Meath 1572-1858 (fragments). (A transcript 1635-1838 in the PRO gives name of testator and year of probate but no address: ref. 1A 42 167).

Ossory 1536-1858 (printed to 1800 by Phillimore. The PRO has a second volume which gives full dates of will and of probate and to whom probate was granted).

Raphoe 1684-1858 (printed to 1858 by Phillimore).

Tuam 1648-1858.

Waterford and Lismore 1648-1858 (printed to 1800 by Phillimore).

Consistorial Administration Bonds

The same circumstances governed the collection, transcription and indexing of the Consistorial Grants of Administrations Intestate as the wills. Here the documents actually indexed were Bonds, since the administrator was required to enter into a bond for a specified sum of money as security that he would duly administer the estate of the intestate person: the administrator was normally either the next of kin or principal creditor. The original bonds were destroyed in 1922 as were the books into which they had been transcribed, with the exception of the Grant Books for Cashel (1840-45), Derry and Raphoe (1812-21, but badly damaged) and Ossory (1848-58).

The Indexes to the Administration Bonds survived, but unlike the Indexes to Wills are not arranged in alphabetical order, but in chronological order under the initial letter of the surname of the deceased. They give only the surname and christian name of the deceased, with address, possibly occupation, and the year in which the bond was made.

List of Indexes to Consistorial Administration Bonds

Ardagh 1697-1850.

Ardfert 1782-1858 (printed by Albert Casey in *O'Keif, Coshe Mang etc.*, Vol. 5, 1962).

Cashel and Emly 1644-1858.

Clogher 1660-1858.

Clonfert 1771-1857 (printed by *The Irish Ancestor,* 1970).

Cloyne 1630-1857 (printed by Albert Casey in *O'Keif, Coshe Mang etc.*, Vol. 6, **1963**).

Connor 1636-1858 (the Index to Connor Wills 1810-58 also includes the administrations and shows full date of grant and to whom granted).

Cork and Ross 1612-1858 (printed by Albert Casey in *O'Keif, Coshe Mang etc.*, Vol. 6, 1963).

Derry 1698-1857.

Down 1635-1858.

Dromore 1742-1858, with the Peculiar of Newry and Mourne, 1811-45 (latter printed in *The Irish Ancestor,* 1969).

Dublin and Glendalough 1638-1858 (printed in the appendices to 26th and 30th **Reports DKPRI, 1895 and 1899**).

Elphin 1726-1857.

Ferns 1765-1833.

Kildare 1770-1848 (printed to 1858 in *Journal of the Kildare Archaeological Society,* 1907).

Killala and Achonry 1779-1858 (printed in *The Irish Ancestor,* 1975).

Killaloe 1704-1857.

Kilmore 1728-1857.

Leighlin 1694-1845 (printed by The Irish Ancestor, 1972).

Limerick 1789-1858.

Meath 1663-1857.

Ossory 1660-1857.

Raphoe 1684-1858.

Tuam 1692-1857.

Waterford and Lismore 1661-1857 with the Peculiar of Lismore 1766-1846.

4.   Testamentary Records after 1857

The 1857 Probate Act, which abolished the jurisdiction of the ecclesiastical courts, set up a Principal Registry in Dublin and eleven District Registries. These local Registries retained transcripts of the wills they proved and of the administrations intestate that they granted. Unfortunately, the transcripts of the Principal Registry (which, in addition to acting as successor to the old Prerogative Court, also covered a wide area around Dublin) were stored in the Four Courts and so were lost in 1922, along with the original wills from the District Registries. The transcript Will Books from the District Registries have since been moved to the P.R.O. and to the Public Record Office of Northern Ireland, the latter holding the books from the Registries of Armagh, Belfast and Londonderry.

The surviving Will Books in the P.R.O. are as follows:

Principal Registry:	1874 (G-M)
	1878 (A-Z)
	1891 (G-M)
	1896 (A-F)
Dublin District of	
Principal Registry:	1869 (G-M)
	1891 (M-P)
	1901 (A-F)
District Registries:	Ballina 1859 to date (with gaps 1900-13 and 1919-23)
	Cavan 1858-1909
	Cork 1858-1911

Kilkenny 1858-1911
Limerick 1858-1899
Mullingar 1858-1901
Tuam 1858-1929
Waterford 1858-1902

The P.R.O. also has the Principal Registry Grant Books for 1878, 1883, 1891 and 1893. Some of the Series of Papers leading to Grants of Administration for the post-1857 period were saved and are listed in the *55th Report DKPRI*. Other papers transferred to the P.R.O. after 1922 cover the years 1904-6 for the Principal Registry, and the years 1900-6 for Ballina, Cork, Kilkenny, Limerick, Mullingar and Tuam, and 1901-6 for Cavan and Waterford.

A new system of arrangement was devised as from 1858, with printed, alphabetically-arranged, yearly Calendars to Wills and Administrations: these are kept in the search-room at the P.R.O. There is also a Consolidated Index for 1858-77 which saves examining the Calendar for each of those years in turn. The Calendar entries are very much more informative than the old Indexes to Wills. In addition to the name, address and occupation of the deceased, they also give the place and exact date of death, together with the name(s) and address(es) of the person(s) to whom probate or administration was granted, and frequently their relationship to the deceased, as well as the exact date of probate and the value of the estate. A vast amount of useful genealogical information may be gleaned from the Calendars alone, and they are often the easiest means of obtaining a date of death. The wording is on the following lines:

> "3 June 1869. Administration of the personal estate of William Tatlow, late of 83 Harcourt Street, Dublin, solicitor, who died 26 April 1869 at the same place, was granted at the Principal Registry to John Garnett Tatlow of Crosdoney, Co. Cavan Esq, the son and one of the next of kin. Effects sworn under £4,000."

5.   Will Abstracts and Copies of Wills

With such a devastating loss of original wills and Will Books, intensive efforts have been made since 1922 to accumulate substitutes in one form or another. The P.R.O. in particular has been successful in building up a truly excellent and ever-growing collection from such sources as solicitors, genealogists and private individuals. The content of the substitutes varies widely. It may be a *verbatim* transcript of a will, or a full copy merely shorn of all legal verbiage, or it may be an abstract giving all names and the main provisions, or it may be a stark, Betham-type note. There is no means of telling until the item itself is inspected.

Since 1922 many other repositories have paid particular attention to the will abstracts in their charge, and many researchers who worked at the P.R.O. prior to the burning have donated the abstracts in their possession to various Irish repositories. A number of abstracts have been printed in diverse sources. The result of all this is that the will substitutes are now widely scattered, some even in England. It may therefore be helpful to provide a general guide as to what is available where.

The Public Record Office

The testamentary collection at present held by the P.R.O. is by far the largest of its kind in Ireland. Its T. Series alone currently numbers more than 20,500 items, and this Series contains only a portion of the testamentary records. The general testamentary collection (including the T. Series) is covered by an alphabetical Card Index to Testamentary Records in the search room. This Card Index includes the wills in the few surviving pre-1858 Will Books (but *not* those from the post-1857 District Registries); copious deposits from solicitors' offices and such like; the large selection of detailed abstracts made by Miss Thrift; the Greene Collection (which gives an abstract of almost every Irish Green(e) will). It does not, however, cover any of the Betham material. This card index is continually being added to as new testamentary documents arrive.

There are three other card indexes in the search room that deal with wills:

(1) the index to Dr. Crossle's collection of abstracts, — a large, miscellaneous accumulation of very detailed abstracts, chiefly from the seventeenth and eighteenth centuries, and with a good deal of material from the north-west of Ireland.

(2) the index to the Jennings Collection, which includes most Waterford wills and administrations. Most of these have also been printed and details are given under Printed Sources.

(3) the index to Charitable Donations and Bequests: this supplies information on monies bequeathed for charitable purposes, but mentions only the testator, executor and date of probate, omitting other provisions of the will.

From the Commissioners of Inland Revenue in London, the P.R.O. obtained a series of yearly Indexes to Irish Will Registers, 1828-79, which show the name and address of the testator and the name and address of the executor. They also obtained the actual Irish Will Registers for the years

1828-39, the volume for the first half of 1834 being missing. This series encompasses all Courts (and indeed has items not listed in the Index to any Court). The Registers give not only the exact dates of will and probate but also the exact date of the testator's decease. They also give the name and address of the executor and — in most cases — the main legacies and names of beneficiaries, with an outline inventory showing how the value of the estate was arrived at. In effect, it means that some information can be had on most wills made in Ireland between 1828 and 1839. Sometimes the Registers can produce a really good abstract, like the following:

"James Boswell of Bachelor's Walk, city of Dublin, gent, who died 22 April 1837 — will dated 2 April 1836 — executor James Boswell of No. 27 Bachelor's Walk Esq — proved Prerogative Court 27 July 1837. Sworn under £6,923. Interest in dwelling houses in Townsend Street, Dublin, to wife for life and after her death as she shall by her will appoint between any two of testator's children. £100 to John Boswell son absolutely. Interest in a house in Stephen's Green to William Boswell son for life, with remainder to son James. Annuity of £70 to William Boswell son for 3 years. £1,000 to Joseph Boswell son. £500 each to Jane, Martha, Rebecca and Anna Boswell, daughters, at 24 or marriage. £100 and interest in premises in Fairview to son James for the benefit of John Boswell brother, and after his death to son James Boswell for life. Residue (except household effects at Bachelor's Walk bequeathed to wife) to James Boswell son."

In the same series there are yearly Indexes to Irish Administration Registers for 1828-79, which show the names and addresses of both the deceased and the administrator. The actual Irish Administration Registers for 1828-39 naturally give far fewer particulars than appear for wills, but they, too, include date of death. They generally take the following form:

"25 March 1829. Ardfert. Denny Hoare who died 10 March 1828 — administratrix Alice Hoare, Caherciveen, widow. Sworn under £300. Inventory: Household Goods £30, Securities £10, Stock £201-10-10. Total £251-10-10."

A section of the Betham Collection includes abstracts from almost all Kildare Wills from 1661, the testators' names A-K ending in 1826 and those K-S ending in 1824 (ref. 1A 44 22).

A typescript of T. U. Sadleir's has abstracts from the Ossory Administrations 1738-1804 (ref. 1A 37 33): at present this is *not* covered by the Card Index to Testamentary Records. There are also some wills in the Quit Rent Office Papers.

The P.R.O. has so enlarged its testamentary collection in recent years that old printed lists should be treated with extreme caution as they cannot be regarded as representing the current holdings of the Office.

The Genealogical Office

The Genealogical Office is particularly rich in abstracts from pre-1800 wills, with many from the Courts of Cork and Cloyne and the Prerogative Court. The main collection of abstracts is covered by a manuscript index (G.O. 429), which was printed in 1949 in *Analecta Hibernica,* No. 17. It then contained over 7,000 items but has since been added to. It covers, amongst others, the sizeable collections made by Fisher, Irwin, Sadleir, Swanzy and Welply, but it does *not* by any means include all the abstracts in the Office. Numerous testamentary items are scattered through other manuscript volumes, as, for example, that entitled "Gordons in Ireland" (G.O. 702) which contains abstracts of most Irish Gordon wills; or that styled "Aldworth Wills" (G.O. 535) which has abstracts of 103 Prerogative and Diocesan wills; or the series called "Pogue" (G.O. 695-7) containing a selection of wills from southern Ulster; or the two volumes of "Hill" (G.O. 691-2) with a set of abstracts relating to that surname. The Walsh Kelly notebooks (G.O. 683-6) also include will abstracts, mainly from Ossory. A small illegible volume (G.O. 707) contains numerous abstracts from the Courts of Tuam, Clonfert and Kilmacduagh. Outside the items listed in G.O. 429, and the series of Betham's Sketch Pedigrees from Prerogative Wills and his Abstracts from Prerogative Administrations, the lack of comprehensive indexing makes the task of tracing all available abstracts at the Genealogical Office a difficult one.

The Registry of Deeds

From its foundation in 1708 the Registry accepted wills as well as deeds. Nearly 1,500 wills were registered up to 1785 and two volumes of abstracts of these, edited by P. Beryl Eustace, were published by the Irish Manuscripts Commission in 1954-6. They have excellent indexes to testators, beneficiaries and witnesses as well as to the abundant place-names, but it should be noted that the provisions of the wills are not given although these are shown in the original memorials. A third, post-1785 volume is now in preparation.

From the genealogist's point of view, registered wills should be regarded with caution since a will was usually registered because the chief beneficiary considered it a potential source of legal dispute, generally due to the testator having excluded somebody from its provisions. One should not, therefore, accept such a will as necessarily supplying, for instance, a complete list of

351

Thomas Nolan of Dublin Maltster will dat 4 March 1695-6 — William Nolan of Dublin maltster will dat 28 Sep 1697 — Anne — Mary

Thomas Newton of Drogheda ald[r] will pr about 1698 — Christian — William Newton of Drogheda ald. — Elizabeth — John Graham ald[r] br. to T. N. — Edward Singleton br. to T. N.

William — Elizabeth — Mary — Christian

Edward Naylor of Kilcarhan in co. Clare gent will dat 4 April 1698 — Walter Naylor — James Naylor of Ennis gent father in law to E. N

Henry Nelthorpe of Dublin jeweller will dat 22 June 1696 pr 7 June 1697 — Dorothy — Thomas Bolton of Dublin gold smith

Edward Nelthorpe

Tabular abstracts of Prerogative Wills.
Betham Collection at the Genealogical Office.

175

the testator's offspring, since mention of a disinherited child may well have been avoided.

Registration of wills declined sharply after 1785, and ceased entirely in the early nineteenth century.

The National Library

As there is no separate index to wills at the National Library it is impossible to estimate how many are there, but the number is large. Among the more important collections are Canon Leslie's abstracts from 981 wills (Ms. 1774); a batch of 166 Waterford wills and administrations (D.9248-9413); a typed volume containing about 100 abstracts of almost all eighteenth-century Dawson wills (Mss. 5644-5); 86 wills in the Townley Hall Papers (D.15093-15178); a collection of wills from Co. Sligo, 1705-32 (Ms. 2164); Domville and other wills (Mss. 9384-6 and 11869); some eighteenth-century Huguenot wills (D.6156-6596); Lane-Poole papers with will abstracts from Cos. Wicklow and Dublin (Ms. 5359). There are many others and the manuscript indexes at the Library should be consulted.

Two useful private collections are available on microfilm, namely, the O'Loghlen wills from Co. Clare (P.2543) and the Wilson Collection with abstracts of 195 Prerogative and 135 Consistorial wills (P. 1990). Also available on microfilm (P. 903) is the Carrigan Collection, q.v.

The National Library has a card index to 10,500 wills contained in the records of the Irish Land Commission, a hitherto untapped source. The Commission's documents stem from the Land Purchase Acts of 1881-1909, and many copies of wills — mostly nineteenth-century but some from as early as the seventeenth century — were lodged as evidence of title. The card index gives the following type of information:

"NUGENT Patrick John, of Portaferry, Co. Down. Administration with Will annexed, 1857. Prerog. (Plain Copy). Irish Land Commission Record No. E.C. 2448. Box No. 3611."

"NUTLEY Richard, of The Middle Temple, London, and Dublin City. Will and Grant 1729. Prerog. (Plain copy). Irish Land Commission Record No. E.C. 8325. Box No. 4448.

The Commission's material is at present housed in its archive at 24, Upper Merrion Street, Dublin.

The Royal Irish Academy

Since the Library of the Royal Irish Academy does not list its will abstracts individually, it is hard to assess the total number scattered through their records, but it seems unlikely that the number exceeds 200.

As already mentioned, there are several early wills and at least one seventeenth-century will in Irish. Other abstracts are contained mainly in three sources, viz. (1) The Upton Papers, with emphasis on items from Cos. Westmeath, Cavan and Longford; (2) The MacSwiney Papers, which deal mostly with Cos. Cork and Kerry; (3) T. Westropp's Ms. volumes entitled "Notes on Clare." The volume referenced 3A 39 has over 100 abstracts of wills and administrations from Cos. Clare and Limerick, which are indexed at the end of the book. The volume referenced 3A 40 has 14 transcripts of wills of pre-eighteenth-century Limerick citizens.

The Academy also has a copy of the 1733 will of Rebecca Dingley, friend of Jonathan Swift's Stella (23 N 37).

It should be noted that the list entitled "Westmeath Wills" in the Upton Papers, No. 4, was extracted from the Index to Prerogative Wills, and is not taken from the now missing Index to Meath Wills.

The Representative Church Body Library

This Library has a most valuable collection of will abstracts made by W. H. Welply, consisting of 1,500 wills and 100 administrations, contained in four volumes: in only very rare instances do these duplicate the other Welply abstracts at the Genealogical Office. The Munster items *only* from this collection were printed by Albert Casey in *O'Keif, Coshe Mang etc.,* Vol. 14 (1968).

Other testamentary items include a duplicate typescript of the Swanzy will abstracts (belonging mainly to Clogher and Kilmore) and a typescript containing abstracts of miscellaneous eighteenth-century Prerogative wills made by the Protestant clergy and their families.

The Library of Trinity College, Dublin

Apart from the medieval wills already mentioned, the Library possesses the Stewart-Kennedy Notebooks which contain about 500 will abstracts, ranging in date from the early seventeenth century to the late nineteenth century. Many are wills proved in the Consistorial Courts of Down and Connor, involving about 230 testators and mainly relating to the families of Stewart, Clarke, Cunningham, Kennedy and Wade. The abstracts are, however, apt to omit whether the dates shown are those of will or of probate.

The Society of Friends' Library, Dublin

The Library has a small but choice collection of Quaker wills, many of them from Dublin and east Leinster. A total of 284 items from the seventeenth and eighteenth centuries were printed in *Abstracts of Wills,* edited by P. Beryl Eustace and Olive C. Goodbody (1957), and an additional 50 were included in *Guide to Irish Quaker Records,* by Olive C. Goodbody (1967), both published by the Irish Manuscripts Commission. Short abstracts of a further 28 wills from Co. Armagh, the property of the Lisburn Meeting, were printed in *The Irish Genealogist,* 1950.

Many of these wills do not appear in the Index to any Court of Probate and were probably never proved, though honoured by the Quaker community as if they had been.

The Carrigan Collection

When William Canon Carrigan was preparing his *History and Antiquities of the Diocese of Ossory* (1905), he made copious notes, the originals of which are now in St Kieran's College, Kilkenny. The National Library has a microfilm copy (P. 903). The will abstracts in this collection are almost exclusively from the seventeenth and eighteenth centuries and stem mainly from the Prerogative Court and the Courts of Ossory and Leighlin. Additionally, there are stray testamentary items from many other dioceses, even as far away as Raphoe. The Episcopal wills in the collection were printed in *Archivium Hibernicum,* Vols. 1-4, and other abstracts were included in the Canon's own book, and in the Rev. Hilary Walsh's *Borris-in-Ossory, An Irish Parish and its People* (1969).

An index to the 952 wills in the Carrigan Mss. was printed in *The Irish Genealogist,* 1970, showing dates of will and of probate, court of probate, approximate length of the abstract and the reference numbers of volume and page.

The Collection also includes abstracts of some 200 administrations from Ossory, 1660-1803, and of 28 administrations from Leighlin, 1702-1802: these abstracts were printed in full in *The Irish Genealogist,* 1972.

The Public Record Office of Northern Ireland

Like its Dublin namesake, this Office has made strenuous and well-rewarded efforts in the line of accumulating wills. A valuable collection has been formed and is covered by an ever-growing card index: the wills, moreover, are not necessarily confined to the area which is now Northern Ireland.

The P.R.O.N.I. holds the Will Books from the District Registries of Armagh, Belfast and Londonderry, starting in 1858. It also has several of Betham's transcripts of Consistorial Will Indexes, as well as a copy of his volumes of Sketch Pedigrees from Prerogative Wills, now at the Genealogical Office.

Group sources include a copy of the Stewart-Kennedy Notebooks now in T.C.D.; a duplicate of the Swanzy collection; some 300 Prerogative wills and administrations of the Mathews family (T.681); and abstracts of Hamilton wills from Co. Down (T.702A).

Armagh Library

This repository is the home of the Johnston collection of will abstracts.

Further Printed Sources

This is one of the most complicated fields and only the very broadest guidance can be given.

The Testamentary Records of the Butler Families, edited by Rev. Wallace Clare (1932), contains 311 abstracts of wills and 218 abstracts of administrations dating from before 1800, and being almost all the testamentary records of the Butlers prior to the nineteenth century. The book has an excellent index.

Various periodicals have printed abstracts of wills. *The Irish Genealogist* and *The Irish Ancestor* have, to date, each printed about 300, the bulk of those in the former publication coming from the Irish Genealogical Research Society's collection in London, while the bulk of those in the latter were obtained from individual private sources. In the 1960s *Breifne* printed a number of pre-1820 wills of the Reynolds family. Quite a selection of will abstracts are scattered through the *Journal of the Cork Historical and Archaeological Society,* and wills can also be found in the *Journal of the North Munster Archaeological Society,* the *Journal of the Co. Louth Archaeological Society,* and the *Journal of the Co. Kildare Archaeological Society.* In 1948 the *Journal of the Royal Society of Antiquaries of Ireland* printed abstracts of a dozen pre-1661 Irish wills from the Prerogative Court of Canterbury. The abstracts in the Jennings Collection (already referred to under the Public Record Office) were largely printed in the *Journal of the Waterford and South-East of Ireland Archaeological Society* in 1913, 1914, 1915 and 1920, making a total of about 500 items, arranged at random. In 1981 *Decies* printed an "Index to Wills relating to Waterford" which includes these printed Jennings items, as well as items from the Walsh Kelly collection at the Genealogical Office.

There are a few wills in the later volumes of the *Journal of the Association for the Preservation of the Memorials of the Dead in Ireland.*

Certain family histories include, as a bonus, clusters of will abstracts. There are 46, mainly from Donegal, in *Three Hundred Years in Inishowen,* by Amy I. Young (1929); 8 in *The Waters Family of Cork,* by Eaton W. Waters (1939); 5 in *The Family of Synge or Sing,* by K. C. Synge (1937); 1 in *An Officer of the Long Parliament,* by Richard and Dorothea Townshend (1892), and so on.

In like vein, certain local histories include abstracts of wills, notably Rev. William Burke's *History of Clonmel* (1907). Wills can also turn up in unexpected places: *The History and Antiquities of Kilkenny,* by William Healy (1893) contains a full copy of the marvellous 1619 will of John Rothe, builder of Rothe House, while *The Life and Letters of the Great Earl of Cork,* by Dorothea Townshend (1904) devotes 36 pages to a transcript of that nobleman's 1642 will.

Printed summaries of family collections such as *The Kenmare Papers, The Inchiquin Papers* and the *Calendar of Ormond Deeds,* published by the Irish Manuscripts Commission, include at least a few wills.

All that one can recommend in the welter of printed sources is patience and diligence!

The Prerogative Court of Canterbury

Several mentions have already been made of the Irish wills which have survived by reason of being proved in the P.C.C. These were particularly plentiful and important in the seventeenth century, though they extend back to the fifteenth century and, of course, continued for the life of the Court.

It has been calculated that there are at least 360 wills before 1660 that show either an Irish address, property in Ireland or the testator's death in Ireland. A further minimum of 400 such wills occur in the period 1661-1700.

Between 1559 and 1661 there are at least 550 Irish Administrations on record: after 1661 the Ms. Calendars rarely show the county (or country) of an intestate and thus it becomes impossible to estimate the numbers involved.

The National Library has a pencil-written collection of abstracts of wills from the P.C.C. relating to Irish testators 1636-98 (Ms. 1397).

The Irish Genealogical Research Society, London

Since its foundation in 1936, this Society has assembled a useful collection of will abstracts, which has continued to grow: it is covered by a card index. A few of these abstracts — less than 250 — were printed in the early issues of *The Irish Genealogist.* The Society also has a copy of the Walsh Kelly Manuscripts.

The Society of Genealogists, London

Though this Society is concerned with English genealogy, inevitably some abstracts of Irish wills have strayed into its records: in particular, there is a collection of Prerogative wills made by the Webb family. As Irish abstracts are not separately indexed, they can be difficult to locate as such, though not, of course, difficult to find under the names of individual testators.

CHAPTER 9

Early Genealogical Sources for Attornies and Barristers

P. BERYL PHAIR

It is important for people researching ancestors known to have practised law in Ireland to realise that in addition to genealogical sources of a general nature such as census returns, wills, etc., there is also a specialised body of records to which they can have recourse if need be. This body of records arose from the fact that the practise of law in Ireland was at all times highly professional and rather exclusive thereby ensuring that detailed records were made—and carefully kept—of all legal practitioners. Those who aspired to a career in the law had first of all to prove their suitability for that vocation to a body known as the Society of King's Inns. They were then required to submit to a searching course of training prescribed by the Society before being permitted to practise as attornies or barristers. In Ireland, legal convention, then as now, required the common citizen to submit his complaint quietly, in the first instance, to the attorney—nowadays known as solicitor—who in turn instructed the barrister to plead the cause by legal argument in open Court.

Origin of the Irish Inns of Court

A collegiate association of Irish legal practitioners can be traced back to the reign of Edward I (1272-1307) and seems to have received semi-official recognition. But it is not evident that the Crown at that time granted any site for an inn or residence. Legal Inns were so termed because originally they were places of residence and study for students and apprentices of law. In Ireland, an Inn of Court, called Collett's Inn — perhaps after some official of that name — was situated outside the municipal limits of Dublin, where Exchequer Street and South Great George's Street now stand. In Edward II's time (1307-1327), Sir Robert Preston consigned his residence as a site for an Inn named after him — Preston's Inn. On 31st July 1541,

Henry VIII granted the site of the dissolved monastery of the Friars Preachers [Dominican Order] near Dublin (where the Four Courts was later built) for a term of twenty-one years. This was the foundation of what became known as King's Inns, although by the end of the 16th century the building itself had fallen into utter ruin, and the King's Inns Society had all but perished.

In 1607 efforts were made to restore the prestige of the Society of King's Inns and records of admittances were ordered to be kept. Rules and regulations were drawn up from time to time and in 1794 the Benchers, or senior members of the Inns of Court, published a pamphlet entitled *General Rules*:

> "Having full Power and Authority to make and ordain Rules and Orders, for and concerning the Business and Practise of Attornies, and for their admission into the said Society, and for and concerning the Admission of Students into the said Society . . . for the advancement of Knowledge in the Science and Practise of the Law."

Thus it will be seen that there were two streams in the King's Inns, the apprentices who became attornies, and the law students who became barristers. This arrangement continued until 1866 when the attornies withdrew and formed their own Society — the Incorporated Law Society of Ireland — which received its charter in 1877. Later the Society deposited its old records in the Public Record Office where they were all destroyed in 1922. In recent years the Society moved to new headquarters at Blackhall Place, Dublin.

The present King's Inns in Henrietta Street, Dublin, was built in 1802, and King's Inns Library, on the other side of the street, was completed in 1827, standing on the site of Primate Robinson's house. The Library, which is not open to the public, contains some 110,000 volumes, about one half concerning legal matters.

The legal year was divided into four terms. In Ireland these were Hilary, January 11 to January 31; Easter, April 15 to May 8; Trinity, May 22 to June 12; Michaelmas, November 3 to November 23. These short terms were arranged so that twenty dinners could be attended in Commons. In 1877 longer term sittings were introduced, but "sittings" only concern the legal programme of the Courts.

Admission and Training of Apprentices and Law Students

There were strict rules governing the admittance of the apprentices and the law students to the King's Inns Society. Memorials in writing had to be sent to the Benchers, a group of up to forty-five senior barristers. The bulk of these memorials, written by hand during the early years, and later on printed forms, have survived. An attorney who wished to take an apprentice had to state in his memorial — addressed formally to the Right Honourable Benchers of the Honourable Society of King's Inn — the apprentice's name, the number of apprentices he already had, his own place of abode and whether he attended the Courts in Dublin or not.

The apprentice, in his petition to be taken as an apprentice, had to state the occupation and place of abode of his parents, and submit two affidavits, one as to his age (he had to be sixteen years or over) and the other as to his education. He had to serve twenty whole terms as an apprentice to an attorney before he was admitted into the Society of King's Inns as an attorney. His actual training was largely a matter of what he could learn from the attorney who took him as an apprentice.

A law student had to set out in his memorial the name, occupation and place of abode of his parents, his education and whether he had been in any trade, profession or business. He had to give up any such employment and would not be accepted if he was acting as an attorney or as clerk to an attorney. With a second memorial, submitted when he sought admission to the degree of barrister, he had to lodge a certificate of his having kept eight terms at an Inn of Court in England — for Henry VIII's grant in 1541 had a clause added that such persons as desired to practise the Irish law should have been resident in an English Court of Law. He also had to have kept nine whole terms at King's Inns, and had to state his age and the day on which he attained that age. His two memorials had to be signed by a barrister of at least forty terms standing.

Furthermore, no person would be admitted a member of the King's Inns Society until he had given security by the bond of two sufficient persons, severally bound in the sum of £100, for his obeying and performing all the laws and rules of the Society. These bonds are of special interest because of the signatures attached.

Admission Papers

The Admission Papers were kept in the Tholsel — built in 1683 in Thomas Street — where the Lord Mayor held his Court. About 1804 they were taken to King's Inns. They were removed on open carts with the result that many of the papers were lost in transit. They remained in the custody of the Under Treasurer of King's Inns, their existence largely unknown, until recent years when they were deposited in the Record Room of King's Inns Library in Henrietta Street. They are now arranged in order of surnames.

Admission Papers are only concerned with the start of a career in law. The great value of these papes lies in their genealogical content. There are some 40,800 such original documents in all held in the Library.

Apprentices and Attornies

Admission Papers, 1793-1866

An attorney's Admission Papers consisted of five parts. Four were concerned with his admission as an apprentice, the fifth being his bond and admission to the Society on becoming an attorney. Few bonds have survived except for the period 1785-1804.

1. An attorney presented a Memorial to take the apprentice:
   Memorial of Hezekiah Holland O'Callaghan, Attorney of Court of Exchequer, Common Pleas and King's Bench, of Nassau Street, Dublin, to take Standish Deane O'Grady to be his Apprentice.

2. The apprentice submitted a Petition:
   Petition of Standish Deane O'Grady, first son of John, Castlefarm, Co. Limerick, and Lucinda O'Grady otherwise O'Driscoll his wife; of full age of 16; educated at Schools of Rev. John Higgins and Rev. Michael Fitzgerald . . . to be taken as Apprentice.

3. Affidavit as to Apprentice's age:
   Affidavit of said Hezekiah Holland O'Callaghan as to said Standish Deane O'Grady's age because the residence of said John O'Grady is upwards of 100 miles from Dublin.
   Affidavit of John O'Grady of Castlefarm, Co. Limerick, aged upwards of thirty-five years, maketh oath that Standish Deane O'Grady in the annexed Petition named is of the full age of sixteen years. Sworn 2 November 1805.

4. Affidavit as to apprentice's education:
   Affidavit by Standish Deane O'Grady "he hath been educated by Private Tuition at his Father's house, and at the Schools of Rev. John Higgins and Rev. Michael Fitzgerald; saith he had read Lattin Gramar, Corderius, Ovid and Virgell when he left the same." 12 November 1805.

5. Bond on admission as attorney to the Society of King's Inns:
   Standish O'Grady eldest son of John O'Grady, of Castlefarm, Co. Limerick, John Ryall, Dublin city attorney, and Peter Smithwick of said city gent. Bond 5 December 1812 on admission of said Standish O'Grady as Member of Honble. Society of King's Inns as an Attorney.

In addition to these documents there were often assignments, as when the apprentice's master had died, or had ceased to attend the Courts or, as one apprentice described the situation, "had become deranged in his affairs." The new master had to file a memorial and the apprentice a petition stating the facts. Charles Costley Sullivan changed masters five times during his apprenticeship from 1835 to 1840. Assignments give no genealogical information.

Indentures, as between a master, his apprentice and usually a parent, were frequently drawn up. The *Guide to the Records in the Public Record Office,* Dublin, by Herbert Wood (published by H.M. Stationery Office, 1919) shows that indentures dating back to 1731 were then in the Record Office, but these all perished in 1922. However, a few were found in the Record Room at King's Inns Library. One such is that made between Stephen Cullen and his father Edmund Cullen, Dublin city, Doctor of Physick, of the one part, and Arthur Thomas, Dublin, attorney, of the other, said Stephen putting himself as apprentice and clerk to the said Arthur Thomas, attorney, Exchequer "to learn the art and mystery of an attorney . . . for the full term of five years," promises obedience and that he "shall not play at cards, dice or any other unlawful games, Taverns and Ale Houses he shall not frequent . . . matrimony he shall not contract without the consent of his said master."

The title of "attorney" was abolished by Act of Parliament in 1873, after which the term "solicitor" came into universal use.

Additional Sources of Information on Apprentices and Attornies

1. **In Reading Room, King's Inns Library:** Manuscript volume, Admissions of Attorneys Michaelmas term 1752 to 1792, names only. In the early years Attornies paid an admission fine of 13s. 4d.

2. **In Record Room, King's Inns Library:** Volume 7, Apprentices 1804-1843: Over 3,000 names of apprentices and names of masters.

3. **In Record Room, King's Inn Library:** Manuscript No. 12, a manuscript of 23 pages being "A List of the attorneys admitted and sworn in the Court of Exchequer since Hilary 1767" to June 1789. This list of over 1,000 names shows that some of the attornies admitted to the Court of Exchequer had previously been admitted to the Court of King's Bench or to the Court of Common Pleas.

4. **Public Record Office, Four Courts, Dublin:** Lodge Manuscript, entitled "Alphabetical List of the Society of King's Inns, Dublin, from the Restoration of the said Society in 1607, Sir Arthur Chichester, Lord Deputy, being the first Member, transcribed from the Society's Books,

being five in number." This manuscript was compiled by John Lodge, Deputy Keeper of the Records in the Bermingham Tower, Dublin Castle, and Deputy Keeper of the Rolls. There is a copy of Lodge's list at the College of Arms, London, and a similar list in the Fisher Manuscript (G.O. 288) at the Genealogical Office, Dublin Castle. There are two lists of Members 1607-1771. The second is of "Attornies." Lodge notes that admissions for attornies were not entered in the Books of the Honourable Society [of King's Inns] between 1679 and 1752. He does, however, include many entrants from the year 1732 onwards and sometimes omits dates.

5. **Public Record Office, Four Courts, Dublin:** Exchequer Petitions. "Petitions of Persons [clerks] to be admitted attorneys of the Court of Exchequer" 1711-1726. There are 222 Petitions. Names of Masters under whom the petitioners had served as apprentices are recited. Names are noted as "master" and "clerk" respectively in *King's Inns Admission Papers 1607-1867.*

6. **Public Record Office, Four Courts, Dublin:** Attorney Roll. "Attornies Alphabetical Roll of 1785-1834 and some undated earlier entries." Entries date to 1864. The early undated entries and those for the period 1785-1818 (almost 2,000 names) have been checked. Those names not found elsewhere are indicated by the letter "r" (Roll) in the *King's Inns Admission Papers 1607-1867.*

7. **Royal Irish Academy, Dawson Street, Dublin:** Haliday Pamphlets, Vol. 121. This is a list, alphabetical, not indexed, of Barristers and Attornies 1734-5, extracted from the Rolls of the several Courts of Law and Equity (printed by George Grierson, Dublin, 1735). The list of Attornies 1734-5 is set out to show to which of the Courts the attornies were attached. (The Four Courts were those of Exchequer, King's Bench, Common Pleas and Chancery.) The list is useful because approximate times of admissions of attornies, listed in some cases by name only in the Lodge Manuscript, can be inferred from the fact that they were in practice in 1734-5.

8. **King's Inns Admission Papers, 1607-1867:** As the Admission Papers in the King's Inns Library amount to some 40,800 original documents, and since the Library is not open to the public, abstracts of all these are being published by the Irish Manuscripts Commission under the title of *King's Inns Admission Papers 1607-1867,* by Thomas U. Sadleir, B.L., edited by Edward Keane and P. Beryl Phair. Abstracts were not made after 1867 as civil registration of births, deaths and marriages had come into force.

The admissions for Law Students and Barristers from 1868 are in the Record Room at the Library but are tedious to consult, being tied in bundles in chronological order and unindexed. The late Thomas U. Sadleir spent many years preparing abstracts from the Admission Papers, work which was unfinished at his death. It was found that many Papers, especially for the period 1804-1818, were missing. Other manuscripts and lists in King's Inns Library and elsewhere in Dublin have been examined and entries from these bridge some gaps. In some cases these sources supply only names and dates but even such information can be useful evidence.

Students and Barristers

Admission Papers, Record Room, King's Inns Library 1723-1867

A barrister's Admission Papers should number five documents. Of those now extant, about one-third are complete, and for the others there may be from two to four papers now available.

1. Memorial to be admitted a Student:
   Thomas Thornton Macklin, 3rd son of James Macklin of city of Londonderry, gent., and Elizabeth Macklin otherwise Rogers; senior sophister and scholar in the University of Dublin. Never followed any profession or business. Humbly requests admission *specially* into this Honble. Society of a Student of Laws therein. 26 April 1802. J.B. Scriven signs that he knows Thomas Thornton Macklin and thinks him a fit and proper person to be admitted a student.

2. Bond on admission as Student and to *special* Membership of the Society of King's Inns:
   Bond of Thomas Thornton Macklin, 3rd son of James, Londonderry, bound with John Rose Baker of William Street, Dublin city, and William Marshall of Townsend Street, said city, unto the Hon. Society of the King's Inns in the sum of £100 . . . that said bounden Thomas Thornton Macklin shall . . . conform himself to the Rules, Orders and Regulations of the said Society. Signed by said Thomas Thornton Macklin, John Rose Baker and William Marshall, 17 May 1802.

3. Certificate from an English Inn:
   Certificate that Thomas Thornton Macklin, 2nd son of James Macklin, Londonderry, schoolmaster, was admitted a Member of the Hon. Society of Gray's Inn 22 June 1803. Hath kept eight terms . . . 1 June 1805.
   (Students could keep terms at King's Inns and then be recommended to an English Inn, or could start their legal career at an English Inn and then proceed to King's Inns. By a Statute of 32 George III 1783 admission to an English Inn carried with it formal admission to King's Inns at the same date. The English Inns of Court to which Students were recommended were Gray's Inn, Middle Temple, Lincoln's Inn and Inner Temple.)

4. Memorial for admission *generally* to Membership of the Society of King's Inns and to the degree of Barrister:
    Memorial of Thomas Thornton Macklin, 2nd son of James Macklin, Londonderry, schoolmaster, and Elizabeth Rodgers. Admitted Student E[aster] 1801 [1802] and to Gray's Inn T[rinity] 1803. That he attained the age of 24 years on the 30th October 1804, Hath kept nine terms in this Honble. Society and eight terms in said Society in Great Britain . . . now requests admission *generally* into the Honble. Society, and to the Degree of Barrister therein.
    I certify that I know the above named Thomas Thornton Macklin and think him a fit and proper person to be admitted to the degree of Barrister. W. C. Plunket, 5 June 1805.
    (Note that one of Thomas Thornton Macklin's elder brothers must have died between 1802 and 1805, when he is described as second instead of third son of James Macklin.)

5. "Barrister's Certificate," Oath of Allegiance, Abjuration or "Qualification":
    Certificate. Search being made in the Prothonotary's Office of the Court of King's Bench in Ireland, I find that Thomas Thornton Macklin did on 10 June 1805 take and subscribe the Oath of Allegiance . . . and Oath of Abjuration. Robert Hamilton D[eputy] Pro[thonotar]y.

A Barrister's Certificate, Oath of Allegiance or "Qualification" was a document that had to be signed before a barrister was admitted to his Degree. In 1704 it was decreed that no person was to be admitted to the Bar until he produced an authentic certificate of his receiving the Sacrament according to the usage of the Church of Ireland. In the early years it is quite common to find that only two documents are now available for a barrister — his certificate from an English Inn and pinned to it a certificate signed by a clergyman that he had on a certain date or dates received the Sacraments. As time went on, this Act was relaxed. These certificates contain no genealogical information but can supply the date when a Student became a Barrister in cases where the barrister's memorial (No. 4 above) is missing.

Theobald Wolfe Tone's Admission Papers:

Three papers of Theobald Wolfe Tone, a prominent leader of the 1798 insurrection in Ireland, are extant. His certificate from the Middle Temple states:—

"These are to certify That Mr Theobald Wolfe Tone the eldest son of Peter Tone of Black Hall in the County of Kildare in the Kingdom of Ireland, Gentleman, was specially admitted of the Honourable Society of the Middle Temple on the third Day of February One Thousand seven hundred and eighty

Theobald Wolfe Tone, 1763-1798.

seven Hath kept eight terms Commons in the Dining Hall of this Society and paid for one Term not kept Hath paid for one Candlelight and six Vacation exercises not performed and hath paid all Duties due to the Society and the Officers thereunto belonging In Testimony whereof I have hereunto set my Hand and the Seal of the said Society this Sixteenth Day of April in the twenty ninth year of the Reign of our Sovereign Lord George the Third by the Grace of God of Great Britain France and Ireland King Defender of the Faith and so forth and in the year of our Lord One thousand seven hundred and eighty nine. Jerome Knapp, Treasurer. Witness Wm. Eldred, Sub Trea[sure]r.''

The Memorial of Theobald Wolfe Tone for the Degree of Barrister is addressed to the Right Honourable the Society of King's Inns, Dublin, and

"Sheweth That your Memorialist is the eldest son of Peter Tone of Blackall in the county of Kildare, gent., and of Margaret Tone otherwise Lamport his wife. That your Memorialist's Father and Mother are Protestants of the Church of Ireland as by law established and that your Memorialist is also a Protestant. That your Memorialist has never been bred to follow any trade, business or occupation whatsoever. That your Memorialist was educated in Trinity College Dublin, and obtained therein a Degree of Batchelor of Laws, as appears by his Testimonium. That your Memorialist has kept eight terms in the Middle Temple, London, as appears by his Certificate.''

To this memorial is appended a note, addressed to the Rt. Honourable and Honourable the Benchers of the Honourable Society of King's Inns, Dublin: "I certify that I know the Memorialist and think him a person proper to be called to the Bar, and admitted a member of this Society. M. Beresford.'' On the back of the memorial is the statement "Trinity Term 1789. Memorial of T. W. Tone, Admitted this Term as a Barrister and a Member of the Honble. Society of King's Inns.'' Wolfe Tone's signature does not appear on any of his papers. The third paper still in existence is the printed Certificate of his having taken the Oath of Allegiance and the Oath of Abjuration on 4th May 1789, signed by [Lord] Farnham.

Robert Emmet's Admission Papers

Only two of the Admission Papers of Robert Emmet who inspired the Insurrection of 1803 in Dublin are extant, his Admission as a Student and his Bond on becoming a Member of the Honourable Society of the King's Inns. His memorial, addressed to the Benchers, reads —

"The Memorial of Robert Emmet Junr. Sheweth That he is the second son of Robert Emmet of Stephen's Green in the city of Dublin, Esq., Doctor of Physick, and Elizabeth Emmet otherwise Mason his wife. That he is at present

Facsimile of the bond of Robert Emmet Junr.
Signed by the said Robert Emmet Junr., Robert Emmet and Thomas Addis Emmet.
Courtesy of the Hon. Benchers, Society of King's Inns, Dublin.

a Student in the University of Dublin and of the rank of Junior Sophister therein. That he never followed any Profession or Business. And he now humbly requests Admission specially into this Honble. Society as a Student of Laws therein. (signed) Robt. Emmet.

I certify that I know the above named Robert Emmet Junr. and the contents of the above Memorial to be true and think him a fit and proper person to be admitted a Student in this Honble. Society. (signed) Richard Frankland.''

This memorial is annotated ''The Memorial of Robert Emmet Junr. to be admitted a Student Rec[eive]d 2 Nov. 1795.''

His Bond, of the same date, made by ''Robert Emmet second son of Robert Emmet of Stephen's Green in the city of Dublin, Doctor of Physick, the said Robert Emmet, and Thomas Addis Emmet of said place Esq,'' is signed by all three parties.

Additional Sources of Information on Students and Barristers

1. **In Reading Room, King's Inns Library:** Manuscript Volume, Admissions of Barristers, Michaelmas Term 1732 to 1791, names only. In the early years barristers are shown as paying a fine of £2 13s. 4d. on admission.

2. **Record Room, King's Inns Library:** Manuscript volumes (not Papers).

   Vol. 1. Barristers, Admission to Degrees 1782-1792. Recites father's name and address 1782-90, terms kept at an English Inn 1782-89. Names only 1790-92.

   Vol. 2. Barristers, Admissions 1792-1819 and 1835. Father's name and address to Trinity Term 1816, then names of barristers only. The year 1835 recites father's name and address.

   Vol. 3. Student Admissions 1782-1785, and

   Vol. 4. Student Admissions 1782-1792. Both these supply father's name and address, e.g. Vol. 4, 11 Jan. 1786: Mr Thomas Grady, son of William, Rahon, Co. Limerick, is admitted as a Student in the Honble. Society of King's Inns, Dublin, and hath paid his admission fee (£5).

   Vol. 5. Student Admissions 1792-1818 and 1835. Father's name and address 1792 to April 1819. April 1819 to December 1819 names only. Hilary Term to Michaelmas Term 1835 with father's name and address. This Admission List is incomplete. Names for 14 Terms are missing, e.g. Admissions are not entered after Trinity Term 1811 until Michaelmas 1812.

   The following five volumes supply names only, sometimes the fee paid, but no genealogical information. Entries are not included in *King's Inns Admission Papers 1607-1867:* they are in chronological order, not indexed:

   Vol. 6. Students 1804-1843.

Vol. 8. Students Admitted Michaelmas 1819-1852.

Vol. 9. Barristers and Students 1850-1883.

Vol. 10. Journal Hilary 1847: Barristers, Students, Attorneys taking Apprentices, Assignments, names and fees paid 1847-1864.

Vol. 11. Barristers Stamped Book: Barristers, Admissions 1819-1852. Names, dates, fees paid.

3. **Public Record Office, Four Courts, Dublin:** Lodge Manuscript — see No. 4 under Apprentices and Attornies above. Lodge's first list 1607-1771 is of Members, mainly of barristers whose numbers were augmented by the admittance of persons such as the Lords Lieutenant and their Secretaries and the Archbishops of Dublin.

4. **Royal Irish Academy, Dawson Street, Dublin:** Haliday Pamphlets Vol. 121, List of Barristers 1734-5. See No. 7 under Apprentices and Attornies above.

Judges

The period covered by the reigns of Edward I and Edward II (1272-1327) saw the establishment in Ireland of the three courts of common law that survived under the names of the King's Bench, the Court of Common Pleas and the Court of the Exchequer until the latter half of the nineteenth century. These three courts, together with the superior Court of Chancery established about 1230, were the principal institutions of law administration in Ireland from Norman times onwards. For many centuries the judges who headed these courts were English by birth or descent and the legal system they administered was modelled on that of England.

The predominance of men of Irish birth on the judge's bench in Ireland from the eighteenth century onwards was a direct result of the foundation of the University of Dublin in 1593. The effect of this foundation on appointments to the Irish Bench was gradual as the following figures show. Between 1625 and 1760 one hundred and fifteen men were raised to the Irish Bench. Of these only thirty-four were students of Dublin University. However, between 1760 and the date of the last judicial appointment by England in 1921 one hundred and eleven Dublin University students were numbered among the hundred and forty-five men raised to the Irish Bench during that period.

Up until the reign of George III, residence at one of the English Inns of Court for a specified number of terms was necessary to secure a call to the Irish Bar. Consequently, the names of Irish barristers raised to the Irish Judicial Bench before 1760 will be found as students of one or other of the four London Inns of Court — Inner Temple, Middle Temple, Lincoln's Inn or Gray's Inn. The names of those appointed to judicial office in Ireland over seven centuries together with biographical details of the more outstanding personages will be found in *The Judges in Ireland,* 1221-1921, details of which are given in the bibliography that follows.

Bibliography

Alumni Dublinenses, a Register of the Students, Graduates . . . of Trinity College in the University of Dublin, 1593-1846. 2nd edition with supplement 1846-1860, by George D. Burtchaell and Thomas Ulick Sadleir, Dublin, 1935.

> (Both law students and apprentices to attornies received similar school education, either in one of the larger schools or as pupils of a local clergyman, but almost all barristers were graduates of a university, whereas few, if any, attornies were.)

A Calendar of the Inner Temple Records by F. A. Inderwick, 3 Vols., 1505-1714, London, 1896.

Register of Admissions to the Honourable Society of the Middle Temple by Sir Henry F. Macgeagh, 3 Vols., 1501-1944, London, 1945.

The Records of the Honourable Society of Lincoln's Inn, 2 Vols., 1420-1893, Lincoln's Inn, 1896.

The Register of Admissions to Gray's Inn by Joseph Foster, 1521-1889, London, 1889.

The Judges in Ireland by F. E. Ball, 2 Vols., 1221-1921, London, 1926.

Dublin and Co. Dublin in the Twentieth Century by E. MacDowell Cosgrave, ed. by W. T. Pike, Brighton & London, 1908.

> (contains short biographies, with photographs, of barristers and solicitors.)

CHAPTER 10

R. E. Matheson's Special Report on Surnames in Ireland

DONAL F. BEGLEY

A considerable proportion of the surnames which we share with our fellow countrymen and women on this island — and indeed with millions of people beyond it — are versions of old Irish family names which came to be anglicized piecemeal following the general superimposition of English culture on Ireland in the seventeenth century. Consequently many people in Ireland today have what amounts to two distinct surnames, one English, the other Irish. This phenomenon of the dual-form surname, e.g. John Kelly/Sean O Ceallaigh, is, of course, a product of our bilingualism.

In the evolution of our modern surnames certain patterns of anglicization can be readily identified. As a general rule, anglicization was effected by a phonetic rendering of the parent Irish name into English. For instance, the basic Irish names of O Braonáin, O Dálaigh and O Máille were rendered respectively Brennan, Daly and Malley. In other cases, anglicization was induced by the assimilation of Gaelic family names to existing English surnames, resulting in, for example, O Brolchain giving way to Bradley, O Maoilmhichil to Mitchell and O Muïregain to Morgan. In some cases even direct translation was resorted to, and thus MacGobhan became Smith and O Sionnaigh Fox — from the Gaelic words *gobha* and *sionnach* meaning "smith" and "fox" respectively.

The haphazard nature of the anglicization of surnames in due course produced a bewildering crop of variations and peculiarities which manifest themselves at all levels of our national records. These variations were not only in spelling but entirely different names could be used synonymously by the same person or by members of the same family. Even the same name had a tendency to assume different forms in different districts due to the influence of local accent and dialect. Some of the more baffling variations were in fact corruptions first caused by illiteracy, which makes the task of identifying the original name well nigh impossible.

Towards the end of the nineteenth century the state of flux of surnames

Robert E. Matheson, 1845-1926.

Courtesy Robert O. Matheson.

was such as to give rise to certain problems at the Office of the Registrar-General, who, under the Registration Acts of 1863, was charged with officially recording births, deaths and marriages from 1st of January 1864. He asserted that none but those actually engaged in registration work could have any idea of the practical difficulties encountered by both registrars and persons searching the indexes owing, as he put it, to the great variations in names in Ireland. Two reports by Robert E. Matheson, secretary of the General Register Office, were issued for the guidance of both these categories. The first was printed in 1890 under the title *Varieties and Synonymes of Surnames and Christian Names in Ireland.* The second, entitled *Special Report on Surnames in Ireland,* was printed as an Appendix to the Twenty-ninth Report of the Registrar-General in 1894. It is with the *Special Report* that we are particularly concerned here.

The Report itself is statistical in nature and based upon the births registered in Ireland during the year 1890. Its value lies in the fact that it provides authoritative information as to the numerical strength and distribution of family names throughout the country. In the preliminary schedules, which deal with the most numerous surnames, we are informed, for instance, that there were approximately 62,000 Murphys, 56,000 Kellys, 43,000 Sullivans and 42,000 Walshes in Ireland in 1890. The hundred most numerous surnames are given, the hundredth being Dwyer, with an estimated 8,100 bearers of the name.

The main part of the Report, reprinted below, sets out in tabular form the distribution of surnames on a countrywide basis. The table gives a list of the surnames having five or more entries in the birth indexes for 1890. It shows the distribution over the four provinces — Leinster (L), Munster (M), Ulster (U), Connacht (C) — of each name as well as the counties wherein the names principally occurred. A note states that the estimated number of persons of each surname in the population can be ascertained by multiplying the number of entries in the table by the average birth rate, which for 1890 was 1 to 44.8. Such calculations would, no doubt, be approximately correct in relation to the more numerous surnames, but could not, of course, be relied upon in the case of the names of less frequent occurrence.

The column in the table headed ''Counties in which principally found'', if adroitly used, could certainly be of assistance in family research. It is clear from this column that certain surnames were found only in particular counties. Thunder, for example, appeared only in Dublin; Howlin, Parle and Rossiter in Wexford, and Kearon in Wicklow. McGuane was found only in Clare. Anglin, Bohane, Bransfield, Brickley, Bullman, Dullea, Hornibrook, Keohane, Kidney, Lombard, Lordan, Lowney were in Cork only while Bowler, Brick, Cournane, Culloty, Currane, Kerrisk,

McCrohan, McGillicuddy were only in Kerry. The surname Leo was peculiar to Limerick and Dahill to Tipperary. Exclusive to Antrim were Buick, Drain, Esler, Gaston, Kernohan, McKillen, McMurtry, McNinch, Meharg, Miskelly, Mulvenna, O'Rawe, Picken, Queen, Richard, Snoddy, Warwick, Weatherup and Wharry. Cartmill and McPolin appeared in Armagh only and McGivney in Cavan. The names McGeady, McGettigan and McNellis had representatives in Donegal only, as did Jess and Lightbody in Down, McEldowney in Derry and McAneny in Tyrone. Cloherty, Dirrane, Diskin, Faherty, Gorham, Grealish, Hara and Welby were confined to Galway, and Dever, Forkin, Heffron, Kilbane, Kilgallon, Kirrane, Kitterick, McAndrew, McManamon, McNicholas, Mea, O'Hora, Ractigan and Tougher to Mayo, and Guihen to Roscommon.

The table highlights local patterns in the spelling of surnames, a factor which could, *in extremis* so to speak, be used as a rough guide to the origin of certain families. To take an example of a single surname: the form McTigue occurs in Mayo with McTague in Cavan and McTeague in Donegal.

For those who may be tempted to embark on impossible research projects there are numerous salutory warnings. Members of the Smith/Smyth family, according to a note in the table, were most numerous in Antrim, Cavan and Dublin, but were also to be found in every county in Ireland, ranging from a single entry in Kerry to 134 in Antrim.

Moreover, in using the table it is important to bear in mind that by 1890 considerable movement of population had occurred in Ireland, brought about by such factors as the Famine, emigration, the coming of the railways and the drift towards the towns. Accordingly, the table would not, of course, accurately reflect the distribution of the population over the face of the countryside in pre-Famine days. Some guidance as to the earlier distribution may be obtained from the county Surnames Indexes, based on Sir Richard Griffith's *Primary Valuation of Tenements* and on the Tithe Applotment Books, covering the period 1824-1864. These also provide a statistical breakdown of surnames by civil parish.

A grave limitation of the table in the *Special Report* is that where fewer than five persons of a surname were born during 1890 no account is taken of such names. Since the table lists approximately only 2,500 names it obviously leaves a large body of surnames below the "five births" baseline unaccounted for. Regarding the disposition and distribution of the rarer Irish family names, the printed Birth Indexes *in toto* for the years 1864, 1865 and 1866 are a useful source of information.

Finally, the figure in brackets after a particular name in the table, which now follows, indicates the number who so spelled the name, while an asterisk denotes that there were also other variations of the name.

Table showing the surnames in Ireland (Irl.) having Five Entries and upwards in the Birth Indexes of 1890, together with the number registered in each province — Leinster (L.), Munster (M.), Ulster (U.) and Connacht (C.), and the counties in which the names were principally found.

Names	Irl.	L.	M.	U.	C.	Counties in which principally found
*Abbott (10), ...	11	5	1	3	2	—
Abernethy, ...	6	–	–	6	–	—
*Abraham (8), ...	9	4	–	4	1	Armagh.
*Acheson (17), ...	27	1	2	23	1	Antrim, Armagh, and Down.
Adair, ...	29	1	1	27	–	19 in Antrim, 6 in Down, and 2 in Londonderry
Adams, ...	77	6	5	62	4	Antrim and Londonderry.
Adamson, ...	9	–	–	9	–	Armagh and Down.
Agnew, ...	39	2	–	37	–	25 in Antrim, 6 in Armagh, and 4 in Down
*Ahern (92)– Aherne (15) —Ahearn (9). ..	122	4	117	1	–	Nearly all in Cork and Limerick.
*Aiken (15), ...	19	–	1	18	–	Antrim.
Alcock, ...	5	2	2	1	–	—
Alcorn, ...	6	–	–	6	–	Donegal and Londonderry.
Alderdice	6	–	–	6	–	Antrim and Armagh.
Alexander, ...	53	3	–	49	1	Antrim and Down.
*Allen (158), ...	163	37	15	102	9	A scattered name—chiefly found in Antrim, Armagh, and Dublin.
Allingham	5	–	1	–	4	4 in Leitrim.
Allison, ...	5	1	–	4	–	Antrim.
Ambrose, ...	12	–	11	1	–	6 in Cork and 5 in Limerick.
Anderson, ...	175	36	14	120	5	Antrim, Dublin, Down, and Londonderry.
Andrews, ...	42	11	2	29	–	Antrim and Down.
Anglin, ...	5	–	5	–	–	All in Cork.
Angus, ...	10	1	–	9	–	Down and Antrim.
Annett, ...	8	–	–	8	–	7 in Down and 1 in Antr...
Archbold, ...	8	8	–	–	–	5 in Dublin and 3 in Kildare.
Archer, ...	15	5	–	10	–	Armagh, Antrim, and Dublin.
Archibald, ...	8	–	–	7	1	Londonderry.
Armour, ...	10	1	–	9	–	Antrim.
Armstrong, ...	140	15	2	110	13	Antrim, Fermanagh, Cavan, and Tyrone.
Arnold, ...	22	8	2	11	1	Antrim and Dublin.
Arnott, ...	5	1	3	1	–	Cork.
Arthur, ...	9	3	4	2	–	—
Arthurs, ...	11	1	1	9	–	Antrim and Tyrone.
*Ashe (18), ...	22	4	9	6	3	Kerry and Antrim.
*Aspel (8), ...	11	9	–	1	1	Wexford.
Atkins, ...	6	1	3	1	1	Cork.
Atkinson, ...	37	6	1	28	2	Antrim, Armagh, and Down.
Auld, ...	6	–	–	6	–	3 in Antrim and 2 in Monaghan.
*Austin (19), ...	20	7	3	9	1	Antrim and Dublin.
Aylward, ...	14	6	7	–	1	Waterford and Kilkenny.
Bacon, ...	7	4	1	2	–	—
*Bagnall (6), ...	9	7	–	–	2	King's.
*Bailey (34), Bailie (29), Bayley (7).	80	15	16	44	5	" Bailey," Antrim and Wexford ; " Bailie," Antrim and Down ; " Bayley," Tipperary and Dublin.
Baird, ...	39	4	1	34	–	Antrim and Down.
Baker, ...	30	10	10	8	2	Dublin and Antrim.
Baldwin, ...	10	3	7	–	–	Waterford.
*Balfe (7), ...	9	7	–	–	2	—
Balfour, ...	5	–	–	5	–	Antrim.
Ball, ...	16	9	2	5	–	Antrim, Meath, and Dublin.
*Ballantine (8), Ballentine (8).	19	–	–	17	2	Antrim.
Balmer, ...	8	1	–	7	–	Down.
Bamford, ...	9	1	–	8	–	7 in Antrim.
Banks, ...	8	–	2	2	4	—
Bannister, ...	5	1	1	3	–	—
*Bannon (21), ...	23	6	9	5	3	Tipperary.
*Barber (15), ...	18	2	1	11	4	Antrim.
Barclay, ...	6	–	–	4	2	Antrim and Galway.
Barker, ...	7	4	–	3	–	—
*Barkley (6), ...	9	–	1	8	–	8 in Antrim.
Barlow, ...	7	3	–	–	4	—
*Barnes (22), ...	26	7	2	14	3	Antrim.
Barnett, ...	15	3	2	9	1	—
Barr, ...	60	3	–	57	–	Antrim, Londonderry, and Down.
*Barrett (141), ...	146	17	74	11	44	Dublin, Cork, Kerry, Limerick, Galway, and Mayo.

Names	Irl.	L.	M.	U.	C.	Counties in which principally found
Barrington,	7	4	2	–	1	—
*Barron (41),	43	12	11	20	–	Antrim, Donegal, Wexford, and Waterford.
Barry,	217	22	173	12	10	Cork, Limerick, Waterford—Cork alone containing about half the entries in all Ireland.
*Bartley (8),	10	3	2	3	2	—
Barton,	20	6	4	10	–	Fermanagh and Dublin.
*Bassett (6),	9	1	4	4	–	—
Bateman,	19	5	10	4	–	Cork and Dublin.
Bates,	22	12	1	9	–	Dublin.
Battersby,	5	3	–	2	–	Dublin.
Battle,	6	–	–	–	6	Sligo.
Baxter,	31	4	–	26	1	Antrim.
Beamish,	5	1	4	–	–	4 in Cork.
*Beattie (61), Beatty (36),	101	13	3	80	5	"Beattie," Antrim and Down; "Beatty," Dublin, Armagh, and Tyrone.
Beck,	7	1	–	6	–	Antrim and Down.
Beckett,	6	–	1	5	–	Antrim.
*Beggan (5),	7	1	1	5	–	Monaghan.
Beggs,	30	6	–	24	–	17 in Antrim, 6 in Dublin.
*Begley (36),	39	2	20	12	5	Kerry and Donegal.
*Behan (37),	46	38	6	1	1	Dublin and Kildare.
Beirne,	64	3	3	–	58	38 in Roscommon and 13 in Leitrim.
Bell,	197	22	3	169	3	Antrim, Down, Tyrone, Armagh, and Dublin.
Bellew,	8	6	–	2	–	Louth.
Belton,	12	6	1	–	5	Longford and Louth.
*Bennett (79),	81	26	20	34	1	Cork, Dublin, Antrim, Armagh, and Down.
*Benson (15),	16	3	2	7	4	—
Beresford,	6	2	1	3	–	—
*Bergin (40),	45	29	15	1	–	Tipperary, Queen's, and Dublin.
Berkery,	6	–	6	–	–	4 in Tipperary and 2 in Limerick.
Bermingham (23), Birmingham (17),	40	22	13	–	5	Dublin, King's, and Cork.
Bernard,	6	2	4	–	–	—
Berry,	30	10	2	12	6	Antrim, King's, and Mayo.
Best,	21	–	1	19	1	Armagh and Tyrone.
Bickerstaff,	5	–	–	5	–	3 in Down and 2 in Antrim.
Biggins,	6	1	–	2	3	Mayo.
Bill,	5	1	–	4	–	4 in Antrim.
Bingham,	30	2	–	27	1	12 in Down and 11 in Antrim.
Birch,	9	4	2	3	–	—
*Bird (21),	22	7	8	5	2	Dublin and Cork.
*Birney (6),	7	2	–	5	–	—
Bishop,	9	6	2	1	–	Dublin.
Black,	116	15	1	96	4	Antrim, Armagh, Tyrone, and Down.
*Blackburn (6),	8	4	1	3	–	Antrim.
Blackstock,	5	–	–	5	–	Antrim and Armagh.
Blackwood,	7	–	–	7	–	Antrim.
*Blain (6),	8	–	–	8	–	5 in Antrim and 3 in Down.
Blair,	78	2	2	74	–	47 in Antrim, 12 in Londonderry, and 8 in Tyrone.
Blake,	58	18	20	8	12	Cork, Galway, Clare, Antrim, and Dublin.
*Blaney (7),	9	1	–	6	2	Antrim.
*Bleakley (7),	11	1	–	9	1	Antrim.
Bloomer,	6	1	–	5	–	3 in Antrim and 2 in Tyrone.
*Boal (12),	17	–	–	17	–	12 in Antrim and 4 in Down.
*Bogan (7),	12	7	2	3	–	Wexford.
Bogue,	9	2	–	7	–	Fermanagh.
*Bohan (27),	30	4	4	4	18	Leitrim and Galway.
Bohane,	5	–	5	–	–	All in Cork.
Boland	57	16	24	3	14	Clare, Kildare, and Roscommon.
Boles (7)—Bowles (5),	12	5	1	–	6	—
*Bolger (64),	70	64	3	1	2	Wexford, Kildare, and Wicklow.
Bollard,	7	7	–	–	–	Dublin.
Bolton,	22	10	6	5	1	—
*Bonar (22),	38	–	–	38	–	29 in Donegal.
Bond,	18	9	4	5	–	Dublin.
Bones,	7	–	–	3	4	—
*Booth (14),	17	7	1	7	2	Antrim and Dublin.
Bothwell,	7	1	–	6	–	—
*Boucher (5),	7	2	4	1	–	—
Bourke,	140	20	84	4	32	Tipperary, Limerick, Mayo, Kerry, and Cork.
Bowden,	8	4	–	4	–	—
Bowe,	14	12	2	–	–	Kilkenny.
Bowen,	14	1	11	1	1	Cork.
Bowers,	5	2	–	3	–	—
Bowes,	10	7	2	1	–	Dublin.
Bowler,	14	–	14	–	–	All in Kerry.
Bowman,	11	1	2	8	–	Antrim and Down.
*Boyce (39),	40	7	2	31	–	Donegal, Down, and Londonderry.

Names	Irl.	L.	M.	U.	C.	Counties in which principally found
*Boyd (154),	155	10	1	141	3	Antrim, Down, and Londonderry.
Boylan,	49	22	4	16	7	Dublin, Monaghan, Cavan, and Meath.
Boyle,	273	27	23	189	34	Donegal, Antrim, Mayo, Tyrone, Armagh, and Louth.
Boyne,	7	6	–	1	–	Dublin.
Brabazon,	5	2	1	1	1	—
*Bracken (24),	26	18	–	4	4	Dublin and King's.
*Bradley (132),	135	21	16	89	9	Londonderry, Antrim, Tyrone, Donegal, Dublin, and Cork.
Bradshaw,	25	6	6	11	2	Antrim, Tipperary, and Dublin.
Brady,	261	105	10	125	21	Cavan, Dublin, Antrim, Meath, and Longford.
Brandon,	8	–	1	6	1	
*Brannan (8)—Brannon (7)	18	1	–	14	3	Donegal.
*Brannigan (20)—Branagen (7),	38	16	2	20	–	" Brannigan " Armagh and Monaghan— " Branagan " Dublin.
Bransfield,	5	–	5	–	–	All in Cork.
Bray,	14	5	5	4	–	Cavan and Dublin.
*Brazil (10),	19	8	9	–	2	Dublin and Waterford.
*Breadon (7),	13	1	–	11	1	Fermanagh and Tyrone.
*Breen (110),	112	57	32	23	–	Wexford, Dublin, and Kerry.
*Breheny (7),	16	–	–	–	16	Roscommon and Sligo.
*Brennan (336)	358	178	50	36	94	Kilkenny, Dublin, Sligo, Mayo, Carlow, and Roscommon.
*Brereton (8),	15	12	1	2	–	Dublin and King's.
*Breslin (42),	43	13	1	29	–	Donegal.
Brett,	20	7	4	–	9	Sligo and Dublin.
Brew,	9	–	9	–	–	6 in Clare.
*Brick (9),	10	–	10	–	–	" Brick," all in Kerry.
Brickley,	5	–	5	–	–	All in Cork.
*Bridget (5),	7	2	–	5	–	
Brien,	246	110	122	5	9	Cork, Dublin, Tipperary, Wexford, and Waterford.
*Briggs (16),	17	1	–	15	1	Antrim and Down.
Bright,	7	5	1	1	–	Dublin.
Briody,	13	9	–	4	–	6 in Longford and 4 in Cavan.
Britt,	12	1	10	1	–	6 in Tipperary and 4 in Waterford.
*Britton (9),	13	6	2	4	1	—
Brock,	6	6	–	–	–	
Broder,	11	–	10	–	1	6 in Kerry and 4 in Limerick.
*Broderick (37),	39	10	14	–	15	Galway, Cork, Kerry, and Dublin.
*Brody (6),	7	–	7	–	–	6 in Clare.
Broe,	7	7	1	–	–	4 in Kildare and 3 in Dublin.
Brogan,	33	5	2	16	10	Mayo and Donegal.
*Brolly (7),	8	–	–	8	–	7 in Londonderry and 1 in Tyrone.
*Brooks (20),	25	7	12	6	–	Cork and Dublin.
Brophy,	50	41	8	–	1	Dublin, Kilkenny, Queen's, and Tipperary.
*Brosnan (47),	66	–	66	–	–	55 in Kerry.
Brown,	327	58	39	214	16	Antrim, Londonderry, Down, and Dublin.
Browne,	146	36	51	30	29	Cork, Mayo, Wexford, and Dublin.
Brownlee,	19	1	–	18	–	Antrim and Armagh.
Bruce,	7	2	–	5	–	
Bruen,	10	–	–	1	9	Roscommon.
Bruton,	9	8	–	–	1	Dublin.
*Bryan (38),	47	31	8	4	4	Dublin, Kilkenny, Wexford, Cork, and Down.
Bryans,	16	1	–	15	–	Antrim and Down.
Bryson,	9	–	–	9	–	Londonderry.
*Buchanan (20),	24	–	1	21	2	Tyrone.
*Buckley (176),	184	31	144	5	4	Cork, Kerry, Dublin, Kilkenny, and Tipperary.
Buggy,	12	10	2	–	–	Very few in any other County. Kilkenny and Queen's.
Buick,	7	–	–	7	–	All in Antrim.
Bullman,	5	–	5	–	–	All in Cork.
Bunting,	17	–	1	16	–	11 in Antrim and 4 in Armagh.
*Burchill (6),	7	2	5	–	–	Cork.
Burgess,	19	8	3	7	1	Dublin.
*Burke (353),	357	76	107	32	142	Galway, Cork, Dublin, Mayo, Tipperary, and Waterford.
*Burnett (7),	8	3	–	5	–	Antrim, Down, and Armagh. The Munster
*Burns (215),	219	18	49	140	12	entries are chiefly in Clare, Cork, Kerry, and Tipperary.
Burnside,	8	1	1	6	–	Londonderry and Antrim.
Burrell,	5	1	–	4	–	Armagh.
*Burrows (15),	19	2	5	10	2	Down.
Burton,	10	5	1	4	–	Dublin and Antrim.
Bustard,	7	–	–	7	–	Donegal.
*Butler (168),	172	72	66	9	25	Dublin, Kilkenny, Tipperary, and Waterford
Butterfield,	7	5	1	1	–	Dublin and Kildare.
Byers,	10	1	–	9	–	Cavan.

Names	Irl.	L.	M.	U.	C.	Counties in which principally found
*Byrne (715), ...	734	583	52	53	46	Dublin, Wicklow, Wexford, and Louth. Many are also found in Carlow, Kildare, and Kilkenny; in Cork and Waterford; Donegal; Galway, Mayo, and Roscommon.
Byron, ...	10	3	2	4	1	Dublin and Antrim.
*Caddell (5), ...	6	3	1	2	-	—
Cadden, ...	5	-	-	5	-	
*Cadogan (6), ...	8	-	8	-	-	Cork.
Cafferky (19), ...	25	-	-	-	25	22 in Mayo and 3 in Roscommon.
Cafferty, ...	6	-	-	4	2	Cavan.
*Caffrey (32), ...	35	25	1	6	3	Dublin, Meath, and Cavan.
*Cahalane (13), ...	27	1	22	-	4	Cork and Kerry.
Cahill, ...	147	54	73	8	12	Cork, Kerry, Dublin, Kilkenny, and Tipperary.
*Cain (23), ...	31	8	4	3	16	Mayo.
*Cairns (43), ...	44	3	1	39	1	Antrim, Down, and Armagh.
Calderwood, ...	12	-	-	12	-	10 in Antrim.
*Caldwell (40), ..	42	5	-	37	-	Antrim, Londonderry, and Tyrone.
*Callaghan (243), ..	250	40	133	48	29	Cork, Kerry, and Dublin.
Callan, ...	33	18	-	15	-	Louth and Monaghan.
*Callanan (18)—Callinan (13),	41	-	32	1	8	"Callanan" Galway and Cork: "Callinan" Clare.
Calvert, ..	15	-	-	15	-	Antrim, Armagh, and Down.
*Calvey (7), ..	9	-	-	-	9	Sligo.
Cambridge, ..	5	-	3	2	-	3 in Cork and 2 in Antrim.
Cameron, ..	30	1	-	28	1	17 in Antrim and 7 in Londonderry.
Campbell, ..	349	39	8	279	23	Antrim, Down, Armagh, Tyrone, Londonderry, and Donegal.
Campion, ..	13	11	2	-	-	Kilkenny and Queen's.
*Canavan (22), ..	26	2	7	13	4	—
*Canniff (5), ..	6	-	5	1	-	Cork.
Canning, ..	25	3	2	15	5	Londonderry.
Cannon, ..	49	7	1	21	20	Donegal, Leitrim, and Mayo.
Canny, ...	8	-	3	-	5	Clare and Mayo.
Cantwell, ..	15	8	7	-	-	Tipperary and Dublin.
Canty, ..	23	2	21	-	-	Cork and Limerick.
*Carberry (15), ..	26	11	4	10	1	Antrim.
Cardiff, ..	5	5	-	-	-	—
Cardwell, ..	9	-	-	9	-	Antrim.
Carew, ...	12	1	10	-	1	9 in Tipperary.
Carey, ..	118	36	59	10	13	Cork, Dublin, Tipperary, Mayo, and Kerry.
Carleton, ..	15	3	1	11	-	Antrim.
*Carley (6), ..	8	4	3	-	1	Wexford.
*Carlin (17), ..	20	3	-	15	-	Tyrone and Londonderry.
*Carlisle (22), ..	24	-	-	24	-	16 in Antrim and 5 in Down.
Carmichael, ..	19	2	-	17	-	Antrim.
Carmody, ..	33	1	32	-	-	Clare, Kerry, and Limerick.
*Carney (48), ..	49	7	4	8	30	21 in Mayo.
*Carolan (39), ..	47	19	1	13	14	Mayo and Cavan.
Carpenter, ..	10	8	1	1	-	Dublin.
*Carr (85), ..	90	21	10	35	24	Donegal, Galway, and Dublin.
*Carrick (7), ..	12	2	6	2	2	
Carrigan, ..	9	2	2	4	1	Fermanagh.
*Carroll (374), ..	386	181	125	26	54	Dublin, Kilkenny, Cork, Tipperary, and Limerick, but found in every County of Leinster, Munster, and Connaught.
*Carruthers (7), ..	11	1	-	10	-	
Carry, ...	5	5	-	-	-	Louth.
Carson, ..	77	3	2	71	-	Antrim, Down, and Tyrone.
Carter, ..	38	17	4	7	10	Dublin and Galway.
Carthy, ..	25	13	9	2	1	Wicklow, Waterford, and Cork
Cartmill, ..	5	-	-	5	-	All in Armagh.
*Carton (27), ..	32	24	1	7	-	Dublin, Wexford, and Londonderry.
Carty, ..	68	33	6	3	26	Roscommon, Wexford, Galway, and Longford
*Carvill (8), ..	14	2	-	12	-	Armagh and Down.
*Casey (252), ..	254	61	134	17	42	Cork, Kerry, Dublin, and Limerick.
Cash, ..	12	6	4	2	-	Tipperary and Wexford.
*Cashin (11), ..	21	9	10	-	2	
Cashman, ..	16	-	16	-	-	13 in Cork.
Caskey, ..	6	-	-	6	-	Antrim.
*Cassells (16), ..	17	2	-	11	4	Armagh.
Casserly, ..	16	4	-	3	9	Roscommon.
*Cassidy (140), ..	141	26	3	96	16	Donegal, Dublin, Antrim, and Fermanagh.
Cassin, ..	5	3	1	-	1	—
Cathcart, ..	16	-	-	13	1	Antrim.
Catherwood, ..	9	-	-	9	-	Antrim.
*Caughey (12), ..	13	-	-	13	-	7 in Down and 6 in Antrim.
*Caulfield (55), ..	59	16	4	21	18	Mayo, Antrim and Monaghan.

Names	Irl.	L.	M.	U.	C.	Counties in which principally found
Cawley, ..	17	–	2	–	15	10 in Mayo, and 4 in Sligo.
Chambers,	69	11	6	39	13	Antrim, Mayo, Down, and Armagh.
Chandler,	7	5	1	–	1	Dublin.
Chapman,	19	8	1	10	–	Dublin, Down, and Antrim.
*Charles (7),	8	–	2	5	1	—
Charleton (7)—Charlton (7),	14	2	–	10	2	Tyrone and Antrim.
*Charters (8), ..	10	2	–	8	–	—
Cherry, ..	10	1	–	9	–	Down.
Christian,	12	4	–	6	2	—
Christopher,	6	–	5	–	1	5 in Waterford and 1 in Leitrim.
Christy (17)—Christie (16),	33	6	–	26	1	Antrim.
Church, ..	7	1	–	4	2	—
Claffey, ..	7	4	–	–	3	—
Clancy (95), ..	100	18	43	11	28	Clare, Leitrim, Galway, and Tipperary.
Clare, ..	9	8	1	–	–	Dublin.
*Clarke (327), ..	345	99	17	176	53	Antrim, Dublin, Mayo, Cavan, and Louth. Generally distributed through the Counties of Ulster.
Clarkson,	5	2	3	–	–	—
Clay, ..	5	–	1	3	1	—
Clayton, ..	12	2	2	5	3	—
*Clear (11), ..	12	9	2	–	1	Queen's and Wexford.
*Cleary (122), ..	127	47	59	12	9	Dublin, Tipperary, Clare, Limerick, and Waterford.
Clegg, ..	12	1	–	11	–	Down and Antrim.
*Cleland (9),	14	1	–	13	–	Down and Antrim.
Clements,	25	2	–	23	–	17 in Antrim.
Clenaghan,	5	–	–	5	–	—
*Clendinning (8),	10	1	–	9	–	Antrim.
*Clerkin (11), ..	15	6	–	4	5	—
*Clifford (82), ..	83	10	58	9	6	45 in Kerry.
Clinton, ..	18	10	1	5	2	Dublin and Louth.
*Cloherty (12), ..	13	–	–	–	13	All in Galway.
*Clohessy (10), ..	12	2	10	–	–	Clare and Limerick.
*Cloonan (7), ..	8	1	1	–	6	" Cloonan," 6 in Galway.
Close, ..	16	3	–	13	–	Antrim.
Clune, ..	10	1	9	–	–	Clare.
Clyde, ..	7	–	–	7	–	Antrim and Londonderry.
Clyne, ..	11	6	–	–	5	Leitrim and Longford.
*Coakley (31), Colclough (4),	36	5	29	–	2	" Coakley," 26 in Cork ; " Colclough," all in Leinster.
*Coates (14), ..	15	3	3	9	–	Antrim.
*Coburn (9), ..	10	2	–	8	–	Down, Armagh, and Louth.
*Cochrane (38), ..	42	2	1	37	2	Antrim, Londonderry, Down, and Tyrone.
Codd, ..	10	10	–	–	–	8 in Wexford.
*Code (8), ..	10	7	2	–	1	—
Cody (23), Coady (12), ..	35	19	13	–	3	Kilkenny, Tipperary, Galway, and Cork.
*Coen (21), ..	27	1	2	3	21	Galway and Roscommon.
Coey, ..	6	–	–	6	–	3 in Antrim and 3 in Down.
*Coffey (90), ..	98	22	60	5	11	Kerry, Tipperary, Dublin, Cork, and Roscommon.
Cogan, ..	14	8	5	1	–	Cork and Kildare.
Colbert, ..	11	1	10	–	–	Cork and Waterford.
*Cole (36), ..	37	15	6	13	3	Dublin, Londonderry, Armagh, Down, and King's.
*Coleman (128), ..	138	31	63	14	30	Cork, Roscommon, Dublin, and Waterford.
*Colgan (31), ..	32	17	1	11	3	Dublin, King's, and Antrim.
*Colhoun (20), ..	22	2	–	20	–	8 in Londonderry and 8 in Tyrone.
Coll, ..	28	2	2	21	3	17 in Donegal.
Colleran,	7	–	–	–	7	5 in Mayo and 2 in Galway.
Collier, ..	7	6	1	–	–	Wexford.
Colligan,	5	2	–	2	1	—
*Collins (350), ..	352	60	200	49	43	Cork, Limerick, Dublin, Galway, and Antrim. A good many are also found in Kerry and Clare.
Colvin, ..	6	1	1	4	–	—
Comber ..	5	–	1	–	4	Mayo.
*Comerford (28), ..	30	21	8	1	–	Kilkenny and Dublin.
*Commins (17), ..	20	4	4	2	10	Mayo and Waterford.
*Commons (13), ..	14	7	1	–	6	Kilkenny, Galway, and Mayo.
Compton, ..	5	1	–	3	1	Antrim.
Conaghan, ..	7	–	–	6	1	Donegal and Londonderry.
*Conaty (12), ..	14	1	–	12	1	10 in Cavan.
*Conboy (11), ..	12	1	1	1	9	Roscommon and Sligo.
*Concannon (17), ..	18	–	–	–	18	11 in Galway, 4 in Mayo, and 3 in Roscommon.
*Condon (63), ..	64	9	53	1	1	22 in Cork, 17 in Tipperary, and 9 in Kerry.
*Condron (19), ..	23	22	–	1	–	Carlow, Dublin, Kildare, and King's.
Condy, ..	5	–	–	5	–	4 in Tyrone and 1 in Fermanagh.

Names	Irl.	L.	M.	U.	C.	Counties in which principally found
*Conefry (6),	7	1	–	–	6	6 in Leitrim.
*Conlon (66)—Conlan (36),	107	31	9	25	42	Roscommon, Mayo, and Sligo. Generally distributed in Leinster and Ulster.
Conn,	9	1	–	8	–	Down and Armagh.
*Connaughton (9),	10	1	2	–	7	Galway and Roscommon.
*Conneely (81),	92	–	–	–	92	89 in Galway.
*Connell (236),	242	40	145	23	34	Cork, Kerry, Limerick, Tipperary, and Galway.
*Connellan (6),	8	1	3	3	1	
Conney,	5	–	2	1	2	—
*Connolly (303)—Connelly (43),	381	81	66	146	88	" Connolly," Cork, Monaghan, Galway, Antrim and Dublin ; " Connelly," Galway.
*Connor (423),	432	110	162	68	92	Kerry, Dublin, Mayo, and Cork ; also found to a large extent in Roscommon and Galway and in Antrim and Londonderry.
*Connors (141),	142	42	87	5	8	Cork, Wexford, and Tipperary.
Conroy,	78	45	9	1	23	Nearly all in Galway, Queen's, and Dublin.
*Conry (36),	52	4	11	5	32	Mayo and Roscommon
Considine,	21	1	19	1	–	Clare and Limerick.
*Convery (10),	11	–	–	11	–	10 in Londonderry.
Convey,	5	–	–	2	3	3 in Mayo and 2 in Down.
Conway	169	34	48	29	58	Mayo, Tyrone, and Dublin, and generally in Munster.
Coogan,	23	13	1	7	2	Dublin, Kilkenny, and Monaghan.
*Cooke (74),	89	21	18	33	17	Antrim, Dublin, Cork, Limerick, Galway, and Sligo.
*Cooley (8),	9	–	1	5	3	Antrim and Galway.
Cooney,	76	20	21	9	26	Mayo and Dublin.
Cooper,	36	17	4	15	–	Antrim and Dublin.
Coote,	6	3	–	3	–	Dublin.
Copeland,	17	1	1	15	–	Armagh and Antrim.
Copley,	5	–	4	–	1	Cork.
*Corbett (54),	64	4	34	19	7	Cork, Tipperary, and Galway.
*Corcoran (127),	132	41	49	2	40	Mayo, Cork, Tipperary, Dublin, and Kerry.
Cordner,	5	1	–	4	–	Armagh.
Corish,	5	3	1	–	1	—
*Corkery (12),	15	–	15	–	–	9 in Cork, 3 in Limerick, and 2 in Kerry.
Corkin,	5	–	–	5	–	4 in Down.
*Corless (5),	6	2	–	–	4	Galway.
Corley,	6	2	–	1	3	
Cormack,	18	11	4	1	2	Kilkenny and Tipperary.
*Cormican (8),	10	–	–	2	8	6 in Galway.
Corr,	55	16	3	31	5	Dublin and Tyrone. [Louth.
Corrigan,	74	31	3	26	14	Dublin, Mayo, Fermanagh, Monaghan, and
*Corry (42),	44	5	13	23	3	17 in Antrim, and 12 in Clare.
*Cosgrave (33),	34	17	9	3	5	Dublin and Wexford.
Cosgrove,	40	6	3	16	15	Mayo and Galway. Scattered in Ulster.
*Costello (80)—Costelloe (58),	147	32	45	3	67	" Costello," Mayo, Dublin, and Galway—" Costelloe," Limerick, Galway, and Clare.
Costigan,	8	7	1	–	–	Dublin, Kilkenny, and Queen's.
Cotter,	64	–	58	6	–	43 in Cork.
*Cotton (8),	9	3	1	3	/2 5	
Coughlan (65)—Coghlan (49),	125	34	81	5	5	" Coughlan," Cork—" Coghlan," Cork and Dublin.
*Coulter (44),	45	2	–	42	1	Antrim, Down, and Fermanagh.
Counihan,	8	–	7	–	1	Kerry.
*Cournane (8),	9	1	8	–	–	" Cournane," all in Kerry.
Courtney (55),	59	16	27	10	6	Kerry, Antrim, and Dublin.
Cousins,	18	8	2	8	–	
*Cowan (31),	33	3	–	30	–	Antrim, Down, and Armagh.
*Cowley (14),	15	5	1	2	7	Mayo.
Cox,	75	27	11	15	22	Roscommon and Dublin.
Coy,	5	2	–	1	2	
Coyle,	90	23	–	52	15	Donegal, Cavan, Londonderry, Dublin, Tyrone, and Longford.
Coyne,	54	13	1	1	39	27 in Galway and 8 in Mayo.
Craig,	120	7	1	111	1	Antrim, Londonderry, and Tyrone.
*Crampsy (5),	9	–	–	9	–	Donegal.
Crampton,	7	7	–	–	–	—
Crane,	8	2	–	4	2	
Cranny,	6	3	1	2	–	
Cranston,	9	1	–	8	–	
*Craven (9),	10	5	–	3	2	Armagh and Antrim.
Crawford,	96	8	7	79	2	Antrim, Down, Londonderry, and Tyrone.
Crawley,	19	10	1	3	5	Louth and Roscommon.
Creagh,	17	6	8	1	2	
*Crean (24),	27	4	16	–	7	9 in Kerry, 7 in Cork, and 4 in Wexford.
Creaney,	5	–	–	5	–	4 in Armagh and 1 in Down.
Creaton,	8	2	1	1	4	
*Creed (7),	9	4	5	–	–	Cork.
*Creedon (14),	15	–	15	–	–	12 in Cork.

Names	Irl.	L.	M.	U.	C.	Counties in which principally found
Cregan (20), Creegan (13),	33	10	12	4	7	" Cregan'" Limerick and Meath ; " Creegan," Leitrim and Sligo.
Cregg,	13	1	1	–	11	Roscommon.
*Crehan (15),	17	–	1	1	15	" Crehan,' 14 in Galway.
*Creighton (20),	23	6	–	15	2	Antrim and Dublin.
*Cremin (20),	25	–	25	–	–	11 in Cork and 11 in Kerry.
*Crilly (18),	23	5	–	18	–	Antrim, Londonderry, and Louth.
*Croghan (6),	9	3	3	1	2	—
Croke,	12	1	11	–	–	Tipperary and Waterford.
Cromie (20),	21	–	–	21	–	Armagh and Down.
Crone,	9	1	4	3	1	3 in Cork and 3 in Antrim.
*Cronin (168),	176	6	161	3	6	102 in Cork, 43 in Kerry, and 11 in Limerick
Crooks,	15	–	–	15	–	Antrim and Londonderry.
*Crosbie (15),	28	20	2	3	3	Dublin.
Cross,	19	5	6	8	–	Dublin, Cork, and Armagh.
*Crossan (15),	17	1	–	16	–	Londonderry.
Crothers,	17	1	–	16	–	10 in Antrim and 5 in Down.
Crotty,	26	2	22	1	1	Clare, Waterford, and Cork.
*Crowe (62),	68	14	27	20	7	Antrim, Tipperary, and Clare.
*Crowley (149),	161	12	142	2	5	116 in Cork.
Crozier,	22	2	–	20	–	Armagh.
*Cruise (7),	8	7	–	–	1	Dublin.
Cryan,	15	–	–	–	15	10 in Roscommon.
Crymble,	6	–	1	5	–	Antrim.
*Cuddihy (5),	6	4	2	–	–	Kilkenny.
Cuddy,	8	3	2	1	2	—
*Cuffe (12),	14	5	2	–	7	Mayo and Wexford.
Culbert,	8	1	–	7	–	Antrim.
Culhane,	16	–	16	··	–	13 in Limerick.
Cull,	10	–	4	4	2	—
*Cullen (196),	203	132	13	34	24	Dublin and Wexford.
*Culleton (10),	12	11	–	–	1	Wexford.
Culligan,	5	–	3	1	1	Clare.
*Cullinane (26)-Cullinan (19),	50	4	37	2	7	" Cullinane," Cork and Waterford — " Cullinan," Clare.
Culloty,	6	–	6	–	–	All in Kerry.
*Cully (15),	22	9	–	11	2	Armagh and Antrim.
*Cumiskey (7),	11	5	–	6	–	Cavan, Longford, and Westmeath.
*Cummings (10),	20	4	2	12	2	Antrim.
Cummins,	77	37	25	11	4	Dublin, Cork, and Tipperary.
*Cunnane (16),	18	1	–	–	17	8 in Mayo and 5 in Roscommon.
*Cunniffe (11),	16	1	–	–	15	Galway, Mayo, and Roscommon.
*Cunningham (202),	215	40	35	89	51	Down, Antrim, Dublin, Galway, Roscommon, and Cork.
Cupples,	7	–	–	7	–	6 in Antrim and 1 in Armagh.
*Curley (28),	36	11	–	3	22	Roscommon, Galway, and Dublin.
*Curran (161),	169	42	37	67	23	Donegal, Dublin, Waterford, and Galway.
Currane,	19	–	19	–	–	All in Kerry.
Currid,	6	1	–	–	5	5 in Sligo and 1 in Wexford.
Currigan	9	–	–	–	9	7 in Roscommon and 2 in Mayo.
Curry (60)–Currie (15),	75	15	8	48	4	29 in Antrim.
*Curtin (68),	69	1	68	–	–	All except 2 in Cork, Limerick, Clare, and Kerry.
Curtis,	23	20	2	1	–	Dublin.
Cusack,	46	5	23	11	7	Limerick, Cavan, and Clare.
*Cussen (6),	9	1	7	–	1	3 in Cork and 2 in Limerick.
Cuthbert,	7	4	1	–	–	3 in Dublin and 2 in Londonderry.
Dagg,	7	3	4	–	–	All in Tipperary.
Dahill,	5	–	5	–	–	Antrim.
Dallas,	6	–	1	5	–	Dublin, Waterford, Limerick, Kilkenny, and Westmeath.
Dalton,	75	38	31	2	4	
*Daly (360),	381	109	182	49	41	Cork, Dublin, Kerry, Galway, and King's.
Dalzell,	12	–	–	12	–	Down.
Danaher,	8	2	6	–	–	6 in Limerick and 2 in Dublin.
*Daniel (16),	17	5	10	1	1	Dublin, Tipperary, and Waterford.
*Darby (10),	11	7	–	4	–	
*Darcy (77),	86	40	24	11	11	Dublin and Tipperary.
Dardis,	6	6	–	–	–	—
*Dargan (11),	13	8	2	2	1	Dublin.
Darling,	5	3	–	1	1	—
Darmody,	12	4	7	–	1	Tipperary.
*Darragh (17),	18	–	–	18	–	Antrim.
*Davern (5),	8	1	6	–	1	4 in Tipperary.
*Davey (18)—Davy (12),	31	7	2	10	12	11 in Sligo and 6 in Antrim.
Davidson,	58	6	–	52	–	Antrim and Down.
*Davin (11),	12	–	5	1	6	Tipperary and Galway.
*Davis (95),	104	41	17	34	12	Dublin and Antrim.

Names	Irl.	L.	M.	U.	C.	Counties in which principally found
*Davison (44), ...	45	3	–	42	..	Antrim.
Davitt, ...	8	2	–	2	4	—
Dawson, ...	55	14	10	28	3	Antrim.
Day, ...	13	5	5	3	–	—
Dea, ...	10	1	6	–	3	—
Deacon, ...	5	2	3	–	–	—
Deady, ...	8	1	7	–	–	Kerry.
*Deane (35), ..	45	2	12	19	12	Mayo, Cork, and Donegal.
*Deasy (32), ..	35	–	24	2	9	24 in Cork and 9 in Mayo.
Dee	16	1	14	–	1	Waterford, Cork, and Tipperary.
*Deegan (26), ..	28	23	3	1	1	Dublin, King's, and Queen's.
Deehan, ...	6	·	–	4	2	Londonderry.
*Deely (7), ..	8	–	2	–	6	Galway.
Deeney (8)—Deeny (7),	15	–	–	15	–	Donegal and Londonderry.
Deering, ...	6	3	–	3	–	Monaghan.
Deery, ...	14	–	··	14	·	Tyrone and Monaghan.
*Deevy (7), ..	9	6	1	2	–	Kilkenny.
Delahunt, ...	6	6	–	–	–	Kildare.
Delahunty, ...	10	4	6	–	–	—
Delaney (93)—Delany (65),	158	97	38	10	13	Dublin, Queen's, Tipperary, and Kilkenny.
*Dempsey (108), ..	117	62	21	22	12	Dublin, Antrim, Cork, Wexford, and King's
*Dempster (12), ..	13	1	–	12	–	8 in Antrim and 4 in Down.
*Dennehy (30), ..	36	–	36	–	–	26 in Cork and 9 in Kerry.
*Dennis (7), ..	10	4	4	1	1	Dublin and Cork.
Dennison, ...	6	–	–	6	–	Armagh.
Derby, ...	6	–	1	5	–	Antrim.
Dermody, ...	9	7	1	–	1	—
Dermott, ...	6	–	–	3	3	Leitrim.
Desmond, ...	34	1	32	1	–	32 in Cork.
Devane, ...	16	–	11	–	5	Kerry.
*Devany (15)—Devaney (11)—Devenny (8),	44	2	3	13	26	Mayo, Galway, and Leitrim.
*Dever (8)—Devers (6),	15	1	1	2	11	" Dever," all in Mayo—" Devers," 3 in Mayo.
Devereux, ...	16	12	3	1	–	8 in Wexford.
Devery, ...	5	5	–	–	–	4 in King's and 1 in Dublin.
*Devine (70), ..	81	25	9	35	12	Tyrone, Dublin, and Roscommon.
*Devitt (16), ..	17	7	7	1	2	Clare and Dublin.
*Devlin (102), ..	112	19	3	88	2	Antrim, Tyrone, Dublin, Armagh, and Londonderry.
*Diamond (13), ..	16	3	–	11	2	Londonderry and Antrim.
*Dick (12), ..	13	1	1	11	–	8 in Antrim and 2 in Down.
*Dickey (11), ..	13	–	–	13	–	Antrim.
Digan, ...	5	4	–	–	1	King's.
*Diggin (6) ..	8	–	8	–	–	7 in Kerry.
*Dignan (10), ..	11	10	–	1	–	Westmeath.
Dillane, ...	19	–	14	–	5	11 in Limerick, 5 in Galway, and 3 in Kerry.
*Dillon (116), ..	117	52	27	19	19	Dublin, Limerick, Antrim, and Galway.
Dinan, ...	14	1	12	–	1	7 in Cork.
*Dinneen (22)—Dineen (18),	42	–	39	–	3	29 in Cork.
Dinsmore, ...	6	–	–	6	··	Londonderry.
*Dirrane (13), ..	14	1	–	–	13	" Dirrane," all in Galway.
*Diskin (10), ..	14	–	–	–	14	" Diskin," all in Galway.
Diver, ...	29	–	1	27	1	26 in Donegal.
Dixon (51)—Dickson (49),	100	19	2	68	11	" Dixon," Dublin and Mayo—" Dickson," Down and Antrim.
*Dobbin (17), ..	21	5	1	15	–	Antrim.
Dobbs, ...	6	4	–	2	–	—
Dobson, ...	14	1	2	9	2	—
*Dockery (7), ..	9	1	–	–	8	Roscommon.
Dockrell, ...	5	5	–	–	–	Dublin.
*Dodds (18)—Dodd (12),	31	5	3	18	5	Down and Armagh.
*D o h e r t y (414)—Dogherty (27),	457	29	52	318	58	Donegal, Londonderry, and Mayo—160 of the 414 births of persons named " Doherty," are in Donegal.
Dolan, ...	142	37	3	50	52	Fermanagh, Roscommon, Cavan, Galway, Leitrim, and Dublin.
Dollard, ...	5	4	–	1	–	—
*Donaghy (40), ..	49	–	–	48	1	Antrim, Londonderry, and Tyrone.
Donald, ...	6	–	–	6	–	Antrim.
Donaldson, ...	33	2	–	31	–	Antrim and Armagh.
*Donegan (23), ..	31	15	9	5	2	—
*Donnan (10), ..	11	–	–	10	1	9 in Down.
Donnell, ...	18	–	5	13	–	Londonderry, Tyrone, and Tipperary.
*Donnellan (19)—Donelan(16)-Donlon (14)—Donlan (13),	76	11	13	4	48	" Donnellan," Clare and Mayo ; " Donelan," all in Galway ; " Donlon," Longford ; " Donlan," Galway.
*Donnelly (228), ..	240	64	19	135	22	Antrim, Tyrone, Armagh, and Dublin.
*Donoghue (84), ..	97	6	82	2	7	Kerry and Cork.

Names	Irl.	L.	M.	U.	C.	Counties in which principally found
*Donohoe (137),	162	83	26	28	25	Dublin, Longford, Cavan, and Galway.
Donovan,	211	14	194	2	1	175 in Cork.
Doody,	27	5	22	–	–	Limerick, Cork, and Waterford.
*Doogan (32)—Dougan (13),	53	3	1	41	8	" Doogan," Donegal ; " Dougan," Antrim and Armagh.
Doohan,	11	–	3	7	1	7 in Donegal and 3 in Clare.
*Doolan (35)—Doolin (13),	66	38	21	1	6	Dublin, Louth, Cork, and Tipperary.
*Dooley (49),	60	33	12	5	10	Dublin and King's.
Doonan,	15	2	–	5	8	Leitrim and Roscommon.
Dooney,	5	–	–	–	5	Roscommon.
Doran,	97	60	13	20	4	Dublin, Wexford, Down, and Armagh
Dore,	12	1	11	–	–	9 in Limerick.
Dorgan,	13	2	11	–	–	9 in Cork.
Dorman,	14	1	2	11	–	7 in Down.
*Dornan (10),	11	–	–	11	–	All except 1 in Antrim and Down.
Dorney,	7	–	7	–	–	6 in Cork and 1 in Tipperary.
*Dorrian (5),	7	–	–	7	–	
*Douglas (47),	54	12	–	41	1	Antrim and Londonderry.
*Dowd (64),	84	18	15	16	35	Roscommon, Dublin, Kerry, and Galway.
*Dowdall (17),	20	19	–	1	–	Dublin and Louth.
Dowling,	109	83	15	6	5	Dublin, Kilkenny, and Queen's—half the Leinster entries are in Dublin.
*Downes (35),	47	15	21	8	3	Clare, Limerick, and Dublin.
*Downey (90),	91	16	42	22	11	Cork, Kerry, Antrim, Galway, and Limerick
Downing,	15	4	11	–	–	6 in Kerry and 5 in Cork.
Doyle,	514	391	59	37	27	This name is found in nearly every County of Ireland, but three-fourths of them are in Dublin, Wexford, Wicklow, Carlow, Kerry, and Cork.
Drain,	5	–	–	5	–	All in Antrim.
Drake,	6	1	–	5	–	Down and Monaghan.
Draper,	5	2	3	–	–	
*Drennan (19),	20	5	4	11	–	Antrim and Tipperary.
Drew,	12	7	5	–	–	Louth.
*Driscoll (120),	121	1	120	–	–	100 in Cork.
Drohan,	10	–	10	–	–	6 in Waterford and 4 in Cork.
Drought,	5	3	2	–	–	
*Drum (12),	13	4	1	8	–	Fermanagh
Drummond,	6	1	1	4	–	Antrim.
*Drummy (6),	9	–	5	–	4	Cork and Sligo.
*Drury (10),	11	3	–	2	6	6 in Roscommon.
Duddy,	13	–	–	11	2	Londonderry.
Dudgeon,	6	1	–	5	–	
*Dudley (5),	6	1	5	–	–	
*Duff (41),	45	21	1	21	2	Antrim, Dublin, and Louth.
Duffin,	17	3	4	10	–	Antrim and Waterford.
*Duffy (282),	305	82	2	126	95	Mayo, Monaghan, Donegal, Dublin, Louth, and Roscommon.
*Dugan (18),	20	2	–	16	2	Antrim, Down, and Londonderry.
Duggan,	89	22	54	5	8	Cork, Dublin, Tipperary, and Waterford
Duhig,	7	–	7	–	–	5 in Cork and 2 in Kerry.
*Duignan (21),	22	8	1	1	12	6 in Leitrim and 6 in Roscommon.
Duke,	12	2	1	6	3	Armagh and Roscommon.
Dullaghan	7	6	–	1	–	5 in Louth.
Dullard,	6	6	–	–	–	4 in Kilkenny and 2 in Queen's.
Dullea,	5	–	5	–	–	All in Cork.
*Dunbar (17),	26	11	–	13	2	Wexford, Antrim, Down, and Tyrone.
*Duncan (35),	41	8	1	25	7	Antrim and Tyrone.
Dundon,	12	3	9	–	–	Clare, Limerick, and Dublin.
Dunlea,	11	–	11	–	–	8 in Cork.
*Dunleavy (27),	40	6	5	6	23	Mayo and Sligo.
Dunlop,	35	2	–	33	–	21 in Antrim.
Dunne (313)—Dunn (51),	364	248	55	47	14	" Dunne "—Dublin, Queen's, Kildare, King's, Kilkenny, Cork, and Tipperary ; only 13 of the births registered under the name " Dunne " are found in Ulster—half of these being in Cavan. " Dunn "—Ulster contains 34 of the 51, which are chiefly in Antrim, Down, Londonderry, and Tyrone.
Dunphy,	34	24	10	–	–	Waterford and Dublin.
Dunwoody,	11	–	–	11	–	Antrim.
*Durkan (48),	62	3	–	1	58	35 in Mayo and 15 in Sligo.
*Durnin (6),	10	5	1	3	1	Louth.
*Dwane (11)-Duane (6),	22	2	13	–	7	" Dwane," Tipperary, Cork, and Kerry— " Duane," Galway.
*Dwyer (152),	155	38	107	2	8	80 per cent. are found in Tipperary, Cork, Dublin, Limerick, Kerry, and Kilkenny.
Dyas,	5	4	–	–	1	Dublin.
*Dyer (14),	16	2	–	2	12	Roscommon and Sligo.

Names	Irl.	L.	M.	U.	C.	Counties in which principally found
Eagar (4)–Eager (3), ..	7	3	1	3	–	—
*Eakins (6)–Eakin (5),..	14	2	1	10	1	—
*Earl (5)–Earle (5), ..	16	10	2	3	1	—
*Early (37) , ..	42	11	1	10	20	Leitrim.
Eaton, ...	8	2	2	4	–	Londonderry.
Eccles, ...	15	4	–	11	–	Tyrone and Antrim.
Edgar, ...	17	–	–	17	–	Antrim and Down.
*Edmonds (5), ..	10	2	5	3	–	—
Edwards	36	16	4	13	3	Dublin, Wexford, and Antrim.
*Egan (165), ..	171	60	40	2	69	Galway, Dublin, King's, Mayo, and Roscommon. The 40 in Munster are generally distributed.
*Elder (14), ..	16	5	–	11	–	7 in Antrim, and 4 in Londonderry.
*Elliott (71), ..	76	11	2	59	4	Fermanagh, Antrim, Donegal, and Dublin.
Ellis, ...	38	14	3	21	–	Dublin and Antrim.
Ellison, ..	13	1	–	12	–	8 in Antrim and 3 in Down.
*Elwood (10), ..	11	–	1	4	6	Mayo.
Emerson, ..	18	4	1	13	–	7 in Down and 4 in Antrim.
England, ...	5	1	2	2	–	—
English, ...	53	14	19	17	3	Tipperary, Antrim, and Dublin contain more than 50 per cent.
Ennis, ...	44	36	2	4	2	Dublin and Kildare.
Enright, ...	49	4	43	–	2	21 in Limerick, 11 in Kerry, 8 in Cork, and 3 in Clare.
Erskine, ..	12	–	1	11	–	Antrim.
*Ervine (14), ..	19	–	1	18	–	10 in Antrim and 7 in Down.
*Erwin (18), ..	19	1	–	18	–	15 in Antrim.
Esler, ...	8	–	–	8	–	All in Antrim.
Eustace, ...	9	6	2	–	1	Dublin.
Evans, ...	55	22	11	19	3	Dublin, Londonderry, and Antrim.
*Evers (5), ..	9	7	–	–	2	4 in Longford and 3 in Dublin.
Ewart, ...	14	–	–	14	–	Antrim.
*Ewing (21), ..	24	1	–	23	–	Londonderry, Tyrone, and Antrim.
*Fagan (47), ..	48	42	2	4	–	50 per cent. of those in Leinster are in Dublin.
Faherty, ..	26	–	–	–	26	All in Galway.
Fahy (72)—Fahey (47),	119	6	31	3	79	Galway, Tipperary, and Mayo. Galway alone contains more than 50 per cent.
Fair, ...	6	2	–	2	2	—
*Fallon (68), ..	70	13	1	1	55	Roscommon and Galway.
*Falloon (9), ..	12	–	–	12	–	Armagh.
Falvey, ...	17	1	16	–	–	All except 1 in Cork, Clare, and Kerry.
*Fanning (22)—Fannin (13),	45	16	12	4	13	Wexford, Tipperary, and Waterford.
Farley, ...	7	2	2	3	–	—
Farmer, ...	6	–	1	3	2	—
Farnan, ...	10	5	–	5	–	—
Farr, ...	5	–	–	5	–	Antrim.
*Farragher (7), ..	9	–	–	–	9	5 in Mayo and 4 in Galway.
*Farrar (6), ..	7	7	–	–	–	Wicklow.
*Farrell (302), ..	311	205	30	36	40	Found in every County, but chiefly in Dublin, Longford, Louth, Meath, Westmeath, and Roscommon.
Farrelly, ..	69	32	–	36	1	29 in Cavan, 14 in Meath, and 10 in Dublin.
*Farren (12), ..	13	2	–	11	–	7 in Donegal and 4 in Londonderry.
Farrington, ..	5	1	1	–	3	—
Farry, ...	5	1	1	1	2	—
Faughnan, ..	8	2	–	1	5	Leitrim.
*Faulkner (18), ..	35	11	2	21	1	Antrim.
Fay, ...	27	21	1	5	–	More than 50 per cent. are in Dublin.
Fearon, ...	21	5	–	16	–	Armagh, Down, and Louth.
*Fee (22), ..	22	–	–	21	2	Antrim, Cavan, and Fermanagh.
*Feehan (14), ..	17	7	6	1	3	Louth.
*Feely (28), ..	41	4	4	16	17	Donegal and Roscommon.
*Feeney (46)—Feeny (26),	73	13	5	11	44	"Feeney," Sligo, Mayo, and Galway "Feeny," Galway and Roscommon.
Feerick, ...	13	1	–	–	12	9 in Mayo and 3 in Galway.
Fegan, ...	26	12	–	14	–	Armagh, Dublin, and Louth.
*Fehily (6), ..	11	2	5	–	4	—
*Fenlon (18), ..	28	28	–	–	–	11 in Carlow, 7 in Dublin, and 7 in Wexford.
*Fennell (28), ..	29	12	16	1	–	Clare and Dublin.
*Fennelly (14), ..	15	12	–	3	–	Kilkenny.
Fennessy, ..	8	–	7	1	–	Waterford.
Fenton, ...	19	1	11	6	1	Kerry and Antrim.
Fergus, ...	8	–	–	1	7	7 in Mayo.
*Ferguson (130), ..	133	11	1	107	14	Antrim, Down, and Londonderry.
*Ferris (32), ..	33	1	4	26	2	Antrim.

Names	Irl.	L.	M.	U.	C.	Counties in which principally found
*Ferry (26), ...	27	1	–	26	–	22 in Donegal.
Fetherston, ...	6	3	–	–	3	3 in Dublin and 3 in Roscommon.
*Field (18), ...	29	15	8	6	–	12 in Dublin and 8 in Cork.
*Finan (9), ...	18	4	2	3	9	" Finan," 6 in Roscommon and 3 in Sligo.
*Finegan (52)-Finnegan (39),	115	37	10	38	30	" Finegan," Monaghan, Galway, and Louth— " Finnegan," Armagh and Cavan.
*Finlay (69), ...	76	17	1	54	4	Antrim and Down.
*Finn (110), ...	111	40	34	7	30	Cork, Mayo, Dublin, and Roscommon.
Finneran, ...	9	1	–	–	8	Galway.
*Finnerty (14)-Finerty (10),	28	2	9	-	17	Galway.
*Finney (7), ..	8	1	–	5	2	—
Finucane, ...	10	–	10	–	–	—
Fisher, ...	29	9	4	16	–	Antrim and Wicklow.
*Fitzgerald (327), ..	330	49	257	7	17	Generally distributed throughout Munster, but most numerous in Cork, Limerick, and Kerry. Those in Leinster are for the most part in Dublin.
*Fitzgibbon (31),	34	1	32	–	1	Limerick contains more than 50 per cent.
Fitzmaurice, ...	21	4	10	–	7	Kerry.
Fitzpatrick, ..	249	103	62	64	20	Generally distributed throughout the whole of Ireland, but Dublin and Queen's in Leinster—Cork and Tipperary in Munster —Cavan, Antrim, and Down in Ulster, and Mayo and Galway in Connaught, contain the largest numbers.
*Fitzsimons (70),	80	34	6	38	2	Dublin, Down, and Cavan.
Flack, ...	8	1	–	7	–	—
*Flahavan (6), ..	12	–	12	–	–	Cork and Waterford.
Flaherty, ..	88	4	30	–	54	47 in Galway, and 16 in Kerry.
*Flanagan (173),	219	61	33	52	73	Roscommon, Dublin, Mayo, Clare, and Galway. The only counties in Ulster containing many entries of this name are Fermanagh, Cavan, and Monaghan.
*Flannery 59), ..	64	4	26	1	33	About 80 per cent. are in Mayo, Tipperary Galway, and Clare.
Flattery, ...	6	4	–	–	2	King's.
*Flattley (6), ..	11	1	–	–	10	10 in Mayo.
Flavell, ..	5	–	–	5	–	—
*Fleming (157), ..	170	42	28	63	37	Antrim, Dublin, Galway, Londonderry, Cork, and Mayo.
Fletcher, ...	22	6	6	10	–	Antrim and Dublin.
Flood, ...	64	45	1	15	3	20 in Dublin—Remainder generally distributed.
*Flynn (304), ..	319	71	140	23	85	Cork, Dublin, Waterford, Roscommon, and Leitrim—Cavan is the only Ulster county in which the name is found to any appreciable extent.
*Fogarty (57) ..	61	21	38	–	2	More than half in Tipperary and Dublin.
*Folan (26), ..	28	–	–	–	28	23 in Galway and 5 in Mayo.
*Foley (249), ..	250	57	167	7	19	Kerry, Cork, Waterford, and Dublin.
Folliard, ..	6	–	–	–	6	4 in Mayo and 2 in Roscommon.
*Foran (18), ..	26	8	18	–	–	Dublin, Limerick, and Waterford.
*Forbes (20), ..	22	3	2	14	3	Antrim and Tyrone.
*Forde (114)—Ford (39),	154	26	41	22	65	Galway, Cork, Mayo, and Dublin contain about two-thirds of the entries.
Foreman, ..	5	1	–	4	–	—
*Forkin (7), ..	11	–	–	–	11	All in Mayo.
*Forrest (8), ..	9	1	7	1	–	Cork.
*Forsythe (29),	33	1	1	30	1	Antrim and Down.
Fortune, ..	22	20	1	1	–	17 in Wexford.
*Foster (51), ..	57	13	3	37	4	Antrim and Dublin.
Fowler, ..	17	6	1	10	–	—
*Fox (124), ..	125	53	13	34	25	Dublin, Longford, Tyrone, and Leitrim. Representatives of this name are found in every County in Ireland.
Foy, ...	38	8	2	14	14	Mayo, Cavan, and Dublin.
Fraher, ..	5	–	5	–	–	4 in Waterford and 1 in Limerick.
*Frain (16), ..	20	2	1	–	17	" Frain," 10 in Mayo and 6 in Roscommon.
*Francey (8), ..	10	1	–	9	–	7 in Antrim.
Francis, ..	13	1	5	7	–	—
Franklin, ..	12	2	9	1	–	Limerick and Tipperary.
*Frawley (19), ..	20	–	20	–	–	10 in Clare and 6 in Limerick.
Frazer (27)—Fraser (14),	41	8	5	21	7	Dublin, Antrim, and Down.
*Freeburn (7), ..	9	–	–	9	–	Antrim.
Freeman, ..	20	8	3	4	5	—
*French (23), ..	24	7	3	8	6	Antrim.
*Friel (40), ..	43	–	–	38	5	27 in Donegal, 6 in Tyrone, and 5 in Londonderry.

Names	Irl.	L.	M.	U.	C.	Counties in which principally found
*Frizell (6),	12	–	–	11	1	—
Frost,	7	1	5	–	1	
Fry,	9	6	–	2	1	Dublin.
*Fulham (5),	8	8	–	–	–	7 in Dublin and 1 in King's.
Fuller,	6	2	4	–	–	Cork.
Fullerton,	25	3	–	22	–	Antrim and Down.
Fulton,	32	–	–	32	–	Antrim
Furlong,	36	33	3	–	–	26 in Wexford.
Fury (10)—Furey (7),	17	2	–	2	13	Galway.
Gabbey,	5	–	–	5	–	3 in Down and 2 in Antrim.
*Gaffey (9),	10	–	–	–	10	7 in Roscommon and 3 in Galway.
Gaffney,	68	29	2	20	17	Cavan, Dublin, and Roscommon contain 43 entries.
Gahan,	11	10	1	–	–	Wexford.
Galbraith,	15	2	–	13	–	Antrim.
*Gallagher (471),	488	28	21	295	144	Donegal, Mayo, Tyrone, Sligo, Londonderry, and Dublin ; Donegal alone furnishing two-thirds of those in Ulster.
*Gallen (10),	13	–	–	13	–	7 in Donegal and 4 in Tyrone.
*Galligan (25),	26	2	2	21	1	20 in Cavan.
*Gallivan (31),	32	–	30	1	1	24 in Kerry.
Galloway,	9	–	–	8	1	Antrim.
*Galvin (60),	62	10	40	1	11	Cork, Clare, Kerry, and Roscommon.
*Galway (12),	13	–	2	11	–	8 in Antrim.
*Gamble (38),	40	4	6	29	1	Antrim, Down, and Londonderry.
*Ganley (7),	11	2	–	2	7	—
*Gannon (71),	73	29	–	1	43	Mayo, Dublin, and Leitrim.
Gara,	20	–	–	10	10	9 in Donegal, 6 in Roscommon, 4 in Mayo, and 1 in Down.
*Gardiner (25),	26	6	2	14	4	Antrim and Dublin.
Gardner,	23	1	1	20	1	Antrim.
Gargan,	7	4	–	3	–	—
*Garland (13),	24	10	1	12	1	Dublin and Monaghan.
Garrett,	24	7	3	13	1	Down, Antrim, and Dublin.
Garry,	14	8	1	2	3	—
*Garvey (60),	64	11	21	10	22	Kerry, Mayo, Galway, and Louth.
Garvin,	5	–	–	1	4	—
Gaskin,	5	3	–	2	–	Dublin.
Gaston,	13	–	–	13	–	All in Antrim.
*Gately (10),	11	1	1	–	9	8 in Roscommon.
*Gaughan (25),	26	–	–	–	26	25 in Mayo and 1 in Sligo.
Gaughran,	5	5	–	–	–	4 in Meath and 1 in Louth.
Gaul (6)—Gaule (5),	11	7	4	–	–	4 Wexford, 4 Waterford, 2 Kilkenny, and 1 Kildare.
Gault,	16	1	–	15	–	13 in Antrim.
*Gavaghan (13),	23	5	–	5	13	" Gavaghan," 10 Mayo, and 3 Sligo.
*Gavin (44)—Gavan (19),	66	11	8	3	44	Of the Connaught entries under this name 30 are in Mayo and 12 in Galway.
Gaw,	6	–	–	6	–	4 in Down and 2 in Antrim.
Gawley,	6	–	–	3	3	Sligo.
*Gaynard (5),	6	–	–	–	6	5 in Mayo.
*Gaynor (21),	22	15	2	3	2	Dublin, Westmeath, and Cavan.
Geaney (8)—Geany (7),	15	–	14	–	1	13 in Cork.
*Geary (24),	26	3	18	2	3	Cork.
Geddis,	13	–	–	13	–	Antrim and Down.
Geelan,	6	1	1	–	4	—
*Geoghegan (33),	38	19	4	–	15	Dublin and Galway.
George,	12	1	2	9	–	—
*Geraghty (54),	72	28	2	–	42	Galway, Mayo, and Dublin.
Getty,	8	–	–	8	–	6 in Antrim and 2 in Londonderry.
*Gibb (5),	8	1	2	4	1	—
*Gibbons (76),	78	8	3	10	57	47 in Mayo and 7 in Galway.
*Giblin (29),	30	1	–	–	29	19 in Roscommon and 6 in Mayo.
Gibney,	26	15	–	11	–	Cavan and Dublin.
Gibson,	96	13	2	77	4	Down and Antrim.
*Giffen (8),	10	2	–	8	–	Antrim.
Gilbert,	16	9	1	5	1	Dublin and Antrim.
*Gilchrist (12),	18	4	–	12	2	—
*Gildea (13),	18	1	3	7	7	Donegal and Mayo.
Giles,	6	3	1	1	1	—
*Gilgan (8),	13	1	–	1	11	7 in Sligo.
*Gilhooly (8),	9	–	1	1	7	Leitrim.
Gill,	62	20	5	10	27	More than half are in Dublin, Galway, Mayo, and Longford.
*Gillan (18)—Gillen (16),	40	7	–	23	10	" Gillan," Antrim and Sligo—" Gillen," Antrim, Donegal, and Tyrone.
*Gilleece (6),	14	–	1	13	–	There are six varieties of this name in the Births Index for 1890.
*Gillespie (84),	86	3	–	76	7	Antrim, Donegal, Armagh, and Tyrone.

Names	Irl.	L.	M.	U.	C.	Counties in which principally found
Gillick, ...	9	–	1	8	–	8 in Cavan.
Gilligan, ..	32	14	2	5	11	Dublin.
Gilliland, ...	11	–	–	11	–	Antrim.
Gilmartin, ...	24	–	–	1	23	14 in Sligo and 8 in Leitrim.
*Gilmore (54)—Gilmour (18),	79	5	2	60	12	Antrim.
Gilpin, ...	9	–	–	9	–	7 in Armagh and 2 in Cavan.
Gilroy, ...	16	1	–	7	8	Leitrim and Mayo.
*Gilsenan (6), ...	12	7	–	5	–	—
Ginn, ...	6	1	1	4	–	—
*Ginty (16), ...	19	1	–	–	18	Mayo.
*Girvin (8)—Girvan (6),	15	–	–	15	–	11 in Antrim.
Glancy, ...	5	1	–	1	3	—
Glasgow, ...	7	–	–	7	–	4 in Tyrone, 2 in Antrim, and 1 in Armagh.
Glass, ...	17	–	–	17	–	Antrim and Londonderry.
Glavin, ...	7	–	7	–	–	4 in Cork and 3 in Kerry.
*Gleeson (81), ..	82	18	63	–	1	38 in Tipperary and 13 in Limerick—The remainder are principally in Dublin, Kilkenny, and Cork.
Glenn, ...	12	–	–	12	–	Antrim and Londonderry.
*Glennon (22), ..	28	18	–	3	7	—
Glover, ...	20	3	1	16	–	Antrim.
*Glynn (66), ...	72	15	11	1	45	About 70 per cent. are in Galway Mayo, Dublin, and Clare.
*Godfrey (17), ..	18	3	6	4	5	Mayo, Tipperary, and Kerry.
*Godkin (6,)	7	5	1	–	1	Wexford.
Gogarty, ...	7	5	1	1	–	Meath and Louth.
*Goggin (26), ..	34	4	26	–	4	The Munster entries are nearly all in Cork and Kerry.
*Golden (22), ...	24	2	7	–	15	Mayo, Sligo, Kerry, and Cork.
*Good (16), ...	19	1	12	3	3	11 in Cork.
Goodbody, ...	5	5	–	–	–	—
Goodman, ...	9	2	–	7	–	Armagh and Monaghan.
*Goodwin (24), ..	26	10	2	13	1	Dublin and Monaghan.
Goold, ...	6	–	5	1	–	Cork.
*Gordon (118), ..	122	22	3	82	15	Antrim, Down, and Dublin. More than half the Ulster entries are in Antrim.
*Gorham (11), ...	12	–	–	–	12	All in Galway.
Gorman, ...	140	57	40	33	10	Antrim, Dublin, and Tipperary—but generally distributed in the counties of Leinster and Munster.
*Gormley (31), ..	44	5	1	25	13	Antrim and Tyrone.
Gough (17)—Goff (13),	30	15	10	4	1	Dublin and Waterford.
*Gould (10), ...	12	–	4	8	–	—
*Goulding (15)-Golding (9),	27	9	11	1	6	" Goulding," Dublin and Cork—" Golding," Galway.
*Gourley (20), ..	23	3	–	20	–	Antrim.
Gowen, ...	5	1	4	–	–	Cork.
Grace, ...	36	21	15	–	–	Dublin and Kilkenny.
Gracey, ...	9	–	1	8	–	Down and Armagh.
Grady	68	11	31	1	25	Mayo, Clare, Kerry, and Roscommon.
*Graham (195), ..	204	28	5	166	5	Antrim, Down, Dublin, Tyrone, Armagh, and Monaghan.
*Grainger (9), ...	11	4	3	–	–	—
Grange	6	3	–	3	–	3 in Dublin and 3 in Antrim.
Grant, ...	77	21	13	42	1	Antrim and Donegal.
*Grattan (3), ...	5	–	–	5	–	—
*Graves (5), ...	6	3	2	1	–	—
*Gray (97), ...	117	33	7	70	7	Antrim, Down, Londonderry, and Dublin.
*Graydon (6), ...	7	6	–	1	–	—
Gready, ...	22	5	11	–	6	Tipperary.
*Grealish (6), ...	7	–	–	–	7	" Grealish," all in Galway.
*Greally (9), ...	15	1	–	–	14	9 in Galway and 5 in Mayo.
*Greany (19), ...	30	4	17	–	9	Kerry and Galway.
Greehy, ...	5	–	5	–	–	3 in Waterford and 2 in Cork.
Green (105)—Greene (47),	152	39	37	54	22	Dublin, Antrim, Galway, Tipperary, and Clare.
Greenan, ...	8	2	1	5	–	Cavan.
Greenaway, ...	7	1	–	6	–	Down and Antrim.
Greer, ...	63	2	2	58	1	Antrim, Armagh, and Down—more than half being in Antrim.
Gregan, ...	5	4	1	–	–	—
Gregg, ...	29	6	2	21	–	10 in Antrim and 9 in Down.
Gregory, ...	14	7	1	5	1	—
*Grehan (22), ...	22	11	1	–	11	Mayo, Galway, Sligo, and Westmeath.
*Grennan (18), ..	19	11	–	–	8	Mayo and Dublin.
*Gribben (18), ..	28	1	–	27	–	All except 3 in Antrim, Armagh, and Down.
*Griffin (206), ..	216	31	133	16	36	Kerry, Clare, Cork, Limerick, Galway, Mayo, and Dublin—very few in any other County except Tipperary and Waterford.

Names	Irl.	L.	M.	U.	C.	Counties in which principally found
*Griffith (16),	22	9	3	8	2	—
Grimason,	5	–	–	5	–	Armagh.
Grimes,	39	15	4	13	7	Tyrone and Mayo.
Grimley,	7	1	1	5	–	Armagh.
*Groarke (7),	9	1	–	–	8	Mayo.
*Grogan (39),	44	16	13	5	10	Dublin, Tipperary, Mayo, and Clare.
Groves,	8	–	4	4	–	Kerry and Antrim.
*Gubbins (5),	7	–	5	2	–	Limerick.
*Guerin (11),	12	–	11	1	–	Limerick.
*Guihen (7),	10	-	1	–	9	" Guihen," all in Roscommon.
Guilfoyle,	11	9	–	–	2	Dublin.
*Guinan (13)—Guinane (7),	21	11	7	–	3	"Guinan," 10 in King's Co.—" Guinane," 5 in Tipperary.
*Guiney (16),	17	–	13	4	–	Cork.
Guiry,	8	1	7	–	-	6 in Limerick.
Gunn,	9	4	–	5	–	—
Gunning,	12	4	–	7	1	Antrim.
Gurry,	5	3	–	–	2	—
*Guthrie (9),	11	1	5	4	1	Clare.
Guy,	11	3	–	8	–	Armagh and Londonderry.
*Hackett (30),	34	14	8	11	1	Tyrone, Dublin, and Kilkenny.
*Haddock (10),	12	1	1	10	–	Armagh.
Haddon (8)—Hadden (6),	14	2	2	10	–	—
Hagan (49)	63	12	–	49	2	Antrim, Tyrone, and Armagh.
*Hale (8),	13	–	6	6	1	Cork and Antrim.
*Halfpenny (8),	12	5	2	5	–	Louth.
Hall,	120	37	13	69	1	Antrim, Dublin, and Armagh.
*Hallahan (4),	8	–	8	–	–	Cork.
*Halliday (18),	19	2	–	16	1	Antrim.
Halligan,	27	10	–	8	9	Roscommon, Dublin, Louth, Armagh, and Mayo.
*Hallinan (9),	10	–	6	–	4	Clare.
*Hallissy (6),	12	–	12	–	–	7 in Cork and 5 in Kerry.
*Halloran (65),	67	2	51	–	14	Clare, Galway, and Cork.
Hally,	13	2	11	–	–	Tipperary.
Halpin,	33	18	12	3	–	Dublin and Clare.
Halton,	9	6	–	3	–	Meath.
*Hamill (68),	77	17	2	56	2	Antrim, Armagh, and Louth.
*Hamilton (166)	167	10	8	143	6	Antrim, Down, Tyrone, and Londonderry.
Hammond,	13	1	3	9	–	Donegal.
Hampton,	5	1	–	4	–	—
Hand,	28	18	4	6	–	Dublin.
*Hanifin (6)—Hanafin (5),	17	–	17	–	–	15 in Kerry.
*Hanlon (93),	95	50	24	20	1	Dublin, Kerry, Louth, and Wexford.
Hanly (60)—Hanley (35),	95	10	39	2	44	" Hanly," Roscommon, Galway, Limerick, and Tipperary—" Hanley," Cork.
*Hanna (81),	86	1	1	84	–	34 in Antrim, 26 in Down, and 10 in Armagh.
*Hannigan (25),	30	7	10	12	1	Dublin, Waterford, and Tyrone.
*Hannon (44)—Hannan (32),	92	14	28	10	40	Galway, Roscommon, Limerick, Cork, and Sligo.
Hanrahan,	54	9	42	1	2	Clare and Limerick.
Hanratty,	30	14	–	16	–	12 in Louth, 9 in Armagh, 7 in Monaghan, and 2 in Dublin.
Hanvey,	5	1	–	4	–	—
Hara,	5	–	–	–	5	All in Galway.
*Haran (16)—Haren (11),	37	1	8	11	17	" Haran," Mayo—" Haren," Clare.
Harbison,	11	–	1	10	–	Antrim.
Hardiman,	7	1	–	–	6	Galway.
Harding,	17	8	7	2	–	Dublin and Tipperary.
Hardy,	19	9	1	8	1	Louth, Dublin, and Tyrone.
*Hare (11)—Haire (10),	22	1	3	13	5	Antrim.
*Harford (16),	17	14	–	2	1	11 in Dublin.
*Hargadon (8),	11	–	–	–	11	9 in Sligo, 1 in Leitrim, and 1 in Roscommon
*Hargan (5),	6	–	1	4	1	—
*Harkin (53),	56	3	1	45	7	32 in Donegal and 8 in Londonderry.
Harkness,	13	1	1	10	1	Antrim.
Harley,	7	–	3	3	1	—
*Harmon (7),	12	8	2	2	–	Wicklow.
Harnett,	15	2	13	–	–	10 in Limerick and 3 in Kerry.
Harney,	11	2	4	–	5	3 in Tipperary and 3 in Galway.
Harold (9)—Harrold (6),	15	3	11	1	–	" Harold," Cork—" Harrold," Limerick.
*Harper (32)—Harpur (18),	51	15	2	34	–	" Harper," Antrim—" Harpur," Wexford.
*Harrell (4),	5	4	–	1	–	—
Harrington,	119	7	99	1	12	82 in Cork, 11 in Kerry, and 7 in Mayo.

Names	Irl.	L.	M.	U.	C.	Counties in which principally found
*Harris (58), ...	59	21	21	15	2	Dublin, Cork, and Antrim.
*Harrison (44), ..	48	11	4	27	6	Antrim, Dublin, and Down.
Hart (64)—Harte (58),	122	27	16	28	51	" Hart," Antrim, Dublin, and Cork—" Harte," Sligo, Leitrim, and Roscommon.
Hartigan, ...	16	4	10	–	2	Limerick.
*Hartin (5), ...	10	5	–	5	–	Antrim and Longford.
*Hartnett (24), ..	27	2	25	–	–	10 in Limerick and 13 in Cork.
Hartney, ...	8	2	5	1	–	3 in Limerick and 2 in Clare.
Harty, ...	17	1	16	–	–	Tipperary, Cork, and Kerry.
*Harvey (53), ..	54	12	5	35	2	Antrim, Dublin, Down, and Donegal.
Haslam, ...	6	5	–	1	–	Dublin.
Hassan, ...	7	1	–	6	–	—
Hassett, ...	11	1	10	–	–	Clare and Tipperary.
Hastings, ...	22	4	6	3	9	8 in Mayo and 5 in Clare.
Hatton, ...	7	4	–	3	–	—
Haugh (20)—Hough (7),	27	1	24	2	–	" Haugh," 13 in Clare—" Hough," 4 in Tipperary and 3 in Limerick.
Haughey, ...	14	–	–	14	–	5 in Armagh, and 5 in Donegal.
Haughton, ...	9	5	1	2	1	—
*Hawe (7), ...	10	4	3	3	–	—
Hawes, ...	5	1	3	–	1	—
*Hawkes (6), ..	7	–	5	2	–	Cork.
Hawkins, ...	18	5	3	6	4	Antrim, Galway, and Cork.
*Hawthorne (15), ..	27	2	1	23	1	Antrim, Down, and Armagh.
*Hay (5), ...	6	–	1	5	–	—
*Hayden (43), ..	45	28	9	2	6	Dublin, Carlow, and Tipperary.
*Hayes (271), ...	275	57	181	27	10	Cork, Limerick, Tipperary, Dublin, and Wexford. Antrim is the only County in Ulster, and Galway in Connaught, in which the name is found to any appreciable extent.
Hazlett (10)—Haslett (9).	19	2	–	15	2	Antrim and Londonderry.
*Healy (272), ...	291	50	151	6	84	About two-thirds are found in Cork, Kerry, Dublin, Galway, Roscommon, and Mayo.
*Heaney (39), ..	56	18	2	32	4	Antrim, Armagh, and Louth.
Heanue, ...	14	–	–	5	9	8 in Galway and 5 in Donegal.
Heaphy, ...	8	2	6	–	–	Cork.
Hearne (6)—Hearn (5),	11	2	8	1	–	8 in Waterford.
Hearty, ...	8	6	–	2	–	6 in Louth and 2 in Monaghan.
*Heavey (6)-Heavy (5),	12	7	2	–	3	—
*Heelan (6), ..	7	2	5	–	–	Waterford.
Heenan, ...	6	–	3	3	–	Tipperary.
Heffernan, ...	53	16	36	–	1	Tipperary.
*Heffron (7), ...	20	4	2	–	14	" Heffron," all in Mayo—these 20 entries contain 7 varieties.
Hegan, ...	5	1	–	4	–	Armagh.
*Hegarty (96), ..	100	6	56	27	11	Four-fifths are found in Cork, Donegal, Clare, Londonderry, and Mayo.
*Hehir (24), ..	28	1	22	–	5	18 in Clare and 4 in Limerick.
Hemphill, ...	7	–	–	6	1	Londonderry and Tyrone.
Henderson, ...	72	12	1	57	2	Antrim and Tyrone.
Hendrick, ...	12	10	1	1	–	7 in Dublin.
*Henehan (14)—Heneghan (11).	49	1	2	–	46	Mayo.
*Henneberry (7), ..	13	2	11	–	–	Waterford and Tipperary.
*Hennessy (95), ..	111	31	74	3	3	Cork, Limerick, Tipperary, and Dublin.
*Henry (124), ...	132	17	1	73	41	Antrim, Sligo, and Tyrone.
*Heraghty (12), ..	16	–	–	6	10	Mayo and Donegal.
Herbert, ...	25	8	12	4	1	Dublin and Limerick.
Herdman, ...	6	–	–	6	–	Antrim.
*Herlihy (38), ..	42	1	41	–	–	29 in Cork and 11 in Kerry.
*Hernon (6), ...	8	2	–	1	5	5 in Galway.
Herron (23)-Heron (22),	45	5	1	38	1	13 in Antrim, and 10 each in Donegal and Down.
Heslin, ...	8	3	–	1	4	Leitrim.
*Hession (17), ..	21	–	–	2	19	15 in Galway and 4 in Mayo.
Hester, ...	8	1	–	–	7	4 in Mayo and 3 in Roscommon
*Hetherington (7), ..	8	1	–	7	–	Tyrone.
*Hewitt (36), ..	40	4	5	31	–	Antrim and Armagh.
*Hickey (132), ..	139	45	82	7	5	Cork, Tipperary, Dublin, Limerick, and Clare.
Hicks, ...	10	3	2	5	–	—
*Higgins (203), ..	205	45	32	23	105	Mayo, Galway, Dublin, Roscommon, Cork, and Antrim.
Higginson, ...	8	–	–	8	–	Antrim.
Hill, ...	118	26	14	71	7	Antrim, Dublin, and Down.
*Hilland (6), ..	7	–	–	7	–	6 in Antrim and 1 in Down.
Hilliard	11	6	2	3	–	Dublin.
*Hillis (10), ..	12	5	–	6	1	Antrim.
Hilton, ...	6	2	3	1	–	—

Names	Irl.	L.	M.	U.	C.	Counties in which principally found
*Hinchy (7),	14	3	10	1	–	—
Hinds (14)—Hynds (6),	20	2	–	13	5	Down and Roscommon.
*Hoare (18),	30	8	20	–	2	Kerry, Cork, and Dublin.
Hoban, ..	22	6	4	–	12	10 in Mayo and 6 in Kilkenny.
Hobbs, ..	5	2	1	2	–	—
Hobson, ..	11	3	1	7	–	Antrim.
Hodges (6)—Hodge (6),	12	4	3	5	–	
*Hodgins (11)—Hodgen (5).	19	4	7	8	–	" Hodgins," Tipperary—" Hodgen," Down.
Hodnett,	5	–	5	–	–	4 in Cork and 1 in Tipperary.
Hoey, ..	33	22	4	6	1	Louth and Dublin.
Hogan, ..	193	59	115	5	14	Tipperary, Dublin, Limerick, Clare, and Cork.
*Hogg (17),	18	1	2	14	1	Antrim and Londonderry.
Holden, ..	20	10	4	5	1	Dublin, Waterford, and Antrim.
Holland,	52	10	22	12	8	Cork, Galway, and Dublin.
*Holleran (6), ..	9	–	–	–	9	6 in Galway and 3 in Mayo.
Holly, ..	8	1	3	4	–	Londonderry and Cork.
Hollywood,	9	5	–	4	–	Louth.
Holman,	5	–	2	1	2	—
* Holmes (81), ..	84	24	11	38	11	Antrim and Dublin.
Holt, ..	8	5	–	2	1	—
Homan, ..	5	3	2	–	–	—
Hood, ..	9	2	–	5	2	Antrim.
Hope, ..	6	2	3	–	1	
Hopkins,	44	12	2	6	24	Mayo and Dublin—nearly one-half being in the former County.
Hopper, ..	8	1	–	4	3	Tyrone.
Horan, ..	63	12	26	2	23	Mayo, Kerry, Tipperary, and Roscommon.
Horgan, ..	66	–	66	–	–	40 in Cork and 21 in Kerry.
*Horne (4),	6	2	2	2	–	
Horner, ..	6	1	–	5	–	Antrim.
Hornibrook,	5	–	5	–	–	All in Cork.
Horrigan,	7	–	7	–	–	Cork.
Hosford,	10	1	9	–	–	9 in Cork.
Hosty, ..	6	–	–	–	6	5 in Mayo and 1 in Galway.
*Houlihan (38)—Holohan (11).	71	20	49	–	2	" Houlihan," Kerry, Limerick, Cork, and Clare—" Holohan," Kilkenny.
*Hourigan (17),	22	4	17	1	–	Limerick and Tipperary.
*Hourihane (9),	16	–	16	–	–	15 in Cork.
*Houston (49)—Huston (19).	76	4	3	68	1	Antrim, Londonderry, Armagh, and Down.
Howard,	61	20	25	8	8	Dublin, Cork, Clare, and Limerick.
Howe, ..	16	4	5	6	1	—
Howell, ..	8	3	4	1	–	Cork.
Howlett,	5	5	–	–	–	3 in Wexford and 2 in Dublin.
Howley, ..	14	–	4	1	9	Clare, Mayo, and Sligo.
*Howlin (5),	6	6	–	–	–	All in Wexford.
Hoy, ..	15	1	–	13	1	9 in Antrim and 2 in Down.
*Hoyne (5),	6	6	–	–	–	Kilkenny.
Hudson, ..	23	15	3	3	2	Dublin.
Huggard,	8	3	2	1	2	—
*Hughes (328), ..	334	92	7	180	55	Armagh, Antrim, Dublin, Tyrone, Monaghan, Galway, and Mayo.
Hughey, ..	6	–	–	6	–	Tyrone.
Hull, ..	10	–	–	9	1	Antrim and Armagh.
*Hume (8),	10	1	–	9	–	Antrim.
*Humphries (15),	32	7	7	18	–	Armagh and Dublin.
Hunt, ..	76	14	16	4	42	Mayo, Roscommon, Dublin, and Waterford.
Hunter, ..	95	7	4	80	4	Antrim, Londonderry, and Down.
*Hurley (129), ..	134	15	113	–	6	86 in Cork, 10 in Waterford, 9 in Dublin, and 6 in Galway.
Hurson, ..	5	2	–	3	–	Longford and Tyrone.
Hurst, ..	10	1	–	5	4	—
*Hussey (21), ..	26	7	9	1	9	Kerry, Galway, and Roscommon.
*Hutchinson (44)-Hutchison (15).	64	13	3	45	3	Londonderry, Antrim, Down, and Dublin.
Hutton, ..	15	4	–	11	–	Antrim and Londonderry.
*Hyde (11),	15	1	7	7	–	Cork and Antrim.
Hyland, ..	55	28	9	5	13	Mayo, Dublin, and Queen's.
Hyndman,	14	–	–	14	–	8 in Antrim and 5 in Londonderry.
*Hynes (81),	83	20	20	6	37	Galway, Clare, Mayo, and Dublin.
*Igoe (6),	10	3	–	–	7	3 in Longford, 3 in Mayo, and 3 in Roscommon.
*Ingram (12), ..	13	1	1	11	–	9 in Antrim.
Ireland, ..	21	3	1	17	–	Antrim and Armagh.
*Irvine (66),	68	3	1	62	2	Antrim and Fermanagh.
Irwin, ..	118	3	12	96	7	Armagh, Antrim, Tyrone, and Londonderry
*Ivers (8),	11	8	–	2	1	Dublin and Louth.
*Ivory (8),	9	8	–	1	–	Dublin.

Names	Irl.	L.	M.	U.	C.	Counties in which principally found
Jack,	8	1	2	5	–	—
*Jackson (100),	101	20	12	60	9	Scattered, but chiefly found in Antrim, Armagh, and Dublin. In Munster, Cork contributes the largest number, and in Connaught, Mayo.
*Jacob (9),	11	9	1	1	–	Dublin.
*Jagoe (4),	6	–	5	–	1	5 in Cork.
James,	12	7	2	3	–	—
*Jamison (24)-Jameson (20)—Jamieson (7).	52	10	1	41	–	" Jamison " and " Jamieson," 16 in Antrim and 9 in Down—" Jameson," Dublin.
*Jeffers (12),	16	4	6	3	3	
*Jenkins (25),	29	6	1	19	3	Antrim and Dublin.
Jenkinson,	7	6	–	1	–	Dublin.
*Jennings (61),	63	6	11	12	34	About 75 per cent. in Mayo, Galway, Cork, and Armagh.
Jess,	7	–	–	7	–	All in Down.
Johnson,	58	18	21	16	3	Cork, Dublin, and Antrim. A scattered name.
Johnston (320)—Johnstone (21).	341	43	4	281	13	" Johnston," Antrim, Down, Armagh, Fermanagh, and Dublin, but found in nearly, every county in Ireland. " Johnstone," Cavan and Londonderry.
Jolly,	5	4	–	–	1	Dublin.
Jones,	152	60	38	45	9	Though found in nearly every County, considerably more than half are in Dublin, Cork, Antrim, and Armagh.
*Jordan (91),	98	36	10	21	31	Dublin, Mayo, Antrim, and Galway.
*Joy (14),	15	1	10	3	1	Waterford.
Joyce,	164	15	17	1	131	85 in Galway and 46 in Mayo.
Judge,	30	9	1	6	14	Mayo, Dublin, and Tyrone.
*Kane (175),	190	57	10	96	27	Antrim, Londonderry, and Dublin.
*Kavanagh (230),	274	205	27	22	20	Dublin, Wexford, and Wicklow—Dublin alone containing 50 per cent. of the entries in Leinster.
Keady,	16	2	2	–	12	11 in Galway.
*Keane (185),	202	13	113	6	70	Galway, Clare, Kerry, and Mayo.
*Keany (18),	33	1	–	8	24	Leitrim, Galway, and Donegal.
*Kearney (137),	147	50	31	45	21	Found all over Ireland, but chiefly in Dublin, Cork, and Antrim.
*Kearns (71),	87	35	10	16	26	Dublin and Mayo.
Kearon,	7	7	–	–	–	All in Wicklow.
*Keating (121),	130	43	74	10	3	Cork, Kerry, Tipperary, and Dublin.
*Keaveny (15),	33	–	–	1	32	Galway and Sligo.
Kee,	6	–	–	6	–	—
*Keeffe (93),	110	29	76	1	4	Cork, Waterford, Kerry, and Kilkenny.
*Keegan (93),	95	61	5	8	21	Dublin, Roscommon, Wicklow, and Leitrim.
Keena,	7	4	–	1	2	—
Keenan,	103	34	1	57	11	Antrim, Monaghan, Dublin, and Down.
Keith,	7	–	1	6	–	Antrim and Down.
Kell,	6	–	–	5	1	5 in Antrim.
*Kelleher (92)—Kelliher (24).	148	2	124	5	17	92 in Cork and 23 in Kerry.
*Kellett (7),	8	4	–	4	–	Cavan and Dublin.
Kells,	10	4	–	5	1	
*Kelly (1,238),	1,242	435	211	267	329	Found in every County in Ireland—chiefly, however, in Dublin, Galway, Mayo, Roscommon, and Cork.
Kelso,	7	2	–	5	–	Antrim.
Kemp,	6	–	2	4	–	—
Kempton,	5	–	–	5	–	Antrim.
Kenna,	21	13	7	–	1	Dublin and Tipperary.
*Kenneally (10)—Kennelly (9).	36	1	35	–	–	Cork, Waterford, and Tipperary.
*Kennedy (436),	446	123	149	112	62	Found in every County—largest numbers in Tipperary, Dublin, and Antrim.
*Kenny (211),	216	95	31	19	71	Dublin, Galway, and Roscommon.
Kenrick,	5	1	4	–	–	
Kent,	13	4	9	–	–	Cork.
*Keogh (96)—Kehoe (51).	163	127	25	4	7	" Keogh," Dublin—" Kehoe," Wexford.
*Keohane (21),	25	1	23	1	–	" Keohane," all in Cork.
*Keon (8)—Keown (8),	18	–	–	14	4	Donegal, Down, and Fermanagh.
*Kerin (15),	17	1	14	2	–	Kerry and Clare.
Kerley,	8	6	2	–	–	Louth.
*Kernaghan (11)—Kernohan (8).	26	3	2	20	1	" Kernaghan," Armagh—" Kernohan," all in Antrim.

Names	Irl.	L.	M.	U.	C.	Counties in which principally found
Kerr, ...	142	12	2	123	5	Antrim, Down, and Tyrone—50 per cent. of those in Ulster being in Antrim.
Kerrane, ...	7	–	–	–	7	5 in Mayo and 2 in Galway.
*Kerrigan (37), ..	41	12	1	11	17	Mayo and Donegal.
Kerrisk, ...	5	–	5	–	–	All in Kerry.
Kerwick, ...	5	3	2	–	–	Kilkenny.
*Kevane (13), ..	19	1	16	1	1	14 in Kerry.
Keys (22)—Keyes (10),	32	9	8	15	..	"Keys," Fermanagh and Antrim—"Keyes," Tipperary and Wexford.
Kidd, ...	28	9	1	18	–	Antrim, Armagh, and Dublin.
Kidney, ...	7	–	7	–	–	All in Cork.
*Kielty (6), ..	9	–	–	2	7	Galway and Roscommon.
*Kiely (36)—Keely (27)—Kealy (18)—Keily (10)—Keeley (9).	110	44	51	3	12	"Kiely" and "Keily," Cork, Limerick, and Waterford—"Keely" and "Keeley," Dublin, Wicklow, and Galway—"Kealy," Kilkenny.
*Kiernan (56), ..	70	45	1	14	10	Almost wholly confined to the Counties of Longford, Cavan, Dublin, and Leitrim.
Kilbane, ...	8	–	–	–	8	All in Mayo.
Kilbride, ...	7	3	–	–	4	—
Kilcoyne, ...	15	–	–	–	15	10 in Mayo and 4 in Sligo.
Kilcullen, ...	6	1	–	–	5	5 in Sligo.
Kilduff, ...	5	3	–	–	2	—
Kilgallon, ...	8	–	–	–	8	All in Mayo.
Kilgannon, ...	8	–	–	–	8	4 in Galway and 4 in Sligo.
*Kilkelly (6), ..	7	–	–	–	7	Galway and Roscommon.
Kilkenny, ...	18	1	–	1	16	Leitrim, Mayo, and Roscommon.
Killeen, ...	40	12	16	–	12	Clare, Mayo, and King's.
*Killelea (6), ..	10	–	–	–	10	7 in Galway and 3 in Roscommon.
Killen, ...	14	3	2	8	1	6 in Antrim.
*Killian (13), ..	18	8	–	–	10	8 in Roscommon and 5 in Westmeath.
Killoran, ...	7	–	–	–	7	Roscommon and Sligo.
Kilmartin, ...	22	8	6	–	8	Roscommon.
Kilpatrick	24	–	–	24	–	16 in Antrim.
Kilroy, ...	15	–	–	1	14	6 in Mayo, 5 in Roscommon, and 3 in Sligo.
*Kinahan (7), ..	15	11	3	–	1	Dublin and Louth.
*Kinane (9)—Kinnane (6),	18	1	16	–	1	Tipperary.
King, ...	203	43	47	51	62	Galway, Dublin, Antrim, Mayo, and Limerick.
Kinghan, ...	5	–	–	4	1	4 in Down and 1 in Mayo.
Kingston, ...	40	3	37	–	–	37 in Cork and 3 in Dublin.
Kinnear, ...	5	1	1	3	–	
*Kinsella (75), ..	81	73	6	–	2	Dublin, Wexford, Wicklow, and Kildare.
Kirby, ...	33	5	17	3	8	Mayo, Kerry, and Limerick.
*Kirk (28), ..	38	12	4	19	3	Antrim and Louth.
Kirkland, ...	6	–	–	5	1	—
Kirkpatrick, ..	25	–	1	22	2	16 in Antrim.
Kirkwood, ...	8	–	1	7	–	7 in Antrim and 1 in Limerick.
*Kirrane (6), ..	8	–	–	–	8	"Kirrane," all in Mayo.
*Kirwan (42), ..	59	40	13	3	3	Dublin, Wexford, and Tipperary.
Kissane, ...	19	–	18	–	1	16 in Kerry.
*Kitterick (5), ..	6	1	–	–	5	"Kitterick," all in Mayo.
Knight, ...	13	4	4	3	2	
Knowles, ...	13	7	1	5	–	Dublin and Antrim.
Knox, ...	45	5	6	32	2	Antrim.
Kyle, ...	26	1	1	23	1	Antrim and Londonderry.
Kyne, ...	27	–	–	–	27	26 in Galway and 1 in Mayo.
*Lacey (21)—Lacy (19)—Leacy (8).	50	36	9	1	4	Wexford, Dublin, and Galway.
Laffan, ...	8	3	5	–	–	Limerick, Tipperary, and Wexford.
Lafferty, ...	17	–	–	17	–	10 in Donegal, 5 in Londonderry, and 2 in Tyrone.
*Laffey (5), ..	7	–	–	1	6	4 in Galway and 1 in Mayo.
Lagan, ...	8	–	1	7	–	Londonderry.
*Lahey (4), ..	7	1	3	–	3	—
Lahiff, ...	8	3	5	–	–	Dublin and Clare.
Laird, ...	17	–	–	16	1	Antrim.
*Lally (33), ..	34	1	1	2	30	17 in Mayo and 11 in Galway.
Lamb (37)—Lambe (13),	50	26	6	13	5	Dublin.
Lambert, ...	22	13	1	4	4	Wexford and Dublin.
*Lamont (16), ..	18	2	–	16	–	11 in Antrim.
*Landers (18), ..	19	1	16	–	2	Waterford and Kerry.
Landy, ...	9	1	4	–	4	Tipperary and Galway.
Lane, ...	69	10	49	3	7	38 in Cork and 10 in Limerick.
Lang, ...	15	–	–	10	5	Cavan.
Langan, ...	19	6	1	2	10	Mayo.
Langton, ...	6	4	1	–	1	—

Names	Irl.	L.	M.	U.	C.	Counties in which principally found
*Lanigan (18), ...	21	14	5	1	1	Kilkenny.
*Lannon (7), ...	11	8	1	–	2	Kilkenny.
Lappin, ...	26	2	–	24	–	Armagh, Tyrone, and Antrim.
Larkin, ...	85	34	19	20	12	Dublin, Armagh, Galway, and Tipperary.
*Larmour (15), ..	17	–	–	17	–	9 in Antrim and 6 in Down.
Latimer, ...	8	4	–	4	–	Dublin.
*Lavelle (33), ..	38	–	–	4	34	28 in Mayo and 5 in Galway.
Laverty, ...	26	–	–	26	–	Antrim.
Lavery, ...	51	–	–	51	–	Armagh, Antrim, and Down.
Lavin (28), Lavan (14),	42	1	–	–	41	22 in Mayo and 13 in Roscommon.
*Law (18), ...	19	1	2	16	–	Antrim.
Lawder (3), Lauder (3),	6	4	1	1	–	—
Lawless, ...	42	21	3	4	14	13 in Dublin and 12 in Galway, the remaining 17 being scattered over 14 counties.
Lawlor (59)—Lalor (42)—Lawler (41),	142	115	25	2	–	Dublin, Queen's, Wicklow, and Wexford.
*Lawn (6), ...	7	–	–	7	–	5 in Donegal and 2 in Tyrone.
*L a w r e n c e (1 2),—Laurence (7),	19	12	3	3	1	Dublin and Tipperary.
Lawson, ...	15	3	1	10	1	Dublin, Armagh, and Down.
Lawton, ...	10	1	7	2	–	7 in Cork.
*Leahy (99), ..	105	13	82	7	3	Cork, Kerry, Limerick, and Tipperary.
*Leane (9), ..	11	–	11	–	–	9 in Kerry and 2 in Limerick.
*Leary (185), ..	186	38	142	3	3	93 in Cork, 38 in Kerry, and 21 in Wexford.
*Leathem (8), ..	11	–	2	9	–	Armagh.
*Leavy (22), ..	31	22	6	2	1	Longford and Westmeath.
*Leckey (6), ..	10	–	1	9	–	—
Leddy, ...	15	3	2	9	1	9 in Cavan.
*Ledwith (5), ..	10	9	–	–	1	Dublin.
*Lee (118), ..	120	33	21	43	23	A very scattered name, but 50 per cent. are found in Antrim, Dublin, Galway, and Limerick.
*Leech (28), ..	35	14	4	9	8	Dublin.
Lees, ...	6	2	2	2	–	—
Leeson, ...	6	3	1	2	–	Dublin.
*Legge (6), ..	8	1	2	5	–	—
*Lehane (23), ..	30	–	30	–	–	29 in Cork and 1 in Kerry.
Leigh, ...	8	8	–	–	–	—
*Lemon (13), ..	15	1	1	12	1	Antrim.
*Lennon (102), ..	103	49	6	36	12	Dublin and Armagh.
Lennox, ...	18	3	1	13	1	Antrim and Londonderry.
Leo, ...	5	–	5	–	–	All in Limerick.
Leonard, ...	99	31	15	18	35	Dublin, Sligo, and Cork.
Leslie, ...	15	3	3	9	–	Londonderry.
Lester, ...	5	1	2	2	–	—
L'Estrange, ..	8	8	–	–	–	—
*Levins (6), ..	7	7	–	–	–	—
Lewis, ...	51	16	16	18	1	About 70 per cent. in Dublin, Antrim, Cork and Tipperary.
*Leyden (10), ..	11	1	4	1	5	Sligo and Clare.
*Liddane (6), ..	7	1	5	–	1	Clare.
*Liddy (8), ..	9	–	6	3	–	6 in Clare and 3 in Antrim.
Liggett, ...	6	1	–	5	–	3 in Armagh and 2 in Antrim.
Lightbody, ..	6	–	–	6	–	All in Down.
Lillis, ...	5	–	4	–	1	—
Lilly (8)—Lilley (6), ..	14	–	–	13	1	Antrim and Down.
Linane (10)-Linnane (5),	15	–	13	–	2	Limerick, Kerry, and Clare.
*Lindsay (36), ..	38	5	1	31	1	50 per cent. in Antrim.
*Linehan (50)-Lenaghan (18)-Lenihan (14),	104	7	63	7	27	" Linehan," 41 in Cork—" Lenaghan," Antrim—" Lenihan," Limerick.
Linton, ...	13	1	1	11	–	Antrim.
*Lipsett (6), ..	7	–	2	4	1	—
Liston, ...	12	–	11	–	1	10 in Limerick.
*Little (43)-Lyttle (14),	59	15	1	42	1	Antrim, Dublin, and Fermanagh.
Livingstone (19)—Living-stone (14)—Levingston (10),	43	1	4	37	1	Armagh, Antrim, and Down.
*Lloyd (19), ..	20	4	8	3	5	Tipperary.
*Locke (5), ..	8	4	2	1	1	—
Lockhart, ..	21	2	–	17	2	Armagh and Antrim.
Loftus, ...	34	3	2	–	29	23 in Mayo.
Logan, ...	55	9	3	39	4	Antrim.
Logue, ...	31	–	–	31	–	17 in Londonderry and 9 in Donegal.
*Lohan (12), ..	14	–	1	–	13	11 in Galway.
Lombard, ...	6	–	6	–	–	All in Cork.
*Lonergan (49)—Lon-drigan (5),	56	10	46	–	–	Tipperary, Waterford, Kilkenny, and Cork.
Long, ...	91	19	46	21	5	Cork, Dublin, Limerick, Kerry, and Donegal.
Looby (11)—Luby (5),	16	4	9	–	3	Tipperary.
*Looney (22), ..	23	–	23	–	–	Cork and Clare.

Names	Irl.	L.	M.	U.	C.	Counties in which principally found
Lord, ...	5	2	1	2	–	—
*Lordan (12), ..	13	–	13	–	–	All in Cork.
*Lorimer (7), ..	8	–	1	7	–	6 in Antrim.
*Lougheed (5), ..	7	2	1	3	1	—
*Loughlin (39)-Laughlin (14),	57	18	7	22	10	"Loughlin," Leitrim, Dublin, and Kilkenny "Laughlin," Tyrone and Antrim.
*Loughman (9),	10	4	5	–	1	—
*Loughnane (10), ..	13	1	6	–	6	—
*Loughran (37),	41	6	–	35	–	Tyrone, Antrim, and Armagh.
*Loughrey (12), ..	13	2	1	8	2	—
Love, ...	22	5	2	15	–	Londonderry.
Lovett, ..	9	2	6	1	–	6 in Kerry.
*Lowe (18), ...	21	10	1	9	1	Dublin.
Lowney, ..	6	–	6	–	–	All in Cork.
*Lowry (53), ...	71	21	4	37	9	Dublin, Antrim, and Down.
Loy, ...	5	1	–	4	–	—
Lucas, ...	22	5	5	12	–	Tyrone and Cavan.
*Lucey (29), ..	42	1	41	–	–	35 in Cork and 4 in Kerry.
Luke, ...	9	3	–	6	–	6 in Antrim.
Lundy, ...	12	1	–	7	4	—
Lunn, ...	9	2	–	6	1	Armagh.
*Lunney (11)-Lunny (9),	24	1	–	20	3	Fermanagh.
*Lydon (49), ..	57	1	–	–	56	33 in Galway and 22 in Mayo.
Lyle, ...	5	–	–	5	–	4 in Antrim.
Lynagh, ...	6	1	1	3	1	—
Lynam, ...	22	19	1	–	2	Dublin and King's.
*Lynas (10)-Lyness (9),	23	–	–	23	–	Antrim and Down.
Lynch, ...	444	125	184	94	39	Found in nearly every county, but chiefly in Cork, Cavan, Dublin, Kerry, Limerick, Clare, Meath, and Londonderry.
Lyne, ...	17	–	17	–	–	16 in Kerry.
Lynn, ...	24	6	–	15	3	Antrim.
*Lynskey (9), ..	11	–	–	–	11	6 in Galway and 5 in Mayo.
Lyons, ...	210	34	85	20	71	Mayo, Cork, Galway, Dublin, Kerry, and Limerick. Of the 34 in Leinster, 22 are in Dublin.
*Lysaght (12), ..	13	–	12	–	1	Limerick.
Mack, ...	20	2	11	7	–	Limerick, Tipperary, and Antrim.
Macken (29)—Mackin (9),	38	15	2	8	13	"Macken," Mayo, Louth, and Dublin— "Mackin," Monaghan.
*Mackey (33), ..	38	11	15	10	2	Dublin, Cork, Tipperary, and Antrim.
Mackle, ..	8	–	–	8	–	Armagh.
*Madden (106),	107	21	33	16	37	Galway, Cork, Dublin, and Antrim.
*Maddock (7), ..	10	6	2	1	1	Wexford.
*Madigan (26), ..	27	1	26	–	–	16 in Limerick and 7 in Clare.
Madill, ..	5	1	–	4	–	—
*Magauran (9), ..	10	–	–	10	–	8 in Cavan.
Magee (138)—McGee (55),	193	28	4	150	11	"Magee," Antrim, Armagh, and Down— "McGee," Donegal and Tyrone.
Magill (65)—McGill (19),	84	10	4	69	1	"Magill," Antrim, Armagh, and Down— "McGill," Donegal and Tyrone.
*Magner (12), ..	17	–	17	–	–	15 in Cork and 2 in Limerick.
*Magrane (12)-McGrane (8),	22	20	–	2	–	16 in Dublin.
Maguire (248)-McGuire (74),	322	85	27	156	54	"Maguire," Fermanagh, Dublin, Cavan, and Donegal—"McGuire," Roscommon and Mayo.—This name, however, is generally distributed.
Maher (176)—Meagher (27),	203	91	107	3	2	Tipperary, Dublin, and Kilkenny contain nearly 50 per cent.
*Mahon (85), ..	87	40	3	16	28	Dublin and Galway.
*Mahony (243), ..	276	17	256	–	3	182 in Cork, 37 in Kerry, and 13 in Limerick.
Mahood, ..	8	–	–	8	–	Antrim and Down.
Mailey, ...	6	–	–	6	–	Antrim.
*Mairs (8), ..	12	1	–	10	1	Antrim.
Maitland, ..	7	–	–	7	–	—
Major, ...	12	–	–	12	–	Antrim and Down.
Malcolm, ..	10	2	–	8	–	Antrim.
Malcomson (11)—Malcolmson (3),	14	2	1	11	–	Armagh.
*Malley (65), ..	85	4	2	3	76	62 in Mayo and 14 in Galway.
*Mallon (44), ..	48	7	1	38	2	Armagh, Antrim, and Tyrone.
Malone, ...	100	63	17	11	9	Dublin, Wexford, and Clare.
Malseed, ..	5	–	–	5	–	3 in Donegal and 2 in Londonderry.
*Mangan (50), ..	52	18	22	2	10	Dublin, Limerick, Kerry, and Mayo.
*Manley (15), ..	21	9	7	2	3	Cork and Wicklow.
Mann, ...	19	1	2	16	–	12 in Antrim.
Manning, ..	54	22	27	2	3	Cork and Dublin.

Names	Irl.	L.	M.	U.	C.	Counties in which principally found
*Mannion (73), ...	91	7	1	5	78	Galway and Roscommon.
Mannix, ...	6	–	6	–	–	3 in Cork and 3 in Kerry.
Mansfield, ...	13	2	11	–	–	Cork and Kerry.
Markey, ...	16	7	–	9	–	Dublin and Monaghan.
Markham, ...	5	–	4	–	1	Clare.
*Marks (13), ...	19	–	2	17	–	12 in Antrim.
*Marley (12), ...	14	–	-	9	5	Donegal and Mayo.
Marlow, ...	7	3	–	4	–	Dublin and Tyrone.
*Marron (23)—Marren (6),	31	3	–	21	7	" Marron," Monaghan—" Marren," Sligo.
Marsh, ...	5	4	–	1	–	—
*Marshall (58), ...	59	11	4	42	2	Antrim, Londonderry, Down, and Dublin.
*Martin (325), ...	326	74	34	186	32	Found all over Ireland—principally in Antrim. Down, Dublin, and Monaghan.
Mason, ...	32	10	11	10	1	Dublin.
*Massey (10), ...	11	3	2	6	–	Down.
Masterson, ...	47	31	–	12	4	Dublin, Longford, and Cavan.
*Matchett (12), ...	14	–	–	14	–	Armagh, Antrim, and Down.
Mateer, ...	9	–	–	8	1	7 in Antrim.
Mathers, ...	9	1	1	7	–	Armagh.
*Mathews (5,1)— Matthews (26),	78	38	5	32	3	Louth, Dublin, Antrim, and Down.
Maughan, ...	9	2	–	–	7	Mayo.
Mawhinney (10)— Mawhinny (8),	18	–	–	18	–	Antrim.
Maxwell, ...	68	16	3	46	3	Antrim, Down, and Dublin.
*May (25), ...	28	7	4	6	11	Sligo.
Mayberry (9)-Maybury (3),	12	3	3	4	2	" Mayberry," Antrim—" Maybury," 2 in Kerry and 1 in Limerick.
*Mayes (6), ...	7	–	–	7	–	Antrim and Armagh.
*Mayne (13), ...	16	1	1	14	–	Antrim.
*McAdam (21), ...	25	2	–	23	–	Monaghan.
*McAfee (8), ...	11	–	–	11	–	Antrim.
*McAleavey (5), ...	10	–	–	10	–	Down and Armagh.
McAleer, ...	17	1	–	16	–	13 in Tyrone.
*McAleese (10), ...	12	–	–	12	–	Antrim and Londonderry.
*McAlinden (19), ...	24	–	–	24	–	17 in Armagh.
*McAllen (6)—McCallan (5),	13	–	2	10	1	Antrim.
*McAllister (40)— McAlister (34),	87	7	2	78	–	Antrim.
McAloney, ...	5	–	–	5	-	4 in Antrim and 1 in Down.
McAndrew, ...	16	–	–	–	16	All in Mayo.
*McAneny (9)— McEneaney (8)— McEneany (5),	32	7	–	25	–	" McAneny," all in Tyrone.—" McEneaney" Louth—" McEneany," Monaghan.
*McArdle (45), ...	55	24	–	31	–	Nearly all in Louth Monaghan, and Armagh.
McAree, ...	6	–	–	6	–	3 in Antrim and 3 in Monaghan.
McAtamney, ...	6	–	–	6	–	Londonderry.
McAteer, ...	36	–	–	34	2	Armagh, Antrim, and Donegal.
*McAuley (49)-McCauley (30).	107	6	–	90	11	Antrim and Donegal.
*McAuliffe (39), ...	40	–	40	–	–	29 in Cork.
McBarron, ...	5	–	–	5	–	4 in Fermanagh and 1 in Donegal.
McBratney, ...	5	–	–	5	–	3 in Antrim and 2 in Down.
McBrearty, ...	8	–	–	8	–	Tyrone and Donegal.
McBride, ...	118	10	2	105	1	Antrim, Donegal, and Down.
*McBrien (13), ...	16	1	1	12	2	Fermanagh and Cavan.
*McBurney (11)—McBirney (6).	19	-	1	18	–	Down and Antrim.
McCabe, ...	145	44	8	84	9	Cavan, Monaghan, and Dublin.
*McCafferty (24), ...	25	-	-	25	–	14 in Donegal, 7 in Londonderry, and 4 in Antrim.
*McCaffrey (31), ...	61	5	-	56	–	Fermanagh and Tyrone.
McCahon, ...	6	–	–	6	–	Antrim.
McCallion, ...	24	–	–	24	–	Londonderry and Donegal.
McCambridge, ...	9	–	–	9	–	8 in Antrim and 1 in Donegal.
McCamley, ...	5	1	–	4	–	—
*McCandless (5), ...	7	–	–	7	–	—
*McCann (175)	177	47	3	105	22	Antrim, Armagh, Dublin, and Tyrone.
*McCarroll (9), ...	13	–	–	13	–	Londonderry.
McCarron, ...	33	–	–	32	1	Donegal and Londonderry.
McCarry, ...	5	–	–	5	–	Donegal.
*McCart (5), ...	6	–	–	6	–	Antrim.
*McCartan (21), ...	35	2	–	29	4	Down and Armagh.
McCarter, ...	9	–	–	9	–	Antrim and Londonderry.
*McCarthy (481), ...	498	35	438	19	6	Cork—in which more than one-half are found —Kerry, and Limerick. Dublin and Antrim are the only Counties outside Munster in which an appreciable number is found.

Names	Irl.	L.	M.	U.	C.	Counties in which principally found
*McCartney (44),	53	7	–	46	–	29 in Antrim.
*McCaughan (7),	10	–	–	10	–	Antrim.
*McCaughey (23),	24	–	1	23	–	Antrim and Tyrone.
*McCaul (12)–McCall (11)	24	2	2	20	–	Armagh and Cavan.
McCausland,	16	3	–	13	–	Antrim.
McCaw, ..	9	–	1	7	1	Antrim.
McClafferty,	11	–	–	11	–	10 in Donegal and 1 in Tyrone.
*McClatchey (7),	8	1	–	7	–	Antrim and Armagh.
*McClay (5), ..	7	–	–	7	–	Londonderry and Donegal.
*McClean (54)—McLean (43).	106	15	5	81	5	Antrim and Derry.
*McCleery (14),	19	–	–	19	–	Antrim and Londonderry.
*McClelland (57),	66	7	2	57	–	Antrim, Down, Armagh, Londonderry, and Monaghan.
*McClenaghan (8)—McLenaghan (5).	19	–	1	18	–	Antrim.
McClintock.	25	2	–	23	–	Antrim and Londonderry.
*McClory (10), ..	11	1	–	10	–	Down.
*McCloskey (47)—McCluskey (24).	79	10	1	67	1	" McCloskey," 35 in Londonderry—" McCluskey," Antrim and Dublin.
McCloy, ..	14	–	–	14	–	Antrim.
McClughan,	5	–	–	5	–	3 in Antrim and 2 in Down.
McClung,	7	–	–	7	–	—
McClure,	35	2	2	31	–	Antrim and Down.
McClurg,	10	–	–	10	–	5 in Antrim and 5 in Down.
*McCole (9),	12	1	–	11	–	11 in Donegal.
McColgan,	16	–	–	16	–	Donegal and Londonderry.
*McCollum (10),	19	–	–	19	–	Antrim, Tyrone, and Donegal.
*McComb (23), ..	26	4	–	22	–	Antrim, Down, and Londonderry.
*McConaghy (14),	16	–	–	16	–	Antrim.
McConkey,	17	3	1	13	–	Antrim.
*McConnell (98),	101	8	2	89	2	Antrim, Down, and Tyrone.
McConnon,	9	6	–	3	–	Louth.
*McConville (24),	29	1	–	26	2	Armagh and Antrim.
McCoo, ..	10	–	–	10	–	7 in Armagh and 3 in Antrim.
McCool, ..	22	–	–	22	–	Donegal and Tyrone.
McCord, ..	15	3	–	12	–	Antrim.
*McCormack (111),	118	48	22	20	28	Found in nearly every county — chiefly Dublin, Mayo, Roscommon, and Limerick.
*McCormick (164),	165	40	2	107	16	Antrim, Dublin, and Down.
McCorry,	16	–	–	16	–	Armagh and Down.
*McCoubrey (5),	11	–	–	11	–	7 in Down and 4 in Antrim.
McCourt,	44	13	–	29	2	Louth, Armagh, and Antrim.—12 of the 13 Leinster entries are in Louth.
McCoy, ..	41	7	2	30	2	Antrim, Armagh, and Monaghan.
McCracken,	33	1	1	31	–	15 in Antrim and 8 in Down.
*McCrea (28),	33	2	1	30	–	Antrim and Tyrone.
*McCready (27),	39	6	1	32	–	Down, Antrim, and Londonderry.
McCreary,	5	2	–	3	–	—
McCreesh,	6	–	–	6	–	Monaghan.
McCrohan,	5	–	5	–	–	All in Kerry.
*McCrory (32), ..	34	–	–	33	1	17 in Tyrone and 10 in Antrim.
*McCrossan (13),	14	–	–	14	–	11 in Tyrone.
McCrudden,	8	1	–	7	–	Antrim.
McCrum,	8	2	–	6	–	—
*McCullough (69)—McCullagh (40).	130	16	2	106	6	Antrim, Tyrone, and Down.—The form " McCullough " appears to be peculiar to Antrim and Down.
McCully,	5	1	–	4	–	—
McCune, ..	8	–	–	8	–	6 in Antrim and 2 in Armagh.
*McCurdy (15),	19	–	–	19	–	17 in Antrim and 2 in Londonderry.
*McCurry (11), ..	12	–	–	12	–	Antrim.
McCusker,	19	2	–	17	–	Tyrone.
*McCutcheon (25),	27	1	2	24	–	Tyrone, Antrim, and Down. [Tyrone.
*McDaid (35), ..	48	3	–	45	–	26 in Donegal, 8 in Londonderry, and 7 in
*McDaniel (8), ..	9	1	2	5	1	
*McDermott (176),	189	42	5	55	87	Roscommon, Dublin, Donegal, Galway, and Tyrone,—Half of those in Connaught are in Roscommon.
*McDevitt (13),	15	–	–	14	1	Donegal, Londonderry, and Tyrone.
*McDonagh (100),	174	13	11	9	141	Galway, Roscommon, and Mayo.
*McDonald (173),	191	89	10	88	4	Dublin, Antrim, Cavan, Wexford, and Carlow.
*McDonnell (237),	247	71	49	58	69	Dublin, Mayo, Antrim, Galway, and Cork.—Very generally distributed throughout the entire country.
*McDowell (89),	91	9	–	80	2	Antrim and Down—very few found elsewhere.
McEldowney, ..	6	–	–	6	–	All in Londonderry.
*McElhinney (17),	26	–	1	24	1	Donegal, Tyrone, and Londonderry.
McElligott, ..	24	1	23	–	–	19 in Kerry.

Names	Irl.	L.	M.	U.	C.	Counties in which principally found
McElmeel,	6	–	–	6	–	Monaghan.
McElwee,	7	–	–	7	–	5 in Donegal and 2 in Londonderry.
McEnroe,	9	3	–	6	–	6 in Cavan.
McEntee,	13	2	–	11	–	Monaghan and Cavan.
*McErlain (11)—McErlean (8),	21	–	–	21	–	13 in Antrim and 8 in Derry.
*McEvoy (85),	99	54	6	36	3	Dublin, Louth, Armagh, and Queen's.
*McFadden (72),	79	2	1	73	3	Donegal, Antrim, and Londonderry.
*McFall (20),	24	1	–	23	–	16 in Antrim and 7 in Londonderry.
McFarland,	46	2	–	44	–	Tyrone and Armagh.
*McFarlane (7),	12	4	–	8	–	——
*McFeeters (6),	7	–	–	7	–	Londonderry.
McFerran,	7	1	–	6	–	6 in Antrim.
*McFetridge (8),	9	–	–	9	–	6 in Antrim and 3 in Londonderry.
McGahan,	13	7	–	6	–	7 in Louth.
*McGahey (12),	13	–	–	13	–	Antrim and Monaghan.
*McGann (18),	21	9	3	3	6	——
*McGarry (64),	79	21	–	29	29	Antrim, Dublin, Roscommon, and Leitrim—very few elsewhere.
*McGarvey (28),	30	1	–	29	–	18 in Donegal and 5 in Londonderry.
McGaughey,	7	–	–	7	–	3 in Antrim and 3 in Armagh.
McGeady,	5	–	–	5	–	All in Donegal.
McGeary,	8	1	–	7	–	Tyrone.
*McGeehan (7),	11	–	–	11	–	9 in Donegal.
McGeough,	11	3	–	8	–	Monaghan and Louth.
McGeown,	19	2	–	17	–	12 in Armagh.
McGettigan,	10	–	–	10	–	All in Donegal.
McGillicuddy,	6	–	6	–	–	All in Kerry.
*McGilloway (8),	10	–	–	10	–	5 in Londonderry and 5 in Donegal.
McGimpsey,	8	–	–	8	–	7 in Down and 1 in Antrim.
McGing,	10	–	–	–	10	7 in Mayo and 2 in Leitrim.
*McGinley (45),	47	–	–	46	1	37 in Donegal.
*McGinn (17)—Maginn (13),	31	4	–	25	2	Generally distributed in Ulster.
*McGinty (10),	12	–	1	9	2	Donegal.
McGirr,	12	1	–	9	2	Tyrone.
*McGivern (17),	18	–	–	18	–	7 in Armagh, 7 in Down, and 4 in Antrim.
McGivney,	6	–	–	6	–	All in Cavan.
McGlade,	8	1	–	7	–	Antrim and Londonderry.
*McGlinchey (17),	22	–	–	22	–	Tyrone and Donegal.
*McGloin (14),	16	1	–	7	8	Donegal and Sligo.
McGlone,	12	–	–	11	1	Tyrone.
*McGlynn (26),	39	9	3	16	11	——
McGoey,	5	2	–	1	2	
*McGoldrick (34),	41	3	1	26	11	Tyrone, Fermanagh, and Sligo.
*McGonigle (24),	38	–	–	38	–	Donegal and Londonderry.
McGookin,	7	–	–	7	–	5 in Antrim and 2 in Armagh.
*McGough (8),	11	2	–	1	8	Mayo.
McGourty,	5	–	–	2	3	Leitrim.
*McGovern (92),	102	13	1	65	23	Fermanagh, Cavan, and Leitrim.
*McGowan (112)—Magowan (28),	152	5	2	91	54	Donegal, Leitrim, and Sligo.
McGrady,	6	–	–	6	–	3 in Antrim and 3 in Down.
*McGrath (233)—Magrath (31),	266	49	131	60	26	This name is found in every county, but more than 50 per cent. are in Tipperary, Cork, Waterford, Antrim, and Tyrone.
McGraw,	5	–	–	5	–	11 in Mayo and 6 in Leitrim.
*McGreal (21),	22	–	2	1	19	Down and Antrim.
*McGreevy (16),	18	–	2	11	5	Londonderry.
*McGregor (14),	16	2	2	11	1	Donegal and Londonderry.
McGrory,	12	1	–	11	–	All in Clare.
McGuane,	6	–	6	–	–	Londonderry.
*McGuckin (8),	11	1	–	10	–	Antrim and Tyrone.
*McGuigan (36),	43	–	–	40	3	Sligo.
McGuinn,	5	–	–	1	4	Dublin, Monaghan, and Louth. There are no fewer than 16 varieties in the spelling of this name in the Birth Indexes for 1890.
*McGuinness (47),	128	42	3	69	14	
*McGurk (32)—McGuirk (17),	51	19	–	30	2	"McGurk," Tyrone and Antrim—"McGuirk," Dublin.
McHale,	51	–	1	–	50	50 in Mayo.
*McHenry (14)—McEnry (5),	27	2	11	13	1	"McHenry," Antrim and Londonderry—"McEnry," and other forms in Limerick.
*McHugh (165),	176	18	4	73	81	Mayo, Donegal, Fermanagh, Galway, and Leitrim.
McIlroy (40)—McElroy (39),	79	6	3	69	1	Antrim, Down, Fermanagh, and Londonderry.
*McIlveen (15),	16	1	–	15	–	9 in Antrim and 5 in Down.
*McIlwaine (20),	29	–	–	29	–	Antrim, Down, and Armagh.
*McInerney (40),	64	8	53	1	2	Clare and Limerick.
McIntosh,	7	–	–	6	1	Antrim.
*McIntyre (42),	58	8	1	34	15	Londonderry, Antrim, and Sligo.
*McIvor (19),	24	1	–	23	–	Tyrone and Londonderry.

Names	Irl.	L.	M.	U.	C.	Counties in which principally found
McKane,	8	2	–	5	1	—
*McKay (53),	64	3	1	56	4	Antrim.
*McKeag (11),	16	–	–	16	–	—
McKee,	96	1	2	93	–	Antrim, Down, and Armagh.
*McKeever (30),	34	7	1	26	–	Londonderry and Antrim.
*McKelvey (21),	24	1	–	23	–	—
McKendry,	19	–	–	19	–	17 in Antrim.
McKenna,	201	37	22	134	8	Antrim, Monaghan, Tyrone, Kerry, Armagh, Dublin, and Louth.
*McKenzie (21),	22	7	–	13	2	Antrim and Dublin.
*McKeogh (12),	13	8	4	1	–	Westmeath.
*McKeown (119)— McKeon (40)—Mc- Keone (12).	175	33	2	115	25	" McKeown," Antrim, Down, Armagh, Londonderry, and Louth—" McKeon " and " McKeone," Leitrim and Louth.
*McKernan (12),	18	–	–	17	1	—
McKevitt,	9	6	–	3	–	6 in Louth.
*McKibbin (14),	20	–	–	20	–	13 in Down and 7 in Antrim.
McKiernan,	9	1	–	6	2	—
*McKillen (8),	9	–	–	9	–	" McKillen," all in Antrim.
*McKinley (23),	35	1	2	32	–	Antrim and Donegal.
*McKinney (37)	42	–	–	42	–	Antrim and Tyrone.
McKinstry	11	–	–	11	–	9 in Antrim and 2 in Down.
*McKitterick (5),	9	1	1	7	–	—
McKnight (38),	39	5	3	31	–	Antrim and Down.
McLarnon (8)—McClar- non (5).	13	–	–	13	–	9 in Antrim.
*McLaughlin (191)— McLoughlin (170).	391	62	7	228	94	" McLaughlin," about 75 per cent. in Antrim, Donegal, and Londonderry—a few in Tyrone, but very few elsewhere. " Mc-Loughlin," chiefly in Dublin and the Counties of Connaught, but found scattered throughout Ireland generally.
McLernon,	8	–	–	8	–	—
*McLoone (9),	10	–	–	10	–	8 in Donegal.
*McMahon (236),	241	34	118	86	3	Clare, Monaghan, Limerick, and Dublin.
McManamon,	6	–	–	–	6	All in Mayo.
*McManus (129),	138	19	2	89	28	Fermanagh.
McMaster,	38	–	–	37	1	Antrim and Down.
McMeekin,	7	–	–	6	1	Antrim.
*McMenamin (34),	36	1	–	34	1	22 in Donegal and 10 in Tyrone.
McMichael,	5	–	–	5	–	—
*McMillen (12)—McMil- lan (11).	25	–	–	25	–	Antrim and Down.
*McMinn (12),	13	–	–	13	–	8 in Antrim.
*McMonagle (10),	12	–	–	12	–	Donegal.
McMorrow,	21	–	1	1	19	17 in Leitrim.
*McMullan (80),	108	4	4	99	1	Antrim and Down.
*McMurray (16),	19	–	–	18	1	Antrim and Armag
*McMurtry (6),	7	–	–	7	–	All in Antrim.
*McNabb (8),	10	1	–	7	2	—
McNair,	5	–	–	4	1	Antrim.
*McNally (72)—Mc- Anally (23).	101	27	3	59	12	Antrim, Armagh, Monaghan, and Dublin.
*McNamara (175),	192	28	118	12	34	Clare, Limerick, Mayo, Dublin, and Cork.
McNamee,	40	14	–	26	–	Londonderry.
McNeice (8)—McNiece (8).	16	–	–	15	1	Antrim.
*McNeill (53),	58	5	2	46	5	Antrim and Londonderry.
McNeilly,	7	–	–	7	–	6 in Antrim and 1 in Down.
McNelis,	8	–	–	8	–	All in Donegal.
McNicholas,	32	–	–	–	32	All in Mayo.
*McNickle (10),	13	–	–	11	2	Tyrone.
*McNiff (13),	14	–	–	3	11	9 in Leitrim.
McNinch,	5	–	–	5	–	All in Antrim.
*McNulty (59),	69	4	1	43	21	Donegal and Mayo.
*McPaden (6),	8	–	–	–	8	Mayo.
*McParland (24)— McPartlan (12)— McPartlin (11).	55	3	–	36	16	" McParland," Armagh—" McPartlan " and " McPartlin," Leitrim.
*McPhillips (13),	17	3	–	14	–	Cavan and Monaghan.
McPolin,	5	–	–	5	–	All in Armagh.
*McQuaid (28)— McQuade (25),	55	4	–	49	2	" McQuaid," Monaghan and Fermanagh—" McQuade," Antrim.
*McQuillan (30),	33	6	–	25	2	Antrim and Monaghan.
*McQuinn (5),	7	1	4	2	–	Kerry.
McQuiston,	5	–	–	5	–	Antrim.
McRedmond,	5	5	–	–	–	King's.
McReynolds,	9	–	1	8	–	Antrim.
McRoberts,	9	–	–	9	–	Down and Antrim.
McShane,	34	9	–	25	–	Donegal and Louth.
McSharry,	29	–	–	9	20	13 in Leitrim, 9 in Donegal, and 7 in Sligo.

Names	Irl.	L.	M.	U.	C.	Counties in which principally found
McSherry,	10	1	1	8	–	Armagh.
McSorley,	15	1	–	14	–	Tyrone and Fermanagh.
*M'Stay (9),	10	–	–	10	–	Armagh.
McStravick,	6	–	–	6	–	4 in Armagh and 2 in Antrim.
*McSweeney (13),	29	2	27	–	–	Cork.
*McTernan (16),	20	–	–	1	19	17 in Leitrim.
McTigue (12)—McTague (4)—McTeague (3),	19	–	1	7	11	" McTigue," Mayo—" McTague," Cavan—" McTeague," all in Donegal.
*McVeigh (47), ..	68	9	–	57	2	Antrim and Down.
*McVicker (10),	13	1	–	12	–	9 in Antrim and 3 in Londonderry.
McWatters,	6	–	–	6	–	Antrim.
*McWeeney (6),	8	1	–	–	7	7 in Leitrim.
*McWhinney (6),	7	–	–	7	–	Down and Antrim.
McWhirter,	5	–	–	5	–	3 in Antrim, and 2 in Armagh.
*McWilliams (40),	43	2	1	38	2	Antrim and Londonderry.
*Meade (24),	25	8	17	–	–	Cork.
*Meany (25), ..	34	12	20	2	–	Kilkenny and Clare.
Meara (33)—Mara (21),	54	12	36	–	6	Tipperary.
Mee (10)—Mea (5), ..	15	1	–	4	10	" Mee," Roscommon—" Mea," all in Mayo.
*Meegan (11), ..	12	3	1	6	2	Monaghan.
*Meehan (112),	121	34	25	32	30	Galway, Sligo, Donegal, Dublin, and Clare. Found in nearly every County—10 entries (in Galway) being the largest number.
Meek, ..	7	1	1	5	–	Antrim.
*Meenan (9),	14	1	–	9	4	Donegal and Tyrone.
Meharg, ..	5	–	–	5	–	All in Antrim.
Melia, ..	11	4	–	–	7	Galway.
*Mellon (11),	12	3	–	9	–	Tyrone.
Melody, ..	5	–	2	–	3	—
Melville, ..	6	1	–	5	–	Antrim and Down.
Melvin, ..	11	–	–	2	9	Mayo.
Mercer, ..	22	2	–	20	–	9 in Antrim and 7 in Down.
*Meredith (5), ..	7	3	2	2	–	—
*Merrick (6),	7	2	3	1	1	—
Merrigan,	7	5	2	–	–	Dublin.
*Metcalf (7),	9	4	–	5	–	5 in Armagh.
Meyler, ..	9	8	1	–	–	7 in Wexford.
*Middleton (5),	6	2	1	3	–	—
Millar (87)—Miller (79),	166	22	7	133	4	Antrim, Londonderry, and Dublin—50 per cent. being found in Antrim alone.
Millen, ..	10	–	1	9	–	7 in Antrim.
*Milligan (22)-Milliken (17),	40	–	1	37	2	Half are in Antrim—remainder chiefly in Down and Londonderry.
Mills, ..	59	16	2	34	7	Antrim.
*Minihane (12),	28	1	27	–	–	19 in Cork. Seven varieties of this name are found in the Birth Indexes for 1890.
Minnis, ..	6	–	–	6	–	Antrim.
Minnock, ..	5	5	–	–	–	4 in King's.
*Minogue (16), ..	17	–	15	–	2	11 in Clare.
Miskelly,	5	–	–	5	–	All in Antrim.
*Mitchell (120),	128	26	9	63	30	Antrim, Galway, and Dublin. They are found in nearly every county in Ireland.
Mitten, ..	7	5	–	–	2	—
*Mockler (7), ..	9	2	5	–	2	Tipperary.
Moffatt (17)—Moffat (11)—Moffett (12)—Moffet (10)—Moffitt (11)—Moffit (7),	68	7	–	45	16	Antrim, Sligo, and Tyrone.
*Mohan (11)—Moan (9),	25	1	–	21	3	Monaghan.
*Molloy (127), ..	153	63	8	37	45	Dublin, Galway, Mayo, King's, and Donegal
*Moloney (119)—Molony (34),	187	26	133	3	25	Limerick, Clare, Tipperary, and Waterford.
*Molyneaux (6),	10	2	6	2	–	—
*Monaghan (96)—Monahan (42),	140	36	11	44	49	Galway, Mayo, Dublin, and Fermanagh.
Mongan, ..	6	–	1	–	5	—
Monks, ..	12	12	–	–	–	11 in Dublin.
Monnelly (9)—Munnelly (6),	15	1	–	–	14	14 in Mayo.
*Montague (8), ..	9	1	–	8	–	Tyrone.
*Montgomery (110),	111	12	–	97	2	More than half are in Antrim and Down.
*Moody (12),	13	3	1	9	–	Antrim and Down.
*Moon (6), ..	8	2	1	4	1	—
Mooney, ..	136	77	9	38	12	Dublin, Antrim, and King's.
*Moore (395), ..	396	135	52	185	24	Antrim, Dublin, Londonderry, Cork, Kildare, and Tyrone—Every county in Ireland has representatives of this name—from 1 entry in Westmeath to 93 in Antrim.
*Moorhead (17),	25	3	2	18	2	Antrim.
*Morahan (7), ..	10	–	2	–	8	Leitrim.
Moran, ..	265	82	36	15	132	Mayo, Dublin, Galway, Roscommon, Leitrim, and Kerry—This name, however, is found in nearly every county.

Names	Irl.	L.	M.	U.	C.	Counties in which principally found
Moreland,	11	–	–	11	–	Antrim and Down.
Morey,	7	–	7	–	–	—
Morgan,	132	37	16	67	12	Antrim, Armagh, Down, Dublin, and Louth
Moriarty,	83	4	79	–	–	74 in Kerry.
Morley,	23	2	–	–	21	20 in Mayo.
*Moroney (35),	44	3	41	–	–	Clare, Limerick, and Tipperary.
*Morrin (6),	8	1	3	4	–	—
*Morris (102),	115	49	6	32	28	Dublin, Mayo, Tyrone, and Monaghan—A very scattered name.
*Morrison (93),	111	12	18	66	15	Antrim, Down, and Dublin.
Morrisroe,	7	–	–	–	7	Roscommon.
*Morrissey (62),	90	20	67	–	3	Waterford, Limerick, and Cork.
*Morrow (90),	91	3	1	83	4	Antrim, Donegal, Armagh, and Down.
*Morton (30),	32	6	1	24	1	One half in Antrim.
Moss,	6	1	1	4	–	Tyrone.
Motherway,	5	–	5	–	–	All in Cork.
Moylan,	23	7	12	1	3	Clare, Cork, and Tipperary.
*Moynihan (50),	66	1	64	–	1	36 in Kerry and 24 in Cork.
Muir,	5	–	2	3	–	—
Mulcahy,	76	3	72	1	–	All except 6 in Cork, Limerick, Waterford, and Tipperary.
Muldoon,	26	3	–	14	9	Fermanagh and Galway.
*Muldowney (5),	7	2	–	–	5	—
Mulgrew,	7	–	–	6	1	5 in Tyrone.
Mulnall,	33	32	1	–	–	Dublin, Kilkenny, Carlow, and Queen's.
*Mulhern (8)—Mulherin (7),	21	–	2	13	6	
*Mulholland (71),	73	3	1	65	4	Antrim, Down, and Londonderry.
Mulkeen,	7	–	–	–	7	6 in Mayo and 1 in Roscommon.
*Mulkerrin (5),	10	–	–	1	9	9 in Galway.
*Mullally (8),	14	7	5	1	1	—
*Mullan (92)—Mullen (72)—Mullin (53),	218	39	2	128	49	Tyrone, Londonderry, Galway, and Antrim.
Mullane,	31	–	29	–	2	16 in Cork and 8 in Limerick.
*Mullany (27),	32	1	7	2	22	Roscommon, Mayo, and Sligo.
Mullarkey,	21	–	–	1	20	Mayo, Galway, and Sligo.
Mulligan,	105	32	1	34	38	Dublin, Mayo, and Monaghan.
Mullins,	47	8	35	–	4	Cork and Clare.
Mulqueen,	6	–	6	–	–	4 in Limerick and 2 in Clare.
Mulrennan,	5	1	–	–	4	—
Mulroe,	5	–	–	–	5	3 in Mayo and 2 in Galway.
*Mulrooney (9),	12	4	1	–	7	—
Mulroy,	12	2	–	–	10	10 in Mayo.
Mulry,	5	–	–	1	4	Galway.
*Mulvany (4)-Mulvanny (4),	15	12	–	2	1	—
Mulvenna,	5	–	–	5	–	All in Antrim.
*Mulvey (21),	27	3	4	1	19	13 in Leitrim.
*Mulvihill (18),	21	4	12	1	4	Kerry and Limerick.
Murdock (18)—Murdoch (12),	30	2	1	27	–	Antrim.
*Murnane (13),	14	4	10	–	–	Limerick and Cork.
*Murphy (1385),	1386	476	611	189	110	Generally distributed, but the largest numbers are found in Cork, Dublin, and Wexford. They vary from 5 in each of the counties of Westmeath, Tyrone, and Sligo, to close on 500 in Cork.
*Murray (405),	438	120	65	161	92	Dublin, Antrim, Cork, Down, Galway, and Mayo. There is no county, however, without representatives of this name.
*Murrin (6),	8	5	–	1	2	—
*Murtagh (58),	66	30	1	17	18	Dublin and Sligo.
*Myers (10),	11	4	4	3	–	Wexford and Antrim.
Myles (7)—Miles (5),	12	7	3	2	–	—
*Nagle (32),	39	3	32	3	1	Cork.
Nally,	20	4	–	–	16	Mayo and Roscommon.
Napier,	8	–	–	8	–	Antrim and Down.
*Nash (20),	21	5	15	–	1	Kerry and Limerick.
*Naughton (52),	71	1	19	1	50	Galway, Mayo, Roscommon, and Clare.
Navin,	6	1	–	–	5	Mayo.
*Naylor (5),	6	4	–	2	–	Dublin.
Neal (6)—Neale (4),	10	7	1	2	–	—
*Neary (34),	43	12	2	2	27	Mayo, Roscommon, Dublin, and Louth.
Nee,	17	1	1	–	15	15 in Galway.
Needham,	7	–	1	1	5	5 in Mayo.
*Neely (9),	12	–	–	11	1	—
Neenan,	7	1	6	–	–	Clare.
Neeson,	17	–	–	17	–	Antrim.

Names	Irl.	L.	M.	U.	C.	Counties in which principally found
*Neilan (12)—Nilan (7),	36	3	9	–	24	Galway, Roscommon, and Sligo.
*Neill (215), ...	244	97	78	63	6	Antrim, Cork, Kerry, Carlow, Dublin, and Wexford.
Nelis, ...	5	–	–	3	2	Londonderry and Mayo.
Nelson, ...	72	8	2	59	3	Antrim, Down, Londonderry, and Tyrone.
*Nesbitt (25), ..	30	5	1	23	1	Antrim, Armagh, and Dublin.
*Nestor (13), ..	15	2	5	–	8	Galway and Clare.
*Neville (36), ..	39	8	27	4	–	Limerick and Cork.
*Nevin (22), ..	23	8	2	5	8	—
*Newell (31), ..	34	2	1	27	4	Down and Antrim.
Newman, ...	36	13	20	3	–	Cork, Meath, and Dublin—15 in Cork.
*Neylon (10), ..	13	1	11	–	1	11 in Clare.
Niblock, ...	6	–	–	6	–	Antrim.
*Nicholl (25), ..	49	2	5	40	2	Antrim and Londonderry.
*Nicholson (43), ..	44	10	2	16	16	Antrim, Sligo, and Dublin.
*Nixon (46), ..	47	7	–	37	3	Antrim, Cavan, and Fermanagh.
Noble, ...	25	7	1	15	2	Antrim and Dublin.
*Nolan (313), ..	321	220	57	13	31	Dublin, Wexford, Carlow, Wicklow, Kildare, Kerry, Tipperary, Mayo, and Galway.
*Noonan (69), ..	83	8	66	1	8	Cork, Clare, Limerick, and Tipperary.
*Noone (29), ..	48	7	–	1	40	Galway, Roscommon, and Mayo.
*Normile (5), ..	9	–	9	–	–	Limerick and Clare.
*Norris (21), ..	22	7	8	7	–	—
*North (8), ..	9	5	–	4	–	—
Northridge, ..	5	–	5	–	–	All in Cork.
Norton, ...	11	8	1	–	2	Dublin.
Nugent, ...	75	19	25	30	1	Armagh, Dublin, Cork, Tipperary, and Tyrone.
Nulty, ...	16	8	1	2	5	Meath.
Oakley, ...	5	–	2	1	2	—
*O'Beirne (9), ..	10	4	–	2	4	—
O'Boyle, ..	20	–	–	5	15	14 in Mayo and 5 in Antrim.
*O'Brien (488), ..	502	105	291	56	50	Dublin is the only county in Leinster in which found to an appreciable extent. Each county in Munster is largely represented ; Cavan takes the lead in Ulster, and Galway in Connaught.
O'Byrne, ..	8	6	2	–	–	6 in Dublin.
*O'Callaghan (63), ..	64	8	51	5	–	Cork.
O'Carroll, ..	5	1	4	–	–	—
*O'Connell (128), ..	130	14	100	6	10	Cork, Limerick, Kerry, and Dublin contain about 80 per cent.
*O'Connor (259), ..	266	50	174	13	29	Kerry, Cork, Limerick, Dublin, Clare, and Galway contain about 80 per cent.
*O'Dea (34), ..	35	5	25	–	5	17 in Clare and 6 in Limerick.
*O'Doherty (7), ..	8	4	1	3	–	—
*O'Donnell (292), ..	294	9	102	132	51	Donegal, Mayo, and Galway. Generally distributed in Munster.
*O'Donoghue (28), ..	39	5	34	–	–	Kerry and Cork.
O'Donovan, ..	11	1	9	–	1	7 in Cork and 2 in Limerick.
O'Dowd, ..	15	5	1	–	9	Sligo.
O'Driscoll, ..	13	2	11	–	–	10 in Cork.
O'Dwyer, ..	25	3	21	–	1	Tipperary, Limerick, and Clare.
O'Farrell, ..	19	5	10	2	2	—
O'Flaherty, ..	16	2	10	3	1	—
O'Flynn, ..	5	–	–	3	2	—
*O'Gara (6), ..	7	–	–	–	7	4 in Roscommon and 3 in Mayo.
Ogle, ...	6	–	–	6	–	—
*O'Gorman (22), ..	24	3	21	–	–	Clare.
*O'Grady (46), ..	47	8	29	2	8	Clare, Limerick, Dublin, and Roscommon.
*O'Hagan (32), ..	33	7	–	26	–	Armagh, Louth, and Down.
*O'Halloran (17), ..	25	2	21	1	1	Limerick.
O'Hanlon, ..	22	9	1	12	–	Dublin and Armagh.
*O'Hara (104), ..	105	31	5	31	38	Dublin, Antrim, and Sligo.
*O'Hare (57), ..	59	12	1	45	1	31 in Armagh, 11 in Louth, and 9 in Down.
*O'Hora (6), ..	8	–	–	–	8	All in Mayo.
*O'Kane (27), ..	29	–	1	27	1	Londonderry and Antrim.
*O'Keeffe (76), ..	83	10	68	2	3	Cork, Limerick, and Dublin, more than one-half being in Cork.
O'Kelly, ...	9	3	4	–	2	—
O'Leary, ..	64	5	57	1	1	41 in Cork, 9 in Kerry, and 5 in Limerick.
*Oliver (15), ..	16	3	1	10	2	—
*O'Loughlin (30), ..	40	12	21	3	4	Clare and Dublin.
*O'Mahony (18), ..	25	5	20	–	–	Cork.
*O'Malley (25), ..	30	3	4	3	20	16 in Mayo.
*O'Meara (20), ..	31	11	19	–	1	Dublin, Limerick, and Tipperary.
*O'Neill (359), ..	407	124	110	145	28	Dublin, Antrim, Cork, and Tyrone contain 50 per cent. Found, however, in nearly every county in Ireland.
*O'Rawe (7), ..	10	–	–	10	–	All in Antrim.
O'Regan, ..	16	1	15	–	–	Cork and Limerick.
*O'Reilly (58), ..	62	37	14	9	2	Dublin.

Names	Irl.	L.	M.	U.	C.	Counties in which principally found
O'Riordan, ...	11	–	11	–	–	Cork.
*Ormond (6), ..	8	3	5	–	–	—
Ormsby, ...	10	3	1	3	3	—
*O'Rourke (31), ..	49	10	12	11	16	—
Orr, ...	73	5	2	65	1	Antrim, Down, Londonderry, and Tyrone.
Osborne, ...	23	5	5	12	1	—
O'Shaughnessy, ..	30	8	18	1	3	Limerick.
O'Shea, ...	46	5	36	2	3	Cork, Kerry, and Limerick.
O'Sullivan, ..	136	8	122	–	6	54 in Kerry, 45 in Cork, and 19 in Limerick.
Oswald, ...	5	–	–	5	–	—
*O'Toole (36), ..	39	26	7	6	–	Dublin, Wicklow, and Limerick.
*Owens (84), ..	89	26	9	33	21	Dublin, Roscommon, and Cork. This name has representatives in 23 counties in the Birth Indexes for 1890.
*Padden (5), ..	10	–	–	1	9	Mayo.
Page, ...	15	4	1	7	3	Antrim and Dublin.
Paisley, ...	12	8	–	4	–	Dublin and Antrim.
Palmer, ...	32	5	9	18	–	Antrim.
*Park (15), ..	21	–	–	18	3	Antrim and Tyrone.
Parker, ...	40	6	8	24	2	Antrim and Cork.
Parkhill, ...	8	–	1	7	–	Londonderry.
Parkinson, ..	14	4	3	7	–	Dublin, Antrim, and Down.
*Parks (16), ..	23	5	1	16	1	Antrim and Armagh.
Parle, ...	5	5	–	–	–	All in Wexford.
Parr, ...	5	1	1	2	1	—
Parsons, ...	12	3	1	1	7	—
*Patterson (137), ..	153	14	6	130	3	Down, Antrim, Armagh, Londonderry, and Tyrone.
*Patton (49)—Patten (10), ..	60	2	1	48	9	" Patton," Antrim and Down—" Patten," Mayo.
*Paul (13), ..	14	2	2	10	–	Londonderry and Antrim.
*Payne (25), ..	26	12	2	9	3	Dublin and Antrim.
*Peacock (7), ..	9	2	2	4	1	—
*Pearson (26), ..	31	11	4	16	–	Antrim and Dublin.
*Peel (11), ..	12	3	1	8	–	Antrim.
Pender, ...	25	14	9	1	1	Wexford.
Penny, ...	5	1	–	4	–	4 in Antrim and 1 in Dublin.
Pentland, ...	7	1	–	6	–	Down and Armagh.
*Peoples (9), ..	10	–	–	10	–	Donegal.
Pepper, ...	10	4	1	5	–	Dublin and Antrim.
*Perrott (5), ..	6	1	4	1	–	Cork.
Perry, ...	23	6	5	10	2	Dublin and Down.
Peters, ...	12	1	5	4	2	Tipperary.
Petticrew (7)—Pettigrew (5), ..	12	1	1	9	1	Antrim.
Peyton, ...	11	1	1	1	8	Mayo.
*Phelan (91), ..	92	46	43	2	1	Waterford, Kilkenny, Queen's, and Tipperary contain nearly 80 per cent.
Phibbs, ...	6	1	1	–	4	Sligo.
*Philbin (9), ..	10	–	–	–	10	9 in Mayo and 1 in Galway.
*Phillips (64), ..	77	27	8	21	21	Mayo, Antrim, and Dublin.
*Picken (5), ..	6	–	–	6	–	" Picken," all in Antrim.
*Pidgeon (5), ..	6	6	–	–	–	—
*Pierce (22), ..	38	21	9	6	2	Dublin and Wexford.
*Pigott (15), ..	20	7	11	1	1	Cork and Dublin.
Pilkington, ..	8	3	1	1	3	—
Pinkerton, ..	7	1	–	6	–	Antrim.
Platt, ...	8	1	–	7	–	Londonderry.
*Plunkett (21), ..	28	20	–	6	2	Dublin.
Poland, ...	5	2	–	3	–	—
Pollard, ...	15	12	3	–	–	Dublin and Kilkenny.
*Pollock (39), ..	41	4	–	36	1	Antrim and Tyrone.
Poots, ...	5	–	–	5	–	3 in Down and 2 in Antrim.
Pope, ...	6	4	2	–	–	—
Porter, ...	73	9	–	64	–	Antrim, Down, Londonderry, and Armagh.
Potter, ...	14	4	1	5	4	—
Powell, ...	23	4	7	7	5	—
*Power (271), ..	272	68	196	6	2	All except 17 in Waterford, Cork, Dublin, Tipperary, Wexford, Kilkenny, and Limerick.
Pratt, ...	10	4	2	4	–	—
*Prendergast (46), ..	52	15	16	1	20	Mayo, Dublin, and Waterford—18 in Mayo.
Prentice, ..	8	1	–	7	–	—
*Prescott (5), ..	6	3	–	3	–	—
Preston, ...	17	5	2	10	–	—
*Price (45), ..	47	22	7	12	6	Dublin and Antrim.
Prior, ...	15	1	–	10	4	10 in Cavan.
Pritchard, ..	11	1	1	9	–	Antrim.
Proctor, ...	15	3	–	12	–	Antrim.
Prunty, ...	10	7	–	3	–	6 in Longford.

Names	Irl.	L.	M.	U.	C.	Counties in which principally found
Punch,	6	–	6	–	–	4 in Cork and 2 in Limerick.
*Purcell (76),	79	41	28	3	7	Kilkenny and Dublin contain nearly all the entries in Leinster ; Tipperary, most of those in Munster.
*Purdy (15),	16	1	–	15	–	Antrim.
*Purtill (6),	9	–	9	–	–	Limerick.
Purvis,	8	1	–	4	3	—
Pyne,	11	–	10	1	–	7 in Cork and 3 in Clare.
*Quail (10),	14	5	–	9	–	Antrim and Down.
Quee,	5	–	–	5	–	All in Antrim.
Quigg,	6	–	–	6	–	—
*Quigley (82),	89	23	10	39	17	Londonderry, Dublin, Donegal, Galway Louth, and Sligo.
Quill,	10	–	9	–	1	Cork.
Quilligan,	7	–	7	–	–	5 in Limerick and 2 in Cork.
Quillinan,	5	–	4	1	–	Tipperary.
Quilty,	9	–	8	–	1	5 in Limerick and 3 in Waterford.
*Quinlan (52),	54	10	44	–	–	Tipperary and Kerry.
*Quinlivan (12),	13	2	–	11	–	Clare.
*Quinn (349)—Quin (58),	408	114	63	155	76	Dublin, Tyrone, Antrim, Roscommon, and Galway—Found in every County in Ireland, from 1 entry in Cavan to 44 in Dublin.
*Quirke (27),	40	10	28	–	2	Tipperary and Kerry.
*Rabbit (10),	13	4	1	–	8	
Ractigan,	5	–	–	–	5	All in Mayo.
Radford,	7	5	2	–	–	—
*Rafferty (54),	55	17	–	34	4	Antrim, Tyrone, and Louth.
*Rafter (17),	20	12	–	2	6	Dublin, Queen's, and Mayo.
*Raftery (25),	26	–	–	–	26	20 in Galway and 6 in Roscommon.
Rahilly,	11	–	11	–	–	8 in Kerry and 3 in Cork.
Rainey,	39	1	–	36	2	22 in Antrim and 10 in Down.
Raleigh,	11	2	9	–	–	Limerick and Tipperary.
*Ralph (12),	14	7	2	1	4	
Ramsay (16)—Ramsey (12).	28	5	–	22	1	Antrim.
Rankin,	36	6	–	29	1	Londonderry and Donegal.
Ratigan (4)—Rattigan (4),	8	1	–	–	7	Mayo and Roscommon.
Ray,	7	2	2	3	–	—
Raymond,	6	2	4	–	–	
Rea,	49	3	4	42	–	31 in Antrim and 7 in Down.
*Reaney (5),	9	–	–	3	6	
*Reddan (7)—Reddin (6),	15	6	8	–	1	—
Reddington (7)—Reddington (7),	14	1	1	–	12	7 in Mayo and 5 in Galway.
*Reddy (25),	32	21	7	1	3	Dublin and Kilkenny.
Redfern,	5	1	1	2	1	
Redmond,	79	74	–	5	–	30 in Wexford, 29 in Dublin, and 10 in Wicklow.
Redpath,	9	–	–	9	–	Antrim.
Reel,	5	2	–	3	–	—
Reen,	10	–	10	–	–	7 in Cork and 3 in Kerry.
Regan,	219	20	110	9	80	Cork, Roscommon, and Mayo.
*Reid (181),	206	50	13	137	6	Antrim, Dublin, Down, Tyrone, and Armagh.
Reidy,	49	2	45	–	2	Kerry and Clare.
*Reilly (503)—Rielly (58),	586	254	50	199	83	Cavan, Longford, Dublin, Meath, Mayo, and Cork contain about 65 per cent., but found in every county.
Relihan,	7	–	7	–	–	Cork and Kerry.
*Reville (5),	6	5	1	–	–	Wexford.
*Reynolds (112),	113	30	15	22	46	Leitrim, Dublin, Antrim, and Louth.
Rice,	99	33	18	48	–	Antrim, Armagh, Louth, and Dublin.
Richards,	9	4	2	3	–	
*Richardson (53),	54	14	8	32	–	Dublin and Antrim.
Richmond,	9	–	–	9	–	All in Antrim.
*Rickard (6),	7	6	1	–	–	
*Riddell (8),	12	1	–	11	–	Antrim.
Ridge,	10	–	–	1	9	9 in Galway.
Rigney,	9	7	1	1	–	King's.
Ring,	18	1	14	1	2	12 in Cork.
Ringland,	7	–	–	7	–	6 in Down and 1 in Antrim.
*Riordan (134),	159	4	154	1	–	89 in Cork, 30 in Kerry, and 24 in Limerick.
*Ritchie (23),	24	2	–	22	–	Antrim.
Roarty,	5	–	–	5	–	4 in Donegal and 1 in Tyrone.
Rodd,	21	–	2	19	–	Antrim.

Names	Irl.	L.	M.	U.	C.	Counties in which principally found
Roberts, ..	40	14	10	15	1	—
Robertson,	18	5	3	9	1	—
Robinson,	217	29	9	168	11	Antrim, Down, Dublin, Armagh, and Tyrone.
Robson, ..	5	–	–	5	–	Down.
*Roche (141), ..	183	69	89	3	22	Cork, Wexford, Dublin, Limerick, and Mayo.
*Rochford (16),	18	12	2	–	4	Dublin.
*Rock (17),	23	9	–	8	6	Dublin.
*Rodden (9), ..	11	1	–	9	1	Donegal.
*Roddy (15), ..	17	1	1	6	9	Mayo and Roscommon.
Roe, ..	21	14	4	3	–	—
Rogan, ..	24	6	1	13	4	Antrim, Down, and Leitrim.
*Rogers (100)—Rodgers (68),	170	40	12	98	20	Antrim, Down, Dublin, and Roscommon— Very generally distributed.
Rohan, ..	8	1	7	–	–	7 in Kerry and 1 in Queen's.
Rollins, ..	7	1	–	6	–	4 in Antrim and 2 in Down.
Ronayne (13)—Ronan (12),	25	9	15	–	1	13 in Cork.
Rooney, ..	119	36	3	43	37	Dublin, Leitrim, Down, Antrim, and Mayo.
Rose, ..	10	5	5	–	–	—
Ross, ..	73	8	10	54	1	Antrim, Londonderry, Cork, and Down.
*Rossiter (12), ..	14	14	–	–	–	13 in Wexford and 1 in Wicklow.
Rothwell, ..	10	9	–	1	–	Wexford and Dublin.
*Roulston (8)—Rolston (7),	25	1	3	20	1	Tyrone and Antrim.
*Rountree (5), ..	9	2	–	7	–	Armagh.
*Rourke (90), ..	136	77	17	15	27	Dublin, Leitrim, Roscommon, and Wexford.
*Rowan (15)—Roughan (5),	27	7	4	11	5	—
*Rowland (11),	12	–	1	4	7	Mayo and Galway.
Rowe, ..	21	13	3	4	1	7 in Wexford.
Rowley, ..	11	2	–	4	5	Mayo.
Roy, ..	16	2	–	14	–	Antrim and Down.
*Roycroft (5), ..	7	–	6	–	1	6 in Cork.
*Ruane (35), ..	37	–	–	–	37	29 in Mayo and 6 in Galway.
Rudden, ..	9	1	–	8	–	Cavan.
Ruddle (5)-Ruddell (4),	9	–	4	5	–	4 in Limerick and 4 in Armagh.
Ruddock, ..	6	1	–	5	–	Down and Armagh.
*Ruddy (22), ..	23	1	–	9	13	13 in Mayo, 5 in Donegal, and 4 in Armagh.
Rush, ..	22	1	–	8	13	Mayo.
*Russell (99), ..	101	26	16	57	2	Antrim, Dublin, and Down.
Ruth, ..	6	5	1	–	–	—
*Rutherford (25),	26	1	2	21	2	Antrim, Londonderry, and Down.
*Rutledge (19),	23	3	–	15	5	Tyrone.
Ruttle, ..	6	5	1	–	–	—
Ryan, ..	715	180	473	13	49	Tipperary (which has by far the largest number), Limerick, Dublin, Cork, Waterford, Kilkenny, Wexford, Clare, and Galway.
Ryder, ..	9	2	–	–	7	Mayo.
*Ryle (6), ..	9	–	8	1	–	6 in Kerry.
*Sadlier (6), ..	12	2	5	2	3	—
*Salmon (21), ..	24	7	2	6	9	—
*Sands (17), ..	18	2	1	15	–	6 in Antrim and 6 in Armagh.
Santry, ..	7	–	7	–	–	All in Cork.
*Sargent (7), ..	11	5	1	5	–	—
*Sarsfield (10), ..	11	2	4	–	5	—
*Saunders (22), ..	29	11	8	8	2	Dublin and Antrim.
Savage, ..	61	13	7	38	3	Antrim, Down, Dublin, and Cork.
Sayers, ..	8	1	3	4	–	—
Scallan, ..	10	6	–	–	4	5 in Wexford.
*Scally (24), ..	25	15	2	1	7	Roscommon, Westmeath, and Dublin.
*Scanlon (54)—Scanlan (42),	97	6	60	3	28	Kerry, Clare, Sligo, Limerick, and Cork.
*Scannell (40), ..	42	–	42	–	–	24 in Cork and 15 in Kerry.
Scott, ..	196	27	4	147	18	Antrim, Down, Londonderry, and Dublin.
Scullion, ..	17	–	–	17	–	10 in Antrim and 5 in Londonderry.
Scully, ..	65	32	28	1	4	Cork, Dublin, Carlow, and King's.
Seaton, ..	6	–	1	5	–	—
*Seeds (6), ..	7	–	–	7	–	4 in Antrim and 3 in Down.
*Seery (20), ..	22	18	1	–	3	Westmeath and Dublin.
Semple, ..	19	1	–	18	–	Antrim.
Sewell, ..	6	1	2	3	–	—
Sexton, ..	43	4	31	6	2	30 of the Munster entries are in Cork, Clare, and Limerick. Cavan has 5 out of the 6 in Ulster.
Seymour, ..	15	5	6	4	–	—
*Shally (6), ..	7	2	–	–	5	Galway.
*Shanahan (53),	65	4	58	3	–	Cork, Kerry, Tipperary, Limerick, and Waterford.

Names	Irl.	L.	M.	U.	C.	Counties in which principally found
Shanks, ...	21	–	–	21	–	10 in Antrim and 7 in Down.
*Shanley (14), ...	22	8	2	–	12	Leitrim.
Shannon, ...	72	10	19	29	14	Antrim, Clare, and Roscommon.
*Sharkey (57), ...	58	12	3	26	17	Roscommon, Donegal, Tyrone, Dublin, and Louth contain 49 out of the 58.
*Sharpe (10), ...	17	3	1	12	1	Antrim.
*Shaughnessy (40), ..	41	6	9	–	26	Nearly 50 per cent. in Galway.
Shaw, ...	80	17	8	51	4	Antrim, Down, and Dublin.
Shea, ...	246	24	217	2	3	Kerry, Cork, Kilkenny, Tipperary, and Waterford—Very few found outside these counties—More than one half of the Munster entries are in Kerry.
Shearer, ...	5	1	–	4	–	—
Sheedy, ...	13	1	12	–	–	Clare.
*Sheehan (171)-Sheahan (43),	215	22	190	–	3	Cork, Kerry, and Limerick, more than one half of the Munster entries being in Cork.
*Sheehy (54), ...	55	3	51	1	–	22 in Kerry, 15 in Limerick, and 9 in Cork.
*Sheeran (18), ...	30	18	2	2	8	
*Shelly (16), ...	17	9	5	1	2	Dublin and Tipperary.
*Sheppard (12), ..	22	9	4	9	–	—
*Sheridan (135), ...	145	52	11	45	37	Cavan, Dublin, and Mayo—very generally distributed, however, throughout Ireland.
Sherlock, ...	23	11	4	5	3	Dublin.
Sherman, ...	5	2	–	3	–	—
Sherrard, ...	7	–	–	7	–	4 in Londonderry and 3 in Antrim.
Sherry, ...	25	10	–	15	–	9 in Monaghan, 5 in Dublin, and 3 in Meath.
Sherwood, ...	8	2	2	4	–	—
*Shevlin (8), ...	11	2	–	7	2	—
Shields (36)—Sheilds (19),	55	6	4	45	–	Antrim and Down.
*Shiels (28)—Sheils (28),	88	31	2	45	10	Dublin, Donegal, and Londonderry.
*Shilliday (5), ...	6	–	–	6	–	4 in Antrim and 2 in Down.
Shine, ...	26	2	21	–	3	12 in Cork.
Shirley, ...	7	5	–	2	–	—
*Short (21)—Shortt (8),	30	13	4	12	1	
*Shortall (10), ...	11	9	1	–	1	Dublin and Kilkenny.
Shorten, ...	7	1	6	–	–	5 in Cork.
*Silk (7), ...	8	1	–	–	7	7 in Galway.
Silver, ...	5	–	1	–	4	4 in Galway.
*Simmons (6), ...	11	6	–	5	–	—
*Simms (11), ...	24	6	1	16	1	Antrim.
Simpson, ...	75	8	2	59	6	Antrim.
Sinclair, ...	18	3	–	15	–	Armagh and Londonderry.
Singleton, ...	17	3	6	8	–	Cork and Down.
*Sinnott (22)—Synnott (12),	37	33	2	1	1	" Sinnott," Wexford—" Synnott," Dublin.
*Skeffington (6), ..	8	–	–	4	4	—
*Skehan (7), ...	8	4	4	–	–	—
Skelly, ...	18	11	–	6	1	Dublin and Down.
Skelton, ...	8	4	–	4	–	—
Skillen, ...	6	–	–	6	–	3 in Down and 2 in Antrim.
*Slator (5), ...	10	6	1	1	2	Dublin.
Slattery, ...	69	9	55	–	5	53 of the 55 in Munster are in Tipperary, Kerry, Cork, Clare, and Limerick, each county having about the same number.
*Slavin (11), ...	14	3	–	11	–	—
Slevin, ...	13	7	–	4	2	
*Sloan (44)—Sloane (16),	61	4	1	55	1	34 in Antrim.
Small, ...	30	4	4	19	3	Antrim, Armagh, and Down.
*Smiley (5)—Smylie (5),	13	2	–	11	–	Antrim.
*Smith (471)—Smyth (277),	753	232	62	412	47	Antrim, Cavan, and Dublin have the largest numbers, but they are found in every county, from 1 entry in Kerry to 134 in Antrim.
Smullen, ...	8	8	–	–	–	Dublin.
Snee, ...	7	–	–	–	7	Mayo.
Snoddy, ...	7	–	–	7	–	All in Antrim.
*Somers (29), ...	38	21	6	7	4	Wexford and Dublin.
*Somerville (18), ..	24	4	1	17	2	
*Spain (7), ...	8	2	3	–	3	
Sparks, ...	6	4	–	2	–	
*Speers (17), ...	38	5	–	32	1	Antrim.
*Spelman (24), ...	30	–	1	1	28	Galway, Roscommon, and Mayo.
*Spence (57), ...	58	3	3	52	–	33 in Antrim and 11 in Down.
Spencer, ...	19	10	7	2	–	Dublin and Cork.
Spillane, ...	44	1	42	1	–	23 in Cork and 11 in Kerry.
Spratt, ...	14	–	1	13	–	Antrim.
Spring, ...	6	2	2	–	2	—
Sproule, ...	17	3	–	11	3	10 in Tyrone.
Stacey, ...	5	4	1	–	–	—

Names	Irl.	L.	M.	U.	C.	Counties in which principally found
Stack, ...	54	–	53	–	1	29 in Kerry, 10 in Cork, and 10 in Limerick.
Stafford, ...	33	22	2	9	–	Wexford and Dublin.
*Stanley (20), ...	21	9	8	4	–	Dublin.
Stanton (39)—Staunton (28),	67	6	16	2	43	" Stanton," 17 in Mayo and 14 in Cork—" Staunton," 11 in Mayo and 8 in Galway.
Stapleton, ...	28	18	10	–	–	Tipperary and Kilkenny.
*Starrett (7), ...	10	–	–	10	–	6 in Antrim and 3 in Londonderry.
Steele (37)—Steel (17),	54	3	–	47	4	33 in Antrim and 8 in Londonderry.
Steen, ...	6	–	–	6	–	
Steenson, ...	19	–	–	19	–	Antrim and Armagh.
Stenson, ...	15	–	–	3	12	11 in Sligo.
*Stephens (32), ..	36	12	5	8	11	Mayo.
*Stevenson (81)—Stephenson (20),	106	8	2	92	4	Antrim, Armagh, and Down. [Tyrone.
*Stewart (236), ..	255	11	10	228	6	Antrim, Down, Londonderry, Donegal, and
Stinson, ...	12	–	–	11	1	—
Stirling (9)-Sterling (7),	16	1	–	15	–	14 in Antrim.
Stitt, ...	12	1	–	11	–	9 in Antrim.
St. John, ...	10	1	9	–	–	Tipperary.
*St. Leger (5), ...	7	4	3	–	–	—
Stockman, ...	7	1	–	6	–	—
Stokes, ...	28	10	13	3	2	—
*Stone (7), ...	12	7	1	1	3	—
*Storey (9), ...	13	3	–	10	–	8 in Antrim.
*Strahan (9), ...	11	5	–	6	–	—
Strain, ...	14	–	–	14	–	Down.
Strange, ...	6	1	–	5	–	5 in Antrim.
Stringer, ...	9	4	5	–	–	—
*Strong (12), ...	15	6	2	6	1	—
Studdert, ...	6	–	6	–	–	5 in Clare and 1 in Kerry.
Sturgeon, ...	8	–	–	8	–	—
*Sugrue (21), ...	23	–	23	–	–	22 in Kerry and 1 in Cork.
*Sullivan (838), ...	839	53	753	15	18	In every county of Munster, 373 of the entries being in Cork and 295 in Kerry.—In Leinster, Dublin has the largest number ; in Ulster, Antrim ; and in Connaught, Galway.
Sunderland, ...	7	7	–	–	–	Wexford.
*Supple (5), ...	6	1	5	–	–	—
*Surgeoner (5)—Surgenor (4).	10	–	–	9	1	9 in Antrim.
Sutherland, ...	6	2	2	2	–	—
Sutton, ...	27	19	7	1	–	Dublin, Wexford, and Cork.
*Swan (19), ...	23	9	–	14	–	Dublin and Antrim.
Swanton, ...	7	2	5	–	–	5 in Cork and 2 in Dublin.
*Sweeney (166)—Sweeny (82).	254	29	82	70	73	Cork, Donegal, Mayo, and Kerry.
*Sweetman (6), ...	8	4	4	–	–	Cork and Dublin.
Swift, ...	12	4	1	1	6	Mayo.
Switzer, ...	7	4	3	–	–	—
Swords, ...	8	8	–	–	–	Dublin.
*Taaffe (11), ...	15	7	4	–	4	—
*Taggart (27), ...	42	1	1	39	1	Antrim.
*Talbot (17), ...	18	6	8	–	4	Dublin.
Tallon, ...	15	14	–	1	–	10 in Clare.
Talty, ...	12	–	10	–	2	7 in Kerry and 1 in Cork.
Tangney, ...	8	–	8	–	–	—
Tanner, ...	7	1	2	4	–	—
*Tansey (10), ...	13	–	–	–	13	8 in Mayo, 3 in Roscommon, and 1 in Galway.
*Tarpey (10), ...	12	–	–	–	12	Cork.
*Tarrant (6), ...	7	2	5	–	–	" Tate," Antrim and Down—" Tait," Londonderry.
*Tate (25)—Tait (10), ..	36	8	2	26	–	
*Taylor (150), ...	151	21	21	97	12	Antrim, Down, Londonderry, and Dublin.
*Teague (5), ...	6	–	–	6	–	—
*Teahan (10), ...	11	1	10	–	–	9 in Kerry.
Teeling, ...	6	6	–	–	–	4 in Dublin.
Telford, ...	14	2	–	12	–	10 in Antrim.
Temple, ...	6	3	–	1	2	—
Templeton, ...	18	2	–	15	1	13 in Antrim.
Tennant, ...	5	1	–	2	2	—
Terry, ...	9	2	7	–	–	5 in Cork.
Thomas, ...	28	9	4	14	1	Antrim.
*Thompson (304), ..	317	44	23	239	11	Antrim, Down, Armagh, Londonderry, Dublin, Fermanagh, and Longford. Not many in any other county.
Thornton, ...	54	21	3	6	24	Galway, Dublin, and Mayo.
*Thorpe (5), ...	6	4	–	2	–	—
Thunder, ...	5	5	–	–	–	All in Dublin.
*Tiernan (26), ...	27	13	1	1	12	Louth.
*Tierney (74), ...	78	27	26	11	14	Dublin, Tipperary, and Galway—A very scattered name.

Names	Irl.	L.	M.	U.	C.	Counties in which principally found
Tighe,	33	6	–	5	22	Mayo.
Timlin,	13	–	–	–	13	12 in Mayo and 1 in Sligo.
*Timmins (16),	25	21	2	2	–	Dublin, Kildare, and Wicklow.
*Timony (9),	14	1	1	4	8	—
Tinsley,	5	2	–	3	–	
Tisdall,	6	5	–	1	–	Dublin.
*Toal (19),	20	3	–	17	–	8 in Armagh and 6 in Antrim.
*Tobin (97),	98	27	69	1	1	Waterford, Cork, Tipperary, Limerick. Dublin, and Kilkenny.
Todd,	38	3	1	34	–	20 in Antrim and 8 in Down.
Tolan,	19	1	–	6	12	11 in Mayo.
Toland,	9	–	–	9	–	Antrim.
Toman,	5	–	–	5	–	3 in Down and 2 in Antrim.
*Tomkins (7),	9	8	1	–	–	—
Tomlinson,	5	2	2	1	–	—
*Toner (39),	42	6	–	35	1	Armagh, Londonderry, and Antrim.
Tooher,	5	3	2	–	–	—
Toolan,	10	2	1	–	7	Roscommon.
*Toole (98),	100	61	4	1	34	Dublin, Galway, Mayo, Wicklow, and Kildare contain 75 per cent.
*Topping (8),	10	–	1	9	–	Antrim and Armagh.
*Tormey (9),	11	8	–	2	1	—
*Torrens (8),	9	–	–	9	–	Antrim.
Totten (9)—Totton (8),	17	–	–	17	–	" Totten," 6 in Antrim ; " Totton," 5 in Armagh.
Tougher,	5	–	–	–	5	All in Mayo.
*Towey (28),	30	–	–	1	29	22 in Roscommon and 7 in Mayo.
*Townsend (9),	11	7	–	4	–	—
Trant,	6	–	6	–	–	Kerry.
Travers,	38	14	1	14	9	Donegal, Dublin, and Leitrim.
*Traynor (35)—Treanor (28)—Trainor (12),	77	24	1	48	4	" Traynor," Dublin—" Treanor " and " Trainor," Antrim, Armagh, Monaghan, and Tyrone.
Treacy (37)—Tracey (31)—Tracy (16),	84	30	29	10	15	" Treacy," Tipperary and Galway—" Tracey " and " Tracy," Dublin.
Trimble (12),	13	2	–	10	1	
Trotter,	12	–	–	11	1	
Troy,	31	15	16	–	–	King's, Cork, and Tipperary.
Trueman,	5	1	–	4	–	
Tucker,	10	4	3	–	3	
Tuite,	14	10	1	3	–	
Tully,	45	8	4	14	19	Galway, Dublin, and Cavan.
*Tumelty (5),	10	3	–	7	–	
*Tuohy (22),	40	8	23	–	9	Clare and Galway.—There are 9 varieties of this name in the Birth Indexes for 1890.
Turkington,	12	–	–	12	–	9 in Armagh.
*Turley (7),	9	2	–	4	3	—
Turnbull,	5	3	–	2	–	—
Turner,	67	22	13	30	2	Dublin, Antrim, and Cork.
Turtle,	9	–	–	9	–	7 in Antrim and 2 in Armagh.
Tutty,	5	3	2	–	–	—
Twamley,	6	2	4	–	–	—
*Tweedie (10),	15	1	–	14	–	—
Twohig,	15	–	15	–	–	All in Cork.
*Twomey (63)—Toomey (15),	80	8	72	–	–	" Twomey," 59 in Cork and 4 in Kerry ; " Toomey," Dublin and Limerick.
Tynan,	20	14	5	1	–	Queen's.
Tyner,	6	4	2	–	–	—
*Tyrrell (27),	30	25	1	3	1	Dublin, Kildare, and Wicklow.
*Uprichard (9),	10	–	–	10	–	6 in Armagh and 4 in Antrim.
Upton,	6	3	2	1	–	—
*Usher (6),	8	5	–	3	–	—
*Valentine (8),	9	8	–	1	–	Dublin.
*Vallely (7),	9	1	–	8	–	Armagh.
Vance,	19	1	1	17	–	Antrim.
Vaughan,	35	5	18	9	3	Cork, Clare, Limerick, Antrim, and Down.
Veale,	12	1	11	–	–	Waterford.
Vickers,	5	2	3	–	–	—
Vincent,	8	2	3	3	–	—
Vogan,	5	–	–	5	–	—
Waddell,	12	–	–	12	–	—
Wade,	30	17	6	7	–	Dublin.
Waldron,	43	9	–	–	34	Mayo, Roscommon, and Dublin.
Walker,	123	28	7	84	4	Antrim, Dublin, Down, and Derry.
Wall,	58	31	26	–	1	Dublin, Waterford, Cork, Kilkenny, Limerick, and Tipperary.

Names	Irl.	L.	M.	U.	C.	Counties in which principally found
*Wallace (140),	144	17	26	80	21	Antrim, Galway, Cork, Limerick, Dublin, Down, and Londonderry.
Waller,	6	3	1	1	1	—
Walls,	11	3	–	7	1	—
Walsh (877)—Walshe (55),	932	237	388	58	249	Cork, Mayo, Waterford, Galway, Dublin, and Wexford. Found in large numbers in nearly every county.
*Walters (5),	7	1	2	4	–	—
Walton,	8	4	2	2	–	—
*Ward (211),	213	57	22	87	47	Found in every county in Ireland, but chiefly in Donegal, Dublin, and Galway.
Wardlow,	5	–	–	5	–	4 in Antrim and 1 in Armagh.
Waring,	7	1	–	6	–	—
Warner,	6	1	5	–	–	4 in Cork.
Warnock,	15	–	–	15	–	Tyrone and Down.
*Warren (31),	35	13	16	2	4	Kerry, Dublin, and Cork.
*Warwick (6),	7	–	–	7	–	All in Antrim.
*Wasson (5),	8	–	–	8	–	—
Waters,	47	16	10	8	13	Sligo, Wexford, and Monaghan.
Watkins,	7	3	1	1	2	—
Watson,	120	11	2	104	3	Antrim, Armagh, and Down.
Watt,	33	1	1	31	–	Antrim.
Watters,	22	5	–	17	–	Tyrone, Antrim, and Louth.
Watterson,	14	1	1	12	–	Antrim.
Waugh,	5	–	–	5	–	—
Weatnerup,	6	–	–	6	–	All in Antrim.
Webb,	33	12	5	13	3	Dublin and Antrim.
Webster,	21	12	2	7	–	Antrim and Dublin.
Weir,	56	2	1	50	3	31 in Antrim and 10 in Armagh.
Welby,	5	–	–	–	5	All in Galway.
Weldon,	14	10	3	1	–	—
Wells,	9	2	1	6	–	Armagh.
*Welsh (27),	32	3	2	25	2	Antrim.
West,	26	7	8	9	2	—
Weston,	7	4	–	3	–	—
Wharry,	5	–	–	5	–	All in Antrim.
Wharton,	5	2	3	–	–	—
Wheeler,	14	8	3	3	–	Dublin.
*Whelan (213),	214	135	63	3	13	Dublin, Wexford, Waterford, Tipperary, Carlow, and Queen's.
*Whelehan (5),	8	8	–	–	–	—
Whelton,	11	–	11	–	–	10 in Cork and 1 in Kerry.
White (269)—Whyte (22),	291	82	91	94	24	Found in every county in Ireland—chiefly in Antrim, Cork, Dublin, and Wexford.
Whiteside,	18	1	1	16	–	Antrim and Armagh.
Whitney,	5	5	–	–	–	3 in Longford and 2 in Wexford.
Whittle,	6	1	2	3	–	—
*Whitton (5),	8	4	1	3	–	—
Whitty,	19	17	2	–	–	11 in Wexford.
Wickham,	6	5	–	1	–	Wexford.
Wiggins,	6	2	1	3	–	—
Wightman,	6	–	–	6	–	Down.
Wilkinson,	33	8	1	21	3	Antrim and Armagh.
Williams,	90	40	25	14	11	A scattered name—principally found in Dublin, Cork, Limerick, and Antrim.
*Williamson (56),	57	3	–	54	–	Antrim, Armagh, Londonderry, and Tyrone.
Willis,	33	6	5	22	–	Antrim and Down.
Wills,	9	2	2	4	1	—
*Wilson (365),	366	49	22	287	8	Antrim, Armagh, Down, Tyrone, Dublin, Londonderry, and Fermanagh.
*Winters (15),	18	6	5	5	2	—
Wise (5)—Wyse (3),	8	2	6	–	–	—
Wiseman,	5	1	3	1	–	—
Withers,	6	1	–	4	–	—
Wood,	14	7	3	4	–	—
Woodhouse,	6	2	–	4	–	—
Woods,	137	27	18	84	8	Antrim, Armagh, Down, Monaghan, Tyrone, Dublin, Louth, and Cork—A scattered name.
Woodside,	9	1	–	8	–	8 in Antrim and 1 in Dublin.
Workman,	5	–	–	5	–	4 in Antrim.
*Woulfe (12),	22	4	13	1	4	Limerick.
Wray,	15	1	–	14	–	6 in Donegal and 5 in Londonderry.
Wren,	12	1	10	–	1	—
Wright,	103	20	8	72	3	Antrim, Down, Dublin, and Armagh.
*Wylie (32),	51	–	2	49	–	Antrim.
*Wynne (46),	47	18	9	3	17	Dublin and Sligo.
Yeates (14)—Yates (4),	18	6	3	9	–	"Yeates," 8 in Antrim and 5 in Dublin— "Yates," 3 in Cork.
*Young (131),	132	25	20	87	–	Antrim, Tyrone, Dublin, Cork, Down, and Londonderry.

Gravestone Inscriptions Recorded in Printed Sources

arranged by parish and townland in which the cemeteries are located.

Co. Antrim

Ardclinis: Glynns, Vol. IV, 1976.
Ballykeel: *Gravestone Inscriptions, Co. Antrim,* Vol. I, by George Rutherford, 1977.
Culfeightrin: Irish Ancestor, Vol. II, No. 2, 1970.
Glynn: *Gravestone Inscriptions, Co. Antrim,* Vol. II, by George Rutherford.
Islandmagee: *Gravestone Inscriptions, Co. Antrim,* Vol. I, by George Rutherford, 1977.
Killycrappin: Glynns, Vol. V, 1977.
Kilmore: Glynns, Vol. IV, 1976.
Kilroot: *Gravestone Inscriptions, Co. Antrim,* Vol. II, by George Rutherford.
Lambeg: *Inscriptions on Tombstones in Lambeg Churchyard,* by William Cassidy.
Lisburn Cathedral: *Lisburn Cathedral and its Past Rectors,* by Very Rev. W. P. Carmody, 1926.
Magheragall: Family Links, Vol. I. Nos. 2 and 3, 1981.
Templecorran: *Gravestone Inscriptions, Co. Antrim,* Vol. II, by George Rutherford.

Co. Armagh

Creggan: Seanchas Ardmhacha, Vol. VI, 1976.

Co. Cavan

Castlerahan: Breifne, Vol. II, No. 3, 1925-6.
Crosserlough: Breifne, Vol. V, No. 17, 1976.
Denn: Breifne, Vol. II, No. 2, 1924.
Derver: Breifne, Vol. I, No. 3, 1922.
Drumlane: Breifne, Vol. V, No. 19, 1979.
Kildrumfertan: Breifne, Vol. II, No. 8, 1965.
Lurgan: Breifne, Vol. I, No. 4, 1961.
Magherintemple: Breifne, Vol. II, No. 6, 1963.
Munterconnacht: Breifne, Vol. III, No. 1, 1927-8.
Templeport: Breifne, Vol. IV, No. 14, 1971.

Co. Clare

Killaloe Cathedral: Year Book of St. Flannan's Cathedral.

Co. Cork
Aghinagh: JCHAS, No. 216, 1967.
Ballyclough: *O'Kief, Coshe Mang, etc.,* Vol. 8, 1965.
Ballycurrany: JCHAS, No. 237, 1978.
Ballyvourney: *O'Kief, Coshe Mang, etc.,* Vol. 6, 1963.
Carrigrohanebeg: JCHAS, No. 218, 1968.
Castlemagner: *O'Kief, Coshe Mang, etc.,* Vol. 6, 1963.
Clondrohid: *O'Kief, Coshe Mang, etc.,* Vol. 6, 1963.
Clonfert: *O'Kief, Coshe Mang, etc.,* Vol. 6, 1963.
Clonmeen (and Lyre and Banteer): *O'Kief, Coshe Mang, etc.,* Vol. 7, 1964.
Clonmult: JCHAS, Nos. 223, 224, 225, 1976-7.
Cullen: *O'Kief, Coshe Mang, etc.,* Vol. 6, 1963.
Dangandonovan: JCHAS, No. 229, 1974.
Desertmore: JCHAS, No. 219, 1969.
Drishane: *O'Kief, Coshe Mang, etc.,* Vol. 6, 1963.
Dromagh: *O'Kief, Coshe Mang, etc.,* Vol. 8, 1965.
Dromtariffe: *O'Kief, Coshe Mang, etc.,* Vol. 6, 1963.
Dunderrow: JCHAS, No. 224, 1971.
Fermoy (military stones only): Irish Sword, Nos. 51 and 53, 1977 and 1979.
Inchigeela: *O'Kief, Coshe Mang, etc.,* Vol. 6, 1963.
Kilbrin: *O'Kief, Coshe Mang, etc.,* Vol. 8, 1965.
Kilcorney: *O'Kief, Coshe Mang, etc.,* Vol. 7, 1964.
Kilcrea Friary: JCHAS, No. 226, 1972.
Kilcummin: *O'Kief, Coshe Mang, etc.,* Vol. 6, 1963.
Killeagh: JCHAS, No. 226, 1972.
Kilnaglory: JCHAS, No. 220, 1969.
Kilnamartyra: *O'Kief, Coshe Mang, etc.,* Vol. 6, 1963.
Kilmeen (Barony of Duhallow): *O'Kief, Coshe Mang, etc.,* Vol. 6, 1963.
Lisgoold: JCHAS, No. 237, 1978.
Macloneigh: *O'Kief, Coshe Mang, etc.,* Vol. 8, 1965.
Macroom: *O'Kief, Coshe Mang, etc.,* Vol. 8, 1965.
Mallow: *O'Kief, Coshe Mang, etc.,* Vol. 8, 1965.
Mologga: Irish Genealogist, Vol. II, No. 12, 1955.
Nohovaldaly: *O'Kief, Coshe Mang, etc.,* Vol. 8, 1965.
St. Finbarr's: *St. Finbarr's Cathedral,* by Rev. Andrew C. Robinson, 1897.
Tisaxon: JCHAS, No. 222, 1970.
Titeskin: JCHAS, No. 221, 1970.
Tullylease: *O'Kief, Coshe Mang, etc.,* Vol. 8, 1965.
Youghal (inscriptions in the Collegiate Church): *The Handbook for Youghal,* by
W. G. Field, 1896 (reprinted 1973).

Co. Donegal
Assaroe Abbey: Donegal Annual, Vol. III, No. 3, 1957.
Ballyshannon: Donegal Annual, Vol. XII, No. 2, 1978.
Finner: *Where Erne and Drowes meet the Sea,* by Rev. P. O. Gallachair, 1961.

Co. Down

Gravestone Inscriptions, Co. Down, Vols. 1-19, compiled by R. S. J. Clarke, 1966-1981.

Aghlisnafin: Vol. 9.
Annahilt: Vol. 18.
Ardkeen: Vol. 13.
Ardglass: Vol. 8.
Ardquin: Vol. 13.
Baileysmill: Vol. 2.
Ballee: Vol. 8.
Balligan: Vol. 14.
Balloo: Vol. 17.
Ballyblack: Vol. 12.
Ballycarn: Vol. 3.
Ballycopeland: Vol. 16.
Ballycranbeg: Vol. 13.
Ballycruttle: Vol. 8.
Ballyculter: Vol. 8.
Ballygalget: Vol. 13.
Ballygowan: Vol. 5.
Ballyhalbert: Vol. 15.
Ballyhemlin: Vol. 14.
Ballykinler: Vol. 9.
Ballymacashen: Vol. 6.
Ballymageogh: Vol. 10.
Ballymartin: Vol. 10.
Ballynahinch: Vol. 9.
Ballyphilip: Vol. 13.
Ballytrastan: Vol. 13.
Bangor: Vol. 17.
Barr: *An Ancient Irish Parish,* by Rev. J. D. Cowan, 1914.
Blaris: Vol. 5.
Boardmills: Vol. 2.
Breda: Vol. 1.
Bright: Vol. 8.
Cargacreevy: Vol. 18.
Carrowdore: Vol. 14.
Carryduff: Vols. 1 & 18.
Castlereagh: Vol. 1.
Clandeboye: Vol. 17.
Cloghy: Vol. 14.
Clough: Vol. 9.
Comber: Vol. 5.

Copeland Islands: Vol. 16.
Donaghadee: Vol. 16.
Donaghcloney: *An Ulster Parish,* by Rev. Edward D. Atkinson, 1898.
Donaghmore: *An Ancient Irish Parish,* by Rev. J. D. Cowan, 1914.
Downpatrick: Vol. 7.
Dromara: Vol. 19.
Dromore: Vol. 19.
Drumaroad: Vol. 9.
Drumbeg: Vol. 3.
Drumbo: Vols. 1, 4 & 18.
Dundonald: Vol. 2.
Dunsfort: Vol. 8.
Edenderry: Vol. 3.
Eglantine: Vol. 18.
Gilnahirk: Vol. 18.
Glasdrumman: Vol. 10.
Glastry: Vol. 15.
Gransha: Vol. 1.
Greyabbey: Vol. 12.
Groomsport: Vol. 17.
Hillhall: Vol. 1.
Hillsborough: Vol. 18.
Holywood: Vol 14.
Inch: Vol. 7.
Inishargy: Vol. 14.
Kilcarn: Vol. 5.
Kilclief: Vol. 8.
Kilhorne: Vol. 10.
Kilkeel: Vol. 10.
Killarney: Vol. 2.
Killaresy: Vol. 6.
Killinakin: Vol. 6.
Killinchy: Vols. 5 and 6.
Killough: Vol. 8.
Killybawn: Vol. 1.
Killyleagh: Vols. 6 & 7.
Killysuggan: Vol. 5.

Kilmegan: Vol. 9.
Kilmood: Vol. 5.
Kilmore: Vol. 3.
Kilwarlin: Vol. 18.
Kircubbin: Vol. 12.
Knock: Vol. 4.
Knockbrecken: Vols. 1 & 18.
Knockbreda: Vol. 2.
Legacurry: Vol. 2.
Lisbane: Vol. 13.
Loughaghery: Vol. 18.
Loughinisland: Vols. 9 & 12.
Magheradrool: Vols. 9 & 12.
Magherahamlet: Vol. 9.
Magheralin: Vol. 19.
Maze: Vol. 18.
Millisle: Vol. 16.
Moira: Vol. 18.
Moneyrea: Vol. 1.
Mourne: Vol. 10.
Movilla: Vol. 11.
Newtownards: Vol. 11.
Old Court, Vol. 8.
Portaferry: Vol. 13.
Rademan: Vol. 3.
Raffrey: Vol. 5.
Rathmullan: Vol. 9.
Ravara: Vol. 5.
Saintfield: Vol. 3.
Saul: Vols. 7 and 8.
Seaforde: Vol. 9.
Slanes: Vol. 14.
Tamlaght: Vol. 10.
Templepatrick: Vol. 14.
Tullymacnous: Vol. 6.
Tullynakill: Vol. 1.
Waringstown: *An Ulster Parish,* by Rev. Edward D. Atkinson, 1898.
Whitechurch: Vol. 15.

Co. Dublin
Chapelizod: Irish Genealogist, Vol. V, No. 4, 1977.
Cloghran: *History and Description of Santry and Cloghran Parishes,* by Rev. Benjamin W. Adams, 1883.
Dalkey: Irish Genealogist, Vol. V, No. 2, 1975.
Dublin City: Christ Church Cathedral: *Inscriptions on the Monuments . . . in Christ Church Cathedral, Dublin,* by Rev. John Finlayson, 1878.
St. Andrew's, Westland Row (names on coffin plates): Irish Genealogist, Vol. V, No. 1, 1974.
SS. Michael and John (names on coffin plates): Irish Genealogist, Vol. V, No. 3, 1976.
St. Paul (C. of I.): Journal of the Royal Society of Antiquaries, Vol. CIV, 1974.
Killiney (old churchyard): Irish Genealogist, Vol. IV, No. 6, 1973.
Kill o' the Grange: Irish Genealogist, Vol. IV, No. 5, 1972.
Leixlip: Irish Genealogist, Vol. IV, No. 2, 1969.
Lucan: Irish Genealogist, Vol. V, No. 6, 1976.
Monkstown: Irish Genealogist, Vol. IV, Nos. 3 and 4, 1970-1.
Palmerstown: Irish Genealogist, Vol. V, No. 8, 1978.
Santry: *History and Description of Santry and Cloghran Parishes,* by Rev. Benjamin W. Adams, 1883.
Tallaght: Irish Genealogist, Vol. IV, No. 1, 1968.
Taney: *The Parish of Taney,* by F. Elrington Ball, 1895.

Co. Fermanagh
Aghalurcher: Clogher Record, Vol. II, No. 2, 1958.
Aghaven: Clogher Record, Vol. IV, Nos. 1 and 2, 1960-61.
Devenish: St. Molaise's and Devenish Abbey: *Devenish, its History, Antiquities and Traditions,* by Rev. J. E. MacKenna and F. J. Bigger, 1897.
Donagh: Clogher Record, Vol. I, No. 3, 1955.
Drumully: Clogher Record, Vol. I, No. 2, 1954.
Enniskillen: *Enniskillen Parish and Town,* by W. H. Dundas, 1913.
Galoon: Clogher Record, Vol. X, No. 2, 1980.
Holywell: Clogher Record, Vol. II, No. 1, 1957.
Kinawley: Clogher Record, Vol. I, No. 4, 1956.
Monea: *The Parish of Devenish,* Co. Fermanagh, by Rev. William B. Steele, 1937.
Templenafrin: Clogher Record, Vol. II, No. 1, 1957.
Tullymageeran: Clogher Record, Vol. 11, No. 3, 1959.

Co. Galway
Kilmacduagh: Irish Ancestor, Vol. VII, No. 1, 1975.

Co. Kerry
Aghadoe: *O'Kief, Coshe Mang, etc.,* Vol. 6, 1963.
Aglish: *O'Kief, Coshe Mang, etc.,* Vol. 6, 1963.

Ardfert: *O'Kief, Coshe Mang, etc.,* Vol. 8, 1965.
Ballymacelligott: *O'Kief, Coshe Mang, etc.,* Vol. 8, 1965.
Castleisland: *O'Kief, Coshe Mang, etc.,* Vol. 6, 1963.
Clogherbrien: *O'Kief, Coshe Mang, etc.,* Vol. 8, 1963.
Currans: *O'Kief, Coshe Mang, etc.,* Vol. 6, 1963.
Dysert: *O'Kief, Coshe Mang, etc.,* Vol. 6, 1963.
Kilcummin: *O'Kief, Coshe Mang, etc.,* Vol. 6, 1963.
Killarney and Muckross Abbey: *O'Kief, Coshe Mang, etc.,* Vol. 6, 1963.
Kilnanare: *O'Kief, Coshe Mang, etc.,* Vol. 6, 1963.
Killeentierna: *O'Kief, Coshe Mang, etc.,* Vol. 6, 1963.
Killorglin: *O'Kief, Coshe Mang, etc.,* Vol. 8, 1965.
Nohoval: *O'Kief, Coshe Mang, etc.,* Vol. 8, 1965.
O'Brennan: *O'Keif, Coshe Mange, etc.,* Vol. 8, 1965.
Rathmore: *O'Kief, Coshe Mang, etc.,* Vol. 6, 1963.
Tralee: *O'Kief, Coshe Mang, etc.,* Vol. 8, 1965.

Co. Kilkenny
St. Canice's Cathedral: *The History, Architecture and Antiquities of the Cathedral Church of St. Canice, Kilkenny,* by Rev. James Graves and J. G. A. Prim, 1857.
St. Mary's, Kilkenny: Old Kilkenny Review, 1979, 1980, 1981.

Co. Limerick
Ardcanny: Irish Ancestor, Vol. IX, No. 1, 1977.
Ardpatrick: *Reflections, Historical and Topographical on Ardpatrick, Co. Limerick,* by John Fleming, 1979.
Athlacca: *Dromin Athlacca,* by Mainchin Seoighe, 1978.
Ballingarry: *Records of Ballingarry,* by Rev. G. F. Hamilton, 1930.
Bruree: *Brú Rí: the History of the Bruree District,* by Mainchin Seoighe, 1973.
Dromin: *Dromin Athlacca,* by Mainchin Seoighe, 1978.
Grange: Irish Ancestor, Vol. XII, 1980.
Kilbehenny: Irish Genealogist, Vol. II, No. 11, 1954.
Nantinan: Irish Ancestor, Vol. XII, 1980.
St. Mary's Cathedral: *The Monuments of St. Mary's Cathedral, Limerick,* by Very Rev. M. J. Talbot, 1976.
Tankardstown: *Brú Rí: the History of the Bruree District,* by Mainchin Seoighe, 1973.

Co. Louth
Ardee: Irish Genealogist, Vol. III, No. 1, 1956.
Ballymascanlon: JCLAS, Vol. XVII, No. 4, 1972.
Carlingford: JCLAS, Vol. XIX, No. 2, 1978.
Castlebellingham: *History of Kilsaran Union of Parishes in the Co. of Louth,* by Rev. James B. Leslie, 1908.
Charlestown: *Notes and Jottings concerning the Parish of Charlestown Union,* by G. W. C. L'Estrange, 1912.

Clonkeen: *Notes and Jottings concerning the Parish of Charlestown Union,* by
 G. W. C. L'Estrange, 1912.
Dromiskin: *History of Kilsaran Union of Parishes in the Co. of Louth,* by Rev.
 James B. Leslie, 1908.
Faughart: *Tombstone Inscriptions from Fochart,* Dundalgan Press, 1968.
Faughart (Urnai cemetery): *Urnai,* by Rev. D. MacIomhair, Dundalk, 1969.
Killanny: Clogher Record, Vol. VI, No. 1, 1966.
Kilsaran: *History of Kilsaran Union of Parishes in the Co. of Louth,* by Rev.
 James B. Leslie, 1908.
Manfieldstown: *History of Kilsaran Union of Parishes in the Co. of Louth,* by Rev.
 James B. Leslie, 1908.
Newtownstalaban: JCLAS, Vol. XVII, No. 2, 1970.
Rathdrumin: JCLAS, Vol. XIX, No. 1, 1977.
Seatown, Dundalk: Tempest's Annual, 1967 and 1971-2.
Stabannon: *History of Kilsaran Union of Parishes in the Co. of Louth,* by Rev.
 James B. Leslie, 1908.
Tullyallen: Seanchas Ardmhacha, Vol. VIII, No. 2, 1977.

Co. Meath
Agher: Irish Ancestor, Vol. X, No. 2, 1978.
Arodstown: Ríocht na Midhe, Vol VI, No. 1, 1975.
Athboy: Irish Ancestor, Vol. XIII, Nos. 1 and 2, 1981.
Balsoon: Irish Ancestor, Vol. VIII, No. 2, 1976.
Clonabreany: Ríocht na Midhe, Vol. VI, No. 2, 1976.
Danestown: Ríocht na Midhe, Vol. V, No. 4, 1974.
Drumlargan: Irish Ancestor, Vol. XII, Nos. 1 and 2, 1980.
Duleek: Irish Genealogist, Vol. III, No. 12, 1967.
Dunboyne: Irish Ancestor, Vol. XI, Nos. 1 and 2, 1979.
Kells: Irish Genealogist, Vol. III, No. 12, 1966.
Kilbride: Ríocht na Midhe, Vol. VI, No. 3, 1977.
Killeen: Ríocht na Midhe, Vol. IV, No. 3, 1970.
Kilmore: Ríocht na Midhe, Vol. VI, No. 1, 1975.
Loughcrew: Irish Ancestor, Vol. IX, No. 2, 1977.
Moy: Irish Ancestor, Vol. VI, No. 2, 1974.
Moyagher: Irish Ancestor, Vol. VIII, No. 1, 1976.
Oldcastle: Ríocht na Midhe, Vol. IV, No. 2, 1968.
Rathmore: Irish Ancestor, Vol. VII, No. 2, 1975.

Co. Monaghan
Clontibret: Clogher Record, Vol. VIII, No. 2, 1974.
Donagh: Clogher Record, Vol. II, No. 1, 1957.
Drumsnat: Clogher Record, Vol. VI, No. 1, 1966.
Glaslough: Clogher Record, Vol. IX, No. 3, 1978.
Killanny: Clogher Record, Vol. VI, No. 1, 1966.
Magheross: Clogher Record, Vol. V, No. 1, 1963, and Macalla, Vol. III, No. 4, 1978.

Mullandoy: Clogher Record, Vol. VI, No. 1, 1966.
Rackwallace: Clogher Record, Vol. IV, No. 3, 1962.
Tydavnet: Clogher Record, Vol. I, No. 1, 1954.

Co. Tipperary

Kilmore: Irish Genealogist, Vol. II, No. 10, 1953.
Uskane: Irish Genealogist, Vol. III, No. 2, 1957.

Co. Tyrone

Clogher: *Clogher Cathedral Graveyard,* by John I. D. Johnston, 1972.
Donaghcavey: Clogher Record, Vol. VII, No. 2, 1970.
Drumglass: Seanchas Ardmhacha, Vol. VII, No. 2, 1974.
Kilskeery: Clogher Record, Vol. VIII, No. 1, 1973.

Co. Waterford

Affane: Irish Genealogist, Vol. II, No. 9, 1952.
Clashmore: Irish Genealogist, Vol. II, No. 8, 1950.
Stradbally: Decies, Vol. XVI, 1981.
Waterford: St. Patrick's: *Catholic Record of Waterford and Lismore,* Vol. IV, by
    Rev. P. Power, 1916.
Whitechurch: Irish Ancestor, Vol. V, No. 1, 1973.

Co. Westmeath

Ballyloughloe (Mount Temple): Irish Ancestor, Vol. IV, No. 2, 1972.
Kilcleagh: *Moate, Co. Westmeath: a History of the Town and District,* by Liam
    Cox, 1981.
Killomenaghan: *Moate, Co. Westmeath: a History of the Town and District,* by
    Liam Cox, 1981.
Moate: *Moate, Co. Westmeath: a History of the Town and District.* by Liam Cox,
    1981.
Street: Ríocht na Midhe, Vol. IV, No. 3, 1969.

Co. Wexford

Memorials of the Dead—North Wexford, by Brian J. Cantwell, 1980.

Ardamine	Brideswell	Inch	Leskinfere
Askamore	Bunclody	Kilanerin	Limbrick
Ballinclay	Camolin	Kilcashel	Monaseed
(Quaker)	Castledockrill	Kilcavan	Prospect
Ballindaggan	Castletown	Kilgorman	Riverchapel
Balloughter	Clonatin	Killenagh	Rosminogue
Ballycanew	Clone	Kilmyshall	Scarawalsh
Ballycarney	Craanford	Kilnahue	Templeshanbo
Ballyduff	Donoughmore	Kilnenor	Toberanierin
Ballyfad	Ferns	Kilrush	Toome
Ballygarrett	Gorey	Kiltennel	
Ballymore	Holyfort	Knockbrandon	

Co. Wicklow

Memorials of the Dead, Vol. *I, North-East Wicklow,* by Brian J. Cantwell, 1974.
Memorials of the Dead, Vol. *II, South-East Wicklow,* by Brian J. Cantwell, 1975.
Memorials of the Dead, Vol. *III, South-West Wicklow,* by Brian J. Cantwell, 1976.
Memorials of the Dead, Vol. *IV, North-West Wicklow,* by Brian J. Cantwell, 1978.

Aghold: Vol. 3.
Aghowle: Vol. 3.
Annacurragh: Vol. 3.
Ardoyne: Vol. 3.
Arklow: Vol. 2.
Ashford: Vol. 1.
Askanagap: Vol. 3.
Aughrim: Vol. 3.
Avoca: Vol. 2.
Ballinatone: Vol. 2.
Ballintemple: Vol. 2.
Ballycooge: Vol. 2.
Ballycore: Vol. 4.
Ballymaconnell: Vol. 3.
Ballymaghroe: Vol. 3.
Ballynure: Vol. 4.
Baltinglass: Vol. 4.
Baltyboys: Vol. 4.
Barndarrig: Vol. 2.
Barranisky: Vol. 2.
Blacklion: Vol. 1.
Blessington: Vol. 4.
Bray: Vol. 1.
Burgage: Vol. 4.
Calary: Vol. 1
Carnew: Vol. 3.
Castlemacadam: Vol. 2.
Castletimon: Vol. 2.
Cloghleagh: Vol. 4.
Connary: Vol. 2.
Coolafancy: Vol. 3.
Coronation Plantation
  Obelisk: Vol. 4.
Cranareen: Vol. 4.
Crossbridge: Vol. 3.
Crosschapel: Vol. 4.
Crosspatrick: Vol. 3.
Curraghlawn: Vol. 3.
Curtlestown: Vol. 1.
Davidstown: Vol. 4.

Delgany: Vol. 1.
Derralossary: Vol. 1.
Donard: Vol. 4.
Donoughmore: Vol. 4.
Dunganstown: Vol. 2.
Dunlavin: Vol. 4.
Ennereilly: Vol. 2.
Ennisboyne: Vol. 2.
Enniskerry: Vol. 1.
Glencree: Vol. 1.
Glendalough: Vol. 4.
Glenealy: Vol. 2.
Grangecon: Vol. 4.
Greenan: Vol. 2.
Greystones: Vol. 1.
Hollywood: Vol. 4.
Kilbride: Vols. 1, 2, 4.
Kilcarra: Vol. 2.
Kilcommon: Vols. 2 & 3.
Kilcoole: Vol. 1.
Kilfea: Vol. 1.
Killadreenan: Vol. 1.
Killahurler: Vol. 2.
Killamoat: Vol. 3.
Killavany: Vol. 3.
Killegar: Vol. 1.
Killiskey: Vol. 1.
Killoughter: Vol. 1.
Kilmacanogue: Vol. 1.
Kilmagig: Vol. 2.
Kilmurry: Vol. 1.
Kilpipe: Vol. 3.
Kilquade: Vol. 1.
Kilquiggan: Vol. 3.
Kilranelagh: Vol. 4.
Kiltegan: Vol. 3.
Knockanana: Vol. 3.
Knockanarrigan: Vol. 4.
Knockarigg: Vol. 4.
Knockloe: Vol. 3.

Lackan: Vol. 4.
Laragh: Vol. 4.
Leitrim: Vol. 4.
Liscolman: Vol. 3.
Macreddin: Vol. 3.
Moyne: Vol. 3.
Mullinacuff: Vol. 3.
Newcastle: Vol. 1.
Newtown Mount Kennedy:
  Vol. 1.
Nunscross: Vol. 1.
Powerscourt: Vol. 1.
Preban: Vol. 3.
Rathbran: Vol. 4.
Rathdrum: Vol. 2.
Rathnew: Vol. 2.
Redcross: Vol. 2.
Redford: Vol. 1.
Rossahane: Vol. 3.
Scurlocks: Vol. 4.
Shillelagh: Vol. 3.
Stratford: Vol. 4.
Templeboodin: Vol. 4.
Templemichael: Vol. 2.
Templerainy: Vol. 2.
Tober: Vol. 4.
Tomacrok: Vol. 3.
Tornant: Vol. 4.
Trinity: Vol. 1.
Valleymount: Vol. 4.
Whaley Abbey: Vol. 2.
Wicklow: Vol. 2.
Yewtree: Vol. 3.

Miscellaneous Genealogical Sources

Records and References arranged by date relating to Ireland in General.

Names of the succession of patentee officers in the departments of state in Ireland, 1152-1827.
> *Liber Munerum Publicorum Hiberniae,* Parts 1-4, 1824. Index: 9th Report, DKPRI, Appendix 3, pp. 21-58.

The names of Irish adherents of Richard, Duke of York, 1449.
> *Facsimiles of National Manuscripts of Ireland,* Part 3, fol. 40.

Calendar of *Fiants* or warrants issued to the Irish Court of Chancery for the issue of royal grants, 1521-1547 (Henry VII, Henry VIII), with index.
> 7th Report, DKPRI, pp. 33-110.

Muster-roll of Irish kerne, 1544.
> *Facsimiles of National Manuscripts of Ireland,* Part 3, fol. 76.

Calendar of *Fiants* of Edward VI, 1547-1553, with index of personal names and places.   8th Report, DKPRI, pp. 27-230.

Calendar of *Fiants* of Philip and Mary, 1553-1558, with index—being warrants addressed to the Irish Court of Chancery for the issue of royal grants.
> 9th Report, DKPRI, pp. 59-104.

Names of English settlers in the Pale, 1556-60.
> *Facsimiles of National Manuscripts of Ireland,* Part 4 (1), pp. 62-67.

Calendar of *Fiants* or warrants issued during the reign of Elizabeth I, 1588-1603.
> 11th, 12th, 13th, 15th, 16th, 17th, 18th Reports, DKPRI. Index to same: 21st and 22nd Reports, DKPRI.

Alumni Dublinenses, a Register of the Students, Graduates . . . of Trinity College in the University of Dublin, 1593-1846. 2nd edition with supplement 1846-1860, by George D. Burtchaell and Thomas Ulick Sadleir, Dublin, 1935.

Fee-farm grants from the Duke of Ormond: names of parties and lands granted, 1636-1713.   6th Report, DKPRI, pp. 73-88.

Cromwellian roll of account of 'money received and payed' for public use in Ireland, 1649-1656.
> *Facsimiles of National Manuscripts of Ireland,* Part 4 (11), pp. 141-148.

The Transplantation to Connacht, 1654-58, by Robert C. Simington, Irish University Press, 1970.

Index to persons and places found in the certificates issued to adventurers and soldiers, 1666.
> *Reports of the Commissioners into the Public Records of Ireland:* 15th Report, pp. 403-433; pp. 434-521.

Abstracts of grants of lands, etc. under the Acts of Settlement and Explanation, 1666-1684.

Reports of the Commissioners into the Public Records of Ireland: 15th Report, pp. 45-280. Index to same, pp. 329-337.

Abstracts, with index of persons, of the conveyances of the forfeited estates in Ireland, 1688.

Reports of the Commissioners into the Public Records of Ireland: 15th Report, pp. 348-399.

Index of names and places occurring in the Decrees of Innocents, 17th century.

Reports of the Commissioners into the Public Records of Ireland: 15th Report, pp. 526-575.

Catalogue of Inquisitions: Leinster Counties: names of persons whose estates were the subject of official inquiry, 17th century.

Reports of the Commissioners into the Public Records of Ireland: 8th Report, pp. 432-461.

Catalogue of Inquisitions: Connaught Counties: names of persons whose estates were the subject of official inquiry, 17th century.

Reports of the Commissioners into the Public Records of Ireland: 8th Report, pp. 507-515.

Catalogue of Inquisitions: Munster Counties: Names of persons whose estates were the subject of official inquiry, 17th century.

Reports of the Commissioners into the Public Records of Ireland: 8th Report, pp. 475-507.

Catalogue of Inquisitions: Ulster Counties: Names of persons whose estates were the subject of official inquiry, 17th century.

Reports of the Commissioners into the Public Records of Ireland: 8th Report, pp. 461-475.

Appeals to the Court of Claims, arranged alphabetically by surname, 17th century.

Reports of the Commissioners into the Public Records of Ireland: 6th Report, pp. 248-300.

A list of claims arising out of the 17th century forfeitures in Ireland entered at Chichester House, College Green, Dublin, on or before 10 August 1700.

G.O. Ms. 482.

Names of converts from Catholicism to the Established Church enrolled between 1704-1839.

The Convert Rolls, ed. by E. O'Byrne, Irish Manuscripts Commission, 1981.

Employees of the Irish Revenue in 1709.   *Irish Ancestor,* No. 1, 1974, pp. 6-16.

List of Court of Chancery Answers: Names of plaintiffs and defendants, 1730-1850.

6th Report, DKPRI, Appendix 3, pp. 29-35.

Catholic Qualification Rolls: Names and addresses of Catholics who took oaths prescribed by law in order to enjoy certain rights, offices and privileges, 1775.

42nd Report, DKPRI, pp. 79-81 and 59th Report, DKPRI, pp. 50-84.

Lists of persons who suffered losses to their property in the course of the 1798 Rebellion and who had given in their claims on or before the 6th of April, 1799 to the Commissioners for enquiring into the losses sustained by such of His Majesty's loyal subjects as had suffered in their property by the Rebellion. The lists give the claimant's name, occupation, residence, nature of loss and amount claimed. The lists are arranged by county, one for each of the following counties: Antrim, Carlow,

Clare, Down, Dublin, Galway, Kildare, Kilkenny, King's County (Offaly), Leitrim, Mayo, Meath, Queen's County (Leix), Roscommon, Sligo, Tipperary, Waterford, Westmeath and Wexford.   NLI. JLB.

List of Chancery Bills with the names of plaintiffs and defendants, mainly 18th century.   6th Report, DKPRI, pp. 36-40.

A schedule of deeds and papers, alphabetically arranged by surname, deposited in the Court of Chancery, Ireland, mainly 18th century.
   Reports of the Commissioners into the Public Records of Ireland: 2nd Report, pp. 90-101.

Military, civil and exchequer lists for Ireland, in receipt of payment from the Exchequer, with the names of the parties paid and the services for which they were paid, 1821.
   Report from Commissioners (Parl. Papers), 1822, Vol. 14, pp. (596) 1-59.

List of regular clergy in Ireland, arranged by county, giving the name, place of birth, name of Order and place of residence of each clegyman, 1824.
   Archivium Hibernicum, Vol. 3, pp. 49-86.

Tabular list of Roman Catholic day schools founded or maintained wholly or in part by subscription, arranged by province and by county, giving the exact location and description of each school (e.g. a poor man's kitchen), the names of teachers, etc., 1824.   *Irish Education Inquiry,* 1826, 2nd Report, pp. 96-135.

Tabular list of schools of the Christian Brotherhood and of those connected with sundry religious orders arranged by county, with the name of the parish in which the school was held, together with the name of the master or mistress, 1824.
   Irish Education Inquiry, 1826, 2nd Report, Appendix 9, pp. 86-89.

Tabular list of female schools attached to Nunneries with the name of the townland or parish in which the school was held, the name of the head-mistress, etc., 1824.
   Irish Education Inquiry, 1826, 2nd Report, pp. 90-95.

List of all parochial schools in Ireland, including the name of the townland or place in which the school was held; the name of the master or mistress; total income of the master or mistress; description of the school-house, numbers in attendance, etc., 1824.   *Irish Education Inquiry,* 2nd Report, 1826.

Return of voters registered in each borough in Ireland, stating voters' names and places of abode, 1830-1840.
   Reports from Committees (Parl. Papers), 1837, Vol. 11 (ii), pp. (480) 193-234.

A return of the names of Clerks of the Roads in Ireland, their ordinary places of residence and amount of annual salary in the year 1831.
   Accounts and Papers, 1831-32, Vol. 45, p. (392) 1.

A return of the name, residence and occupation of each person admitted as a Freeman in each Corporation in Ireland (except Dublin) with the date of admission and date of registration of each, together with a statement of the right under which each was admitted, 1831-1837.
   Reports from Committees (Parl. Papers), 1837, Vol. 11 (1), pp. (39) 57-93.

A return of the name, residence and description of each person admitted as a Freeman in each Corporation in Ireland (except Dublin), 1831-1838.
   Reports from Committees (Parl. Papers), 1837-38, Vol. 13 (2), pp. 468-482.

Returns of persons in cities and market towns who made application, or received excise licences, for the sale of spirits in premises under an annual value of £10, 1832-1838.
   Reports from Committees (Parl. Papers), 1837-38, Vol. 13 (2), pp. 558-601.

Return of the number of rentcharges registered 1832-1837, stating the name and residence of each person so registered, the barony and denomination of land on which the charge was granted and the name of the person granting same.

Reports from Committees (Parl. Papers), 1837, Vol. 11 (1), pp. (39) 94-125.

Additional return of names and residences, specifying the streets and numbers of houses, of all individuals in the towns of Ireland which return members to serve in Parliament who have made application or received excise licences for the sale of spirits in premises under an annual value of £10, 1832-1838.

Reports from Committees (Parl. Papers), 1837-38, Vol. 13 (2), pp. 602-607.

Tithe Compositions in Ireland: names of owners of tithes and their entitlement to same, 1834.   *Accounts and Papers,* 1834, Vol. 43, pp. (309) 1-45.

List of persons, arranged by county, discharged from gaols before the expiration of their sentences, 1835-1837.

Accounts and Papers (Parliamentary Papers), Vol. 45, pp. (194) 3-47.

Returns of convicts under sentence of transportation, discharged or sentences commuted to imprisonment, 1835-1837.

Accounts and Papers (Parliamentary Papers), Vol. 45 (196), pp. 3-21.

Names of the Commissioners, and their occupations, of the following towns:— Athlone, Athy, Ballinasloe, Ballymena, Ballyshannon, Banbridge, Bandon, Belturbet, Callan, Carrick-on-Suir, Cashel, Cavan, Charleville, Clonakilty, Clonmel, Coleraine, Downpatrick, Dromore, Dundalk, Dungannon, Ennis, Fethard, Kinsale, Lisburn, Longford, Loughrea, Lurgan, Mallow, Maryborough (Portlaoise), Mitchelstown, Monaghan, Nenagh, Newry, Newtownards, Portadown, Roscommon, Strabane, Tipperary, Tralee, Wicklow, Youghal, 1836-1843.

Accounts and Papers, 1843, Vol. 50, pp. (632) 1-26.

Names and addresses of tenants holding tenements under £5 yearly value, 1837.

Reports from Committees (Parl. Papers), 1837, Vol. 11 (1), pp. (39) 211-215.

Return of the number of rentcharges registered in each county together with the name and residence of each person so registered, 1832-1838.

Reports from Committees (Parl. Papers), 1837-38, Vol. 13 (2), pp. 523-545.

Names of Presbyterian clergymen and their parishes in the following counties: Antrim, Armagh, Down, Donegal, Fermanagh, Tyrone, Cork, Dublin, King's County (Offaly), Louth, Westmeath and Mayo, 1837.

New Plan for Education in Ireland, 1838, Part 1, pp. (27.8) 200-205.

Names, stations and assignments of magistrates serving in Ireland, 1839-1841.

Accounts and Papers (Parliamentary Papers), 1844, Vol. 43, pp. (131) 1-13.

Constabulary List for Ireland.   H.M.S.O., Dublin, 1840.

Names of persons prosecuted, their addresses and occupations, nature of offences, penalties, etc., in the court of the Exchequer in Ireland, 1841, 1842, 1843.

Accounts and Papers, 1843, Vol. 50, pp. (607) 2-11.

Criminal prosecutions with parties' names and nature of offences: Connaught and Munster circuits, Spring Assizes, 1842.

Accounts and Papers, 1843, Vol. 50, pp. (619) 34-41.

Return of the names of the officers of each yeomanry corps in Ireland, indicating the rank of each officer and date of commission, arranged by county, 1843.

Accounts and Papers, 1843, Vol. 50, pp. (408) 3-11.

Names and addresses of Irish Volunteers for the Papal Army, 1860.

59th Report, DKPRI, pp. 85-105.

Calendar of Patent and Close Rolls of Chancery in Ireland by James Morrin, Vols. I and II, Dublin, 1861, 1862.

General Index: Births registered in Ireland, 3 vols., 1864, 1865, 1866, with index of names and Registration District of each birth, Dublin, 1873.

Records and References relating to individual counties

Co. Armagh

A list of the freeholders of Co. Armagh, c. 1738.   NLI P. 206.

Poll Book for Co. Armagh, 1753.   G.O. Ms. 443.

A list of the registered freeholders of Co. Armagh, 1821-31.   PRONI T. 862.

Co. Clare

List of voters at the Parliamentary election, Co. Clare, 1745.   TCD MS. 2059.

Rental of the Roxton estate, Inchiquin Barony, Co. Clare, 1834.   PRO M.5764.

Rental of the estate of O'Callaghan-Westropp, Barony of Tulla Upper, Co. Clare. NLI Ms. 867.

Return of the deaths in the Kilrush and Ennistymon Workhouses, Hospitals, Infirmaries, etc., from 25th March 1850 to 25th March 1851, with the name, age, sex, cause of death, date of death, and the date of admission.
Accounts and Papers (Parliamentary Papers), 1851, Vol. 49, pp. (484) 1-47.

Co. Cork

A return of the names, in alphabetical order, of all persons registered as householders in the city of Cork, 1830-1837.
Reports from Committees (Parl. Papers), 1837-38, Vol. 13 (2), pp. 554-557.

A list of registered voters in the city of Cork: voters' names, residences, valuations, date of registration and elections voted at, 1832-1837.
Reports from Committees (Parl. Papers), 1837-38, Vol. 13 (1), pp. 320-321.

List of persons and their addresses in the city of Cork appearing on the Treasurers' Books as exempt from Rates, who voted in 1832, 1835 and 1837.
Reports and Committees (Parl. Papers), 1837-38, Vol. 13 (1), pp. 309-314.

List of persons, including addresses and occupations, appearing in the Registry as £10 householders in the city of Cork, 1837.
Reports from Committees (Parl. Papers), 1837-38, Vol. 13 (1), pp. 301-308.

List of non-resident Freemen, city of Cork, with those who voted at the Election of 1837 marked off.
Reports from Committees (Parl. Papers), 1837-38, Vol. 13 (1), pp. 315-317.
Several lists of waste and poor in various parishes in the city of Cork, 1837.
Reports from Committees (Parl. Papers), 1837-38, Vol. 13 (1), pp. 327-334.

List of waste and poor in the parishes of St Ann's, St Mary's, St Peter's and St Nicholas in the city of Cork exempted from City Rate by the Grand Jury at July Assizes 1837.
Reports from Committees (Parl. Papers), 1837-38, Vol. 13 (1), pp. 324-326.

Co. Donegal

Register of freeholders in Co. Donegal, 1767.   NLI P. 975.

Names of owners of freeholds entitled to the vote, c. 1770.   NLI Mss. 987-8.

Co. Dublin

Index to Christ Church Deeds, 1174-1684.   27th Report, DKPRI, pp. 6-96.

Rental of the Commons of Holy Trinity, Dublin, with the names and addresses of tenants, 1542.   24th Report, DKPRI, pp. 137-138.

Brethren admitted to the Guild of Smiths, Dublin, by marriage right, 1777-1830.
Reports from Committees (Parl. Papers), 1837, Vol. 11 (ii), pp. (480) 182.

List of freeholders in Co. Dublin, 1767.   PRO M.4912.

A return of the names of all persons admitted to the several guilds or corporate bodies of the City of Dublin: Apothecaries, Bakers, Surgeons, Carpenters, Smiths, Merchants, Tailors, etc., 1792-1837.
Reports from Committees (Parl. Papers), 1837, Vol. 11 (ii), pp. (480) 161-191.

Dublin City and County freeholds: names and addresses, 1830.   NLI Ms. 11,847.

Alphabetical list of 501 freeholders of the City of Dublin, stating place of residence, occupation, parish and description of property held, c. 1830.
Reports from Committees (Parl. Papers), 1837, Vol. 11 (ii), pp. (480) 146-175.

Number and names of Freemen, City of Dublin, 1832.
Reports from Committees (Parl. Papers), 1837, Vol. 11 (1), pp. (39) 159-175.

An alphabetical list of the registered voters in Parliamentary elections for the City of Dublin registered prior to 1st Feb. 1833, with situation of property and by what right entitled to the vote.
Reports from Committees (Parl. Papers), 1837, Vol. 11 (ii), pp. (480) 1-145.

Dublin County freeholders and leaseholders, 1835, 1837, 1852.   NLI Ms. 9363.

Co. Fermanagh

The names of freeholders residing in Co. Fermanagh, c. 1770.   NLI Mss. 787-8.

Names of registered voters in Enniskillen, Co. Fermanagh, 1832.
Reports from Committees (Parl. Papers), 1837-38, Vol. 13 (2), pp. 554-557.

Freeholders list for Co. Fermanagh, with names of freeholders and dates of registration, 1837.
Reports from Committees (Parl. Papers), 1837, Vol. 11 (1), pp. (39) 7-21.

Co. Galway

Council book of the Town of Galway: copy of page with record of the names of the Mayor, Sheriffs, Recorders and Council elected, Sept. 1632.
Facsimiles of National Manuscripts of Ireland, Part 4 (11), fol. 49.

Description of the County of Galway with the names of the principal inhabitants, 1599.   NLI P.1707.

Wages book of the Bellew estate, Mountbellew, 1679-1775.   NLI Ms. 9200.

Names of former and new tenants of the forfeited lands in the Liberties of Galway.
The History of the Town and County of Galway by James Hardiman, Dublin, 1820. Appendix VI.

The names and residences of several persons in the city of Galway who were discharged from the payment of local rates and taxes by reason of their tenements being of less annual value than £10, 1837.
Reports from Committees (Parl. Papers), 1837, Vol. 11 (1), pp. (39) 206-210.

Rental of the Trench estate in Co. Galway, 1840-1850.   NLI Ms. 2577.

Galway Castles and Owners.
Journal of the Galway Archaeological and Historical Society, Vol. 1, pp. 109-123.

Co. Kilkenny
A list of Co. Kilkenny freeholders, 1809-1819.   NLI Ms. 14181.

Names of Co. Kilkenny land owners, 1775.   G.O. Ms. 443.

Co. Leitrim
Names of the registered freeholders of Co. Leitrim, 1791.   G.O. Ms. 665.

A list of the freeholders or voters in Co. Leitrim, c. 1820.   NLI Ms. 3830.

Co. Leix (Queen's Co.)
Printed list of freeholders in Co. Leix, 1758-1775.   G.O. Ms. 443.

Co. Limerick
List of mayors, bailiffs and sheriffs of the City of Limerick, 1509-1690.
The Diocese of Limerick, Vol. 2, by John Canon Begley, 1927.

Names of gentlemen and freeholders in Co. Limerick, 1569.   NLI P.1700.

Rental of lands in Limerick City and County, 1660.   NLI Ms. 9091.

List of freeholders voting in a parliamentary election in Limerick City, 1761.
NLI Ms. 16092.

Names and addresses of freeholders voting in a parliamentary election, 1761.
NLI Ms. 16093.

Names of the owners of freeholds entitled to vote, 1776.   PRO M.1321-2.

List of freeholders in the Barony of Coshlea, c. 1840.   NLI Ms. 9452.

Survey of households in connection with Famine relief, 1846.   NLI Ms. 582.

Rate book for Clanwilliam Barony, Co. Limerick, 1870.   PRO M.2434.

Co. Longford
Rent book of the Adair estate for the parish of Clonbroney, 1738-1767.
NLI Ms. 3859.

Registration book of the freeholders of Co. Longford, 1747-1806.   PRO M.2745.

Names of the owners of freeholds in Co. Longford, c. 1790.   PRO M.2486-8.

Printed list of the Co. Longford freeholders, 1800-1835.   G.O. Ms. 444.

Collection of freeholders' certificates for Co. Longford, 1828-1836.   PRO M.2781.

Rental of the Aldborough estates in Co. Longford, 1846.   PRO M.2971.

Co. Louth
Drogheda Methodist Baptismal Register, 1829-1865.
Journal of the County Louth Archaeological and Historical Society, No. 2, 1974,
pp. 132-139.

List of the electors of Co. Louth who voted in the General Election of 1852.
NLI Ms. 1660.

Rental of the Trench estate at Drogheda, Co. Louth.   NLI Ms. 2576.

Co. Meath
List, compiled for election purposes, of the owners of freeholds in Co. Meath,
c. 1770.   NLI Mss. 787-8.

Alphabetical list of the freeholders of Co. Meath, 1794.
RIA, Upton Papers, No. 12.

Roll Books of Model School, Trim, Co. Meath, 1851, 1852, 1853.
NLI Ms. 3287.

Co. Roscommon

Names of the freeholders resident in Co. Roscommon, c. 1780.   G.O. Ms. 442.

About thirty lists of freeholders, some arranged by barony, 1790-1799.
NLI Ms. 10130.

Co. Sligo

An alphabetical list of voters in Sligo town and county, including addresses, 1790.
NLI Ms. 2169.

Names of freeholders resident in Co. Sligo, 1795.   NLI Ms. 3136.

Names of persons in Co. Sligo prosecuted at the Spring Assizes, 1842.
Accounts and Papers (Parliamentary Papers), 1843, Vol. 50, pp. (619) 34-35.

Co. Tipperary

Names of the freeholders in Co. Tipperary, 1595.   NLI P.1700.

The names of soldiers and adventurers who received land in Co. Tipperary under the Cromwellian Settlement, 1653.
The Cromwellian Settlement of Ireland, by John Prendergast, Dublin, 1922, pp. 386-400.

Cause list of Chancery Pleadings of the Palatine Court, Co. Tipperary, with the names of plaintiffs and defendants, 1662-1690.
6th Report, DKPRI, Appendix 5, pp. 47-72.

Fines levied in the Palatinate of Tipperary: parties' names and dates, 1664-1715.
Appendix to 5th Report, DKPRI, pp. 41-68.

A register of the freeholders residing in Co. Tipperary, 1776.   PRO M.1321-2.

Names of all persons qualified to serve as Jurors in the Northern Division of the County of Tipperary, 1840-1844.
Accounts and Papers (Parliamentary Papers), 1844, Vol. 43, pp. (380) 1-29.

List of persons charged at Nenagh Spring Assizes, 1843.
Accounts and Papers (Parliamentary Papers), 1843, Vol. 50, p. (619) 33.

Co. Waterford

Rent roll of estates in Co. Waterford, 1564.   NLI Ms. 9034.

Freeholders' rental for the parish of Dungarvan, 1844-1859.   NLI Ms. 6178.

Co. Westmeath

The names of owners of freeholds in Co. Westmeath, compiled for electoral purposes, 1761-1788.   NLI Mss. 787-788.

Co. Westmeath Poll Book, 1761.   G.O. Ms. 443.

Co. Wexford

Rent books relating to the estate of Baron Farnham at Bunclody, 1775-1820.
NLI Mss. 5504-5506.

Copies of rent lists for Co. Wexford, 18th century.   NLI Ms. 1782.

Names of tenants on the Alcock estate at Clonmore, c. 1820.   NLI Ms. 10169.

Return of the names of the Masters, Owners, Crew and Ships belonging to New Ross prosecuted for smuggling tobacco; also the names of magistrates who heard the cases, decisions, etc., 1840-1843.
Accounts and Papers (Parliamentary Papers), 1843, Vol. 42, p. 299.

List of Irish Libraries, Archives and Record Offices

General Repositories

Department of Folklore,
University College,
Belfield,
Dublin 2.

Genealogical Office,
Dublin Castle,
Dublin 2.

General Register Office,
The Custom House,
Dublin 1.

Linen Hall Library,
17 Donegall Square North,
Belfast BT1 5GD.

Marsh's Library,
St. Patrick's Close,
Dublin 8.

National Library of Ireland,
Kildare Street,
Dublin 2.

Ordnance Survey (Maps),
Phoenix Park,
Dublin 8.

Public Record Office,
The Four Courts,
Dublin 7.

Public Record Office of Northern
   Ireland,
66 Balmoral Avenue,
Belfast BT9 6NY.

Maynooth College Library,
Maynooth,
Co. Kildare.

Registry of Deeds,
King's Inns,
Henrietta Street,
Dublin 1.

Representative Church Body Library,
Braemor Park,
Rathgar,
Dublin 14.

Presbyterian Historical Society,
Church House,
Fisherwick Place,
Belfast BT1 69W.

Royal Irish Academy,
19 Dawson Street,
Dublin 2.

Society of Friends' Library,
6 Eustace Street,
Dublin 2.

State Paper Office,
Lr. Yard,
Dublin Castle,
Dublin 2.

Trinity College Library,
College Street,
Dublin 2.

University College Library,
Western Road,
Cork.

University College Library,
Galway,
Co. Galway.

City and County Libraries

North-Eastern Education & Library
   Board,
County Library,
Demesne Avenue,
Ballymena,
Co. Antrim BT43 7BG.

Central Library,
Royal Avenue,
Belfast BT1 1EA.

Southern Education & Library Board,
Library Headquarters,
Brownlow Row,
Legahory,
Craigavon BT65 8DP,
Co. Armagh.

Carlow County Library,
Dublin Street,
Carlow.

Cavan County Library,
Casement Street,
Cavan.

Clare County Library,
Mill Road,
Ennis,
Co. Clare.

Cork City Library,
Grand Parade,
Cork.

Cork County Library,
The Courthouse,
Washington Street,
Cork.

Donegal County Library,
The Courthouse,
Lifford,
Co. Donegal.

South-Eastern Education & Library
   Board,
Library Headquarters,
Windmill Hill,
Ballynahinch,
Co. Down BT24 8DH.

Dublin City and County Library,
Central Public Library,
Pearse Street,
Dublin 2.

Western Education and Library Board,
Fermanagh Divisional Headquarters,
Darling Street,
Enniskillen,
Co. Fermanagh.

Galway County Library,
The Courthouse,
Galway.

Kerry County Library,
Moyderwell,
Tralee,
Co. Kerry.

Kildare County Library,
Athgarven Road,
Newbridge,
Co. Kildare.

Kilkenny County Library,
John Street,
Kilkenny.

Laois County Library,
Church Street,
Portlaoise,
Co. Laois.

Leitrim County Library,
The Courthouse,
Ballinamore,
Co. Leitrim.

Limerick City Library,
Pery Square,
Limerick.

Limerick County Library,
58 O'Connell Street,
Limerick.

Northern Ireland Western Education
and Library Board,
Londonderry Divisional Headquarters,
Christ Church School,
Windsor Terrace,
Londonderry BT48 7HQ.

Louth County Library,
Chapel Street,
Dundalk,
Co. Louth.

Mayo County Library,
Mountain View,
Castlebar,
Co. Mayo.

Meath County Library,
Railway Street,
Navan,
Co. Meath.

Monaghan County Library,
The Diamond,
Clones,
Co. Monaghan.

Offaly County Library,
Tullamore,
Co. Offaly.

Roscommon County Library,
Abbey Street,
Roscommon.

Sligo County Library,
Stephen Street,
Sligo.

Tipperary County Library,
Castle Avenue,
Thurles,
Co. Tipperary.

Northern Ireland Western Education
and Library Board,
Library Headquarters,
Dublin Road,
Omagh,
Co. Tyrone BT78 1HG.

Waterford County Library,
Lismore,
Co. Waterford.

Longford/Westmeath County Library,
Dublin Road,
Mullingar,
Co. Westmeath.

Wexford County Library,
County Hall,
Spawell Road,
Wexford.

Wicklow County Library,
Greystones,
Co. Wicklow.

Periodicals

The Irish Genealogist,
c/o F. B. Payton,
The Irish Genealogical Research
Society,
Glenholme,
High Oakham Road,
Mansfield, Notts.,
England.

The Irish Ancestor,
Editor: Miss Rosemary ffolliott,
Pirton House,
Sydenham Villas,
Dundrum,
Dublin 14.

Genealogical Research Agencies

Genealogical Office,
Dublin Castle,
Dublin 2.

The Ulster-Scot Historical Foundation,
66 Balmoral Avenue,
Belfast BT9 6NY.

Hibernian Research Co. Ltd.,
Windsor House,
22 Windsor Road,
Rathmines,
Dublin 6.

INDEX